Design Patterns Formalization Techniques

Toufik Taibi
United Arab Emirates University, UAE

IGI PUBLISHING
Hershey • New York

Acquisition Editor:	Kristin Klinger
Senior Managing Editor:	Jennifer Neidig
Managing Editor:	Sara Reed
Assistant Managing Editor:	Sharon Berger
Development Editor:	Kristin Roth
Copy Editor:	April Schmidt and Lanette Ehrhardt
Typesetter:	Jamie Snavely
Cover Design:	Lisa Tosheff
Printed at:	Yurchak Printing Inc.

Published in the United States of America by
IGI Publishing (an imprint of IGI Global)
701 E. Chocolate Avenue
Hershey PA 17033
Tel: 717-533-8845
Fax: 717-533-8661
E-mail: cust@igi-pub.com
Web site: http://www.igi-pub.com

and in the United Kingdom by
IGI Publishing (an imprint of IGI Global)
3 Henrietta Street
Covent Garden
London WC2E 8LU
Tel: 44 20 7240 0856
Fax: 44 20 7379 0609
Web site: http://www.eurospanonline.com

Library of Congress Cataloging-in-Publication Data

Design patterns formalization techniques / Toufik Taibi, editor.
    p. cm.
Summary: "This book focuses on formalizing the solution element of patterns, providing tangible benefits to pattern users, researchers, scholars, academicians, practitioners and students working in the field of Design patterns and software reuse; it explains details on several specification languages, allowing readers to choose the most suitable formal technique to solve their specific inquiries"—Provided by publisher.
  Includes bibliographical references and index.
  ISBN 978-1-59904-219-0 (hardcover)—ISBN 978-1-59904-221-3 (ebook)
  1. Software patterns. 2. Formal methods (Computer science) 3. Software architecture. I. Taibi, Toufik, 1969-
  QA76.76.P37D47 2007
  005.1—dc22

British Cataloguing in Publication Data
A Cataloguing in Publication record for this book is available from the British Library.

Design Patterns Formalization Techniques

Table of Contents

Foreword

Software design is a fledgling discipline. When the "software crisis" came to be acknowledged during the late 1960s, software development projects have been marred by budget overflows and catastrophic failures. This situation has largely remained unchanged. Programmers still create poorly-understood systems of monstrous complexity which suffer from a range of problems directly linked to the lack of abstraction: lack of means of communicating design decisions, absence of effective pedagogic tools for training novice programmers, and inadequate means for maintaining gigantic software systems. In the recent years, we have witnessed an explosion of loosely-related software technologies, techniques, notations, paradigms, idioms, methodologies, and most of all proprietary and poorly-understood ad-hoc solutions, driven by market forces more than by design, planning, or research.

Design patterns were introduced to programming practices at the end of the 1980s as a result of dissatisfaction with software's state of affairs. The few means of abstraction in existence at the time, such as algorithms and data structures, narrowly-suited procedural programming, poorly fitting with the growing use of object-oriented programming paradigm. For the first time, an abstraction technique at hand was general enough to be useful for practitioners and academics alike, specific enough to enter textbooks, broad enough to be useful during any stage in the development process, and generic enough to support any programming paradigm. The introduction of Design patterns marks a turning point in the history of software design.

In 1995, we witnessed the publication of a catalogue (Gamma, Helm, Johnson, & Vlissides, 1995) of 23 Design patterns written by four experienced object-oriented designers. The catalogue, which came to be known as the "Gang of Four" catalogue, was an immediate success. The abstractions described offer a rich vocabulary for abstractions for conceptualising, designing, brain-storming, communicating, documenting, understanding, maintaining, and teaching about software. Each pattern captures a design motif that is common enough to deserve wide recognition, described in clarity and sufficient detail to indicate the consequences of choosing to apply it. Patterns help novices avoid common pitfalls and encourage experienced programmers to build better software. As a result, Design patterns entered textbooks and became the subject matter of scientific papers, conferences, and intensive efforts for providing tool-support by a broad range of industrial software development environments. In the decade since they have entered the zeitgeist, Design patterns have revolutionized software design.

Early on, the attempt to reason about and provide tool support for Design patterns have led many to recognize that verbal descriptions and case studies are not enough. The software engineering community came to realize that conceptual clarity and automation require a formal specification language. The central problem in software design has therefore shifted from seeking suitable abstractions to providing precise means for capturing and representing them. But existing modelling notations which were designed for documenting design decisions tailored for specific programs, proved inadequate for the purpose of modelling abstract design motifs. This shortcoming has motivated the investigation in formal modelling techniques which is the subject matter of this book.

Mathematics is the most successful conceptual tool for capturing, representing, understanding, and using abstractions. Effective mathematical analysis and modelling is the hallmark of modern science and a mark of maturity of an engineering discipline. The research in formal techniques for modelling Design patterns is therefore the next natural step in the progress of software design. This line of investigation is vital for achieving conceptual clarity and ever more potent means of abstraction. This book provides a summary of this investigation.

A convergence of formalization techniques for Design patterns, expected to evolve within a decade or two, is vital for establishing a sound foundation for using and understanding patterns. Convergence is also crucial for communicating about and teaching patterns. Given the central role of Design patterns, such an achievement is widely taken to be the most important vehicle of progress for software design and a prerequisite for a regimented engineering discipline. The next generation of software design techniques may very well depend on accomplishing convergence. We hope this book shall speed and facilitate this process.

Amnon Eden

Layer-de-la-Haye, December 2006

Amnon H. Eden *is a lecturer with the University of Essex and a research fellow with the Center For Inquiry. He is investigating the problem of modelling Design patterns since 1996. In 1998, Eden received his PhD from the Department of Computer Science, at Tel Aviv University, for his dissertation on language for patterns uniform specification (LePUS) and the building-blocks of object-oriented design. Eden's contributions also include the intension/locality hypothesis, the notion of evolution complexity, and the ontology of software. Eden lives with his partner in Layer-de-la-Haye, UK.*

Reference

Gamma, E., Helm, R., Johnson, R., & Vlissides, J. (1995). *Design patterns: Elements of reusable object-oriented systems*. Addison-Wesley Professional.

Preface

Christopher Alexander was the first to introduce patterns as a form of describing accumulated experiences in the field of architecture. He defines a *pattern* as a construct made of three parts: a *context*, a set of *forces* and a *solution* (Alexander, Ishikawa, & Silverstein, 1977). The *context* reflects the conditions under which the pattern holds (Alexander, 1979). The *forces* occur repeatedly in the context and represent the *problem(s)* faced (Alexander, 1979). The *solution* is a configuration that allows the forces to resolve themselves (i.e., balances the forces) (Alexander, 1979). Alexander's patterns comprise commonly encountered problems and their appropriate solutions for the making of successful towns and buildings in a western environment. Alexander called a set of correlated patterns a *pattern language*, because patterns form a vocabulary of concepts used in communications that take place between experts and novices.

Ward Cunningham and Kent Beck (1987) were inspired by Alexander's work and decided to adapt it to software development. Their first five patterns dealt with the design of user interfaces. This marked the birth of patterns in the software field. Nowadays, software patterns are so popular that they are being applied in virtually every aspect of computing. Moreover, the concept of patterns is being adapted to many other fields, such as management, education, and so forth.

There are many kinds of software patterns based on different categorizing criteria. If the focus is on the software design phase, patterns are classified according to their abstraction level into architectural patterns, Design patterns, and idioms. This book mainly focuses on Design patterns. As such, in this preface, the terms Design patterns and patterns can be used interchangeably.

A pattern can be defined as a description of a proven (successful or efficient) *solution* to a recurring *problem* within a *context*. The above definition keeps the essence of Alexander's original definition by mentioning the three pillars of a pattern (context, problem, and solution). Reusing patterns usually yields better quality software within a reduced time frame. As such, they are considered artifacts of software reusability.

Patterns are published mostly within collections or catalogs. However, the most influential publication of Design patterns is the catalog by the "*Gang of Four*" (GoF) (Gamma, Helm,

Johnson, & Vlissides, 1995), which listed 23 patterns classified under three categories: creational, structural, and behavioral. All patterns recorded in the GoF catalog were described in great detail and share an identical format of presentation.

Patterns are used as a way of improving software design productivity and quality for the following reasons:

- Patterns capture previous design experiences, and make it available to other designers. Therefore, designers do not need to discover solutions for every problem from scratch.
- Patterns form a more flexible foundation for reuse, as they can be reused in many ways.
- Patterns serve as a communication medium among software designers.
- Patterns can be considered microarchitectures, from which bigger software architectures can be built.

Well-established engineering disciplines have handbooks that describe successful solutions to known problems. Though as a discipline, software engineering is a long way from that goal, patterns have been useful for software engineers to reuse successful solutions.

Currently most patterns are described using a combination of textual descriptions, object-oriented (OO) graphical notations such as unified modeling language (UML) (Rumbaugh, Jacobson, & Booch, 1998), and sample code fragments. The intention is to make them easy to read and use and to build a pattern vocabulary. However, informal descriptions give rise to ambiguity, and limit tool support and correct usage. Tool support can play a great role in automated pattern mining, detection of pattern variants, and code generation from pattern specification.

Hence, there is a need for a formal means of accurately describing patterns in order to achieve the following goals:

- Better understand patterns and their composition. This will help know when and how to use them properly in order to take full advantage of their inherent benefits.
- Resolve the following issues regarding relationships between patterns such as duplication, refinement, and disjunction. Resolving the above-mentioned questions will ease the process of pattern repository management.
- Allow the development of tool support in activities related to patterns.

Many formal approaches for pattern specification have been emerging as a means to cope with the inherent shortcomings of informal descriptions. Despite being based on different mathematical formalisms, they share the same goal, which is accurately describing patterns in order to allow rigorous reasoning about them, their instances, their relationships and their composition and facilitate tool support for their usage. It is important to note that formal approaches to Design pattern specifications are not intended to replace existing informal approaches, but to complement them.

Currently, there is no single avenue for authors actively involved in the field of formal specification of Design patterns to publish their work. There has been neither a dedicated conference nor a special journal issue that covers precisely this field. Since this book contains chapters describing different Design pattern formalization techniques, it will contribute to the state-of-the-art in the field and will be a one-stop for academicians, research scholars, students, and practitioners to learn about the details of each of the techniques.

The book is organized into XVI chapters. A brief description of each of the chapters follows. These were mainly taken from the abstracts of the chapters.

Chapter I describes Balanced pattern specification language (BPSL), a language intended to accurately describe patterns in order to allow rigorous reasoning about them. BPSL incorporates the formal specification of both structural and behavioral aspects of patterns. The structural aspect formalization is based on first-order logic (FOL), while the behavioral aspect formalization is based on temporal logic of actions (TLA). Moreover, BPSL can formalize pattern composition and instances of patterns (possible implementations of a given pattern).

Chapter II describes the Design pattern modeling language (DPML), a notation supporting the specification of Design pattern solutions and their instantiation into UML design models. DPML uses a simple set of visual abstractions and readily lends itself to tool support. DPML Design pattern solution specifications are used to construct visual, formal specifications of Design patterns. DPML instantiation diagrams are used to link a Design pattern solution specification to instances of a UML model, indicating the roles played by different UML elements in the generic Design pattern solution. A prototype tool is described, together with an evaluation of the language and tool.

Chapter III shows how formal specifications of GoF patterns, based on the rigorous approach to industrial software engineering (RAISE) language, have been helpful to develop tool support. Thus, the object-oriented design process is extended by the inclusion of pattern-based modeling and verification steps. The latter involving checking design correctness and appropriate pattern application through the use of a supporting tool, called DePMoVe (design and pattern modeling and verification).

Chapter IV describes an abstraction mechanism for collective behavior in reactive distributed systems. The mechanism allows the expression of recurring patterns of object interactions in a parametric form, and to formally verify temporal safety properties induced by applications of the patterns. The authors present the abstraction mechanism and compare it to Design patterns, an established software engineering concept. While there are some obvious similarities, because the common theme is abstraction of object interactions, there are important differences as well. Authors discuss how the emphasis on full formality affects what can be expressed and achieved in terms of patterns of object interactions. The approach is illustrated with the Observer and Memento patterns.

In **Chapter V**, authors have investigated several approaches to the formal specification of Design patterns. In particular, they have separated the structural and behavioral aspects of Design patterns and proposed specification methods based on first-order logic, temporal logic, temporal logic of action, process calculus, and Prolog. They also explore verification techniques based on theorem proving. The main objective of this chapter is to describe their investigations on formal specification techniques for Design patterns, and then demonstrate using these specifications as the methods of reasoning about Design pattern properties when they are used in software systems.

Chapter VI presents the SPINE language as a way of representing Design patterns in a suitable manner for performing verification of a pattern's implementation in a particular source language. SPINE is used by a proof engine called HEDGEHOG, which is used to verify whether a pattern is correctly implemented.

Chapter VII presents a viewpoint based on intent-oriented design (IOD) that yields simple formalisms and a conceptual basis for tools supporting design and implementation from an intent-oriented perspective. The system for pattern query and recognition (SPQR) is an automated framework for analysis of software systems in the small or the large, and detection of instances of known programming concepts in a flexible, yet formal, manner. These concepts, when combined in well-defined ways to form abstractions, as found in the Design patterns literature, lead to the automated detection of Design patterns directly from source code and other design artifacts. The chapter describes the three major portions of SPQR briefly, and uses it to facilitate a discussion of the underlying formalizations of Design patterns with a concrete example, from source code to completed results.

Chapter VIII describes techniques for the verification of refactorings or transformations which introduce Design patterns. The techniques use a semantics of object-oriented systems defined by the object calculus and the pattern transformations are proved to be refinements using this semantics.

Chapter IX describes a UML-based pattern specification language called role-based metamodeling language (RBML), which defines the solution domain of Design patterns in terms of roles at the metamodel level. The chapter discusses benefits of the RBML and presents notation for capturing various perspectives of pattern properties. The OBSERVER, INTERPRETER, and ITERATOR patterns are used to describe RBML. Tool support for the RBML and the future trends in pattern specification are also discussed.

In **Chapter X**, the formal specification of a Design pattern is given as a class operator that transforms a design given as a set of classes into a new design that takes into account the description and properties of the Design pattern. The operator is specified in the SLAM-SL specification language, in terms of pre- and postconditions. Precondition collects properties required to apply the pattern and post-condition relates input classes and result classes encompassing most of the intent and consequences sections of the pattern.

Chapter XI describes a formal, logic-based language for representing pattern structure and an extension that can also represent other aspects of patterns, such as intent, applicability, and collaboration. This mathematical basis serves to eliminate ambiguities. The chapter explains the concepts underlying the languages and shows their utility by representing two classical patterns, some concurrent patterns and various aspects of a few other patterns.

Chapter XII introduces an approach to define Design patterns using Semantic Web technologies. For this purpose, a vocabulary based on the Web ontology language OWL is developed. Design patterns can be defined as RDF documents instantiating this vocabulary, and can be published as resources on standard Web servers. This facilitates the use of patterns as knowledge artefacts shared by the software engineering community. The instantiation of patterns in programs is discussed, and the design of a tool is presented that can x-ray programs for pattern instances based on their formal definitions.

Chapter XIII presents a novel approach allowing the precise specification of patterns as well as retaining the patterns' inherent flexibility. The chapter also discusses tools that can assist practitioners in determining whether the patterns used in designing their systems have been implemented correctly. Such tools are important also during system maintenance and evolution to ensure that the design integrity of a system is not compromised. The authors also show how their approach lends itself to the construction of such tools.

Chapter XIV introduces the user requirements notation (URN), and demonstrates how it can be used to formalize patterns in a way that enables rigorous trade-off analysis while maintaining the genericity of the solution description. URN combines a graphical goal language, which can be used to capture forces and reason about trade-offs, and a graphical scenario language, which can be used to describe behavioral solutions in an abstract manner. Although each language can be used in isolation in pattern descriptions (and have been in the literature), the focus of this chapter is on their combined use. It includes examples of formalizing Design patterns with URN together with a process for trade-off analysis.

Chapter XV describes an extended compiler that formalizes patterns, called pattern enforcing compiler (PEC). Developers use standard Java syntax to mark their classes as implementations of particular Design patterns. The compiler is then able to use reflection to check whether the classes do in fact adhere to the constraints of the patterns. The checking possible with our compiler starts with the obvious static adherence to constraints, such as method presence, visibility, and naming. However, PEC supports dynamic testing to check the runtime behavior of classes and code generation to assist in the implementation of complex patterns. The chapter gives examples of using the patterns supplied with PEC, and also examples of how to write your own patterns and have PEC enforce these.

Chapter XVI presents Class-Z, a formal language for modelling OO Design patterns. The chapter demonstrates the language's unique efficacy in producing precise, concise, scalable, generic, and appropriately abstract specifications modelling the GoF Design patterns. Mathematical logic is used as a main frame of reference: the language is defined as a subset of first-order predicate calculus and implementations (programs) are modelled as finite structures in model theory.

References

Alexander, C. (1979). *The timeless way of building*. Oxford University Press.

Alexander, C., Ishikawa, S., & Silverstein, M. (1977). *A pattern language: Towns, buildings, construction*. Oxford University Press.

Beck, K., & Cunningham, W. (1987). Using pattern languages for object-oriented programs (Tech. Rep. No. CR-87-43). Tektronix Inc, Computer Research Laboratory.

Gamma, E., Helm, R., Johnson, R., & Vlissides, J. (1995). *Design patterns: Elements of reusable object-oriented systems*. Addison-Wesley Professional.

Rumbaugh, J., Jacobson, I., & Booch, G. (1998). *The unified modeling language reference manual*. Addison-Wesley Professional.

Acknowledgment

The editor would like to acknowledge the help of all those who contributed to this one year long project. Without their help and support, the project could not have been satisfactorily completed.

Most of the authors of chapters included in this book also served as referees for articles written by other authors. Many thanks to all those who provided constructive and comprehensive reviews. Special thanks also go to all the staff at IGI Global, whose contributions throughout the whole process from inception of the initial idea to final publication have been very invaluable. In particular, to our development editor, Kristin Roth, whose continuous communication via e-mail kept the project on schedule.

I wish also to thank all of the authors for their insights and excellent contributions to this book.

Finally, I want to thank my wife and children for their love and support throughout this project.

Toufik Taibi, PhD
Al Ain, UAE
December 2006

Chapter I

An Integrated Approach to Design Patterns Formalization

Toufik Taibi, United Arab Emirates University, UAE

Abstract

A Design pattern describes a set of proven solutions for a set of recurring design problems that occur within a context. As such, reusing patterns improves both quality and time-to-market of software projects. Currently, most patterns are specified in an informal fashion, which gives rise to ambiguity, and limits tool support and correct usage. This chapter describes balanced pattern specification language (BPSL), a language intended to accurately describe patterns in order to allow rigorous reasoning about them. BPSL incorporates the formal specification of both structural and behavioral aspects of patterns. Moreover, it can formalize pattern composition and instances of patterns (possible implementations of a given pattern).

Introduction

A Design pattern describes a set of proven solutions for a set of recurring design problems that occurs within a certain context. Hence, reusing patterns yields better quality software within reduced time frames.

Currently, most patterns are described using a combination of textual descriptions, object-oriented (OO) graphical notations such as unified modeling language (UML) (Rumbaugh, Jacobson, & Booch, 1998), and sample code fragments. The intention was to make them easy to read and use, and to build a pattern vocabulary. However, informal descriptions give rise to ambiguity, and limit tool support and correct usage. Tool support can play a great role in automated pattern mining, detection of pattern variants, and code generation from pattern specification.

The pattern community mostly focuses on the solution element of a pattern and not on its other elements, such as the problem solved, the context, the important forces (Alexander, Ishikawa, & Silverstein, 1977) acting within the problem, or the way the pattern resolves these forces. Indeed, the verbal description of the solution element is the most coherent and the easiest to formalize. As such, this work also focuses on specifying the solution element of patterns.

Most formal approaches for pattern specification lack in the area of approachability due to the assumption that complex mathematical notations are necessary to achieve precision, thus favoring mathematically mature modelers rather than normal modelers (Taibi & Ngo, 2003b). Another problem of formal approaches is that they are not comprehensive enough to describe both aspects (structural and behavioral) of patterns. Additionally, only a few of the formal approaches attempted formalizing pattern composition (Taibi & Ngo, 2003b).

Balanced pattern specification language (BPSL) (Taibi & Ngo, 2003a) was developed in order to formally specify the structural as well as behavioral aspects of patterns at three levels of abstraction: pattern composition, patterns, and pattern instances.

First order logic (FOL) (Smullyan, 1995) is used as the formal basis for specifying the structural aspect of patterns, because relations between pattern participants can be easily expressed as predicates. Temporal logic of actions (TLA) (Lamport, 1994) is used as the formal basis for specifying the behavioral aspect of patterns, because it is best suited to describe the collective behavior of objects. BPSL has been successfully used to specify patterns for stand-alone systems (Taibi & Ngo, 2003a) and also for distributed object computing systems (Schmidt, Stal, Rohnert, & Buschmann, 2000; Taibi & Ngo, 2004).

The design of component-based software involves the composition of different components. Patterns are special types of components offering a flexible means of reuse. Since each pattern represents a well-tested abstraction that has many instances, patterns can be considered building blocks from which reusable and flexible software designs can be built. Checking the correctness of pattern composition allows detecting problems early in the lifecycle, which saves time and the cost of fixing errors at later stages. Thus, if formalized, pattern composition can lead to ready-made architectures from which only instantiation is required to build robust implementations. Since the specification of the structural and behavioral aspects of patterns uses two different formalisms (FOL and TLA), pattern composition is formalized independently for each aspect.

The rest of the chapter is organized as follows. Next, the chapter gives a detailed description of BPSL's concepts and constructs, while the following section describes BPSL's composition process. The chapter then provides case studies on applying BPSL for formally specifying patterns and their composition. This is followed with a description of how BPSL can be used to specify pattern instances and related work. Finally, the chapter concludes, providing future research directions.

Balanced Pattern Specification Language (BPSL)

Structural Aspect Formalization

The structural aspect of patterns is specified using a first-order language called S_{BPSL}, where "S" stands for "structural." The following are the formation rules that define the syntax of formulas in S_{BPSL}:

- A *term* is either a *constant* like *2* or a *variable* like *x*.
- An *atom* is a dyadic (binary) *predicate* symbol applied to two arguments, each of which is a term.
- A *formula* is either an atom, $A \wedge B$ (*A* and *B* are formulas), or any formula *A* and any variable *x* in $\exists x\, A$.

As it can be seen from the above formation rules, S_{BPSL} is a very simple first-order language having the following characteristics:

- Each formula is a well-formed formula.
- Each formula is a sentence, as it does not contain free variables.
- S_{BPSL} does not support function symbols, restricts predicates to have two arguments and requires only the usage of the existential quantifier ($\exists$).

Variables and constants of S_{BPSL} are many-sorted. Variable and constant symbols represent classes, typed variables and methods. The sets of classes (or references to classes), typed variables and methods are designated *C, V,* and *M,* respectively. Typed variables represent variables of any predefined or user-defined types except elements of set *C*. Binary predicate symbols represent permanent relations among them. BPSL defines a set of *primary* permanent relations based on which other permanent relations can be built (Table 1). The term "permanent" is used to differentiate these relations with "temporal" relations, defined below.

In Table 1, $M \times C$ is the Cartesian product of *M* and *C*. Primary permanent relations represent the smallest set (in terms of cardinality), on top of which any other permanent relation can be built. For example, the permanent relation *Forwarding* is a special case of *Invocation*, where the actual arguments in *Invocation* are the formal arguments defined for the first method. This can be formally specified as follows: *Forwarding*(m_1,m_2)$\Leftrightarrow$ *Invocation*(m_1,m_2)$\wedge$*Argument*(a_1,m_1) $\wedge...\wedge$*Argument*(a_n,m_1) $\wedge$*Argument*(a_1,m_2)$\wedge...\wedge$ *Argument*(a_n,m_2), where $m_1, m_2 \in M$ and $\{a_1,..., a_n\} \subset C\cup V$, which means that the elements of the set $\{a_1,..., a_n\}$ can either be references to classes or typed variables.

Let us take an example of permanent relations from the *Observer* pattern (Gamma, Helm, Johnson, & Vlissides, 1995). The permanent relations *Reference-to-one(concrete-observer, concrete-subject)* and *Reference-to-many(subject, observer)* depict, in this case, that the *concrete-observer* class has only one reference to the *concrete-subject* class, while the *subject* class has many references to the *observer* class. This is due to the fact that a subject could have many observers attached to it, while each observer is attached to only one subject.

Brief Summary of TLA

The behavioral aspect of patterns is specified using TLA as the formal basis. This part of BPSL is called, B_{BPSL}, where "B" stands for "behavioral." Since, the syntax and semantics of B_{BPSL}, derive completely from TLA, this section provides a brief summary of TLA (Lamport, 1994).

In TLA, a semantic is given by assigning a semantic meaning $[\![F]\!]$ to each syntactic object *F*. The semantics of TLA is defined in terms of *states*, where a state is an assignment of

Table 1. Primary permanent relations and their intent

Name	Domain	Intent
Defined-in	$M\times C$	Indicates that a method is defined in a certain class.
	$V\times C$	Indicates that a typed variable is defined as an attribute in a certain class.
Reference-to-one (-many)	$C\times C$	Indicates that one class defines a member whose type is a reference to one (many) instance(s) of the second class.
Inheritance	$C\times C$	Indicates that the first class inherits from the second.
Creation	$M\times C$	Indicates that a method contains an instruction that creates a new instance of a class.
	$C\times C$	Indicates that one of the methods of a class contains an instruction that creates a new instance of another class.
Invocation	$M\times M$	Indicates that the first method invokes the second method.
	$C\times M$	Indicates that a method of a class invokes a specific method of another class.
	$M\times C$	Indicates that a specific method of a class invokes a method of another class.
	$C\times C$	Indicates that a method of a class invokes a method of another class.
Argument	$C\times M$	Indicates that a reference to a class is an argument of a method.
	$V\times M$	Indicates that a typed variable is an argument of a method.
Return-type	$C\times M$	Indicates that a method returns a reference to a class.

values to variables. A state s assigns a value $s(x)$ to a variable x. The collection of all possible states is denoted St. As such, a state is a function from the set of variables Var to the set of values Val.

Thus, $s[\![x]\!]$ denotes $s(x)$. The meaning $[\![x]\!]$ of variable x is a mapping from states to values.

A state function is a non-Boolean expression built from variables and constant symbols. The meaning $[\![f]\!]$ of a state function f is a mapping from the collection St of states to the collection Val of values. A postfix functional notation is used letting $s[\![f]\!]$ denote the values that $[\![f]\!]$ assigns to state s as follows: $s[\![f]\!] \triangleq f(\forall \; 'v':s[\![v]\!]/v)$, where $f(\forall \; 'v':s[\![v]\!]/v)$ denotes the value obtained from f by substituting v by $s[\![v]\!]$ for all variables v. The symbol $\triangleq$ means equal by definition.

A state predicate (or predicate) is a Boolean expression built from variable and constant symbols. $[\![P]\!]$ is a mapping from states to Booleans, so $s[\![P]\!]$ equals true or false for every state s. A state s satisfies a predicate P if and only if (iff) $s[\![P]\!]$ equals true.

An action is a Boolean-valued expression formed from variables, primed variables, and constant symbols. An action represents a relation between old states and new states, where the unprimed variables refer to the old state and the prime variables refer to the new state. The meaning $[\![A]\!]$ of an action A is a function that assigns a Boolean $s[\![A]\!]t$ to a pair of states s,t. $s[\![A]\!]t$ is obtained from A by substituting each unprimed variable v by $s[\![v]\!]$ and each primed variable v' by $t[\![v]\!]$ as follows:

$$s[\![A]\!]t \triangleq A(\forall 'v:s[\![v]\!]/v,t[\![v]\!]/v').$$

A pair of successive states is called a step. The pair of states s,t is called an "A step" iff $s[\![A]\!]t$ equals true. A predicate P can also be viewed as an action that does not contain primed variables. Thus $s[\![P]\!]t$ is a Boolean which equals $s[\![P]\!]$ for any states s and t. A pair of states s,t is a P step iff it satisfies P.

For any state function or predicate F, we define F' to be the expression obtained by replacing each variable v in F by the primed variable v' as follows: $F' \triangleq F(\forall 'v':v'/v)$.

If P is a predicate symbol then P' is an action and $s[\![P]\!]t$ equals $t[\![P]\!]$ for any state s and t. An action A is said to be valid, written as $\vDash A$, iff every step is an A step. Formally $\vDash A \triangleq \forall s,t \in \mathbf{St} : s[\![A]\!]t$. A special case of this is $\vDash P \triangleq \forall s \in \mathbf{St} : s[\![P]\!]$. A valid action is true regardless of the values substituted for primed and unprimed variables. Thus, the validity of an action expresses a theorem about values.

For any action A, $EnabledA$ is a predicate that is true for a state iff it is possible to take an A step starting in that state. Semantically, $EnabledA$ is defined by: $s[\![EnabledA]\!] \triangleq \exists t \in \mathbf{St} : s[\![A]\!]t$ for any state s.

A temporal formula is built from elementary formulas using Boolean operators (basically $\wedge$ and $\neg$ as the others are derived from these two) and the unary operator $\square$ (read always). The operator $\lozenge$ (read eventually) can be derived from $\square$ by $\lozenge F \triangleq \neg \square \neg F$. The following defines $\lozenge F$ and $\square F$:

$$\langle s_0, s_1, s_2, \ldots \rangle [\![\Box F]\!] \triangleq \forall n \in \textbf{\textit{Nat}} : \langle s_n, s_{n+1}, s_{n+2}, \ldots \rangle [\![F]\!]$$
$$\langle s_0, s_1, s_2, \ldots \rangle [\![\Diamond F]\!] \triangleq \exists n \in \textbf{\textit{Nat}} : \langle s_n, s_{n+1}, s_{n+2}, \ldots \rangle [\![F]\!]$$

A behavior is an infinite sequence of states. A temporal formula is interpreted as an assertion about behaviors. Formally, the meaning $[\![F]\!]$ of a formula F, is a Boolean-valued function on behaviors. Let $\sigma [\![F]\!]$ denote the Boolean value that formula F assigns to behavior σ, and we say that σ satisfies F iff $\sigma [\![F]\!]$ equals true. $\vDash F \triangleq \forall \sigma \in \textbf{\textit{St}}^\infty : \sigma [\![F]\!]$, where $\textbf{\textit{St}}^\infty$ denotes the collection of all behaviors (infinite sequences of elements of $\textbf{\textit{St}}$).

Another component of TLA syntax is the *stuttering* operator on actions. A stuttering on action A under the vector of variables f occurs when either the action A occurs or the variables in f remain the same (while either some other independent action occurs or the system remains idle).

The stuttering operator and its converse the *angle* operator are given by: $[A]_f \triangleq A \vee (f' = f)$ and $\langle A \rangle_f \triangleq A \vee (f' \neq f)$.

Reasoning about *fairness* is an important aspect when modeling concurrency. Fairness is concerned with progress properties, facts that ensure that no process is consistently neglected. In TLA, two types of fairness properties are defined: a process is said to satisfy the *weak fairness* condition if at all times either it is eventually executed or it eventually becomes disabled, and it is said to satisfy the *strong fairness* condition if at all times either it will eventually be executed or eventually it will be disabled at all later states. The definitions for these two conditions are given as: $WF_f(A) \triangleq (\Box \Diamond \langle A \rangle_f) \vee ((\Box \Diamond \neg Enabled \langle A \rangle_f)$ and $SF_f(A) \triangleq (\Box \Diamond \langle A \rangle_f) \vee ((\Diamond \Box \neg Enabled \langle A \rangle_f)$.

In TLA, systems are usually represented as a conjunction of an initial condition, an action that is continually repeated under stuttering, and a set of fairness conditions. As such, TLA formulas can be written as $\Phi \triangleq Init_\Phi \wedge \Box [N]_f \wedge F$, where:

- $Init_\Phi$ is a predicate specifying the initial values of variables.
- N is the system's next-state relation (disjunction of actions).
- f is an n-tuple of variables.
- F is the conjunction of formulas of the form $SF_f(A)$ and/or $WF_f(A)$, where A represents an actions of a disjunction of actions.

Behavioral Aspect Formalization

We describe the behavioral aspect of a pattern as a sequence of steps, each producing a new state by changing the values of one or more variables (object attributes and typed variables) and predicates (temporal relations). Thus, the semantics of the behavioral aspect of a pattern is the collection of all its possible sequences of steps. Reasoning about the behavioral aspect of a pattern will therefore require reasoning about sequences of states.

B_{BPSL} uses a special type of predicates called temporal relations. A temporal relation can be defined as follows: $TR(C_1 <cardinality>, C_2 <cardinality>)$, where TR is the name of the temporal relation, C_1 and C_2 are classes involved by this relation, and *cardinality* represents the number of instances (objects) of each class that participate in the relation. Cardinality can be represented as either a closed interval $<n..m>$, where n and m represent any two positive integers or $<*>$ to depict any possible number of instances. When used in actions, temporal relations can take different forms, each of which have a different semantics, as described below:

- $TR(o_1, o_2)$ depicts that an object o_1 of a class C_1 is currently linked through TR with an object o_2 of a class C_2.
- $\neg TR(o_1, o_2)$ depicts that objects o_1 and o_2 are no longer linked through TR.
- $TR(o_1, C_2)$ depicts that object o_1 is linked with all objects of the class C_2.
- $\neg TR(o_1, C_2)$ depicts that object o_1 is not linked through TR with any object of class C_2.
- $\neg TR(C_1, C_2)$ depicts that no object of class C_1 is linked through TR with any object of class C_2.

Let us take an example of temporal relations and actions from the *Observer* pattern (Gamma et al., 1995). Table 2 represents a portion of its B_{BPSL} formula.

In the above example, *TR* is the set of all temporal relations. The temporal relation *Attached(concrete-subject<0..1>,concrete-observer<*>)* reflects the fact that a *concrete-observer* is associated with a *concrete-subject* whenever it is interested in its content. The cardinality shows that many *concrete-observers* might be attached to zero or one *concrete-subject*. The temporal relation *Updated(concrete-subject<0..1>,concrete-observer<*>)* reflects the fact that each *concrete-subject* needs to know to which *concrete-observers* its contents have been delivered since the last modification. Thus, *concrete-subjects* are associated with *concrete-observers* that have already been updated. Action *Attach* sets the temporal relation *Attached* between *concrete-subject* and *concrete-observer* objects. In the current state, the objects are not linked by the temporal relation *Attached* and in the next state the objects become linked by this temporal relation.

Temporal relations can be replaced by Boolean expressions made of variables (primed and unprimed) and constant symbols. However, this will involve implementation details rather that staying at design level, which is the level of abstraction of patterns.

In the action *Attach*, instead of using the temporal relation *Attached*, we could use a list handled by a subject (we call this set *List*) and containing the object references of the observers attached to it. As such, action *Attach* could be written as: $Attach \triangleq o \notin List \wedge List' = List \cup \{o\}$.

Table 2. A portion of the B_{BPSL} formula of the Observer pattern

Attached(concrete-subject<0..1>,concrete-observer<*>),Updated(concrete-subject<0..1>,concrete-observer<*>)∈ TR; s∈ concrete-subject; o∈ concrete-observer; d∈ V;
Attach $\triangleq \neg$Attached(s,o)$\wedge$ Attached'(s,o)
...

Structure of BPSL Formulas

BPSL uses three compartments (boxes) to specify a pattern (see Table 3). The first contains the S_{BPSL} formula, the second contains declaration of temporal relations and variables used in the B_{BPSL} formula, while the third contains the B_{BPSL} formula. In Table 3, $PR_1...PR_q$ are permanent relation symbols, $TR_1(z_1<cz_1>,t_1<ct_1>),...,TR_m(z_m<cz_m>,t_m<ct_m>)$ are temporal relation symbols, and $A_1...A_r$ are action symbols. In the notation $TR_i(z_i<cz_i>,t_i<ct_i>)$, z_i and t_i are variables representing classes, while $<cz>$ and $<ct>$ are the cardinalities of z_i and t_i respectively. The notation "*Member of C*" means that $u_1,...,u_n$ are objects of specific classes (belonging to the set C). In all specifications, we follow a convention in which only relations (permanent and temporal) and actions start with a capital letter. Actions in BPSL represent either individual operations (methods) or a group of operations.

Formal Specification of Pattern Composition

Component-based software development focuses on building software systems by assembling previously developed and well-tested or even formally validated components rather than developing the entire software from scratch (Chessman & Daniels, 2000). This leads to an apparent reduction in time, cost and effort. However, the assembly can lead to software failures if it is not done with prior knowledge of the relevant properties of each component (D'Souza & Willis, 1998).

Component integration plays a central role in this process. Ensuring the correctness of this integration will allow problems to be detected and fixed early in the lifecycle instead of waiting to solve them at late and expensive stages of the lifecycle. Formalization facilitates the automation of error avoidance and detection and ensures the correctness of the composition at design stage. The correctness of pattern composition is satisfied by both of the following fundamental rules:

1.   The composition does not make a component lose any of its properties.

2.   The composition does not add new properties to any component.

Table 3. Structure of a BPSL formula

$\exists\, x_1,...,x_{q1},y_1,...,y_{q2} \subset C\cup V\cup M \wedge_i PR_i(x_j,y_k)$ $\{1<=i<=q,\ 1<=j<=q_1;1<=k<=q_2\}$
$TR_1(z_1<cz_1>,t_1<ct_1>),...,TR_m(z_m<cz_m>,t_m<ct_m>)\in TR;\ \{z_1,...,z_m,t_1,...,t_m \in C\}$ $u_1,...,u_n \subset (Member\ of\ C)\cup V;$
$Init_\Phi \triangleq P$ *{P is the initial predicate}* $N \triangleq A_1\vee...\vee A_r$ $\{A_1...A_r\ are\ actions\}$ $u \triangleq \langle u_p,...,u_j\rangle$ $\{1<=i<=n\ and\ 1<=j<=n\}$ $\Phi \triangleq Init_\Phi \wedge \Box [N]_u \wedge WF_u(A)$ $\{A=A_{i1}\vee...\vee A_{i2},1<=i_1<=i_2<=r\}$

Design patterns are considered design components, allowing a great deal of reuse flexibility to the designer. They are therefore considered microarchitectures from which more reusable and flexible designs can be built. Thus, if formalized, pattern composition can lead to ready-made architectures from which only instantiation is required to build robust implementations. Since the specification of the structural and behavioral aspects of patterns uses two different formalisms (FOL and TLA), the specification of pattern composition is done independently for each aspect.

Name mapping is applied during composition of patterns. Name mapping associates properties defined in the patterns to be composed with properties defined in the composition. For the structural aspect properties represent terms and predicates, while for the behavioral aspect they represent predicates, variables, and actions. In the following we assume the composition of two patterns. However the underlying theory can be generalized to more than two patterns.

Let P_1 and P_2 denote sets containing properties of the patterns to be composed and let Q denote a set containing properties of the composition of P_1 with P_2. Name mappings are defined as:

$$C_1: P_1 \rightarrow Q$$
$$C_2: P_2 \rightarrow Q$$

The correctness rules defined above (informally), can be formalized as follows (f represents any property):

1. $f \in (P_1 \cap P_2) \Rightarrow C_1(f) = C_2(f)$
    $f \in (P_1 \cup P_2) \Rightarrow (C_1(f) \in Q) \vee (C_2(f) \in Q)$
2. $f \notin (P_1 \cup P_2) \Rightarrow (C_1(f) \notin Q) \wedge (C_2(f) \notin Q)$

Note that (2) means that Q can contain new properties not related to P_1 and P_2. The name mapping functions defined above can be represented by *substitutions*. In FOL, a substitution list $Theta = \{v_1/t_1, .., v_n/t_n\}$ means to replace all occurrences of variable symbol v_i by terms t_i (variables or constants in S_{BPSL}). Substitutions are made from left to right in the list. For example, $subst(\{x/Pasta, y/John\}, eats(y,x)) \equiv eats(John, Pasta)$. In BPSL, we restrict the terms t_i to variable and constant symbols only, that is, function symbols are not supported. Substitutions can also be applied to TLA actions in a similar way as described above. If A_1 is an action involving variables $x_1, \ldots, x_n$, then A_2 an action involving variables $y_1, \ldots, y_n$ can be defined based on A_1 as follows: $A_2 \triangleq subst(\{x_1/y_1, \ldots, x_n/y_n\}, A_1)$.

Following are declarations needed for the composition formulas given below:

- P_1 and P_2 are the patterns to be composed and P is the result of the composition.
- $P_i(p,q)$ is a temporal relation of P_1, $Q_j(s,t)$ is a temporal relations of P_2 and $R_k(w,z)$ is a temporal relation of P. The cardinalities have been omitted and $\{p,q,s,t,w,z\} \subset C$.

- Φ is the S_{BPSL} formula of P, Φ_1 is the S_{BPSL} formula of P_1, Φ_2 is the S_{BPSL} formula of P_2 and Φ_3 is an S_{BPSL} formula representing the extra variables, constants, and permanent relations of the composition itself.

- Ψ is the B_{BPSL} of P, Ψ_1 is the B_{BPSL} formula of P_1, Ψ_2 is the B_{BPSL} formula of P_2.

- $u_1...u_n, v_1,...,v_m \in C \cup V \cup M$

- $x_1...x_n, y_1...y_n \in (Member\ of\ C) \cup V$

$$\Phi \equiv subst(\{u_1/v_1,...,u_n/v_m\},\Phi_1 \wedge \Phi_2) \wedge \Phi_3 \qquad \{structural\ aspect\}$$
$$R_k(w,z)=subst(\{p/w,q/z\},P_i(p,q))\ or\ R_k(w,z)=subst(\{s/w,t/z\},Q_j(s,t)) \quad \{temporal\ relations\}$$
$$\Psi \equiv subst(\{x_1/y_1,...,x_n/y_n\},\Psi_1 \wedge \Psi_2) \qquad \{behavioral\ aspect\}$$

The temporal relations of the pattern composition represent the union of the temporal relations of the patterns to be composed. Moreover, the substitutions made in formula $\Phi_1 \wedge \Phi_2$ also take effect in the temporal relations of the pattern composition. We have shown substitutions in temporal relation here just for clarity. In the formula of the pattern composition, we do not explicitly show the substitutions in temporal relations.

The formula defining the structural aspect composition is straightforward. However, the one defining the behavioral aspect composition needs to be explained, in particular the meaning of the TLA conjunction $\Psi_1 \wedge \Psi_2$ (Lamport, 1994).

If Ψ_1 is defined as:

$Init_{\Psi1} \triangleq P$

$\qquad\qquad\qquad\qquad\qquad \{initial\ predicate\}$

$M \triangleq A_1 \vee ... \vee A_{m1}$

$\qquad\qquad\qquad\qquad\qquad \{actions\}$

$u \triangleq \langle u_1,...,u_{m2} \rangle$

$\qquad\qquad\qquad\qquad\qquad \{variables\}$

$\Psi_1 \triangleq Init_{\Psi1} \wedge \Box [M]_u \wedge WF_u(A) \qquad \{A \equiv A_{i1} \vee ... \vee A_{j1}, 1<=i1<=j1<=m1\}$

If Ψ_2 is defined as:

$Init_{\Psi2} \triangleq Q \qquad\qquad\qquad\qquad \{initial\ predicate\}$
$N \triangleq B_1 \vee ... \vee B_{n1} \qquad\qquad\quad \{actions\}$
$v \triangleq \langle v_1,...,v_{n2} \rangle \qquad\qquad\qquad \{variables\}$
$\Psi_2 \triangleq Init_{\Psi2} \wedge \Box [N]_v \wedge WF_v(B) \qquad \{B \equiv B_{i2} \vee ... \vee B_{j2}, 1<=i2<=j2<=n1\}$

Then Ψ will be defined as follows:

$Init_\Psi \triangleq subst(\{...\}, Init_{\Psi1}) \wedge subst(\{...\}, Init_{\Psi2})$
$W \triangleq C_1 \vee ... \vee C_{m1+n1}\ \{C_i=subst(\{...\},A_j)\ or\ C_i=subst(\{...\},B_k), 1<=i<=m1+n1, 1<=j<=m1,$
$1<=k<=n1\}$

$$w \triangleq u \cup v$$
$$\Psi \triangleq Init_\Psi \wedge \square [W]_w \wedge WF_w(A) \wedge WF_w(B)$$

In the notation $C_i = subst(\{...\}, A_j)$, $\{...\}$ represents any substitution list. It is to be noted that common permanent relation, initial predicates and actions will only appear once in the composition formulas as by simple logic $P \wedge P \equiv P$ and $P \vee P \equiv P$.

Case Studies

This section shows how BPSL was successfully used to specify patterns and their composition. Most findings of the previous section will be applied here.

Observer Pattern

In the *Observer* pattern (Gamma et al., 1995), there are (concrete) subjects and (concrete) observers. Each subject has data whose content can be modified. Each observer can be interested in the content of a subject's data. The pattern describes how subjects and observers are connected with each other and how they communicate in order to preserve data consistency. A subject notifies its observers whenever a change occurs that could make their data inconsistent with its own. After being notified of the change, observers query the subject to get the latest values of the subject data.

Figure 1 depicts the UML class diagram of the *Observer* pattern, while Table 4 depicts its BPSL specification. The semantics of the formulas given in Table 4 can be easily understood from the explanations given in second section.

In Table 4, actions $Init_{\Psi 1}$, *Attach* and *Update* are straightforward. In the current state of actions *Detach* and *Notify*, expression "$Attached(s,o) \vee (Attached(s,o) \wedge Updated(s,o))$" reflects that a *concrete-observer o* is either attached to a *concrete-subject s* (if it has just joined the list of *concrete-observers* attached to s) or it is an old member of the list and it has received the latest update.

Figure 1. Class diagram of the Observer pattern

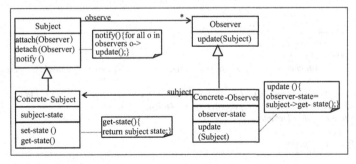

Mediator Pattern

In this variant of the *Mediator* pattern, there are (concrete) colleagues that connect to a mediator. Connected colleagues can communicate with each other by putting messages into the mediator (using a mailbox), which then lets the colleagues get the messages addressed to them. When connection is no longer needed, colleagues may disconnect from the mediator. Whenever a colleague receives a message, the message has been explicitly sent to it by a colleague who is still connected to the mediator. We prefer to use this variant of the Mediator patterns because the original version given in Gamma et al. (1995) is too abstract and too generic (there are neither attributes nor methods defined in that version) to give any room for formal specification. Figure 2 depicts the UML class diagram of the *Mediator* pattern, while Table 5 depicts its BPSL specification. The semantics of the formulas given in Table 5 can be easily understood from the explanations given in section 2.

Observer-Mediator Pattern Composition

Figure 3 depicts the UML class diagram of the *Observer-Mediator* pattern composition, while Table 6 depicts its BPSL specification. The keyword *List* is used in the method *put()* to reflect the fact that the message is addressed to a list of *Observer Colleagues*. The *Observer-Mediator* pattern combination allows subjects and observers to either communicate directly (as in the *Observer* pattern) or to communicate through a mediator which provides a mailbox for the communication (as in the *Mediator* pattern).

Table 4. BPSL specification of the Observer pattern

$\Phi_I \equiv \exists$ *subject, concrete-subject, observer, concrete-observer* $\in C$; *subject-state, observer-state* $\in V$; *attach, detach, notify, get-state, set-state, update* $\in M$: *Defined-in(subject-state, concrete-subject)$\wedge$ Defined-in (observer-state, concrete-observer) $\wedge$Defined-in(attach, subject) $\wedge$Defined-in (detach ,subject) $\wedge$Defined-in (notify, subject) $\wedge$Defined-in(set-state, concrete-subject) $\wedge$Defined-in (get-state, concrete-subject) $\wedge$ Defined-in (update, observer) $\wedge$ Reference-to-one(concrete-observer, concrete-subject) $\wedge$ Reference-to-many(subject, observer) $\wedge$ Inheritance(concrete-subject, subject) $\wedge$ Inheritance(concrete-observer, observer) $\wedge$ Invocation(set-state, notify) $\wedge$ Invocation(notify, update) $\wedge$ Invocation(update, get-state) $\wedge$ Argument(observer, attach) $\wedge$ Argument(observer, detach) $\wedge$ Argument(subject, update)*
Attached(concrete-subject<0..1>,concrete-observer<*>),Updated(concrete-subject<0..1>,concrete-observer<*>) $\in TR$; $s \in$ *concrete-subject*; $o \in$ *concrete-observer*; $d \in V$;
$Init_{\psi_I} \triangleq \neg Attached(s, concrete\text{-}observer)$ $Attach \triangleq \neg Attached(s,o) \wedge Attached'(s,o)$ $Notify \triangleq Attached(s,o) \vee (Attached(s,o) \wedge Updated(s,o))) \wedge ((s.subject\text{-}state)' = d) \wedge \neg Updated'(s,concrete\text{-}observer)$ $Update \triangleq Attached (s,o) \wedge \neg Updated(s,o) \wedge ((o.observer\text{-}state)' = (s.subject\text{-}state)) \wedge Updated'(s,o)$ $Detach \triangleq Attached(s,o) \vee (Attached(s,o) \wedge Updated(s,o)) \wedge \neg Attached'(s,o)$ $M \triangleq Attach \vee Notify \vee Update \vee Detach$ $u \triangleq \langle s,o \rangle$ $\Psi_I \triangleq Init_{\psi_I} \wedge \square [M]_u \wedge WF_u (Update)$

Figure 2. Class Diagram of the Mediator pattern

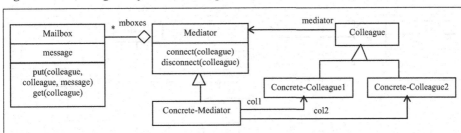

Let us now check the correctness of the composition from both aspects (structural and behavioral) as per the rules defined in the third section.

The *Observer* pattern has four classes, the *Mediator* pattern has six classes, while the *Observer-Mediator* pattern composition has eight classes. This means that there are two common classes (which have been mapped to *Observer-Colleague* and *Subject-Colleague*). These mappings have been reflected in the substitutions shown in compartment 1 of Table 6 (*concrete-colleague1/observer-colleague, concrete-colleague2/subject-colleague,concrete-observer/observer-colleague,concrete-subject/subject-colleague*). Moreover, all terms and predicates belonging to either *Observer* or *Mediator* patterns have been mapped to themselves (remained unchanged) in the *Observer-Mediator* pattern composition, except the *Concrete-*

Table 5. BPSL specification of the Mediator pattern

$\Phi_2 \equiv \exists$ *mediator, concrete-mediator, colleague, concrete-colleague1,concrete-colleague2, mailbox* $\in C$; *message* $\in V$; *connect, disconnect, put, get* $\in M$:
Defined-in (connect ,mediator) $\wedge$ *Defined-in (disconnect, mediator)* $\wedge$ *Defined-in(message, mailbox)* $\wedge$
Defined-in (put ,mailbox) $\wedge$ *Defined-in(get, mailbox)* $\wedge$ *Reference-to-one(colleague, mediator)* $\wedge$
Reference-to-one(concrete-mediator, concrete-colleague1) $\wedge$ *Reference-to-one(concrete-mediator, concrete-colleague2)* $\wedge$ *Reference-to-many(mediator, mailbox)* $\wedge$ *Inheritance(concrete-mediator, mediator)* $\wedge$ *Inheritance(concrete-colleague1, colleague)* $\wedge$ *Inheritance(concrete-colleague2, colleague)* $\wedge$
Argument(colleague, connect) $\wedge$ *Argument(colleague, disconnect)* $\wedge$ *Argument(colleague, put)* $\wedge$ *Argument (message, put)* $\wedge$ *Argument(colleague, get)*

Owned (mailbox<0..1>, colleague<0..1>),Connected (colleague<*>,concrete-mediator <0..1>), Accessed (mailbox<*>, colleague<*>) $\in TR$;
$m \in$ *concrete-mediator;* $c_1 \in$ *concrete-colleague1;* $c2 \in$ *concrete-colleague2;mb* $\in$ *mailbox;d* $\in V$;

$Init_{\psi 2} \triangleq \neg Connected(colleague, m) \wedge \neg Owned(mailbox, colleague)$
$Connect \triangleq \neg Connected(c_1, m) \wedge Connected'(c_1, m)$
$Acquire \triangleq Connected(c_1, m) \wedge \neg Owned(mb, colleague) \wedge Owned'(mb, c_1)$
$Release \triangleq Owned(mb, c_1) \wedge \neg Accessed(mb, colleague) \wedge \neg Owned'(mb, c_1)$
$Put \triangleq Owned(mb, c_1) \wedge Connected(c_2, m) \wedge (mb.message)' = d \wedge Accessed'(mb, c_2)$
$Get \triangleq Accessed(mb, c_1) \wedge (d = mb.message) \wedge \neg Accessed'(mb, c_1)$
$Disconnect \triangleq Connected(c_1, m) \wedge \neg Owned(mailbox, c1) \wedge \neg Connected'(c_1, m) \wedge \neg Accessed'(mailbox, c_1)$
$N \triangleq Connect \vee Acquire \vee Release \vee Put \vee Get \vee Disconnect$
$v \triangleq \langle mb \rangle$
$\Psi_2 \triangleq Init_{\psi 2} \wedge [N]_v \wedge WF_v(Get)$

Figure 3. Class diagram of the Observer-Mediator pattern composition

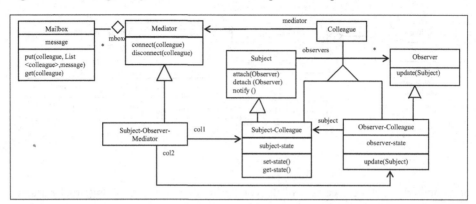

Mediator class, which has been renamed *Subject-Observer-Mediator*. Based on the above discussion, condition (1) holds. Since no new terms or predicates about either the *Observer* or the *Mediator* pattern have been added by the composition, rule (2) also holds.

As for the behavioral aspect specification, it can be seen that it follows exactly the composition formula described in the third section. The *Observer* and *Mediator* patterns have no common variables, temporal relations or actions. Temporal relations, initial predicates, and actions of the composed pattern are based on those of the original pattern with some straightforward substitutions of variables. Hence rule (1) holds. The changes required on actions of the *Observer-Mediator* pattern composition are as follows:

- Only a *Subject Colleague* can own a *mailbox*.
- A *Subject Colleague* can put messages for a group of *Observer Colleagues*.

Since no new variables, predicates or actions about either the *Observer* or the *Mediator* pattern have been added by the composition, rule (2) also holds.

Formal Specification of Instances of Patterns

BPSL specification of instances of patterns is done by applying substitutions on the specification of the original pattern. Following are declarations needed for pattern instantiation formulas given below:

- P_1 is a pattern and P is an instance of P_1.
- $Q_i(p,q)$ is a temporal relation of P_1, $R_j(s,t)$ is a temporal relations of P. The cardinalities have been omitted and $\{p,q,s,t\} \subset C$.

Table 6. BPSL specification of the Observer-Mediator pattern composition

$\Phi \equiv subst(\{concrete\text{-}mediator/subject\text{-}observer\text{-}mediator, concrete\text{-}colleague1/subject\text{-}colleague, concrete\text{-}colleague2/observer\text{-}colleague,\ concrete\text{-}observer/observer\text{-}colleague,\ concrete\text{-}subject/subject\text{-}colleague\},\Phi_1 \wedge \Phi_2)$

$Init_\psi \triangleq subst(\{s/sc,\ concrete\text{-}observer/observer\text{-}colleague\},Init_{\psi_1}) \wedge subst(\{m/som\},Init_{\psi_2})$

$Observer\text{-}Attach \triangleq subst(\{s/sc,o/oc\},\ Attach)$

$Subject\text{-}Notify \triangleq subst(\{s/sc,o/oc,concrete\text{-}observer/observer\text{-}colleague\},Notify)$

$Observer\text{-}Update \triangleq subst(\{s/sc,o/oc\},Update)$

$Observer\text{-}Detach \triangleq subst(\{s/sc,o/oc\},\ Detach)$

$Colleague\text{-}Connect \triangleq subst\ (\{(c_1/sc)\vee(c_1/oc),\ m/som\},\ Connect)$

$Subject\text{-}Acquire \triangleq subst(\{c_1/sc,m/som\},Acquire)$

$Subject\text{-}Release \triangleq subst(\{c_1/sc\},Release)$

$Subject\text{-}Put \triangleq subst(\{\ c_1/sc,\ c_2/observer\text{-}colleague,\ m/som,\ d/sc.subject\text{-}state\},Put)$

$Observer\text{-}Get \triangleq subst(\{c_1/oc,\ d/oc.observer\text{-}state\},Get)$

$Colleague\text{-}Disconnect \triangleq subst(\{(c_1/sc)\vee(c_1/oc),\ m/som\},\ Disconnect)$

$W \triangleq Observer\text{-}Attach \vee Subject\text{-}Notify \vee Observer\text{-}Update \vee Observer\text{-}Detach \vee Colleague\text{-}Connect \vee$
$Subject\text{-}Acquire \vee Subject\text{-}Release \vee Subject\text{-}Putt \vee Observer\text{-}Get \vee Colleague\text{-}Disconnect$

$w \triangleq \langle\ sc,oc,mb\rangle$

$\Psi \triangleq Init_\psi \wedge \square [W]_w \wedge WF_w(Observer\text{-}Update) \wedge WF_w(Observer\text{-}Get)$

- Φ_1 is the S_{BPSL} formula of P_1, Φ is the S_{BPSL} formula of P.
- Ψ_1 is the B_{BPSL} formula of P_1, Ψ is the B_{BPSL} formula of P.
- Φ_2 is an S_{BPSL} formula representing extra required variables and permanent relations for P.
- $u_1 \ldots u_m,\ v_1,\ldots,v_m \in C \cup V \cup M$
- $x_1 \ldots x_n,\ y_1 \ldots y_n \in (Member\ of\ C) \cup V$

$\Phi \equiv subst(\{u_1/v_1,\ldots,u_n/v_n\},\Phi_1) \wedge \Phi_2$ {*structural aspect*}

$R_j(s,t)=subst(\{p/s,q/t\},Q_i(p,q))$ {*temporal relations*}

$\Psi \equiv subst(\{x_1/y_1,\ldots,x_n/y_n\},\Psi_1)$ {*behavioral aspect*}

Now, we will apply the above formulas to specify an instance of the *Observer* pattern (see Figure 4) that was given in the sample code section in Gamma et al. (1995). In this pattern instance, the class *Clock Timer* is a concrete subject for storing and maintaining the time of the day. The method *set-time()* gets called by an internal timer every second. The method *set-time()* updates the *Clock Timer*'s internal state and calls the method *notify()* to inform concrete observers of the change. The classes *Digital Clock* and *Analog Clock* are concrete observers used to display the time in a digital and analog fashion, respectively. When the time ticks, the two clocks will be updated and will redisplay themselves appropriately. Table 7 depicts BPSL specification of this instance of the *Observer* pattern. Since the S_{BPSL} formula of the *Observer* pattern includes only one *Concrete Observer*, it is obvious that we need to add an extra class and an extra inheritance permanent relation to accommodate the other concrete observer (analog-clock). In Table 7, the substitution *"concrete-observer/observer"* is done to make it possible for an object of *concrete-observer* to be substituted for either an object of *digital-clock* or *analog-clock*.

Figure 4. Class diagram of an instance of the Observer pattern

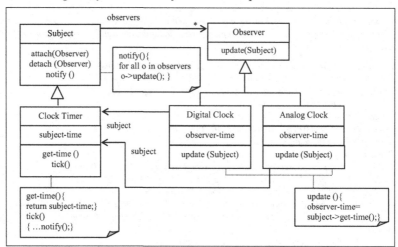

Related Work

Formal Specification of Patterns

Based on a comparison done on formal specification languages for Design patterns (Taibi & Ngo, 2003b), it was found that the most promising alternatives for specifying Design patterns are language for patterns' uniform specification (LePUS) (Eden & Kazman, 2003), and distributed co-operation (DisCo) (Jarvinen & Kurki-Suonio, 1991).

As such, BPSL is based to a certain extent on both mathematical backgrounds of LePUS (Eden & Kazman, 2003) and DisCo (Jarvinen & Kurki-Suonio, 1991), which are FOL and TLA, respectively. LePUS uses higher-order logic (HOL) as a formal basis and focuses only on specifying the structural aspects of Design patterns. We preferred to use a small fraction of FOL because approachability was paramount in the design of BPSL. If the users of a formal specification language for Design patterns cannot easily understand it, how are they supposed to understand Design patterns formally specified by this language? DisCo uses TLA as the formal basis and was designed to specify reactive systems, which are in constant interaction with their environment and therefore have a predominant behavioral aspect. DisCo has little (almost no) support for specifying the structural aspect.

Formal Specification of Pattern Composition

In Saeki (2000), the author used language of temporal ordering specification (LOTOS) (Van Eijk, Vissers, & Diaz, 1989) to specify pattern composition. The formal semantic of

Table 7. BPSL specification of an instance of the Observer pattern

$\Phi_2 \equiv \exists$ *analog-clock* $\in$ *C: Inheritance(analog-clock, observer)* Φ=*subst({ concrete-subject/clock-timer ,concrete-observer/digital-clock, subject-state/subject-time,get-state/get-time,set-state/set-time,observer-state/observer-time},* Φ_1)∧ Φ_2
Attached(concrete-subject<0..1>,concrete-observer<*>)≡ subst(concrete-subject/clock-timer, concrete-observer/observer),Updated(concrete-subject<0..1>,concrete-observer<*>)≡ subst(concrete-subject/clock-timer, concrete-observer/observer)∈ TR;
Ψ=*subst({concrete-subject/clock-timer, concrete-observer/observer, subject-state/subject-time, observer-state/observer-time},* Ψ_1)

LOTOS is based on Calculus of Communicating Systems (CCS) for behavior specification and on algebra of abstract data type (ADT) for data specification. LOTOS was originally devised by the International Organization for Standardization (ISO) to specify the layers and their interaction for the open system interconnection (OSI) model. LOTOS has been adapted in Saeki (2000) to be used for specifying patterns that appeared in Gamma et al. (1995) and their composition. While LOTOS is best suited for network layers specification, its adaptation to patterns did not yield simple and clear specifications, as expected by any formal specification language. Saeki used LOTOS to formally specify the *Command* and *Composite* patterns and their composition using very lengthy LOTOS specifications from a purely behavioral aspect.

In Dong, Alencar, and Cowan (2000), the authors used FOL *theories* to specify the structural aspect of patterns and TLA to specify their behavioral aspect. The same techniques were used to specify pattern composition. The specification of the structural aspect of a pattern used predicates for describing classes, state variables, methods, and their relations. More precisely, the *sorts class* and *object* denote the *first-class* objects in a pattern. They also make use of other *sorts,* such as *bool* and *int.* Each pattern is described using a *signature* that contains predicate names, their domain, and their range (*bool*). Each pattern is specified by an FOL theory that is derived from its signature. From a structural aspect, pattern composition is performed using *name mapping,* which associates the classes and objects declared in a pattern with the classes and objects declared in the pattern composition. From a behavioral aspect, pattern composition is the conjunction of the TLA formula representing each of the participating patterns. In Dong et al. (2000), composition proofs (for both structural and behavioral aspect) are done on the specific example, and not on the general case.

In Mikkonen (1998), the author used a variation of DisCo (Jarvinen & Kurki-Suonio, 1991) to specify the behavioral aspect of patterns. The specification of pattern composition was done using as example the *Observer-Mediator* pattern composition. The correctness of the specification of the pattern composition is ensured using the concept of *refinement.* Actions of the pattern composition must refine actions from both patterns, which guarantee to satisfy their characteristic properties. The technique does not use the concept of name mapping, nor common things between patterns. Moreover, the composition is solely done from a behavioral aspect with little focus on the structural aspect composition.

Conclusion and Future Research Directions

Patterns are gaining increasing acceptance and usage. They capture design experience in such a way that they become a learning aid for novice designers. However, the inherent benefits of patterns cannot be fully exploited by the existing informal means of specifying them. Formal specification of patterns allows precise specifications and facilitates tool support. BPSL was developed to cope with the shortcomings of the existing formal approaches for pattern specification. BPSL's ultimate purpose is to complement (not replace) informal approaches in order to allow users to know exactly *when* and *how* to use patterns. This was achieved by providing well-defined formulas that specify patterns in order to allow rigorous reasoning about them. Since patterns are seldom used in isolation but composed to build bigger systems, BPSL was also used to formalize pattern composition. The composition was applied on the *Observer-Mediator* pattern composition.

We have developed a tool for generating skeleton Java code from BPSL specifications of pattern instances (Taibi & Mkadmi, 2006). We are also working on developing a pattern repository management tool in which BPSL specifications of well-established patterns are stored and candidate patterns are checked against them to see whether they can be added as new patterns or classified as refinements of well-established patterns.

References

Alexander, C., Ishikawa, S., & Silverstein, M. (1977). *A pattern language: Towns, buildings, construction*. USA: Oxford University Press.

Cheesman, J., & Daniels, J. (2000). *UML components: A simple process for specifying component-based software*. Addison-Wesley Professional.

Dong, J., Alencar, P.S.C., & Cowan, D.D (2000). Ensuring structure and behavior correctness in design composition. In *Proceedings of the 7th IEEE International Conference and Workshop on the Engineering of Computer Based Systems* (pp. 279-287). IEEE Computer Society Press.

D'Souza, D.F., & Wills, A.L. (1998). *Objects, components, and frameworks with UML: The catalysis approach*. Addison-Wesley Professional.

Eden, A.H., & Kazman, R. (2003). Architecture, design, implementation. In *Proceedings of the 25th International Conference on Software Engineering* (pp. 149-159). IEEE Computer Society Press.

Gamma, E., Helm, R., Johnson, R., & Vlissides, J. (1995). *Design patterns: Elements of reusable object-oriented systems*. Addison-Wesley Professional.

Jarvinen, H.M., & Kurki-Suonio, H.M. (1991). Disco specification language: Marriage of actions and objects. In *Proceedings of the 11th IEEE International Conference on Distributed Computing Systems* (pp. 142-151). IEEE Computer Society Press.

Lamport, L. (1994). The temporal logic of actions. *ACM Transactions on Programming Languages and Systems, 16*(3), 872-923.

Mikkonen, T. (1998). Formalizing Design patterns. In *Proceedings of the 20th International Conference on Software Engineering* (pp. 115-124). IEEE Computer Society Press.

Rumbaugh, J., Jacobson, I., & Booch, G. (1998). *The unified modeling language reference manual*. Addison-Wesley Professional.

Saeki, M. (2000). Behavioral specification of GoF Design patterns with LOTOS. In *Proceedings of the 7th Asia Pacific Software Engineering Conference* (pp. 408-415). IEEE Computer Society Press.

Schmidt, D.C., Stal, M., Rohnert, H., & Buschmann, F. (2000). *Pattern-oriented software architecture: Patterns for concurrent and networked objects*. John Wiley & Sons.

Smullyan, R.M. (1995). *First-order logic*. New York: Dover Publications.

Taibi, T., & Mkadmi, T. (2006). A java code generator from BPSL specifications of Design patterns. In *Proceedings of the 7th UAEU Research Conference* (pp. 46-54). Al Ain: UAE. UAEU Press.

Taibi, T., & Ngo, D.C.L. (2003a). Formal specification of Design patterns-A balanced approach. *Journal of Object Technology, 2*(4), 127-140.

Taibi, T., & Ngo, D.C.L. (2003b). Formal specification of Design patterns: A comparison. In *Proceedings of the 1st ACS/IEEE International Conference on Computer Systems and Applications (AICCSA)* (pp. 77-86). IEEE Computer Society Press.

Taibi, T., & Ngo, D.C.L. (2004). Towards a balanced specification language for distributed object computing patterns. *IASTED International Journal of Computers and Applications, 26*(1), 63-70.

Van Eijk, P.H.J., Vissers, C.A., & Diaz, M. (Eds.). (1989). *The formal description technique LOTOS*. The Netherlands: Elsevier Science Publishers B.V.

Chapter II

A Visual Language for Design Pattern Modeling and Instantiation

David Maplesden, Orion Systems Ltd., New Zealand

John Hosking, University of Auckland, New Zealand

John Grundy, University of Auckland, New Zealand

Abstract

In this chapter we describe the Design pattern modeling language, a notation supporting the specification of Design pattern solutions and their instantiation into UML design models. DPML uses a simple set of visual abstractions and readily lends itself to tool support. DPML Design pattern solution specifications are used to construct visual, formal specifications of Design patterns. DPML instantiation diagrams are used to link a Design pattern solution specification to instances of a UML model, indicating the roles played by different UML elements in the generic Design pattern solution. A prototype tool is described, together with an evaluation of the language and tool.

Introduction

Design patterns are a method of encapsulating the knowledge of experienced software designers in a human-readable and understandable form. They provide an effective means for describing key aspects of a successful solution to a design problem and the benefits and tradeoffs related to using that solution. Using Design patterns help produce good design, which helps produce good software (Gamma, Helm, Johnston, & Vlissides, 1994).

Design patterns to date have mostly been described using a combination of natural language and UML-style diagrams or complex mathematical or logic based formalisms, which the average programmer finds difficult to understand. This leads to complications in incorporating Design patterns effectively into the design of new software. To encourage the use of Design patterns, we have been developing tool support for incorporating Design patterns into program design. We describe the Design pattern modeling language (DPML), a visual language for modeling Design pattern solutions and their instantiations in object-oriented designs of software systems. We have developed two prototype tools, DPTool and MaramaDPTool, realising DPML and integrating it within the Eclipse environment. Significant contributions of this work include the introduction of *dimensions* as a proxy for collections of like Design pattern participants and the instantiation of patterns into designs rather than directly into code. These both fit naturally with model driven design approaches.

We begin by describing previous work in Design pattern tool support. We then overview DPML and describe its use in modeling Design pattern solutions and pattern instantiation. We discuss two prototype tools we have developed to support the use of DPML, together with an evaluation of their usability. We then discuss in more detail the rationale and implications of the design choices we have made in designing DPML and the potential for more general applicability of some of those design features, before summarising our contributions.

Previous Work

Design patterns, which describe a common design solution to a programming problem, were popularised by the seminal "Gang of Four" book (Gamma et al., 1994) and Coplien's *software patterns* (Coplien, 1996). Design patterns have become very widely used in object-oriented software development, and their influence has spread to areas of software development other than design, such as the development of analysis patterns (patterns in the analysis phase) and idioms (language specific programming patterns). Design patterns are typically described using a combination of natural language, UML diagrams, and program code (Gamma et al., 1994; Grand, 1998). However, such descriptions lack Design pattern-specific visual formalisms, leading to pattern descriptions that are hard to understand and hard to incorporate into tool support. The UML standard for modeling Design patterns relies upon UML profiles and the UML metamodel (Object Management Group, 2006). This presents difficulties for modeling Design patterns, particularly because they are constructed using similar concepts to object models, and hence are simply prototypical examples of that object model. This does not allow enough freedom to model patterns effectively. Design pattern representations look like existing UML models and linking pattern elements to standard UML elements is often not supported. Several attempts have been made to improve Design pattern representation with UML (e.g., Fontoura, Pree, & Rumpe, 2002; Guennec, Sunye, & Jezequel, 2000; Mak, Choy, & Lun, 2004) but all use conventional UML diagram representations or minimal extensions. Stereotypes and related approaches to delineating patterns make the diagrams considerably more complex, and discerning pattern elements from standard UML elements is difficult.

Lauder and Kent (1998) propose an extension to UML to aid in "precise visual specification of Design patterns." They use a 3-layer model with a visual notation for expressing models. The notation is an amalgam of UML and "constraint diagrams," a notation to visually specify constraints between object model elements. A second notation expresses object dynamic behaviour and can represent generalised behaviour of Design patterns. We found their notation difficult; the differentiation between the diagrams at different levels was unclear and it seemed difficult to understand the reason why some abstractions were made at one level and not another.

There have been a number of approaches proposed for alternative visual representations for Design patterns. LePUS (Eden, 2002) uses a textual higher order monadic logic to express solutions proposed by Design patterns. Primitive variables represent the classes and functions in the Design pattern, and predicates over these variables describe characteristics or relationships between the elements. A visual notation for LePUS formulae consists of icons that represent variables or sets of variables and annotated directed arcs representing the predicates. LePUS' basis in mathematics and formal logic makes it difficult for average software developers to work with and provides a weak basis for integrated tool support, being well removed from typically used design and programming constructs. LePUS tool support is based on Prolog and lacks support for the visual notation and while diagrams are compact, they are difficult to interpret with a high abstraction gradient. LePUS concentrates solely on defining Design pattern structures, and has no mechanism for integrating instances of Design patterns into program designs or code. Mak, Choy, and Lun (2003) have proposed an extension to LePUS which addresses pattern composition.

Florijn, Meijers, and van Winsen (1997) represent patterns as groups of interacting "fragments," representing design elements of a particular type (e.g., class, method, pattern). Each fragment has attributes (e.g., classname), and roles that reference other fragments representing pattern relationships, for example, a class fragment has method roles referencing the method fragments for methods of that class. The fragments actually represent instances of patterns. Pattern definitions are represented by prototype fragment structures, a one-level approach to defining patterns where the patterns, kept in a separate repository, are identical to the pattern instances in the fragment model. This approach lacks support for the definition of Design patterns and a strong visual syntax. The single level architecture means patterns are only defined as prototypical pattern instances. We argue that concepts exist at the pattern level that do not at the pattern instance level, and thus patterns can't be specified in the most general way using only prototypical instances, that is, you cannot specify all patterns in the most general way using only prototypical instances. Their approach to pattern definition also has no formal basis. It is limited to defining patterns only relative to Smalltalk programs represented in the fragment model. We feel it would be advantageous to define an exact unambiguous meaning for the pattern representation in use so that it can be discussed without confusion and applied appropriately to a range of programming languages.

RBML (France, Kim, Ghosh, & Song, 2004; Kim, France, Ghosh, & Song, 2003) adopts a similar approach to ours, and has been influenced by the initial work we have presented in this area (Maplesden, Hosking, & Grundy, 2002). It uses a metamodeling approach to the specification of pattern representation, extending the UML metamodel to achieve this. They place more emphasis on behavioural specification than we have in the development of DPML, which has focused more on structural representations of patterns. They also adopt a cardinality approach to specification of multiplicities as opposed to our dimension concept. The tradeoffs involved are discussed further in the penultimate section of this chapter.

Some approaches use textual rather than visual languages (e.g., Reiss, 2000; Sefika, Sane, & Campbell, 1996; Taibi & Ngo, 2003). While these present useful concepts, our interest is in a visual language for modeling Design patterns. Domain-specific visual languages like DPML offer a higher level of abstraction and representation, particularly for design-level constructs. We are also particularly interested in applying to Design pattern modeling the approach UML (Object Management Group, 2006) takes to object modeling, that is, providing a common formalism that is accessible to the average designer or programmer, while abstracting away from lower levels of design.

Overview of DPML

DPML defines a metamodel and a notation for specifying Design pattern solutions and solution instances within object models. The metamodel defines a logical structure of objects, which can be used to create models of Design pattern solutions and Design pattern solution instances, while the notation describes the diagrammatic notations used to represent the models visually. It is important to stress that DPML can only be used to model the generalised *solutions* proposed by Design patterns, not complete Design patterns. A complete Design pattern also contains additional information, such as when the solution should be applied and the consequences of using the pattern.

DPML can be used as a stand-alone modeling language for Design pattern solutions or, more commonly, in conjunction with UML to model solution instances within UML design models, that is, where in the UML model the pattern is used, and the various bindings that result from that usage. DPML supports incorporation of patterns into a UML model at design-time, rather than instantiation directly into program code. We feel design-time is the vital stage at which to include Design patterns in the software engineering process, the assumption being that if Design patterns can be effectively incorporated into the UML object model, then converting the object model into code is, relatively speaking, straightforward.

There were three primary goals for the development of the DPML. Firstly, to provide an extension to the UML so that Design patterns could be raised to first class objects within the modeling process. Secondly, to provide for Design patterns some of the same benefits that the UML provides for object oriented modeling (a common language to facilitate the exchanging of models, a formal basis for the understanding of such models, and a basis to facilitate the provision of automated tool support for modeling). By raising Design patterns to first class objects in the design process, the DPML allows Design patterns to become an integral part of the design process. Thirdly, we have aimed for a formalism to express De-

Figure 1. Core concepts of DPML

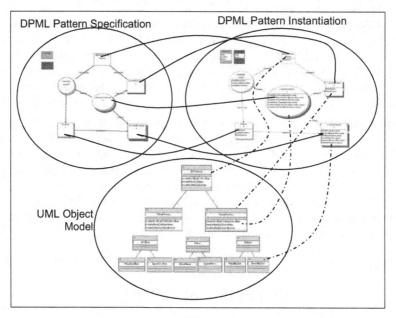

sign patterns that is *accessible* to typical programmers. Our aim is for sufficient formalism to provide a robust representation, while avoiding complex mathematical formalisms that restrict the use of our approach to a very small set of mathematically inclined programmers. This is a similar approach to formalism as has been taken in the development of UML. We feel that by providing an easy-to-use, yet powerful, method for creating and instantiating Design pattern solutions, designers will be encouraged to think at higher levels of abstraction about the problems they are facing and come up with more general, reusable solutions which can, in an iterative manner, be abstracted and then encapsulated in a Design pattern for future use.

The secondary goals of the DPML include, firstly, a common standard language for the definition of Design patterns that will allow patterns to be exchanged among designers in a more readily accessible manner than written text and diagrams, and thus hopefully spreading useful design abstractions and robust designs, and improving program design, and secondly, providing a basis for tool support for Design patterns. DPML has been developed specifically with automated tool support in mind. It is designed to be relatively easy to implement, particularly in conjunction with UML. We have carried out a detailed investigation into the implementation issues for the DPML and the processes that can be supported for working with the DPML, and have developed two proof-of-concept tool implementations.

The intended uses of the DPML, then, is to capture areas of good design within an OO model in a Design pattern and to reuse them within the same and different models. Specifying the constructs in the Design pattern that capture the essential parts of the good design ensures that these elements exist every time the Design pattern is employed. Indeed, by encouraging more experienced designers to create the Design patterns to be used by less experienced designers in their work, the DPML provides a practical way to encapsulate and reuse the expertise of good designers.

The core concept of DPML (as shown in Figure 1) is that a Design pattern specification model is used to describe the generalised design structures of Design patterns that are of interest to or useful to the user. This entails modeling the participants (interfaces, methods, etc.) involved in the pattern and the relationships between them. The user can then use the UML to create an object-oriented (OO) model of a system they are interested in or developing. During the OO modeling process, if the user sees an opportunity to use a Design pattern they have previously defined, they can create an instance of that Design pattern from the original definition. The instantiation process consists of linking the roles of the elements in the Design pattern with members from the OO model, or creating new model members where required. The well-formed rules at this stage define which members from the OO model are eligible for fulfilling each role. In this way, the user can be sure of creating a valid instance of the Design pattern and so be sure of gaining the benefits of using the Design pattern.

The Design pattern instance model also allows each individual Design pattern instance to be tailored. By default, a Design pattern instance contains members for all objects and constraints on these objects specified by the pattern definition. However, certain parts of the pattern may be relaxed or extended on a case-by-case basis, allowing pattern instances that are variations on the base pattern. This recognises the fact that pattern instantiation often involves small adaptations of the pattern to suit the particular context it is being applied to (Chambers, Harrison, & Vlissides, 2000).

Modeling Design Pattern Solutions

Pattern Specification

In DPML, Design pattern solution models are depicted using Specification Diagrams, the basic notation for which is shown in Figure 2. It should be emphasised that the surface syntax is relatively unimportant (and we have used at least two variants of this in our work), but we have aimed for a notation that is sufficiently different from UML so as not to be confused with it (i.e., DPML diagrams are readily identified as such). In addition, in our MaramaDPTool, the surface appearance can be altered by the user by use of a metatool designer. Of much more importance is the abstract metamodel, which is described as a UML class diagram in Figure 3. DPML models Design pattern solutions as a collection of participants (dimensions associated with the participants and constraints on the participants). A participant represents a structurally significant feature of a Design pattern, that when instantiated, will be linked to objects from the object model to realise the pattern. Constraints represent conditions that must be met by the objects filling the roles of the participants in a Design pattern instance for it to be considered a valid instance of the Design pattern. Dimensions are constructs associated with participants to indicate that the participant potentially has more than one object linked to it in an instantiation. They indicate that a participant represents a set of objects in the object model, instead of just a single object.

Figure 2. Basic DPML notation

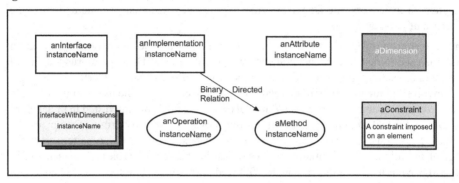

Participants can be interfaces, implementations, methods, operations, or attributes. An interface (a lighter and thicker bordered rectangle) represents a role that must be played by an object that declares some behaviour that is it exhibits an interface or signature in the object model. In a traditional UML class model, this means an interface or a class can fill an interface role, as both declare a set of operations that provide behaviour. An implementation (a darker, thinner bordered rectangle) represents a role played by an object that defines or actually implements some behaviour. In a conventional UML model an implementation would map to a class. The key concept with an implementation is that it defines no interface itself: its type or the declaration of its behaviour is defined entirely by the interfaces it is said to implement. This is different from the traditional concept of a class, which embodies both an interface and an implementation in the one object. This split is designed to allow a clearer definition of roles of the participants in a design. Modelers can specify precisely whether an object is intended to be a declaration of type, an interface, or a definition of behaviour, an implementation. A single object, in the case of a class, can play the roles of both an interface and an implementation.

A relationship similar to the one between interfaces and implementations exists between operations and methods. An operation (a lighter thicker bordered oval) is the declaration of some form of behaviour, while a method (a darker thinner bordered oval) is the definition or implementation of that behaviour. An operation represents a role that must be played by an object in the object model that declares a single piece of behaviour, for example, it can be played by a method or an abstract method in a conventional UML model. A method can only be played by an object that actually defines behaviour and so must be played by a concrete UML method. An attribute (rounded rectangle) is a declaration of a piece of state held by an implementation and defines a role played by a class attribute in the UML model.

Constraints are either simple constraints or binary directed relations. Simple constraints (plain text inside a grey box) define a condition specified in either natural language or OCL to be met by the object bound to a single participant. Binary directed relations (lines with arrowheads) define a relationship between two participants, implying a relationship must exist between the objects in the object model playing the roles each of the participants define. The type of the binary directed relation determines the exact relationship that is implied.

Figure 3. DPML specification diagram metamodel

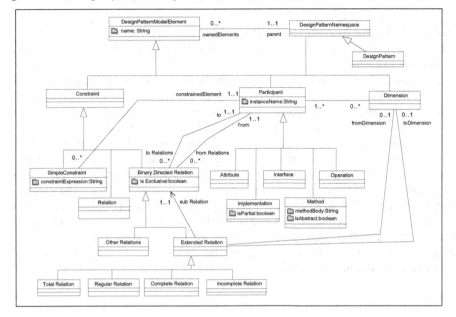

For example, the "implements" relationship between an implementation and an interface implies the object filling the role of the implementation must implement the object filling the role of the interface. Other examples of binary directed relations are *extends*, *realises*, *creates, declared in, defined in, return type,* and *refers to.*

A more complex subclass of binary directed relations is the set of extended relations. These define the mappings of a binary directed relation between participants that have dimensions associated with them. Because these participants have sets of objects associated with them, we need to specify how the base relation maps between the sets of objects involved. There are four possible mappings: the relation exists between every possible pair of objects (a *total* relation), exactly once for each object (a *regular* relation), for every object in one set but not necessarily the other (a *complete* relation), and only between one pair of objects (an *incomplete* relation). Extended relations are more fully specified as expressions of the form *extendedRelationName(fromParticipantDimension, toParticipantDimension, subRelation-Specification)*. An example later in this section will illustrate this further.

Dimensions (indicated by a coloured rectangle and coloured shading of participant icons to indicate they are associated with a dimension) specify that a participant can have a set of objects playing a role. The same dimension can be associated with different participants in a pattern and this specifies not only that these participants can have some multiple number of objects associated with them but that this number of objects is the same for both participants.

Pattern Specification Examples

Consider modeling the Abstract Factory Design pattern from Gamma et al. (1995) (Figure 4). This pattern is used by designers when they have a variety of objects ("Products") which are subclasses of a common root-class to create. A set of "Factory" objects are used to create these related "Product" objects. In this pattern there are six main participating groups of objects. The abstract factory interface declares the set of abstract create operations that the concrete factories will implement. This can be modeled by the DPML with an interface named *AbstractFactory* and an operation named *createOps*. The *createOps* operation represents a set of operations so it has an associated dimension (*Products*) because there is one operation for each abstract product type we want to create. There is also a complete *Declared_In* relation running from *createOps* to *AbstractFactory*. This relation implies that all methods linked to the *createOps* operation in an instantiation of the pattern must be declared in the object that is linked to the *AbstractFactory* interface. The *Products* interface has the *Products* dimension associated with it to imply there is the same number of abstract product interfaces as there are abstract *createOps* operations. A regular *Return_Type* relation runs from *createOps* to *Products*, implying that each of the *createOps* operations has exactly one of the *Products* as its return type.

Figure 4. Example specification of abstract factory pattern using DPML

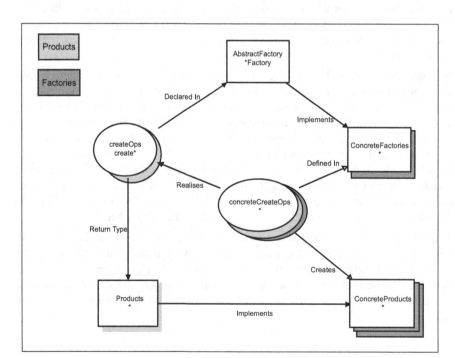

The above set of participants defines the abstract part of the Abstract Factory pattern. The other set of participants define the concrete part of the pattern: the factory implementations, the method implementations that these factories define, and the concrete products that the factories produce. These are modeled by a *concreteFactories* implementation, a *concrete-CreateOps* method, and a *concreteProducts* implementation, respectively.

The *concreteFactories* implementation has a dimension, *Factories,* to indicate it represents a number of concrete implementations, one for each type of Factory implemented. A complete *Implements* relation runs from *concreteFactories* to *AbstractFactory*, implying all the *concreteFactories* must implement the *AbstractFactory* interface. The *concreteCreateOps* method represents all methods from the set of *ConcreteFactories* that implement one of the sets of *createOps,* so it is associated with both the *Factories* and *Products* dimensions. It has a regular relation with a complete sub relation that has a *Defined_In* sub relation running from it to the *concreteFactories* implementation. This extended relation sounds complicated, but it implies simply that for every concrete factory there is a set of concreteCreateOps that it defines, one member of that set for each *Product*. This can be stated in a more compact expression form, as:

regular(Factories, Factories, complete(Products, , Defined_In)),

where we see that the regular relation is associated with the *Factories* dimension, that is, for each of the Factories the complete subrelation holds. This subrelation is between the *Products* dimension on the *concreteCreateOps* side and no dimension on the *concreteFactories* side, and specifies that every *concreteCreateOp* associated with a Product is defined in each *concreteFactory*.

Similarly, there is a regular relation with a complete sub relation which has a *Realises* sub relation running from *concreteCreateOps* to *createOps,* which implies that for every *cre-*

Figure 5. Object structure implied by defined in and realised relations associated with ConcreateCreateOps methods

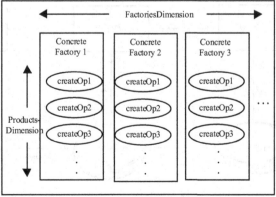

ateOps operation there is a set of methods in *concreteCreateOps* that realise it (one in each concrete factory). This can be stated in a more compact expression form, as:

regular(Products,Products , complete(Factories, , Realises).

The overall effect of the two extended relations can be seen in Figure 5, which shows the object structure implied by them.

Finally, the *concreteProducts* implementation has both *productsDimension* and *factoriesDimension* dimensions associated with it. This is because there is exactly one *concreteProduct* for each abstract product, and concrete factory that is each concrete factory produces one concrete product for each abstract product interface. The *concreteProducts* implementation also takes part in an *Implements* extended relation (regular, complete, Impelments) with the *Products* interface and a *Creates* extended relation (regular, regular, Creates) with the *concreteCreateOps* method. These specify that each *concreteProduct* implements one *Product* interface and each *concreteProduct* is created (instantiated) in exactly one of the *concreteCreateOps* methods.

As can be seen, the full name of a relation in expression format can be long and can clutter the diagram when the base relation is the important part. So for ExtendedRelations, just the name of the base relation can be used on the diagram to improve readability of the diagram, which means the full ExtendedRelation needs to be specified elsewhere (in our proof of concept tools, this is specified in a property window). Generally, the type of the ExtendedRelation can be deduced from the diagram because relations tend to follow common patterns. Usually (but not always) a relation between two Participants with the same Dimension will be a RegularRelation and between a Participant with a Dimension and a Participant without a Dimension will be a CompleteRelation. Occasions when TotalRelations and IncompleteRelations are used are much less common, and it is advisable in these cases to show the full ExtendedRelation name in the diagram.

Figure 6. Specification diagram for the Adapter pattern

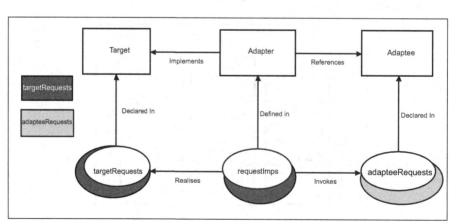

Figure 6 shows another specification diagram, this time for the adapter Design pattern, also from Gamma et al. (1995). This specifies how an *Adapter* implementation can be used to map operations specified by a *Target* interface to an *Adaptee*, which has different signatures for its operations. Here we see that the *Target* interface declares a set of *targetRequests*, the set being associated with the *targetRequests* dimension. The *Adapter* implements *Target's* interface, in the process defining a set of *requestImps* methods, also associated with the *targetRequests* dimension. A regular *Realises* relation between *requestImps* and *targetRequests* specifies that each *targetRequests* operation is realised by one *requestImps* method. The *Adapter* has a *References* relation with the *Adaptee* interface. The *Adaptee* declares a set of *adapteeRequests,* one for each member of the *adapteeRequests* dimension. The *Invokes* relation between *requestImps* and *adapteeRequests* indicates that each of the *requestImps* may invoke one or more of the *adapteeRequests*.

Behavioural Specification

In designing DPML, we have concentrated on structural specification. However, more dynamic aspects, such as method calling mechanisms, can be represented using an extended form of UML sequence or collaboration diagram. Figure 7 shows an example sequence diagram for the Adapter pattern. This uses standard sequence diagram notation, but includes participants acting as proxies for the final bound objects. Dimensions, as is the case in the specification diagram, are represented using coloured shading, in this case, the *targetRequests* and *requestImps* invocations are annotated with the *targetRequests* dimension colour, and the *adapteeRequests* invocation is annotated with the *adapteeRequests* dimension colour. This component of the formalism needs further development. In particular, it should be possible to use dimensions to indicate looping constructs with a similar set of invocation relationships having a similar set of extended relationship variations as for the structural diagrams. This remains as further work.

Figure 7. Behavioural specification for Adapter pattern

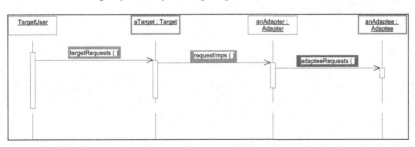

Pattern Instantiation

Instantiation diagrams provide a mapping from the pattern specification to its realisation in a UML design model. In addition, as mentioned earlier, the instantiation process can adapt a pattern solution through addition of extra participants or modification of existing participants, an important part of our DPML design. Pattern solutions are rarely instantiated directly, and the instantiation almost always involves some measure of adaptation or refinement. Accordingly, instantiation diagrams have a very similar look and feel to specification diagrams. The basic notation is very similar and, in fact, all of the modeling elements (except addition of new dimensions) that are used in specification diagrams may also be used in instantiation diagrams. These modeling elements are used to model the pattern adaptations. In addition, however, an instantiation diagram also includes *proxy* elements (which will typically be the majority of the diagram's elements). These represent the original participant specifications

Figure 8. Additional notational elements for instantiation diagrams

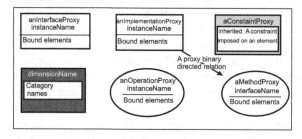

Figure 9. DPML Instantiation Diagram metamodel

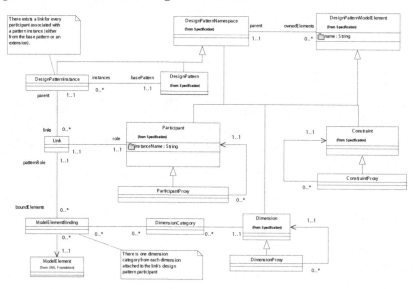

in an instantiated pattern, but are elaborated with information about the actual UML design elements that they are bound to in this particular instantiation of the pattern. Figure 8 shows the proxy element notation. As can be seen, the syntactic form is similar to that of the specification diagram equivalents. In the case of interface, implementation, operation, method, and relation proxies, they differ from the originals by having dashed borders or lines and lists of bindings. For constraints, an "inherited" keyword precedes the constraint expression, and for dimensions, a list of the names of the category bindings for that dimension.

Figure 9 shows the metamodel for instantiation diagrams. In a DesignPatternInstance (i.e., the model for an instantiation diagram) every Participant (whether they are a "proxy" or "real") has a Link associated with it that maintains a binding from the Participant to some number of UML model elements in an object model (*UMLModelElement* is part of the UML Foundation Package). The names of the bound UMLModelElements are those displayed in the bound elements lists in the proxy participant icons. When model elements are bound to Participants with Dimensions, each model element is associated with a DimensionCategory for each Dimension. These DimensionCategories are specified as a simple list of their names, which are displayed in the Dimension proxy. The number of DimensionCategories for a Dimension establishes the "size" of the Dimension for the Instance.

Figure 10. Instantiation diagram for GUIFactory

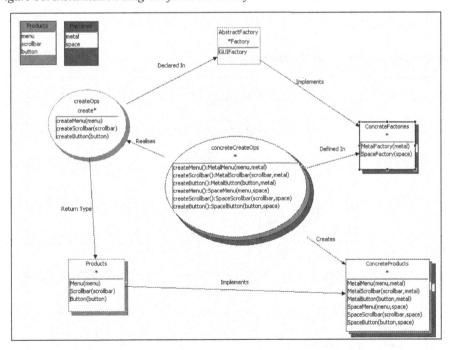

Pattern Instantiation Example

As an example, consider the Instantiation of the Abstract Factory pattern shown in Figure 10. Assume we are implementing a GUI toolkit that allows programmers to create a GUI with windows, menus, icons, buttons, and so forth, which users can change the look and feel of at runtime, and that we want to use the Abstract Factory Design pattern to do this. The instantiation diagram illustrates the bindings for this. The *GUIFactory* UML interface is bound to the AbstractFactory interface participant, and this interface is implemented by two *ConcreteFactories, MetalFactory,* and *SpaceFactory*, one for each dimension category (metal, space) in the Factories dimension (the relevant dimension category name is shown in brackets after the bound element name). *GUIFactory* declares three operations: *createMenu, createScrollbar,* and *createButton.* There is one for each of the product dimensions (menu, scrollbar, button), each of which has a return type of the corresponding *Product* type (*Menu, Scrollbar, Button*). The *concreteCreateOps* method participant has six bound elements, a set of three methods (each creating a corresponding *ConcreteProduct*) for each of the two *ConcreteFactories.*

Figure 11 shows a UML class diagram representing the UML model elements bound in Figure 10. This could have been independently developed and bindings made manually in the instantiation diagram. Alternatively, having specified the dimension category names for each dimension, and some other key bindings (in this case only the *GUIFactory* binding) simple regular expressions (defined in the specification diagram) specifying naming convention patterns combined with the extended relation expressions, and a small amount

Figure 11. UML design for GUIFactory

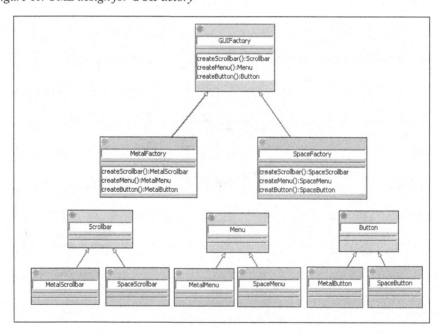

of manual intervention (notably for incomplete relations) could be used to directly *generate* the bound element names and from them, the bound elements themselves, and hence the equivalent UML model for those elements. For example, the *ConcreteFactories* bindings may be generated by pre-pending the string "Factory" with the Factory dimension category name with its first letter capitalised, while the *ConcreteProducts* bindings may be generated by the cross product of the Factory dimension category names (first letter capitalised) and the Products dimension category names (first letter capitalised). The asterisks in the examples indicate names or parts of names which can be generated in this way.

Tool Support

We have developed two proof of concept tools to support the use of DPML for pattern modeling and instantiation. The first, reported in Maplesden et al. (2002), is a standalone tool, DPTool, implemented using our JViews/JComposer metatoolset. Figure 12 shows this tool in use. The second, MaramaDPTool, is an Eclipse (Eclipse Foundation, 2006) plugin generated using our Ponamu/Marama metatoolsets (Grundy, Hosking, Zhu, & Liu, in press; Zhu, Grundy, & Hosking, 2004), and which use Eclipse's EMF and GEF frameworks for model and view support, respectively. The bulk of the diagrams presented earlier in this chapter were generated using MaramaDPTool. Three views of this tool in use are shown in Figure

Figure 12. The prototype DPTool in use

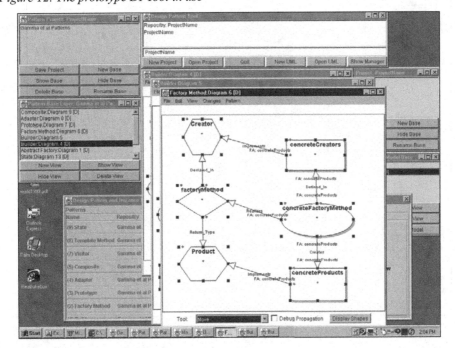

13. Of the two implementations, DPTool is the most developed in terms of functionality. However, MaramaDPTool, based as it is on the Eclipse framework, has far better potential for integration with other programmer productivity toolsets.

Both tools provide the following functionality:

- Modeling views for specification, instantiation, and UML class diagrams, including specification of naming convention patterns

- For each type of view, multiple views can be modeled, with consistency maintained between the views, meaning that complex patterns or UML models can be broken down into a collection of partial specifications, each contributing to an underlying model

- Support for instantiation of a pattern, through generation of an instantiation diagram with the same layout as the specification diagram it is derived from, but with participants replaced by proxies

Figure 13. Three views using the MaramaDPTool: (top) Design pattern specification diagram, (centre) Design pattern instantiation diagram, (bottom) UML class diagram

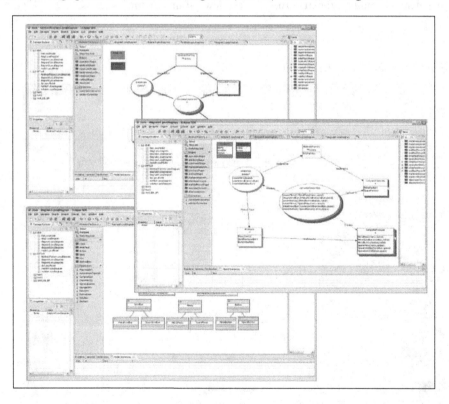

- Consistency management between specification and instantiation views, so changes to a specification are reflected in each of the instantiations
- Support for binding UML model elements to instantiation diagram participants and proxies.
- Consistency management between UML class diagram views and instantiation diagram bindings so that changes to the pattern instantiation can be reflected in the UML class diagrams, and vice versa
- Support for instantiation of multiple, overlapping patterns into a UML model through the use of multiple instantiation diagrams contributing to a common UML model
- Model management support, to allow saving and loading of models (DPML and UML), undo-redo, and so forth

In addition, the JViews based DPTool has better support for pattern realisation and model validation, together with better repository support through provision of a library of predefined patterns. Realisation support includes recommendations on UML model elements that could be validly bound to participants. Validation support checks validity of UML models against the pattern specification, checking for incompleteness, that is, participants that aren't bound, and inconsistency, that is, violations of the DPML or UML well formedness rules and violations of the participant naming convention patterns. Errors discovered are displayed in a window, as shown in Figure 14. Validation in the DPTool is a user instigated operation. In our MaramaDPTool, we are implementing an Argo critic style of validation support which can execute in the background generating a to-do list of identified errors (Robbins & Redmiles, 1999).

Pattern abstraction is the process of identifying a useful or interesting structure or design in an object model and abstracting from that object structure to a suitable DesignPattern model. This mechanism forms the third leg (the first two being pattern instantiation and pattern realisation) of a complete round trip engineering process for Design patterns. In Pattern Abstraction, a group of elements from an object model are identified and used as a blueprint for creating a DesignPattern model. This is not currently well supported in either of our tools. Currently, this requires manual construction of Instantiation and Specification diagrams and binding of participants to the UML model. In our MaramaDPTool we are developing complementary support to the pattern instantiation mechanisms permitting selection of UML model elements and generation of a pattern instantiation diagram, which in turn can be automatically abstracted to a Pattern Specification diagram. This is more complex than the pattern instantiation process, however. In general, it is impossible to create a fully accurate and defined Design pattern automatically from a collection of object model elements.

Figure 14. The error display in the DPTool

Error Type	Description	ModelElement	Pattern Instance
Model Warning	No view of base model element	MetalFactory.createCar():Car	
Model Warning	No view of base model element	MetalFactory.createScrollBar...	
Pattern Instance Error	The FROM bound element 'MetalFactory.createCar():Car' does not satisfy this relation.	Proxy for Method: createMeth...	TestInstance
Pattern Instance Error	The element "car():Car" has a name which does not match the participant's 'instancename' pattern	Proxy for Operation: createOp	TestInstance

This is because there are any number of ways certain arrangements of elements could be abstracted to a Design pattern model. A particular difficulty is the recognition of repeating sets of elements as elements that should be represented by Participants with Dimensions. Accordingly, the abstraction support will only be able to automatically perform parts of the abstraction process, requiring manual assistance from the user for aspects such as dimension identification. An additional diagram type more explicitly showing binding relationships between DPML and UML elements may be a useful component in solving this problem.

Evaluation

We have evaluated DPML, and, in particular, the DPTool via an end user based usability study and a cognitive dimensions assessment (Green & Petre, 1996). Results of these evaluations have been reported in Maplesden et al. (2002). In brief, the user study, which was qualitative in its nature, showed that the tool was regarded favourably by the survey group, as was much of the language and notation used by the tool. The explicit separation between Design patterns, Design pattern instances, and object models was easy to follow and effective in managing the use of Design patterns and users found the tool useful and usable for its primary tasks of creating and instantiating Design patterns models. Weaknesses and difficulties noted included a difficulty in understanding the dimension and dimension category concepts due to poor visualisation of these and the lack of annotation capability. Both of these have been addressed in MaramaDPTool, the former by having explicit iconic representation of dimensions and dimension category bindings (these were not in the original notation) and the latter by supporting textual annotations. Pattern abstraction support was also highlighted as a desirable feature, which we are currently addressing in MaramaDPTool. The integration of DPML support into Eclipse via MaramaDPTool allows code generation and consistency management between UML models and target code to be maintained. It also potentially allows us to use MaramaDPTool pattern descriptions with third party UML tools via their XMI-based UML metamodels.

The cognitive dimensions assessment highlighted the strong abstraction gradient and difficult mental operations introduced by the dimension concept. These have been mitigated, as noted above, by more explicit iconic representation of dimensions. However, it is worth noting that DPML is already better in both aspects than other, more formal notations, such as Kent and Lauder's (1998) or LePUS (Eden, 1998). DPML exhibits good closeness of mapping and consistency, and DPTool provides good progressive evaluation support via its validation mechanism. Hidden dependencies are an issue, as is the case with any multiview tool. Secondary notation capability in DPTool is poor, but has been addressed through the enhanced annotation capability in MaramaDPTool.

Discussion and Future Work

As described in the introduction, we feel that in addition to DPML (particularly the DPML meta model) and the prototype tool support we have developed for it, our most significant contributions have been in the area of dimensions and instantiation of patterns into designs. These both have some novel characteristics which have more general applicability. Accordingly, it is instructive to understand how we developed these concepts in comparison to alternatives.

In the DPML metamodel we wanted a concept that would allow us to create models including groups of objects of arbitrary size. There were various other approaches we could have taken besides using the Dimension concept. One simple approach would have been to allow the cardinality of a Participant to be specified directly, indicating how many objects it represents. This is the approach taken in RBML (Kim et al., 2003). This would have allowed groups of objects to be detailed by a single Participant, but it lacked a certain expressive power. One could not, for example, express the fact that a Participant represents objects that can be classified into sets by multiple criteria, and that it effectively has sets of sets of objects. Another method we considered was the set-based approach of LePUS. This would have allowed us to create a set of objects and then a set of sets of objects, and so forth. The main drawback is that it implies an unnecessary ordering on the groupings of the objects, as you must group them into sets according to some criteria first and then group the sets into sets according to a second criteria, and so forth. The order in which you apply the criteria is arbitrary but fixed, and once specified you cannot go back and reorder the groupings to suit the different relationships the groupings may be involved with.

We came up with the concept of a Dimension to get around this problem. Designers can specify that a Participant has a certain number of dimensions but no ordering of those Dimensions is (nor should be) implied. The objects linked to a Participant then can be classified according to their position within a particular Dimension, and we can consider the Dimensions in any order we wish, each order creating a different sequence of classifications. No order then is implied by the specification of the Dimensions, because its simply that this Participant has another Dimension in which the objects attached to it can (and indeed must) take up a position. Another advantage of the Dimension concept is that the same Dimension can be applied to different Participants to imply they have a similar cardinality in that one direction. This enables us to easily specify constraints, such as two Participants having exactly the same cardinality, by giving them both the same Dimension. Also, if one Participant has a Dimension and another Participant has that Dimension plus a second Dimension, then we are saying the second Participant represents a group of objects for every object in the first Participant.

The proxy elements were also an interesting design decision. We considered, initially, replicating a Design pattern's structure in a Design pattern instance by simply linking the original objects from the Design pattern into the instance. However, this technique would result in an unnecessarily messy and inelegant object structure in our DPML models. The same object would have been linked into many instances and would have had potentially many different instance-specific alterations added to it. The proxy elements allow us to maintain a certain separation between the instances and the original pattern, while still having a mechanism for keeping the structures consistent. It is not possible in the metamodel to express the fact that, in an implementation of the DPML, the proxy elements should listen to their base element and make changes, when required, to maintain consistency with that base element. However, you can specify that, in a correct model, proxy elements must be consistent with their base elements. The proxy elements then take part in all the relationships and activities that have instance-wide scope, while alterations and relationships that have pattern-wide scope take place in the pattern and, in a tool implementing the DPML, can be propagated to the instances via the proxy elements. Proxy elements help us maintain the self-contained nature of the original Design pattern models so that they can be used independently from models of their instances (although not vice versa!).

In both cases, dimensions and proxies, we feel that the approach we have taken is more generally applicable, in particular to any model driven development situation where an element in the model can represent and be instantiated as a multiply-categorised set and where models have multiple, tailored instantiations, respectively. We are, for example, exploring the use of dimensions in our meta tool model specification languages as an alternative to the cardinality approaches we are currently using.

The decisions about what object structures to model as Participants and what to model by using Constraints or Relations were the most difficult ones we made. The set of Participants we came up with was fairly standard by most measures. However, arguments can be made for modeling an Attribute as a Constraint on an Implementation, rather than as a Participant as we have done, or for modeling constructs, such as Associations as Participants, rather than with a BinaryDirectedRelation, which is the approach we took. We were largely influenced in our decisions by what structures in an OO design have a clear definition in an implementation (such as a class, a method, or an attribute) because these fell naturally into roles as Participants. If associations between classes in a mainstream programming language are ever given a clearer, more encapsulated definition than as a pair of object references, our perception of associations could well change. This would be an argument for having Associations as Participants rather than as a condition that exists between two other Participants.

Another area that requires further work is pattern composition. It is obvious after working with DPML for a while that some combinations of Participants or mini-patterns are very common and are repeatedly reused in design after design. This was an aspect also noted by our survey respondents. While our model and tool support instantiation of multiple patterns into a UML model, there is no support for composing patterns from other patterns. In the DPML metamodel the direct superclass of DesignPattern and DesignPatternInstance, DesignPatternNamespace, is a direct subclass of DesignPatternModelElement. We gave some consideration to making DesignPattern a subclass of Participant to facilitate a form of Design pattern composition. With the ability to include a whole DesignPattern as a Participant of another pattern, one could specify a simple mini-pattern in a DesignPattern and use it in many other patterns, even with Dimensions to specify multiple groups of the DesignPattern. There are complicating issues that arise with this addition to the metamodel, however, particularly in the changes required to the instantiation metamodel and in the semantics of linking additional Constraints to the Participants involved in the sub-pattern, which leads to the whole notion of visibility of Participants from outside the DesignPattern. We have not been able to address these issues satisfactorily yet and so we have not as yet been able to incorporate this idea for pattern composition into our metamodel or tool support. By contrast, Mak et al. (2003) have developed an extension to LePUS (exLePLUS), which provides pattern composition capability. Noble and Biddle (2002) provide a deeper discussion of the relationships that exist between patterns that provides a useful basis for further developing pattern composition tool support.

Generalising, it can be seen that other, for example, more domain specific, participants could be selected, creating a variety of DPML-like variants for use in model driven development. Our metamodel is readily adaptable to this approach, and the metatoolset-based implementations we have been using for implementation likewise allow for rapid adaptation to incorporate new participant types and related icons. We thus see our developing MaramaDPTool as an underlying framework for rapidly developing domain specific modeling languages that support instantiation into UML designs as part of an overall model driven development approach. In this respect, we have similar aims to those behind the development of Microsoft's DSLTool meta toolset (Microsoft, 2006). This type of approach is likely to suit constrained situations, such as product line configuration, where domain specific visual notations afford a more accessible approach for end user configuration than existing conventional coding approaches.

Conclusion

We have described DPML and associated toolset for specifying and instantiating Design patterns. Patterns specified using DPML can be instantiated into UML designs. The instantiation process supports customisation to adapt the pattern instance for the particular context it is applied to. Two proof-of-concept tools have been developed supporting the use of DPML. Evaluations, both user and cognitive dimensions based, demonstrate the usefulness and effectiveness of the language and tool support. Of particular novelty is our approach to specifying multiplicity of participants in a Design pattern, using the dimension concept combined with binary extended relations that interpret the dimensions in a particular context. We feel these have broader applicability in other areas of model driven development.

Acknowledgment

Support for this research from the New Zealand Public Good Science Fund and the New Economy Research Fund is gratefully acknowledged. David Maplesden was supported by a William Georgetti Scholarship.

References

Chambers, C., Harrison, B., & Vlissides, J. (2000). A debate on language and tool support for Design patterns. In M. Wegman & T. Reps (Eds.), *Proceedings of the 27th ACM SIGPLAN-SIGACT Symposium on Principles of Programming Languages* (pp. 277-289). Boston: ACM Press.

Coplien, J.O. (1996). *Software patterns*. SIGS Management Briefings. SIGS Press.

Eclipse Foundation (2006). *Eclipse*. Retrieved November 9, 2006, from http://www.eclipse.org/

Eden, A.H. (2002). A visual formalism for object-oriented architecture. In *Proceedings of Integrated Design and Process Technology*, Pasadena, CA.

Florijn, G., Meijers, M., & van Winsen, P. (1997). Tool support for object-oriented patterns. In *ECOOP '97 Proceedings of the 11th European conference on Object Oriented Programming* (LNCS 1241, pp. 472-495).

Fontoura, M., Pree, W., & Rumpe, B. (2002). *The UML profile for framework architectures*. Addison-Wesley.

France, R.B., Kim, D.-K., Ghosh, S., & Song, E. (2004). A UML-based pattern specification technique. *IEEE Transactions on Software Engineering, 30*(3), 193-206.

Gamma, E., Helm, R., Johnston, R., & Vlissides, J. (1994). *Design patterns*. Addison-Wesley.

Grand, M. (1998). *Design patterns and Java*. Addison-Wesley.

Green, T.R.G., & Petre, M. (1996). Usability analysis of visual programming environments: A "cognitive dimensions" framework. *Journal of Visual Languages and Computing, 7*, 131-174.

Grundy, J.C., Hosking, J.G., Zhu, N., & Liu, N. (in press). Generating domain-specific visual language editors from high-level tool specifications. In *Proceedings of the 2006 ACM/IEEE Conference on Automated Software Engineering*.

Guennec, A.L., Sunye, G., & Jezequel, J. (2006). Precise modeling of Design patterns. In *Proceedings of UML'00* (pp. 482-496).

Kim, D., France, R., Ghosh S., & Song, E. (2003). A UML-based metamodeling language to specify Design patterns. In *Proceedings of the Workshop on Software Model Engineering (WiSME), at UML 2003*, San Francisco.

Lauder, A., & Kent, S. (1998). Precise visual specification of Design patterns. In *Proceedings of the ECOOP'98 Workshop Reader on OO Technology* (LNCS 1445, pp. 114-134).

Mak, J.K.H., Choy, C.S.T., & Lun, D.P.K. (2003). Precise specification to compound patterns with ExLePUS. In *Proceedings of the 27th Annual International Computer Software and Applications Conference* (pp. 440-445).

Mak, J.K., Choy, C.S.T., & Lun, D.P.K. (2004). Precise modeling of Design patterns in UML. In *Proceedings of the 26th International Conference on Software Engineering (ICSE'04)* (pp. 252-261).

Maplesden, D., Hosking, J.G., & Grundy, J.C. (2002). Design pattern modelling and instantiation using DPML. In *Proceedings of Tools Pacific 2002*, Sydney, Australia. IEEE CS Press.

Microsoft (2006). *Domain-specific language tools*. Retrieved November 9, 2006, from http://msdn.microsoft.com/vstudio/DSLTools/

Noble, J., & Biddle, R. (2002). Patterns as signs. In *Proceedings of the European Conference on Object Oriented Programming (ECOOP)* (pp. 368-391). Spain: Springer-Verlag.

Object Management Group (2006). *Unified modelling language (UML) specification v 2.0*. Retrieved November 9, 2006, from www.omg.org/technology/documents/formal/uml.htm

Reiss, S.P. (2000). Working with patterns and code. In *Proceedings of the 33rd Annual Hawaii International Conference on System Sciences, Volume: Abstracts* (pp. 243-243).

Robbins, J.E., & Redmiles, D.F. (1999). Cognitive support, UML adherence, and XMI interchange in Argo/UML. In *Proceedings of CoSET'99* (pp. 61-70). University of South Australia.

Sefika, M., Sane, A., & Campbell, R.H. (1996). Monitoring compliance of a software system with its high-level design models. In *Proceedings of the 18th International Conference on Software Engineering* (pp. 387-396). Berlin, Germany.

Taibi, T., & Ngo, D.C.L. (2003). Formal specification of Design patterns—A balanced approach. *Journal of Object Technology, 2*(4), 127-140.

Zhu, N., Grundy, J.C., & Hosking, J.G. (2004). Pounamu: A meta-tool for multi-view visual language environment construction. In *Proceedings of the IEEE Visual Languages and Human Centric Computing Symposium* (pp. 254-256). Tokyo.

Chapter III

A Generic Model of Object-Oriented Patterns Specified in RSL

Andrés Flores, University of Comahue, Argentina

Alejandra Cechich, University of Comahue, Argentina

Gabriela Aranda, , University of Comahue, Argentina

Abstract

Object-oriented patterns are a promising technique for achieving widespread reuse of software architectures. They capture the static and dynamic structures of components and frameworks in successful solutions to problems for a wide range of domains. However, patterns are invariably described informally in the literature, which makes it difficult to give any meaningful certification of pattern-based software. The design process could be enhanced by means of an automatic support for modeling and verification with a proper formal foundation. In this chapter, we show how formal specifications of GoF patterns, based on the RAISE language, have been helpful in developing that tool support, where we have adopted the well-known Java language upon its portability facet. Thus, the object-oriented design process is extended by the inclusion of pattern-based modeling and verification steps, the latter involving checking design correctness and appropriate pattern application through the use of the supporting tool, called DePMoVe (design and pattern modeling and verification).

Introduction

Design patterns are descriptions of communicating objects and classes that are customized to solve a general design problem in a particular context (Gamma, Helm, Johnson, & Vlissides, 1995). By their very definition, Design patterns result in reusable object-oriented design because they name, abstract, and identify key aspects of a common design structure. Design patterns are a promising technique for achieving widespread reuse of software architectures. They capture the static and dynamic structures and collaborations of components in successful solutions to problems that arise when building software in domains like business data processing, telecommunications, graphical user interfaces, data-bases, and distributed communication software. Patterns aid the development of reusable components and frameworks by expressing the structure and collaboration of participants in a software architecture at a level higher than source code or object-oriented design models that focus on individual objects and classes. Thus, patterns facilitate reuse of software architecture, even when other forms of reuse are not feasible.

However, patterns are invariably described informally in the literature, generally using natural language narrative together with a sort of graphical notation, which makes it difficult to give any meaningful certification of pattern-based software. Particularly, patterns in the GoF catalogue (Gamma et al., 1995) are described by using a consistent format which is based on an extension of the object modeling technique (OMT) (Rumbaugh, Blaha, Premerlani, Eddy, & Lorensen, 1991). This form of presentation gives a very good intuitive picture of the patterns, but it is not sufficiently precise to allow a designer to conclusively demonstrate that a particular problem matches a specific pattern or that a proposed solution is consistent with a particular pattern. Moreover, it is difficult to be certain that patterns themselves are meaningful and contain no inconsistencies. In some cases, descriptions of patterns are intentionally left loose and incomplete to ensure that they are applicable in a range as wide as possible. This reduces understanding and interpretation upon appropriate patterns usage. Nevertheless, the availability of a more formal description could help alleviate these problems.

Formal methods are gaining prominence in software engineering as a way to insure that a specification is consistent with its intended meaning, and that two formally-rendered artifacts (e.g., a specification and an implementation) are consistent with each other in some precise way. Formal methods in the arena of software architecture tend to manifest themselves in representation technology. In sum, formal methods are useful to help a human organize thought patterns into a more disciplined form, thus heading off conceptual errors.

In a previous work (Cechich & Moore, 1999a, 1999b; Moore, Cechich, Reynoso, Flores, & Aranda, 2002), we have presented a formal model of a generic object-oriented design that was developed in RSL (the RAISE specification language) (RAISE Group, 1992, 1995), and based upon the extended OMT notation given on the GoF catalogue. We have shown how designs can be formally linked with patterns in this model, and how properties of individual patterns can be specified in the model, thus giving a basis for formally checking whether a given design and a given pattern are consistent with each other. Although we have mainly focused our attention to GoF patterns, the whole model is general enough to be applied in a similar way to formalize other patterns based on object-oriented notations, including compound GoF patterns as we have experienced (see Aranda & Moore, 2002; Buccella & Cechich, 2002).

Basically, the formal model has been organized into seven main RSL schemas, which describe a metamodel of a generic object-oriented design with the addition of a mechanism to link pattern descriptions to elements of a design. Such mechanism is also called *pattern instantiation* for which one of the following three approaches might be used on a design process. Figure 1 shows a schema for a design-pattern linkage (Flores & Moore, 2000).

- **Top-Down:** Given a pattern, generate its appropriate components at the design level
- **Bottom-Up:** Given a (subset of a) design and a pattern, perform the binding or verify the matching
- **Mixed:** Given a pattern and a (subset of a) design that only partly matches it, generate the missing pattern components at the design level

Our model of patterns was separated into three working units according to the purpose classification given by the GoF catalogue. Thus, the formal metamodel for OO design was used to formalize Creational, Structural, and Behavioral Design patterns from the GoF catalogue.

These formal specifications were used to build a supporting tool focused on the learning process about pattern application, which is composed of two basic steps, modeling and verifying (Flores, Cechich, & Ruiz, 2006; Reynoso, Aranda, Buccella, & Flores, 2002). This lets designers gain a useful insight into design principles and heuristics and also learn about diverse pattern properties. Through a formal specification of patterns, a designer may certify when and how a pattern is being appropriately applied to solve a specific design problem. Furthermore, the design process may be improved with a precise technique supported by this tool: any error detected during verification can help designers improve their designs and reason about information that can be vital to correctly apply a particular pattern.

The focus of this chapter is mainly on the definition of our formal specification of the individual GoF patterns. We have achieved a model that precisely allows and describes valid

Figure 1. Design-pattern levels linkage

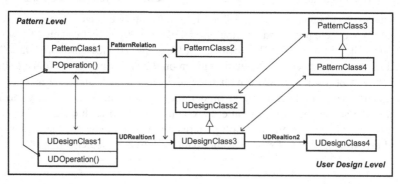

variations of patterns applications. Thus, in this chapter we also present remarks of different variants on the use of patterns, which can be performed by means of our formal basis.

Related Work

In previous work (Flores & Fillottrani, 2003), we have carried out an evaluation of eight formal models of patterns, where seven different languages were used on their construction: *Disco* (Disco Project, 2006; Mikkonen, 1998), *LePUS* (Eden, 2002; Eden, Gil, & Yehudai, 1997), *RAISE*, *VDM++* (Lano & Goldsack, 1996; Lano, Bicarregui, & Goldsack, 1997), *Sigma(σ)+Rho(ρ)-Calculus* (Abadi & Cardelli, 1995; McC. Smith & Stotts, 2002), *UML+OCL* (Le Guennec, Gerson, & Jèzèquel, 2000; UML Consortium, 2006a, 2006b), *UML+Constraints Diagrams* (Gil, Howse, & Kent, 2001; Lauder & Kent, 1998), and *Contracts* (Helm, Holland, & Gangopadhyay, 1990). To do so, fourteen characteristics, such as mathematical foundation, visual representation, structural/behavioral description, OO support, and refinement (among others) were used to classify languages. Similarly, 10 characteristics, such as precision, flexibility, and design heuristics (among others) were used to classify existing formal models of patterns. For these characteristics to be evaluated, we have assumed in general a not supported, poorly supported, up to very well supported value.

RAISE is one of such languages under evaluation because it was the one we have used to build our model of pattern instantiation. Although RAISE is a general-purpose formal language, our motivation of its use precisely came from the results of this analysis. We have compared our model and the used language in order to understand benefits and drawbacks by observing other viewpoints. As brief remarks, we could see that languages satisfying the characteristics with an acceptable degree are LePUS, RAISE, VDM++, and UML. If a visual notation is a prerequisite, then the choice is centered on LePUS and UML. However, whether the formal foundation must be rigorous, we must take into account that UML presents serious lack on semantics.

Contracts and DisCo are found to be fairly similar as much on style as on usability of their formal apparatus and comprehension of generated specifications. Their design orientation is quite particular (interaction-oriented and action-oriented, respectively) and should be applied when the requisite is describing interactions rather than representing participating entities. That is, it should be more centered on behavior and very little on structure. Sigma(σ)+Rho(ρ)-Calculus has gotten the lowest degree on the analysis from the perception of a less usable (rather rigid) formal apparatus. It is more difficult to remember and therefore less useful as a communicating artifact.

Indeed, RAISE is not a language with object-orientation characteristics, although its formal constructors allow both the ability to easily develop an OO design metamodel and to accurately represent such object-orientation aspects, as we have experienced. Opposite to Contracts and DisCo, our model has been found in Alagar and Lämmel (2002) as quite syntactic, because no emphasis on dynamic interactions is given. Despite that aspect, our formal basis for pattern application satisfies the framework's characteristics with a fairly high degree, because its level of completeness on solving problems of imprecision is much higher than the other models. This has been achieved at the design level by remarking principles and heuristics, and also at the pattern level by precisely describing their deeply analyzed properties.

In the next section, we present our formalization of a pattern instantiation model, where the characteristics of the framework will be remarked upon. In this way, the reader may understand the requirements for an approach of pattern instantiation and its likely benefits when applied to a design process.

A Formal Model of Patterns Specified in RSL

The formal specification of the model is quite long, so we present an overview by briefly describing the main building blocks of the model. RSL type definitions from every particular element, as well as functions representing the well-formedness conditions that these types must satisfy, are introduced in the following. A full description can be seen in Flores, Reynoso, and Moore (2000).

Table 1 lists the seven main RSL schemas in which was divided the whole formal model, and the identifier that was used on other schemas to make a reference—that is, like an inclusion of schemas.

Design_Structure

A design is composed of a collection of classes and a collection of relations between those classes. This is formalized as follows:

Design_Structure = C.Classes × R.Wf_Relations

We assure a consistency on the link between classes, and also include heuristics on a design. To do so, the *Design_Structure* type is constrained to establish a well-formed (wf) type by

Table 1. RSL schemas as the formal basis

Scheme	Description	Identifier
Types	General definitions to the model.	G
Methods	operations or methods that form a class' interface.	M
Classes	Structure and behavior of classes in a OO design.	C
Relations	Set of valid relations that link classes on a design.	R
Design_Structure	Consistent link between classes and their inter-relations.	DS
Renaming	Correspondence between names from design to those from a pattern – that is, setting of pattern roles played by design entities.	DR
Design_Pattern	Set of generic functions that sum the previous ones and help to formally describe any Design pattern.	

the function is_*wf_design_structure*, which is composed of different subfunctions, each addressing a particular design aspect.

Wf_Design_Structure = {| ds : Design_Structure • is_wf_design_structure(ds) |}

is_wf_design_structure : Design_Structure → Bool
is_wf_design_structure(ds) ≡
   is_correct_design_class(ds) ∧ is_defined_class(ds) ∧ is_correct_name_relation(ds) ∧
   is_correct_name_rel_in_subclass(ds) ∧ correct_state_hierarchy(ds) ∧ not_allowed(ds) ∧
   correct_multiple_inheritance(ds) ∧ is_correct_invocation(ds) ∧ is_rqst_instantiation(ds) ∧
   *is_implemented_signature(ds) ∧ is_impl_error_interf_inherited(ds) ∧ is_correct_res_f_*
param(ds)

Design_Class

A design class is composed of a set of *methods* that form its interface, a set of properties that represent its *state*, and a type which can be "*concrete*"or "*abstract.*" Every design class has a name that is unique on the entire design. Thus, we use the RSL map type to describe the correspondence between a class name and its definition.

Wf_Design_Class =
   G.Class_Name $\overrightarrow{m}$ *Design_Class,*

Design_Class ::
   class_state : G.State
   class_methods : M.Class_Method
   class_type : G.Class_Type

Methods

Every method has a unique *name* into the interface of a class that, together with a list *of parameters* and a *result*, forms the method's signature. A method may be only *defined* by its signature or may express a concrete functionality, that is, being *implemented*. A special case is a method that describes a situation of *error*.

Class_Method = {| m : Map_Methods •
      is_wf_class_method(m) |}

Map_Methods = G.Method_Name $\overrightarrow{m}$ *Wf_Method*

Method ::
   f_params : G.Wf_Formal_Parameters
   meth_res : Result
   body : Method_Body

An implemented method helps describe collaborations between classes. Changes on the state of a class (by its variables) and some assignments for returning *results* are described by mapping variable_change. They are mainly produced by specific requests, such as *invoca-*

tion of methods (belonging to a given class) or instantiation to create objects. A request-list describes the order of their occurrence into the body of an implemented method.

Method_Body ==   *defined | error |*
                         implemented(variable_change : Variable Change,
                                   request_list : Request*)

Variable_Change = {| m : G.Wf Vble Name-set   Request_or_Var •
                         is_wf_vchange(m) |}

Request = Invocation | Instantiation | _

Design_Relation

A relation is described by the classes it connects, which are identified by means of their class names. The relation has a specific type that may be inheritance, association, aggregation, or instantiation. All relations are represented in the model as binary relations, by identifying source and sink classes. We have applied constraints to the definition of a relation as well as to the set of possible relations that can be modeled in a design.

Wf_Relations = {| rs : Wf_Relation-set • wf_relations(rs) |}

Design_Relation ::   *Relation_Type ==*
    relation_type : Relation_Type   *inheritance | association(as_ref: Ref)*
    source_class : G.Class_Name   *instantiation | aggregation(ag_ref : Ref),*
    sink_class : G.Class_Name,   *Ref :: relation_name : G.Wf_Vble_Name ..,*

Renaming

The link from design elements (classes, variables, methods, and parameters) with corresponding elements of a pattern is defined by means of a mapping of names. A design class may play more than one pattern role, and so can do the rest of the design elements. A method or a variable (a relation name or a state variable) may play pattern roles, depending on a given class role—similarly, for parameters with respect to methods. Then a design matches a particular pattern if all the elements in a design playing a pattern role satisfy its properties.

Renaming = G.Class_Name $\vec{m}$ ClassRenaming-set,

ClassRenaming :: classname : G.Class_Name
            methodRenaming : Method_and_Parameter_Renaming
            varRenaming : VariableRenaming,

Then a design, together with a renaming map which defines its correspondences to a given pattern, is described by the simple cartesian product type Design_Renaming. This type is properly constrained in order to complement the model with some consistency conditions.

Design_Renaming = DS.Wf_Design_Structure × Wf_Renaming

This has been so far a brief summary of the formalization concerning our formal metamodel of OO Design and the mechanism for pattern applications. We encourage interested readers to see a likely *instantiation* in Flores, Moore, and Reynoso (2001), where proper explanations are given according to the types and functions described in this section, in order to understand whether or not consistency conditions are appropriately accomplished. We continue by presenting precise descriptions of patterns, together with a deep analysis of their constituents, in order to give a solution on patterns understanding.

A Formalization of Design Patterns

Various common properties of the GoF Design patterns were specified in the Metamodel as generic RSL functions, and these, appropriately instantiated and combined, can be used to formalize the properties of the patterns.

Our model of patterns was separated into three working units according to the *purpose* classification given by the GoF catalogue. Thus, the formal metamodel for OO design was used to formalize *Creational, Structural,* and *Behavioral* Design patterns from the GoF catalogue. The reader may see the complete formalization of patterns in Aranda and Moore (2000), Flores and Moore (2000), and Reynoso and Moore (2000). In this section, we illustrate such a formalization through a quite complete definition of the **Decorator** pattern (*structural*), and for brevity reasons only extracts of the **Observer** pattern (*behavioral*) and the **Abstract Factory** pattern (*creational*).

Decorator

The **Decorator** pattern makes a component being enclosed inside another object taking care to add a decoration (by means of an additional behavior). The enclosing object, called decorator, conforms to the interface of the component it decorates so that its presence is transparent to their clients. It forwards requests to the component and may perform additional actions (related with the new responsibility) before or after forwarding. Decorators may be

*Figure 2. Structure of **Decorator** pattern*

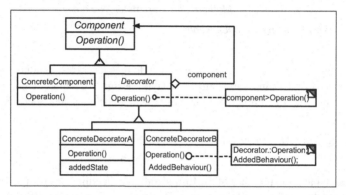

recursively nested, which effectively allows an unlimited number of added responsibilities. Figure 2 shows the structure of a **Decorator** pattern.

From Figure 2, names of classes in the pattern, together with names of their methods and state variables, are defined as RSL constants, as follows. A full description concerning the formalization of this pattern can be seen in Flores and Moore (2000).

Classes and relations in the **Decorator** pattern satisfy the following properties:

1.   There is a hierarchy with root class playing the Component role that is only played once in the pattern, which has leave classes playing either the ConcreteComponent or the ConcreteDecorator role. Every class in this hierarchy can play only one role in the pattern (because they have different properties) and no class in the hierarchy can play the Client role. In a particular design, we may have a class playing the ConcreteComponent role that has subclasses also playing the same role. This is the design heuristic which encourages to "factor out" common behavior and properties from related classes into a superclass—the process of generalization or classification (Martin & Odell, 1995; Rumbaugh et al., 1991). Hence, we allow intermediate additional classes between the root and the leaves, which may play the same roles as the leaves, that is, ConcreteComponent or ConcreteDecorator. These properties are specified using the generic function hierarchy from the *Design_Pattern* scheme, where dr denotes the Design_Renaming type:

one_component_in_hierarchy(dr) ≡

        hierarchy(Component, {ConcreteComponent, ConcreteDecorator}, {Client}, dr),

2.   Decorator class also forms the root of a hierarchy, where the leaves and possible intermediate classes may only play the ConcreteDecorator role. However, since Decorator is an abstract superclass which factors out a common interface, it should be a direct subclass of Component (i.e., without intermediate classes). We explicitly specify that

Decorator class is abstract whereas this is not needed for Component, since it contains an abstract method (Operation) which makes the class being abstract as well—this property is built into our general model of object-oriented design.

has_parent_component(dr) ≡ *has_parent_direct(Decorator, Component, dr)*

is_abstract_decorator(dr) ≡ *is_abstract_class(Decorator, dr)*

3. When a class role must be represented at the design level, we state this explicitly. This is the case for the ConcreteComponent and ConcreteDecorator roles where we use the function *exists_role*. As these classes represent actual components and decorators in the system, they must be concrete, which is formalized by means of the function *is_concrete* that checks if a class is a concrete subclass of a given class – in this case Component and Decorator, respectively.

exist_concrete_component(dr) ≡ *exists_role(ConcreteComponent, dr)*,

is_concrete_component(dr) ≡ *is_concrete(Component, ConcreteComponent, dr)*,

4. **Decorator** pattern provides a structure which allows a Client to refer to objects without knowing whether they are decorated or not – all objects are accessed uniformly through Operation methods in the Component interface. Clients should therefore be linked to the Component class by either an *aggregation* or an *association* relation.

decorator_client(dr) ≡

has_assoc_aggr_reltype(Client, Component, AssAggr, G.one, dr) ∧

use_interface(Client, Component, Operation, dr)

5. For the previous interaction, one abstract method (*defined*) playing the Operation role is needed in the Component class. Operation methods must be implemented in ConcreteComponent, Decorator, and ConcreteDecorator classes. Decorator class has a specific implementation that simply forwards the method call to its component state variable, specified by the function *deleg_with_var*.

Ct_has_operation_defined(dr) ≡ *has_def_method(Component, Operation, dr)* ∧

has_all_def_method(Component, Operation, dr),

Dec_has_impl_operation(dr) ≡

deleg_with_var(Decorator, Operation, component, Component, Operation, dr),

CCt_has_impl_operation(dr) ≡ *has_all_impl_method(ConcreteComponent, Operation, dr)*,

6. The unique relation between the Decorator and Component classes is an *aggregation*. It has cardinality *one-one* because its purpose is to add *one* and not many responsibilities

at a time (Gamma et al., 1995). The name of this relation, component, is a unique state variable which refers to the object that is being decorated.

$decorator\_relation(dr) \equiv$
$\quad$ $has\_unique\_assoc\_aggr\_relation(Decorator, Component, dr) \land$
$\quad$ $has\_assoc\_aggr\_var\_ren(Decorator, Component, Aggregation, component, one, dr),$

$store\_unique\_component(dr) \equiv store\_unique\_vble(Decorator, component, dr)$

7. Finally, we refer to the Operation methods in ConcreteDecorator classes. These classes provide the "decoration" to ConcreteComponent classes, which can be done either by adding new state variables or by adding new methods. In the first case, an Operation in ConcreteDecorator might override a corresponding method in a superclass, making an invocation to that method (*super*) and additionally invoking other methods on the addedState variables. In the second case, there could be an additional invocation to local (*self*) AddedBehaviour methods (as Figure 2 shows), which requires that at least one of those additional methods should be concrete (*implemented*).

$CDec\_has\_extended\_interface(dr) \equiv$
$\quad$ $(CDec\_has\_impl\_added\_behaviour(dr) \lor CDec\_stores\_added\_state(dr)) \land$
$\quad$ $(CDec\_has\_impl\_added\_behaviour(dr) \Rightarrow CDec\_has\_super\_self\_operation(dr)) \land$
$\quad$ $(CDec\_stores\_added\_state(dr) \Rightarrow CDec\_has\_super\_operation(dr)),$

The formalization of the **Decorator** pattern is represented by the function *is_decorator_pattern*, which collects all of the properties that were recognized and properly analyzed. This helps to distinguish whether or not a design matches this pattern.

$is\_decorator\_pattern: Wf\_Design\_Renaming \rightarrow Bool$
$is\_decorator\_pattern(dr) \equiv$
$\quad one\_component\_in\_hierarchy(dr) \land one\_decorator\_in\_hierarchy(dr) \land$
$\quad is\_abstract\_decorator(dr) \land has\_parent\_component(dr) \land decorator\_client(dr) \land$
$\quad decorator\_relation(dr) \land store\_unique\_component(dr) \land$
$\quad exist\_concrete\_component(dr) \land is\_concrete\_component(dr) \land$
$\quad exist\_concrete\_decorator(dr) \land is\_concrete\_decorator(dr) \land$
$\quad Ct\_has\_operation\_defined(dr) \land CCt\_has\_impl\_operation(dr) \land Dec\_has\_impl\_operation(dr) \land$
$\quad CDec\_has\_impl\_operation(dr) \land CDec\_has\_extended\_interface(dr)$

An instantiation of **Decorator** pattern can be seen in Flores and Moore (2000). The case study used on such instantiation has been extracted from the *Motivation* and *Sample* sections of the GoF Catalogue. In later sections we also present another case study of this pattern, which is used to present the process of designing enhanced by our automatic tool for modeling and verification.

Observer

The **Observer** pattern, which is also known both as Dependents and as Publish-Subscribe, is used when an abstraction has two aspects, one dependent on the other, for example, when a change to one object requires changing others, the number of objects needing to be changed is unknown, and when an object should be able to notify other objects without making assumptions about what those objects are (Gamma et al., 1995). The structure is shown in Figure 3.

As can be seen from the pattern structure in Figure 3, the pattern comprises four class roles, six method roles, and six variable roles, which are formalized as constant names as follows. A full description concerning the formalization of this pattern can be seen in Reynoso and Moore (2000).

Subject, ConcreteSubject, Observer, ConcreteObserver : G.Class_Name

Attach, Detach, Notify, GetState, SetState, Update : G. Method_Name

observers, subjectState, subject, observerState, observer_param, subjectState_param : G. Variable_Name

Classes and relations in the **Observer** pattern satisfy the following main properties. Those properties similarly formalized on **Decorator** pattern are omitted here for brevity reasons.

1.   The class playing the Subject role contains exactly one method playing the Attach role that is implemented and has a single parameter playing the observer_param role and which is of type Observer. This method contains an invocation to an observers state variable of the primitive *collectionadd* method with observer_param sent as parameter. Similarly, for the Detach role and the primitive *collectionremove* method;

Figure 3. Structure of the Observer

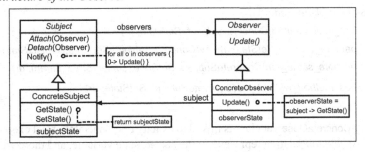

Attach implemented(dr) ≡

unique_method(Subject, Attach, dr) ∧ *has impl method(Subject, Attach, dr)* ∧
one_image_ren_pars_in_design(Subject, Attach, Observer, observer_param, dr) ∧
deleg_with_var_coll_aparam_ren(Subject, Attach, observers, G.collectionadd, observer_param, dr)

2.   The Subject class contains exactly one method playing the Notify role, which is implemented and contains an invocation to the variable, playing the observers role of the
Update method in the Observer class;

Notify_implemented(dr) ≡

    unique_method(Subject, Notify, dr) ∧ *has_impl_method(Subject, Notify, dr)* ∧

    deleg_with_var (Subject, Notify, observers, Observer, Update, dr

3.   Every ConcreteSubject class contains at least one method playing the GetState role
which is implemented, has no parameters, and returns a non-empty subset of the state
variables playing the subjectState role. Each subjectState variable belongs to the result
of at least one GetState method;

GetState_implemented(dr) ≡

    has_impl_method(ConcreteSubject, GetState, dr) ∧

    has_all_impl_method(ConcreteSubject, GetState, dr) ∧

    no_parameter_in_design(ConcreteSubject, GetState, dr) ∧

    results_of_Get State(ConcreteSubject, GetState, subjectState, dr)

4.   Every ConcreteSubject class contains at least one SetState method which is implemented, has no result, and has at least one parameter, and all the parameters play
the subjectState_param role. This method simply assigns each of the parameters to
a different **subjectState** variable, and each subjectState variable appears in such an
assignment in at least one SetState method.

SetState_implemented(dr) ≡

    has_impl_method(ConcreteSubject, SetState, dr) ∧

    params_vars_in_SetState_many(ConcreteSubject, SetState, subjectState, dr) ∧

    all_pars_same_ren(ConcreteSubject, SetState, subjectState_param, dr) ∧

    has_method_without_res(ConcreteSubject, SetState, dr)

5.   Every ConcreteObserver class is linked to exactly one ConcreteSubject class by a *one-
one association* relation representing the subject state variable, and there are no other
relations between such classes. Additionally, every ConcreteSubject class has a link
of this form from at least one ConcreteObserver class.

concrete_Observer_relation(dr) ≡

  has_assoc_var_ren(ConcreteObserver, ConcreteSubject, subject, G.one, dr) ∧

  has_unique_assoc_aggr(ConcreteObserver, ConcreteSubject, dr) ∧

  class_connected(ConcreteSubject, ConcreteObserver, dr)

6. Every ConcreteObserver class has at least one state variable playing the observerState role, and the number of such variables is not greater than the number of state variables playing the subjectState role in the ConcreteSubject class represented by its subject state variable.

store_ObserverState(dr) ≡

 store_vble(ConcreteObserver, observerState, dr) ∧

 less_quantities_of_variables(ConcreteObserver, observerState, ConcreteSubject, subjectState, dr)

7. The Update method is implemented in every ConcreteObserver class and returns no result. Its body consists of a series of assignments to subsets of the observerState state variables from the result of invoking some GetState method on the subject state variable, and each observerState state variable is set by at least one such assignment.

Update_implemented(dr) ≡

  Update_state_var_change_deleg_var(ConcreteObserver, Update, observerState,

      subject, ConcreteSubject, GetState, dr)

Finally, the formalization of the **Observer** pattern is represented by the function *is_observer_pattern*, which collects all of the properties that were recognized and properly analyzed. This helps to distinguish whether or not a design matches this pattern.

is_observer_pattern(dr) ≡

 Subject_hierarchy(dr) ∧ *Observer_hierarchy(dr)* ∧ *exists_concrete_ Subject(dr)* ∧

 exists_concrete_Observer(dr) ∧ *Observer_relation(dr)* ∧ *concrete_Observer_relation(dr)* ∧

 store_subject(dr) ∧ *store_observers(dr)* ∧ *store_ObserverState(dr)* ∧ *is_abstract_Subject(dr)* ∧

 Attach_implemented(dr) ∧ *Detach_implemented(dr)* ∧ *Notify_implemented(dr)* ∧

 GetState_implemented(dr) ∧ *SetState_implemented(dr)* ∧ *Update_defined(dr)* ∧

 Update_implemented(dr) ∧ *is_concrete_Observer(dr)* ∧ *is_concrete_Subject(dr)*

Abstract Factory

The **Abstract Factory** pattern provides an interface for creating families of related or dependent objects without specifying their concrete classes. The main feature of the pattern is the idea of a family of products, which means a set of products that are designed to work together. The structure participants are shown in Figure 4.

From the pattern structure in Figure 4 can be seen that there are five class roles and one method role, which are described as constant names as follows. A full description concerning the formalization of this pattern can be seen in Aranda and Moore (2000).

AbstractFactory, ConcreteFactory, AbstractProduct, ConcreteProduct, Client: G.Class_Name

CreateProduct: G. Method_Name

The main properties of the **Abstract Factory** are as follows.

1. Families of products are represented by many hierarchies, each representing one kind of product. The root of each hierarchy is an abstract class playing the AbstractProduct role, so there can be more than one class playing this role in a design. Leaves in each hierarchy must all play the ConcreteProduct role and other extra classes in these hierarchies either play the ConcreteProduct role or play no role in the pattern – for example, neither one of the factory roles nor the Client role.

    AbstractProduct_hierarchies(dr) ≡

       exists_role_AbstractProduct(dr) ∧

         is_hierarchy(AbstractProduct, {ConcreteProduct}, {AbstractFactory, ConcreteFactory, Client}, dr)

2. Every AbstractProduct class has at least one subclass playing the ConcreteProduct role and every ConcreteProduct class is a concrete subclass of a unique class playing the AbstractProduct role. Additionally, ConcreteProduct classes cannot extend the public interface defined by an AbstractProduct, because the Client uses this public interface and any extension will then be invisible.

Figure 4. Structure of the Abstract Factory

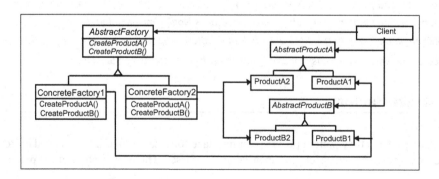

exists_ConcreteProduct(dr) ≡

   has_subclass_playing_role(AbstractProduct, ConcreteProduct, dr) ∧

   is_concrete_of_ a(AbstractProduct, ConcreteProduct, dr) ∧

   no_extends_operation_interface(ConcreteProduct, AbstractProduct, dr)

3.   AbstractFactory contains at least one method playing the CreateProduct role which return a result and all such methods must be abstract (*defined*) because they represent the common interface for every ConcreteFactory subclass. The amount of CreateProduct methods must be the same as the number of different kinds of products—that is, classes playing the AbstractProduct role. This is because each factory creates one of each kind of product—that is, one product from each products hierarchy.

Afactory_has_CreateProduct_def(dr) ≡

   has_all_def_method(AbstractFactory, CreateProduct, dr) ∧

   has_method_with_res(AbstractFactory, CreateProduct, dr) ∧

   balance_methods_classes(AbstractFactory, CreateProduct, AbstractProduct, dr)

4.   Every ConcreteFactory class has at least one method playing the CreateProduct role. Each of such methods is implemented and "instantiates" a class playing the ConcreteProduct role and no two methods instantiate ConcreteProduct classes in the same products hierarchy. Similar to ConcreteProduct, ConcreteFactory classes cannot extend the interface defined by the AbstractFactory class.

Cfactory_has_CreateProduct_impl(dr) ≡

      has_impl_method_with_result_class(ConcreteFactory, CreateProduct, Concrete-Product, dr) ∧

         dif_methods_dif_hierarchies(ConcreteFactory, CreateProduct,

                  ConcreteProduct, AbstractProduct, dr) ∧

   no_adds_method_role(ConcreteFactory, AbstractFactory, CreateProduct, dr)

5.   Every ConcreteFactory class has as many instantiation relations to ConcreteProduct classes as there are classes playing the AbstractProduct role and no two ConcreteProduct classes that are instantiated by the same ConcreteFactory class belong to the same family of products or products hierarchy. Additionally, every ConcreteProduct class is instantiated by a unique class which plays the ConcreteFactory role.

Cfactory_instantiate_Cproduct(dr) ≡

 instantiate_one_class_from_each_hierarchy(ConcreteProduct,

                  ConcreteFactory, AbstractProduct, dr) ∧

  is_instantiated_by_unique_class(ConcreteProduct, ConcreteFactory, dr)

6.   There is at least one class playing the Client role, and every one of these classes uses the interfaces defined by the AbstractFactory and AbstractProduct classes. In the case of AbstractFactory, the interface relates to CreateProduct methods, but in the case of AbstractProduct, the interface is unknown. Client class interacts with AbstractFactory and AbstractProduct classes through *association* or *aggregation* relations.

Client_use_interface(dr) ≡

  exists_role(Client, dr) ∧ has_assoc_aggr_reltype(AbstractFactory, Client, AssAggr, G.one, dr) ∧

  has_assoc_aggr_reltype(AbstractProduct, Client, AssAggr, G.one, dr) ∧

  use_some_known_interface(Client, AbstractFactory, CreateProduct, dr) ∧

  use_some_unknown_interface(Client, AbstractProduct, dr)

Eight properties were formalized, and they are then combined in the function *is_abstract_factory_pattern* which checks whether a given design matches the **Abstract Factory** pattern.

is_abstract_factory_pattern(dr) ≡

  AbstractFactory_hierarchy(dr) ∧ AbstractProduct_hierarchies(dr) ∧

  exists_ConcreteFactory(dr) ∧ exists_ConcreteProduct(dr) ∧

  Afactory_has_CreateProduct_def(dr) ∧ Cfactory_has_CreateProduct_impl(dr) ∧

  Cfactory_instantiate_Cproduct(dr) ∧ Client_use_interface(dr)

Discussion

In the previous sections, we have presented a more accurate description of a general object-oriented design and patterns, based on the use of the RSL formal language. However, one of the common concerns expressed about formal descriptions of Design patterns is that they could make the usage of patterns too inflexible. As patterns were defined to be general enough for a widely application on different contexts, the question is whether applying formality could narrow this scope. Nevertheless, we can positively claim that, far from reducing the range of use, we have achieved a model that precisely allows and describes valid variations of patterns applications. Thus, in the following we present different variants of the use of our pattern specifications, as it is generically depicted in Figure 5.

The following list may help designers learn possibilities that could be poorly described in a consistent format description. Each item in the following list is presented without a specific order, and references some specific sections from the consistent format description given in the GoF catalogue.

1.   **Hierarchy:** A pattern structure usually shows an inheritance relationship between two classes. However, it does not mean there are only two levels in the hierarchy. In fact,

Figure 5. Different generic applications of patterns on a design

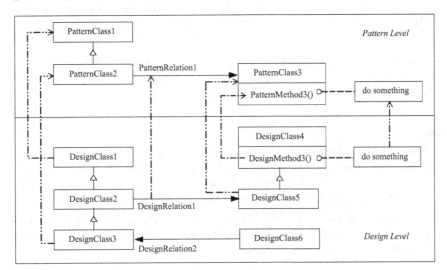

it usually signifies an inheritance hierarchy. Figure 5 depicts this issue in a generic way.

Example

* **Composite:** Figure 6 shows the *Sample* section for this pattern where the design level presents an intermediate class between Component class and Composite leaf-classes. Further explanations in Flores and Moore (2000).

Figure 6. Composite—Pattern and design levels

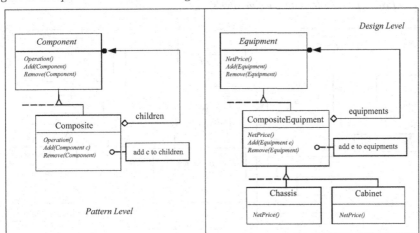

- **Prototype:** ConcretePrototype classes showed in the *Motivation* section of this pattern (Figure 7) are not connected directly to Graphic class, but through the MusicalNote class.

2. **Association vs. Aggregation:** In some cases, an association relationship between two participant classes can be replaced by an aggregation relationship in a particular design without changing the intent of the pattern.

Example

- **Prototype:** A Client class asks a Prototype class to clone itself through an association relationship. However, on the design level of Figure 7, GraphicTool is connected to Graphic using an aggregation relationship, which is stronger than association, and is not inadequate because the intent is still being satisfied.

  Note: In the application of the formal general basis to the specification of each pattern, we have analyzed when it is possible to change a relation type. Full details can be seen in Flores and Moore (2000).

3. **Additional Design Methods:** It is always possible to include methods in the design that have no counterparts in the pattern. They are important to the domain in which the pattern is being applied, but they do not change the behavior of the pattern participants.

Example

- **Prototype:** In the *Motivation* of this pattern (Figure 7), the Draw method does not play any method role in the pattern, but it represents an added method in design, which is domain-specific for graphical editors.

Figure 7. Prototype—Pattern and design levels

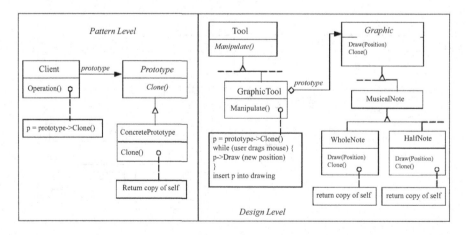

4.   **Minimal set of Methods:** Although the set of methods represented in a pattern structure seems to be the minimal set that a design should include, it is possible to omit few of them.

Example

- **Singleton:** SingletonOperation and GetSingletonData are specific methods which may or may not have a representative in design without losing the features of a Singleton class. Further details are in Aranda and Moore (2000).

- **Observer and Composite:** Those methods related to the management of an object collection (Attach, Dettach in Observer; Add, Remove, GetChild in Composite) are not completely necessary when there is another class in charge of building their object structure.

5.   **Additional Design Parameters:** If no parameters are included in a method definition of any class in a pattern structure, it does not mean they are not allowed in a correct design. The fact that they are not shown only means they are not significant for the family of designs the pattern represents.

Example

- **Builder:** The Sample section of this pattern presents an implementation of the Maze problem. Although the method BuildPart is showed without parameters in the pattern, its counterparts in design, BuildRoom and BuildWall, do have some parameters. For a precise description, see Aranda and Moore (2000).

6.   **Additional Design Hierarchy:** Although a particular concrete participant could be shown in a pattern structure as a "stand-alone" class, it can be part of a hierarchy for a particular design. That is, hierarchies in the structure of a pattern are shown when the aspect that varies in the pattern can only be designed using inheritance; however, it does not mean that other participants can be included in domain-specific hierarchies.

Example

- **Prototype:** As can be seen in Figure 7 of this pattern, that GraphicalTool representing the Client is in fact a leaf in the hierarchy with root Tool.

   Note: Our formal model includes this possibility, as can be seen in Aranda and Moore (2000).

7.   **Implicit Relations:** In some patterns, the name of some methods and classes reveals relations between classes involving semantic aspects.

Example

- **Visitor:** The way each method of the Visitor class is named (VisitConcreteElementA, VisitConcreteElementB) indicates that each one is related to a particular ConcreteElement (Reynoso & Moore, 2000).

- **Abstract Factory:** There is a relation of amounts between ConcreteFactory and Product using two different indexes (numbers and letters). For instance, the CreateProductA method of ConcreteFactory1 class instantiates the ProductA1 (Aranda & Moore, 2000).

  Note: Our model does not implement this feature by restricting names of methods. Instead, we constrain the way classes playing these roles are related, as we have shown in the specification of this pattern in the previous section.

8. **Inherited Methods:** A method is shown as part of a given participant class in the pattern structure. Though, that method in design can be either defined in the owned interface of the design class playing the pattern role, or inherited from a superclass. This feature is shown in a general way in Figure 5.

Example

- **Composite:** In Figure 6, methods Add and Remove in the Composite leaves classes (e.g., Chassis) are inherited from the design CompositeEquipment class where they are implemented (Flores & Moore, 2000).

9. **Factorized Relations:** An association, aggregation, or instantiation relation between two classes in the pattern structure may be modeled in design by means of a factorization. Let us define PA and PB pattern participants, and DA and DB, their counterparts in design. If there is a relation from PA to PB in a pattern, in design the relation can be from DA to DB, as well as from a superclass of DA to DB. See a generic drawing in Figure 5.

Example

- **Composite:** In Figure 6, the relation with variable name children in the pattern is factored out in design to the CompositeEquipment class.

A Supporting Tool

We have developed a tool for graphical modeling where the formal model serves as an instrument to verify whether the patterns are properly applied and the design satisfies the required modeling principles. For this, we have translated the formal building blocks into an OO metamodel by means of the Java language (Flores et al., 2006; Reynoso et al., 2002).

Basically, the tool is divided into two layers, the Modeling layer, whose result is a specification of an OO design model provided by a graphical component, and the Verification layer, which carries out the process of checking the correctness of the design model and also the matching of a design subset that was linked to a specific pattern. We have selected a non-commercial tool called FUJABA (Fujaba, 1998; Fujaba Home Page, 2006; Nickel, Niere, Wadsack, & Zündorf, 2000; SUN) that was developed in the Java language.

Figure 8 shows in a diagrammatic way the whole process for correctness verification when modeling a design by means of the tool support. Briefly, the process involves a designer drawing the design elements (classes, methods, etc.), and also selecting a specific pattern from which the setting of roles could be carried out. After that, the designer may choose to export an *eXtended Java Specification* from where the verification tasks can be initiated.

The designer may choose to check only the design for correctness on heuristics and design principles. The other option also includes checking whether the pattern has been correctly applied. For both options, the first step is to generate an object structure from the *eXtended Java Specification* by means of an ad-hoc parser component. Then, the verification of design is carried out by invoking the proper services. If no error occurs, this step is considered successful; otherwise, a set of errors is returned to be shown on the Fujaba's GUI. When the selected option is verifying a pattern application, the next step (in the case that the design checking has been successful) is to instantiate the objects representing the selected pattern. Then the checking is initiated by invoking the ad-hoc services on the previously generated objects. The results (successful or error) are shown in the Fujaba's GUI. Thus, the designer may correct what is needed (in case of error).

Because we are aware of the current running Fujaba projects (Fujaba Home Page, 2006), we expect to move forward to transform our deployed product into a plug-in, which any current Fujaba users could download to improve the tool they already use. For identification purposes, the plug-in is named design and pattern modeling and verification (DePMoVe).

Figure 8. Internal process of design and pattern verification

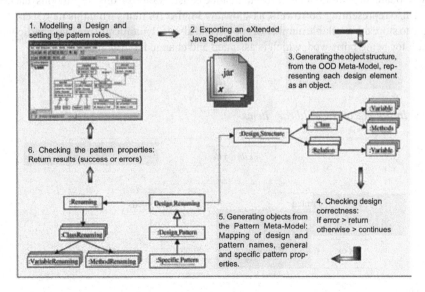

A Case Study

Imagine a management system for a library. The library contains books and magazines that correspond to printed items. In addition, recorded material is available as video and DVD. All these items can be lent to people in two ways, first by being accessible only to be managed into the library, or being able to take them outside for some days. Such ways of lending are dynamically defined according to decisions made by librarians on different moments. In such a way, items can sometimes exhibit one or even the two lending forms. Information from borrowers is recorded in order to keep track of items' destinations. From this domain description, the software system should provide information to be properly displayed on a user interface, for example, the number of items currently available in the library, those that have been lent inside the library, and those that have been taken away for few days.

We could start modeling our design by considering only library items without taking into account lending procedures. Figure 9 shows a possible hierarchy of items classified according to the material source (printed/recorded). Objects in this hierarchy should include the number of copies for each library item and the responsibilities to display their stored information.

On a second step, we can focus on the conditions that make an item available to be lent. Here, we could think that the responsibility to manage the information concerning the current number of copies, and the destination of lent items, corresponds particularly to those items.

However, an item can be borrowed in two ways, so two responsibilities should be added to the representative classes. Additionally, librarians may dynamically assign one lending way at one time, and then change to the other at another time, or even make the item lent on the two ways as well. Hence, such responsibilities should be incorporated to the objects in a dynamic form, thus making us think about the application of a "pattern." Thus, we start searching the appropriate pattern and we decide that the right choice should be the **"Decorator"** pattern.

Thus, we update the diagram in Figure 9 to include considerations from the previous discussion and also representing borrowers, as shown in Figure 10. Items from this model can be managed to store the available number of copies, and also to dynamically receive a particular condition for being borrowed, which is assigned and changed by librarians.

Figure 9. Initial hierarchy of library items

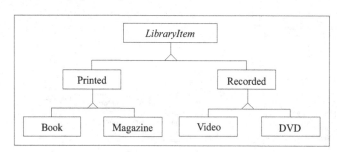

*Figure 10. Model of library with application of **Decorator** pattern*

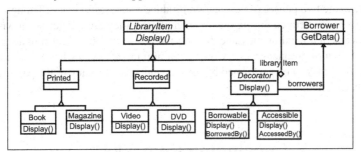

Since we would like to know whether this pattern has been properly applied, we use our tool to select the use of this pattern and then set their roles on the corresponding design elements. Figure 11 shows the display screen displayed to a designer when modeling the current case study. From the menu "Patterns" or the ad-hoc tool bar we can select the pattern and assign pattern roles (for classes, relations, state variables, and methods).

Now, we must check whether the design model and the applied pattern exhibit the expected adequacy. To do so, we select the option to "Export eXtended Java Specification" and then "Check Design&Pattern" from the menu "Patterns" or the ad-hoc tool bar. These selections trigger the whole process of verification described in Figure 8 at the beginning of this section.

Figure 11. The whole library model displayed by the tool

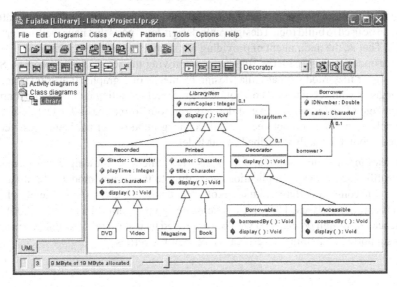

In this case, we have correctly satisfied the required aspects both at the design and at the pattern levels, so the two phases of verification produce a successful result. Though in case any kind of error is generated during one of such phases, they are explicitly shown to the designer by means of a window message. It helps the designer understand situations where a variation of a pattern produces a bias from the pattern intent. Even when the selection of the pattern is still a task to be performed by the designer, the accuracy of the pattern usage might be fairly satisfied.

Concluding Remarks

Design patterns are a valuable tool for OO designers because of their pragmatic benefits, though, of course, there are also a number of common problems. For example, some Design patterns are simply too difficult for the average OO designer to learn. In some cases, the pattern is inherently complex; in other cases it is given a name and a description that are not obvious. Whatever the cause, pattern understanding is a practical problem when they are adopted by an organization.

In practice, an OO designer needs personal time and personal initiative to become skilful in Design patterns. For example, a Design pattern may be used in a toy example before it can be used in the real case, a real case may be verified against the application of pattern's properties, and so forth. The main issue here is that every OO designer should learn how to apply Design patterns.

Learning processes might be facilitated through improving the understanding of the semantics behind the patterns. Although the reasons to formalize patterns were discussed in this chapter, current formal notations for characterizing pattern models mainly rely on descriptive concerns (Flores & Fillottrani, 2003); that is, the formal notation suggests a more specific meaning of a pattern's elements as modeling building blocks.

Verification of a pattern's properties adds another reason to exploit the use of formal notations. Patterns can be used to build robust designs with design-level parts that have well-understood trade-offs. That is, the main intent of providing our supporting tool is facilitating a learning process for understanding patterns, and hence improving the whole design process. Since an OO designer may model a particular design by means of a graphical user interface, we allow designers with regular skills on both OO graphical modeling and Design patterns to take advantage of a rigorous back-end derived from our formal basis for OO design and pattern application. They do not need to have a background on formal languages, yet still may benefit from a formally described MetaModel.

Besides, learning how to apply patterns is also facilitated by allowing experimentation, which identifies semantics of applications according to the formal model behind the tool. This helps us to compare different situations on several different contexts, and detect whether a pattern is appropriately used to solve a specific design problem (Flores et al., 2006). As a consequence, the design process as a whole is improved by using a reuse technique, patterns, which is supported by automatic verification of their properties.

Diversity of uses is remarkable during experimentation. Naïve OO designers may test different aspects of patterns through systematically using our supporting tool during their training period. Then, trainees will iteratively learn and check new knowledge, which facilitate understanding. Expert OO designers might take advantage of this process too. They could use the tool to improve current designs by experimenting with "what-if" situations on different alternatives. Information collected from experiences in the different cases will increase knowledge on the use of patterns, which in turn improves future use of the tool. Patterns and their variations are stored for future analysis; hence, sharing knowledge among OO designers is also possible.

So far, the tool has been used in the context of training students. Results show a time reduction in learning, compared to similar courses without using the tool. Additionally, the number of errors introduced in the design decreases significantly. However, we are aware that more empirical evaluation is needed to quantify advantages of the use of the tool. To do so, it is currently being checked on academic, as well as industrial, environments.

Acknowledgment

Our work was developed under the research projects 04/E032, 04/E048, and 04/E059 at the GIISCo Research Group (http://giisco.uncoma.edu.ar), University of Comahue, Neuquen, Argentina, and the research project "Formalization of GoF patterns using RSL" at the International Institute for Software Technology, United Nations University (UNU/IIST), Macau, South China (http://www.iist.unu.edu/home/Unuiist/newrh/II/1/2/11/page.html).

References

Alagar, V., & Lämmel, R. (2002, October 21-25). Three-tiered specification of microarchitectures. In *Proceedings of the 4th ICFEM'02, International Conference on Formal Engineering Methods*, Shanghai, China (LNCS 2495, pp. 92-97). Springer-Verlag.

Abadi M., & Cardelli, L. (1995). A theory of primitive objects: Second-order systems. *Science of Computer Programming, 25*(2-3), 81-116.

Aranda, G., & Moore, R. (2000, August). *GoF creational patterns: A formal specification* (Tech. Rep. No. 224). P.O. Box 3058, Macau, China: UNU/IIST. Retrieved November 14, 2006, from http://www.iist.unu.edu

Aranda, G., & Moore, R. (2002, July 15-19). A formal model for verifying compound Design patterns. In *Proceedings of the 14th SEKE'02 International Conference on Software Engineering and Knowledge Engineering*, Ischia, Italy (pp. 213-214). ACM Press.

Buccella, A., & Cechich, A. (2002, February 18-21). A precise semantics of behavioural properties of analysis patterns. In *Proceedings of the 20th IASTED'02 International Conference on Applied Informatics* (pp. 351-196). Innsbruck, Austria: ACTA Press.

Cechich, A., & Moore, R. (1999a, December 7-10). A formal specification of GoF Design patterns. In *Proceedings of the APSEC'99 Asia Pacific Software Engineering Conference*, Takamatsu, Japan (pp. 248-291).

Cechich, A., & Moore, R. (1999b, January). *A specification of GoF Design patterns* (Tech. Rep. No. 151). PO Box 3058, Macau, China: UNU/IIST. Retrieved November 14, 2006, from http://www.iist.unu.edu

DisCo Project. (2006). *Home page.* Retrieved November 14, 2006, from http://disco.cs.tut. fi

Eden, A.H. (2002, June 22-28). LePUS: A visual formalism for object-oriented architectures. In *Proceedings of the 6th IDPT'02 World Conference Integrated Design and Process Technology*, Pasadena, CA (pp. 26-30).

Eden, A.H., Gil, J., & Yehudai, A. (1997, November 2-5). Precise specification and automatic application of Design patterns. In *Proceedings of the 12th ASE'97 International Conference on Automated Software Engineering, Lake Tahoe, Nevada* (pp. 143-152). IEEE Computer Society Press.

Flores, A., Cechich, A., & Ruiz, R. (2006). Automatic verification of OOD pattern applications. In J. Garzás & M. Piattini (Eds.), *Object-oriented design knowledge: Principles, heuristics, best practices.* Hershey, PA: Idea Group Inc.

Flores, A., & Fillottrani, P. (2003, October 6-10). Evaluation framework for Design pattern formal models. In *Proceedings of the CACIC'03 IX Argentinean Conference on Computer Science*, La Plata, Argentina (pp. 1024-1036). RedUNCI.

Flores, A., & Moore, R. (2000). *GoF structural patterns: A formal specification* (Tech. Rep. No. 207). PO Box 3054, Macau, China: UNU/IIST. Retrieved November 14, 2006, from http://www.iist.unu.edu

Flores, A., Moore, R., & Reynoso, L. (2001, March 14-15). A formal model of object-oriented design and GoF Design patterns. In *Proceedings of the FME'01 Formal Methods Europe* (LNCS 2021, pp. 223-241). Berlin, Germany: Springer Verlag.

Flores, A., Reynoso, L., & Moore, R. (2000). *A formal model of object oriented design and GoF Design patterns* (Tech. Rep. No. 200). PO Box 3058, Macau, China: UNU/IIST. Retrieved November 14, 2006, from http://www.iist.unu.edu

Fujaba (1998). FUJABA: From UML to Java and back again. *Crossroads Student Magazine.* Software Engineering Group, University of Paderborn, Germany. Retrieved November 14, 2006, from http://www.uni-paderborn.de/cs/fujaba

Fujaba Home Page. (2006). *University of Paderborn, Software Engineering Group.* Retrieved November 14, 2006, from http://wwwcs.uni-paderborn.de/cs/fujaba/

Gamma, E., Helm, R., Johnson, R., & Vlissides, J. (1995). *Design patterns: Elements of reusable object-oriented software* (pp. 144-192). Boston: Addison-Wesley Longman Publishing.

Gil, J., Howse, J., & Kent, S. (2001, 5-7). Towards a formalization of constraint diagrams. In *Proceedings of the HCC'01 International Symposium on Human-Centric Computing Languages and Environments*, Stresa, Italy (pp. 72-79). IEEE Computer Society Press.

Helm, R., Holland, I., & Gangopadhyay, D. (1990, October 21-25). Contracts: Specifying behavioral compositions in object-oriented systems. In *Proceedings of the ECOOP/ OOPSLA '90 European Conference on Object-Oriented Programming, and Conference on Object-Oriented Programming Systems, Languages, and Applications*, Ottawa, Canada (pp.169-180). ACM SIGPLAN Notices, 25(10).

Lano, K., Bicarregui, J., & Goldsack, S. (1997, July 14-15). Formalising Design patterns. In *Proceedings of the 2nd BCS-FACS Northern Formal Methods Workshop, eWICS Series*, Ilkley, UK. BCS, British Computer Society.

Lano, K., & Goldsack, S. (1996, March 25-26). Integrated formal and object-oriented methods: The VDM++ approach. In *Proceedings of the 2nd Methods Integration Workshop, eWIC Series*, Leeds, UK. BCS, British Computer Society.

Lauder, A., & Kent, S. (1998, July 20-24). Precise visual specification of Design patterns. In *Proceedings of the 12th ECOOP '98 European Conference on Object-Oriented Programming*, Brussels, Belgium (LNCS 1445, pp.114-134). Springer-Verlag.

Le Guennec, A., Gerson, S., & Jézéquel, J.M. (2000, October 2-6). Precise modeling of Design patterns. In *Proceedings of the UML '00 3rd International Conference oo Unified Modeling Language, Advancing the Standard*, York, UK (LNCS 1939, pp. 482-496). Springer-Verlag.

Martin, J., & Odell, J. (1995). *Object oriented methods: A foundation*. Englewood Cliffs, NJ: Prentice Hall.

McC. Smith, J., & Stotts, D. (2002, December 5-6). Elemental Design patterns: A formal semantics for composition of OO software architecture. In *Proceedings of the 27th SEW-27'02 Annual NASA Goddard Software Engineering Workshop*, Greenbelt, MD (pp. 183-192). IEEE Computer Society Press.

Mikkonen, T. (1998, April 19-25). Formalizing Design patterns. In *Proceedings of the 20th ICSE '98 International Conference on Software Engineering*, Kyoto, Japan (pp. 115-124). IEEE Computer Society Press.

Moore, R., Cechich, A., Reynoso, L., Flores, A., & Aranda, G. (2002). Object-oriented Design patterns. In H. Dang Van, C. George, T. Janowski, & R. Moore (Eds.), *Specification case studies in RAISE* (Formal Approaches to Computing and Information Technology Series, pp. 287-314). Springer FACIT.

Nickel, U., Niere, J., Wadsack, J., & Zündorf, A. (2000, May 11-12). Roundtrip engineering with FUJABA. In *Proceedings of the WSR '00 2nd Workshop on Software Re-engineering*, Bad Honnef, Germany.

RAISE Group (1992). *The RAISE specification language (BCS Practitioner Series)*. Hemel Hempstead, UK: Prentice-Hall International.

RAISE Group (1995). *The RAISE development method (BCS Practitioner Series)*. Hemel Hempstead, UK: Prentice-Hall International.

Reynoso, L., Aranda, G., Buccella, A., & Flores, A. (2002). Component-based tool for verifying applications using object-oriented patterns. *JCS&T '02, Journal of Computer Science and Technology, 2*(7), 42-48. Retrieved November 14, 2006, from http://journal. info.unlp.edu.ar/journal

Reynoso, L., & Moore, R. (2000). *GoF behavioural patterns: A formal specification* (Tech. Rep. No. 201). PO Box 3058, Macau, China: UNU/IIST. Retrieved November 14, 2006, from http://www.iist.unu.edu

Rumbaugh, J., Blaha, M., Premerlani, W., Eddy, F., & Lorensen, W. (1991). *Object-oriented modelling and design.* Englewood Cliffs, NJ: Prentice Hall.

SUN. The source for developers. *Sun Developer Network.* Sun Microsystems, Inc. Retrieved November 14, 2006, from http://java.sun.com/

UML Consortium (2006a). *UML home page.* Retrieved November 14, 2006, from http://www.rational.com/uml

UML Consortium (2006b). *OCL: Object constraint language specification.* Retrieved November 14, 2006,from http://www.rational.com

Chapter IV

Patterns of Collective Behavior in Ocsid

Joni Helin, Tampere University of Technology, Finland

Pertti Kellomäki, Tampere University of Technology, Finland

Tommi Mikkonen, Tampere University of Technology, Finland

Abstract

This chapter presents an abstraction mechanism for collective behavior in reactive distributed systems. The mechanism allows the expression of recurring patterns of object interactions in a parametric form, and the formal verification of temporal safety properties induced by applications of the patterns. The abstraction mechanism is defined and compared to Design patterns, an established software engineering concept. While there are some obvious similarities, because the common theme is abstraction of object interactions, there are important differences as well. The chapter discusses how the emphasis on full formality affects what can be expressed and achieved in terms of patterns of object interactions. The approach is illustrated with the Observer and Memento patterns.

Introduction

The motivation for Design patterns is to improve the quality of software by improving its structure. Taking this one step further, the motivation for *formalizing* Design patterns is to improve their quality. Here, the premise of formalization is twofold. First, the commonly acknowledged benefits stemming from rigorous *specification* are the decrease of ambiguities and the flagging of hidden assumptions. In the case of patterns, this reduces problems that arise from their inappropriate application due to misunderstandings. Second, the possibility to mechanically reason about important properties of patterns contributes to better quality by finding errors and inconsistencies.

The interests driving this chapter are somewhat orthogonal to the issues addressed by the well known object-oriented Design patterns. Since Design patterns have their roots in the object-oriented programming community, it is natural that many patterns deal with object-oriented concepts. There are patterns for organizing inheritance hierarchies, traversal of structures composed of objects, and so forth. Many of these patterns are concerned with static organization of code rather than its *behavioral properties*, which are the focus of our approach.

The fundamental goal behind this chapter's approach is the modularization of distributed behavior, which involves coordinated cooperation of objects over time. The units of behavior to be modularized are usually below the level of complete distributed algorithms. They are pieces of behavior that ensure that the system has some meaningful *temporal properties*. The background for the work of this chapter is in stepwise refinement, where the temporal properties of interest are often *invariants* that link abstractions with their implementations. Another concern that comes up in the context of distribution is atomicity.

Focusing on behavioral properties leads to somewhat different territory than the mainstream Design pattern work. A popular figure of speech when talking about the quality of code is "code smell," which is a somewhat subjective, non-quantifiable property. Design patterns help to remove these smells by qualitatively improving the code. Temporal properties, on the other hand, are very clear cut. For example, an interaction either is atomic or it is not, and there are no intermediate degrees of atomicity.

Patterns are often described using UML (Rumbaugh, Jacobson, & Booch, 1998). For the purposes of this chapter, the problem with the UML mechanisms for describing behavior (i.e., sequence diagrams and collaboration/communication diagrams) is that, at least at the present time, they do not specify atomicity except at a very detailed level. This means that one cannot reliably reason about what happens when *concurrent* activities described using abstract diagrams interact, which defeats the goal of this chapter.

This chapter develops an approach based on *views*, which allow to modularize specifications based on their behavioral properties. Classes of similar views can be abstracted using *view templates*, which are parametric descriptions of *collective* behavior. Verification effort can be reused by verifying behavioral properties at the template level. The approach is embodied in the experimental *Ocsid* language (Helin & Kellomäki, 2004, 2005).

To avoid confusion, patterns of collective behavior are referred to as *Ocsid patterns* in the following, and the term *Design pattern* refers to patterns as understood by the object-oriented community.

In the rest of the chapter, first the commonalities and differences between Ocsid patterns and Design patterns are discussed. Then, it is illustrated how collective behavior is expressed in Ocsid by using the *Observer* and *Memento* patterns (Gamma, Helm, Johnson, & Vlissides, 1995), which contain enough object interactions to make them nontrivial. It is also shown how the patterns are composed in a way that guarantees that certain behavioral properties of the patterns are preserved.

Background

The background of our approach to pattern formalization is in formal specification of reactive distributed systems. It is based on separation of *behavioral concerns* using *closed world* modeling and atomic *joint actions*, pioneered in the DisCo method (Disco home page, 2006; Järvinen & Kurki-Suonio, 1991; Järvinen, Kurki-Suonio, Sakkinen, & Systä, 1990). These facilitate modularization of a reactive system in a way that is aligned with its behavioral properties, which makes separate verification of modules possible.

The methodological background is in the incrementality facilities of the DisCo language (Mikkonen, 1999). Specifications are composed using a mechanism which is in some sense the inverse of *projections* (Lam & Shankar, 1984) and *program slicing* (Weiser, 1984). Instead of creating abstractions of a system by removing variables and associated operations, such abstractions are composed to produce a specification of the system.

Formal Basis

The formal basis of Ocsid is *linear time temporal logic*, where behavior is modeled as infinite sequences of discrete states. Linear time temporal logic is simple, yet expressive enough for specification and verification of behavioral properties of distributed systems.

There is a plethora of modeling approaches based on linear time temporal logic. For example, Temporal Logic of Actions (Lamport, 1994), TLA+ (Lamport, 2000), Compositional TLA (Herrmann, Graw, & Krumm, 1998), Unity (Chandy & Misra, 1988), the B Method (Abrial, Lee, Neilson, Scharbach, & Sørensen, 1991) and DisCo all share the same formal basis.

The approaches differ in the kind of modularity they provide. At one extreme Temporal Logic of Actions is very close to conventional mathematics, and provides little explicit support for modularity. This also means that it places few restrictions on how specifications can be structured. The B method and Compositional TLA have a somewhat component oriented flavor, although both are general enough to be used in a variety of ways. A number of approaches, including Unity and DisCo, are based on *superposition* (Dijsktra & Scholten, 1980), where behavior is described in *layers*. This more or less imposes a particular style of specification on the designer.

Ocsid combines linear time temporal logic with a composition mechanism similar to that of the Hyperspace approach (Tarr, Ossherr, Harrison, & Sutton, 1999) and Hyper/J (Tarr, Ossher, & Sutton, 2002). A system is described using a set of partially overlapping *views* that are merged to produce a composed specification. Formal details are given later in the chapter.

Temporal Properties

Temporal properties are classified as *safety properties* or *liveness properties*. The violation of a safety property can be determined from a finite prefix of a behavior, so informally safety properties can be characterized as "something bad never happens." Liveness properties, on the other hand, are of the form "something good eventually happens," so it is not possible to detect a violation from a finite prefix.

Work on Ocsid has concentrated on safety properties, mainly invariants. Reasoning about safety properties applies standard temporal reasoning techniques. For fully formal verification, a formalization of temporal logic in the PVS (Owre, Rajan, Rushby, Shankar, & Srivas, 1996) theorem prover has been used. Later in the chapter we describe how composition in Ocsid preserves safety properties. This is imperative for our interests, because it allows modular reasoning about safety properties.

Atomicity

The behavior of a system is specified using *joint actions*, which specify atomic state changes that may cross object boundaries. There is no explicit flow of control in the execution model. A joint action may take place any time the guard of the action (a boolean expression) evaluates to true for a particular combination of participating objects. An action thus describes the effect it has on the local states of the participants, but it does not prescribe any particular implementation of the state change.

Formally, a behavior is a sequence of action executions, but the interleaving interpretation of concurrency allows concurrent execution of independent actions.

Closed World Principle

One key to being able to compose facets of behavior without breaking temporal properties is the concept of a *closed system*. A closed-system description is *behaviorally complete* with respect to some set of variables. In other words, it contains all the operations that modify the variables in the set, which makes it possible to reason about temporal safety properties. Because all other operations by definition leave the relevant variables unchanged, it is sufficient to check that the operations listed in the closed-system description do not violate the safety property of interest.

The closed-system approach puts some constraints on how *composition* can be defined. When two closed-system descriptions of a system are composed, the behaviors allowed by the result need to be allowed by both component descriptions. In other words, the result of composition needs to be a *refinement* of all the composed modules.

In the DisCo language, this is achieved by only allowing assignments to any given variable in one of the modules. The rest of the modules can only read the value of the variable. Ocsid relaxes this by allowing several modules to assign to a variable, as long as the assignments are compatible.

Comparison to Related Approaches

To differentiate Ocsid from our previous work on DisCo, it is necessary to summarize the main similarities and fundamental differences. Both languages, along with a number of others already mentioned, share the underlying principles of temporal logic, joint actions and closed systems. From a formal view point, this is all. In particular, the defining characteristic of DisCo, the superposition layer, is replaced with the view concept, which has been created to simplify rigorous reasoning and to ease reuse of already composed proofs.

The main advantage to using views instead of layers is not in how they are used to model an aspect of a system, but in how they allow more flexibility and thus lend themselves to *generalization* via parametrization. In fact, methodologically, both concepts are used in a similar fashion. This is due to the way decomposition is performed, that is, horizontally into behaviorally complete closed systems. However, the composition of views and the superimposition of layers are two distinctly different operations, which fundamentally separate Ocsid and DisCo.

From the view point of applicability to Design pattern formalization, the downside to superposition layers is that while suited for plain formalization, they are not a good match to parametrization. Instead of stating assumptions of and requirements to application context, they are explicitly dependent on other layers. Of course, this matter could be changed by replacing dependencies with explicitly enumerated contextual requirements, but this would present a new problem. Generalization would become very difficult because there is already a level of indirection. Circumventing these complications, views provide a natural match to parametrization.

The conceptual simplicity of Ocsid also means that implementing tool support is significantly less costly. Taken together, they provide for a flexible platform to incorporate research ideas. For example, this has been a major factor in incorporating a more versatile expression language and type system.

Comparison to other approaches with regard to various aspects of formalization is discussed in the next section.

Patterns and Formalization

Formalization of Design patterns can have several different goals. One may want to synthesize new designs by successive application of patterns, or one may want to do *post hoc* analysis of patterns in an existing design. The choice of formalism and the degree of rigor depend on what one wants to achieve by formalization. A partial list of concerns that may be addressed by a formalization is:

- structure (classes, relations, data members, method signatures, ...),
- behavior (call sequences, invariants, ...),
- instantiation of patterns,
- contextual dependencies,
- verification of patterns and pattern instances,
- composition of patterns and pattern instances.

We discuss these in detail in the following, and compare our approach to some of the other approaches. The purpose of this section is to show where the strengths of our approach are to be found. This section should not be taken as a deep analysis of what can be formalized, but rather as a showcase of aspects considered important for Design patterns.

Structure

Formalization of structure is relatively easy, as it can be captured by UML class diagrams. Classes in a pattern are formal placeholders for actual classes in a particular design.

Our formalization considers classes and data members, but does not address methods directly. This is due to joint action modeling, which specifies behavior in terms of atomic state changes. It is possible to refine the abstraction level of a joint action specification down to the level of individual method calls, but in our experience it does not really provide any additional benefits.

Because structural aspects are already handled quite effectively by UML, we are satisfied with minimal support for this concern. As will be discussed next, our main interest lies in behavior, so it is important to keep unnecessary details from distracting.

Behavior

There is much more variation in how behavior is described in the various approaches. Ocsid uses linear time temporal logic explicitly, but temporal logic is implicitly used by any approach where reasoning is based on sequences of method calls or messages (Soundarajan & Hallstrom, 2004). Process algebraic methods can also be used (Dong, Alencar, & Cowan, 2004), which enables the use of model checkers for verifications.

However, the ability to reason about behavior is not enough with respect to Design patterns. The formalism must also provide concepts and syntactic elements suitable to represent patterns and their instances. In addition, pattern composition needs to be supported in order to be of use with patterns. If handling composition is impossible or excessively difficult, the value of formalization is decreased.

Instantiation

Instantiation links the formal description of a pattern with its application in a specific design. In our approach, patterns are used for synthesis, and the link is provided by the instantiation process. This is analogous to how the code generated from a template is related to the template. Thus, in our process, it is guaranteed by construction that pattern instances have the desired properties.

If patterns are used for analysis or checking, then the design needs to be annotated with information that links the design back to the pattern. This can of course be done even when the design is initially instantiated from a pattern.

Contextual Dependencies

A pattern focuses on a subset of a design, where the objects involved cooperate to achieve some common goal. Fulfilling the goal often requires that the rest of the design behaves in a benign way with respect to the pattern. The description of a pattern needs to express the assumptions it makes of its environment.

In our case, assumptions about the context are expressed by the implicit closed world assumption and nondeterministic actions that model the effects of the environment on the closed world. In Soundarajan and Hallstrom (2004), the closed world assumption is made explicit by placing requirements on the effects of methods not mentioned in the pattern.

Verification

One of the main reasons Design patterns are used is that they describe solutions that have worked well in the past. This reuse of design effort provides opportunities for verification reuse as well.

Verification can take place at two levels: at the pattern level or at the instance level. Pattern level verification requires a richer language for expressing behavioral properties, as the properties need to be given in a *quantified* form. At the instance level it is sufficient to talk about concrete objects and their communication.

Patterns can be verified by pen and pencil proofs, or by using tool support. Coming from the formal specification and verification community, we are biased toward verification tools.

Our emphasis is on pattern level verification, and we have used the PVS (Owre et al., 1996) theorem prover and its logic for expressing and verifying behavioral properties. Theorem proving is a labor intensive activity, but the cost of verification can be amortized over all the uses of a pattern. Instance level verification can utilize more automated verification tools, such as model checking, but it seems to us that their usefulness is quite limited in pattern level verification.

Composition

In our view, the real difficulty in dealing with patterns is in composition. It is relatively easy to reason about the properties of a pattern and its instances in isolation, but patterns can interact in unexpected ways when composed together.

One way to deal with the problem is to perform composition and verify that the result has the desired properties, as in Dong et al. (2004). In this approach, verification effort is not reused, however. Only the formulation of the properties to be verified is obtained from the patterns to be composed.

Our solution is to specify the composition operation in such a way that it preserves temporal safety properties. This way a temporal safety property can be verified for a pattern, and by construction an instance of the property holds for an instance of the pattern. Since composition preserves safety properties, the result of composing a number a pattern instances satisfies all the safety properties of the patterns.

It is also desirable to be able to do composition at the template level to produce larger units of reusable behavior. Template composition is performed by grouping a set of template instantiations in a new template which uses its formal parameters to instantiate the component templates, thus binding them together.

Ocsid Patterns

In this section we describe how the Ocsid language addresses the issues outlined in the previous section, using the *Observer* and *Memento* patterns for illustration.

Ocsid patterns share some properties with Design patterns. Both provide solutions to recurring problems by introducing objects and their interactions to the design. They also describe the context in which the solutions are applicable.

Both Design patterns and Ocsid patterns are detailed, but in slightly different senses of the word. Design patterns are intentionally somewhat sketchy descriptions of solutions that have worked well in practice. However, the sketches are accompanied with sometimes very involved discussion about the ramifications of using a particular pattern, implementation alternatives, and so forth. These details are not formalized, because their purpose is to help the designer apply the pattern in a sensible way.

Ocsid patterns, on the other hand, resemble templates in programming languages, and are subject to formal manipulation. They are very explicit, because formal verification requires all relevant details to be formalized. This makes them more rigid than Design patterns, but enables us to give formal guarantees of the result of applying a particular pattern.

Joint Actions and Temporal Semantics

Our formalism is state-based and builds upon TLA, the Temporal Logic of Actions (Lamport, 1994). At any moment of time, the *state* of a system is composed of the values of the *state variables* of interest. A *behavior* is an infinite sequence of states. The set of all possible behaviors σ is denoted by Σ^∞, where Σ is the state space.

In a temporal logic without objects, such as TLA, state variables are functions from state to the approriate type. In Ocsid, state variables are data members of objects. This means that there is one level of indirection via the enclosing object when accessing the value of a variable.

Actions, action *functions,* and *joint actions* are defined as follows.

An *action* is a predicate on a pair of states.

An *action function* is a function that maps a tuple of objects into an action. The tuple of objects lists the objects whose local state is referenced or modified in the action.

As used in our approach, an action function is complete with respect to a set of data members. That is, for every member m in the data set and every object o, the function gives the next state value of data member m of object o.

A *joint action* is an action constructed by existentially quantifying over the parameters of an action function. For example, if $A(p, q)$ is an action function, then $\lambda s_1, s_2: \exists p, q : A(p,q)(s_1, s_2)$ is a joint action (λ refers to the lambda form for defining anonymous functions).

Syntactically, a joint action in Ocsid consists of a parameter list, a guard and a body. The parameter list makes explicit the state variables which are accessible in the body; all other state variables implicitly stutter (retain their previous values). The semantics of the guard of an action is that it must be true in the current state for the action to be executed. Operationally, the guard determines whether the joint action is eligible for execution. Intuitively, the semantics of a body is that, when evaluated in the current state, the right-hand sides of assignments must produce values identical to those of the left-hand sides in the next state.

Joint action systems have an interleaving semantics, that is, actions are executed in some sequential order. However, in implementation terms it is the atomicity that counts. If two actions do not have any common participants, it is permissible to execute them concurrently.

Ocsid Views

An Ocsid specification consists of several *views*, like the one in Figure 1. A view is a complete description of some aspect of the world. It enumerates the classes and state variables of interest, along with all the joint actions that assign to the variables.

Semantically, a view is a predicate on behaviors, which specifies the desired operation of the intended system. Formally, the semantics of a view v is:

$\lambda (\sigma : \Sigma^\infty)$:
  $\sigma[0] \Rightarrow initial\_condition(v)$
  $\vee \ \forall \ (n : Nat)$:

      $\exists \ (a : actions(v)) : a(\sigma[n], \ \sigma[n+1]) \vee (stutter(\sigma[n], \sigma[n+1])$

Views are *mutationally* complete, meaning that all changes to state variables are defined by a view, either explicitly or by the implicit stuttering.

Figure 1 illustrates how an instance of the *Observer* pattern is expressed as an Ocsid view. The view first declares classes ConcreteObserver and ConcreteSubject and their variables (data members), and then gives the joint actions that implement the desired functionality.

As described in Gamma et al. (1995), the *Observer* Design pattern does not explicitly specify what happens if the state of the subject changes while observers are being notified. Several possibilities are discussed, for example a new round of notifications may be started, the state change may be delayed, or the state change may not be possible at all. Each of the alternatives leads to different behavioral properties.

An Ocsid action is an atomic unit of behavior, so Figure 1 explicitly specifies one of the alternatives. Since the guard of action SubjectStateChange is true only when there are no observers to notify, it precludes state changes while observers are being notified.

Often in refinement-like situations, a view is insensitive to the actual values assigned to a variable. This can be denoted by using an underscore for the right-hand side in an assignment, as in action SubjectStateChange.

Most of the behavior specified by a view is usually described operationally. However, sometimes the operational mechanism that satisfies an invariant can be quite complex. In order to improve modularization, a view can *assume* invariants which can be used when verifying invariants for the view. The assumed invariants need to be established by other views when the final specification is constructed.

Sometimes the exact actions that modify a variable are not of interest for the invariants provided by a view. In such a case, declaring a variable to be *volatile* allows every action to change the variable in arbitrary ways. It is basically shorthand for including an underscore assignment in every action. The values of volatile variables can be constrained by assumed invariants, which provides a convenient declarative way to describe the behavior of the environment.

View Composition

The complete specification is constructed by integrating all of its views in such a way that the result is a refinement of every view of the specification. Each action of the specification includes one action from each of the views as a component. This trivially ensures that all invariants of the views are invariants of the specification. If a view does not include an action, then the view contributes the implicit stuttering (state preserving) action as a component.

Figure 1. An instance of Observer in Ocsid

```
view AnObserverInstance is
  class ConcreteObserver;
  variable ConcreteObserver.observerState : integer;
  type ObserverRef = ref ConcreteObserver;

  class ConcreteSubject;
  variable ConcreteSubject.subjectState : integer;
  variable ConcreteSubject.observers : set[ObserverRef];
  variable ConcreteSubject.toNotify : set[ObserverRef];

  initially init:
    forall (cs : ConcreteSubject) :
      empty?(cs.observers) and empty?(cs.toNotify);

  action Attach by cs : ConcreteSubject, co : ConcreteObserver
  when true do cs.observers := cs.observers + {reference(co)};
  end

  action GetState by cs : ConcreteSubject, co : ConcreteObserver
  when member(reference(co), cs.observers)
  do co.observerState := cs.subjectState;
  end

  action Detach by cs : ConcreteSubject, co : ConcreteObserver
  when member(reference(co), cs.observers) do
    cs.observers := cs.observers - {reference(co)};
    cs.toNotify := cs.toNotify - {reference(co)};
  end

  action SubjectStateChange by cs : ConcreteSubject
  when empty?(cs.toNotify) do
    cs.subjectState := _;  cs.toNotify := cs.observers;
  end

  action UpdateGetState by cs : ConcreteSubject, co : ConcreteObserver
  when member(reference(co), cs.toNotify) do
    co.observerState := cs.subjectState;
    cs.toNotify := cs.toNotify – {reference(co)};
  end
end
```

For example, view AnObserverInstance can only be composed with other views where the only action assigning to variable ConcreteSubject.subjectChange is SubjectStateChange. In practice this leads to a somewhat constraint-oriented style of development. Action Subject-StateChange in AnObserverInstance does not constrain the value assigned to cs.subjectState, but it constrains when the assignment can take place. Some other view may then specify what the exact value assigned in the action is.

Structure-wise, the classes and state variables of the specification are the unions of the classes and variables of the views, respectively. This implies that the types of composed variables must match.

To facilitate behavioral reasoning, view composition is defined so that a composed action implies its component actions. That is, an execution of the composed action is equivalent to some execution of each of the component actions, when interpreted in the corresponding view. This preserves temporal safety properties; any execution of the composed system is allowed by each of the views. Liveness properties are not preserved by the composition.

Action composition is defined semantically in terms of action functions. The composition operator $\oplus$ for action functions a_1, a_2,..., a_n is defined as:

$$\oplus (a_1, a_2, ..., a_n):$$
$$\lambda(p_u): \lambda(s_1, s_2 : STATE): \ a_1(p_1)(s_1,s_2) \wedge .(a_2(p_2)(s_1,s_2) \wedge ... \wedge a_n(p_n)(s_1,s_2),$$

where $p_1, p_2,..., p_n$ are tuples of objects by which $a_1, a_2,..., a_n$ are parameterized respectively, and p_u is the result of merging the tuples such that each participant occurs exactly once.

For example, let $A_1(p, q)$ and $A_2(q, r)$ be action functions. Their composition is:

$$\lambda(p,q,r):\lambda(s_1,s_2): A_1(p,q)(s_1,s_2) \wedge A_2(q,r)(s_1,s_2)$$

When composing views, one needs to deal with behavioral compatibility at two levels. In order for composition to be possible at all, the views must agree on which variables are modified by each of the actions. This requirement arises from the closed-world interpretation of views. This is a syntactic constraint. Semantically, there is no problem in composing incompatible actions, but it results in identically false actions. An attempt to compose incompatible views is flagged as an error by the Ocsid compiler.

When views are composed, actions from different views are matched by name. At this level, values assigned to matching variables need to be equal, which is a semantic rather than syntactic requirement. Because of this, the guards of actions are strengthened to ensure that the condition holds.

The guard of the composed action is the conjunction of the guards of the component actions, which provides a simple way for views to influence each other. If an action has a precondition that is relevant to only one view, the precondition can be given in the guard of the action in that view. Other views may be oblivious of the precondition, yet it is present in the result of composition.

For data members that only occur in one of the views, merging of assignments in action bodies is straightforward. For a shared member, the composed action needs to assign the member a value compatible with the component actions. There are basically three cases, depending on how flexible the component actions are. Let v denote a shared data member, and e_1 and e_2 denote the right-hand sides of the assignments to v in the component actions.

In the general case, e_1 and e_2 are syntactically different expressions. In some cases this may be a design error which should be flagged, but unfortunately it is computationally impossible to determine whether the values of two arbitrary expressions are equal or not. Instead of attempting to do so, we augment the guard of the composed action by the conjunct $e_1 = e_2$. This preserves safety properties with the possible expense of liveness. In the extreme case, e_1 and e_2 are never equal, and the action is never enabled. Such an unintended restriction of liveness can only be detected by simulation or examination of the composed action.

The component actions may allow a range of values to be assigned to v. This can be expressed in Ocsid by using an action parameter as the right-hand side of the expression, and placing constraints on the parameter in the guard of the action. For example, let e_1 and e_2 be references to parameter *amount*, and let the guards of the component actions include the conjuncts *MIN* < *amount* and *amount* < *MAX*, respectively. The composed action ensures that the value assigned to v is between *MIN* and *MAX*.

One of the component actions may refrain from constraining the value assigned to v at all, which makes merging of assignments trivial. This typically happens when views are used in a stepwise refinement fashion. One of the actions then describes the high level "business logic," while the other one is a part of an implementation mechanism on which the high level functionality is built.

Figure 2. An instance of Memento

```
view ConcreteSubjectMemento is
  class ConcreteSubject;
  class Memento;
  class Caretaker;

  variable ConcreteSubject.subjectState : integer;
  variable Memento.origstate : integer;
  variable Memento.originator : ref ConcreteSubject;

  initially forall (m: Memento): m.originator = null;

  action CreateMemento by o: ConcreteSubject; m: Memento
  when m.originator = null do
    m.originator = ref(o);
    m.origstate = o.subjectState;
  end

  action SubjectStateChange by o: ConcreteSubject; m:  Memento      //SetMemento
  when m.originator = ref(o) do
    o.subjectState = m.origstate;
  end

  action SubjectStateChange by o: ConcreteSubject                   //overloading
  when true do
    o.subjectState = _;
  end
end
```

To illustrate composition via an example, Figure 2 shows another instance of a pattern, namely *Memento*. The instance is adapted for composition with the view AnObserverInstance. The interaction between the two pattern instances can be seen in the first SubjectStateChange action. Composition ensures that whenever originator state is restored from a memento, the observers are duly notified. The second, overloaded SubjectStateChange action is required for allowing normal, nonrestorative state changes. Without it, the only allowable change to the state of the subject would be to restore it from a memento.

As is clearly evident, working at the pattern instance level has its limitations. In the next section, a template mechanism is introduced for representing the patterns themselves. An important quality of the composition operation is that it can be performed also at the template level, allowing the composition of parametrized patterns. This is a key property of our approach in facilitating the construction of specifications from verified, reusable building blocks, themselves possibly similarly (de)constructed.

Templates

Views are a convenient mechanism for modularizing behavior, but additional parametrization is needed for describing recurring patterns of behavior in a more generally applicable fashion. Generalization of views into *view templates* is defined so that all instantiated views exhibit concrete versions of the parametrized temporal properties of the view template by construction. This ensures that invariant proofs are applicable across all instantiations.

A view template is a collection of *action templates* which operate on parametric data. The types, classes, variables and functions referenced in a template are declared as formal parameters. By substituting these placeholders with concrete specification-level entities, one can instantiate suitable concrete views from the template.

Action templates are patterns for generating concrete actions, and their syntax is identical to actions in views. The participants of an action template can be renamed in instantiation to adjust the result to a particular specification. The designer is free to pick and choose suitable actions from the template for manipulating the state variables of the view. Not all actions in the template need to be instantiated, and some actions may be instantiated multiple times.

Figure 3 illustrates how a particular variant of the Observer pattern is expressed as an Ocsid template. Notes:

1. Template parameter list contains formal placeholders for entities to be supplied in instantiation. This includes types, classes, variables, and functions. Function parameters are an important mechanism for achieving flexibility at the template level.

2. Variable parameters are responsible for the actual binding between the concrete state space of a view and the parametric state changes described by action templates.

3. Variables internal to a template are not operationally different from variable parameters, but each instance of a template has unique copies of them.

Figure 3. The Observer template

```
template ObserverPattern<
  type T;                                                        // Note 1
  class FormalObserver;
  variable FormalObserver.observerState : T;                     // Note 2
  class FormalSubject;
  variable FormalSubject.subjectState : T >
is
  type FormalObserverRef = ref FormalObserver;
  variable FormalSubject.observers : set[FormalObserverRef];     // Note 3
  variable FormalSubject.toNotify : set[FormalObserverRef];

  initially init:
    forall (fs: FormalSubject) :
      empty?(fs.observers) and empty?(fs.toNotify);

  invariant inv:                                                 // Note 4
    forall (fs: FormalSubject) : empty?(fs.toNotify) =>
      forall (fo: FormalObserver) :
        member(reference(fo), fs.observers) =>
          fo.observerState = fs.subjectState;

  action AttachTemplate by fs: FormalSubject, fo: FormalObserver //Note 5
  when true do fs.observers := fs.observers + {reference(fo)};
  end

  action GetStateTemplate by fs: FormalSubject, fo: FormalObserver
  when member(reference(fo), fs.observers) do
    fo.observerState := fs.subjectState;
  end

  action DetachTemplate by fs: FormalSubject, fo: FormalObserver
  when member(reference(fo), fs.observers) do
    fs.observers := fs.observers - {reference(fo)};
    fs.toNotify := fs.toNotify - {reference(fo)};
  end

  action StateChangeTemplate by fs: FormalSubject
  when empty?(fs.toNotify) do
    fs.subjectState := _;
    fs.toNotify := fs.observers;
  end

  action UpdateGetStateTemplate by fs: FormalSubject, fo: FormalObserver
  when member(reference(fo), fs.toNotify) do
    fo.observerState := fs.subjectState;
    fs.toNotify := fs.toNotify - {reference(fo)};
  end
end
```

4.   Invariant templates describe the abstract properties which are to hold for all instances of the view template. Ensuring this amounts to proving that each action template preserves the invariant, that is, the invariant proof is structured into *preservation lemmas*.

5.   The fact that action templates are the means to introduce desired behavior into an instance is reflected in the naming scheme. For this particular action template, the trivially true action guard entails that observers are free to attach at any point, including during notification.

Figure 4 illustrates how the template is instantiated. View InstantiatedObserver first declares the classes and variables of the view, and then instantiates the ObserverPattern template using them. The instantiation lists the actions to be obtained from the template instance, which allows for renaming of actions and the formal participant roles of actions. Notes:

6.   The structure of the resulting view has to be specified before instantiation.

7.   Concrete entities given as arguments must be compatible as defined by the template parameter declarations. For example, the class containing the variable observerState must match with the class given as argument for the formal parameter FormalObserver. In general, the enforced consistency is uniform substitution.

8.   Another constraint regarding instantiation is that a variable cannot be bound to more than one formal variable. This is a syntactic restriction originating from the fact that allowing this would in most cases lead to identically false specifications. The view template designer would have to deliberately account for aliasing effects.

9.   Action instantiations introduce behavior into a view and adapt the action templates for the particular design. Action templates may be instantiated multiple times or not

Figure 4. Instantiating Observer

```
view InstantiatedObserver is
  class ConcreteObserver;                                              // Note 6
  variable ConcreteObserver.observerState : integer;
  class ConcreteSubject;
  variable ConcreteSubject.subjectState : integer;
  instantiate ObserverPattern <
      integer,
      ConcreteObserver,
      ConcreteObserver.observerState,                                  // Note 7
      ConcreteSubject, ConcreteSubject.subjectState >                  // Note 8
  action Attach is AttachTemplate <cs, co>                             // Note 9
  action GetState is GetStateTemplate <cs, co>
  action Detach is DetachTemplate <cs, co>
  action SubjectStateChange is StateChangeTemplate <cs>
  action UpdateGetState is UpdateGetStateTemplate <cs, co>;
end
```

instantiated at all. For example, if the ObserverPattern was to be applied to a specification with two actions modifying subjectState, two copies of the action template StateChangeTemplate would be needed.

Using Ocsid

After discussing how the Ocsid language can be used to formalize Design patterns, we give an outline of the engineering process and show the practical side of using Ocsid. Tool support, which has until now been only mentioned in passing, plays a significant part.

As Ocsid is a specification language, its role in software engineering is mostly in the first phases of development. Outside the scope of Design patterns, the primary usage is to clearly formulate the problem space and ensure it exhibits the desired properties. This consists of decomposing the system into views concern-wise and stating and proving invariants of the views.

Unlike in traditional, module-centric, or process-centric approaches, decomposition is not performed along structural boundaries into interfaces and implementations. Instead, the focus is on collective behavior from the perspective of a particular set of related variables. The purpose is to package together variables and the invariants that constrain their changes over time, and the actions that bring about those changes. This package is the view concept.

Each view should be minimal in the sense that it only contains those variables that are significant for the collective behavior. Due to the closed world interpretation of views, this works to keep the view from unnecessarily restricting the context in which it can be composed with other views. For the same purpose, behaviorally the view should be designed to be as relaxed as possible as long as the invariants can still be satisfied.

After the views have been defined, the complete specification is derived by composing the views. In this step, incompatibilities between views must be resolved; otherwise the resulting specification will not be the one intended because of identically false composed actions. Composition is performed mechanically by the Ocsid compiler and the result is a view which contains all the elements from individual views. This all-encompassing view is referred to as the specification and should now reflect the entire system. Ocsid compiler also checks that all assumed invariants have been provided by other views. If this is not the case, the specification is lacking an operational description of some inherent concern.

Before verification takes place, the views and the complete specification should ideally be validated, that is, made certain that the behaviors exhibited by the system indeed reflect correct interactions. Validation can be undertaken with the animation tool, which depicts a system visually and allows for action execution to drive the system, either manually or randomly. The user can keep track of which actions are enabled at each step and examine which participating combinations are viable. The tool also checks that invariants are not violated. In practice, the visualization is an important vehicle for communicating the operational details and dynamics of a specification.

Once the correct views have been specified, their invariants are verified. This entails the need for theorem proving support to rigorously show that actions do not violate invariants. Here a general purpose theorem proving system can be exploited by producing a mechanization of Ocsid onto a host logic. Currently, the Ocsid compiler produces shallow embeddings of views, view templates, and specifications onto the logic of the PVS proof system. This embedding also comprises appropriate lemmas and theorems that must be discharged in order to prove that the invariants hold. How the proofs are carried out is outside the scope of this chapter.

Templates and their use in the formalization of Design patterns extend the above process by additional steps. First, we have to consider how templates come about. Templates are parametrized views, so they are the result of a generalization process. And as in all generalization, it is first necessary to detect similarities, that is, those similar interactions that are actually the recurring manifestations of a more general pattern. This is a highly intellectual task and typically requires solid domain knowledge and iteration.

Once the potential for generalization and reuse has been identified, it becomes a matter of incorporating the essential, characteristic similarities shared by all instances to the view template. Necessary variation between instances is then supported by defining template parameters so as to allow change in those aspects that do not directly affect the invariants of the view template. These parameters include types, classes, variables, and functions which can later be replaced with concrete elements specified by the instantiating view.

Verification of invariants can also be performed on a view template. By construction, this reasoning also applies on all valid instance views. Thus, an Ocsid template may be used to express the structure and behavior of a Design pattern in a way that allows for reuse of both the specification and the verification effort. As verification is typically a highly demanding and resource-intensive task, this has the potential to save a significant amount of work, or alternatively, extend verification to areas where it would otherwise not have taken place.

Once a collection of templates has been accumulated, the specification process then includes the task of detecting reuse possibilities. In comparison to how Design patterns are informally used, the Ocsid compiler helps ensure that assumptions and contextual requirements of a template are complied with when the template is instantiated.

Instances of Design patterns rarely occur isolated in a design. Normally, the burden of ensuring their compatibility and consistent combination must be handled in an *ad hoc* manner. However, composition in Ocsid can be used to create view templates that exhibit common combinations of Design patterns. These can be used in a more efficient fashion, especially when the component templates deal with very basic aspects of behavior needed to support more complex patterns of interaction.

As already explained, views are specifications and as such, they do not prescribe particular implementation decisions. Thus, how Ocsid specifications are implemented is an extralingual matter, and highly depends on the environment and non-functional requirements of the solution.

Trends

In this section, we briefly mention promising avenues where the principles of our approach might be extended. Here the goal is to narrow the gap between full formality and practical software engineering.

Some of the ideas discussed in this chapter can be found applied in a UML pattern tool (Hammouda, Koskinen, Pussinen, Katara, & Mikkonen, 2004). There, UML models correspond to the formal models presented in this chapter, and patterns (or templates in Ocsid terminology) are modeled with metalevel templates of collective behavior that can be instantiated to augment existing designs. The tool provides a designer with assistance on pattern instantiation process, which is an important usability factor and could in fact also be used in connection with Ocsid as such. Indeed, from both a practical and research perspective, it would be interesting to study the possibilities to provide similar support on the formal side as well. A longer term goal of this research is to connect formal descriptions and UML using patterns as the common element. Some groundwork has already been laid in Pitkänen and Selonen (2004), where a UML profile is introduced for expressing formal properties not unlike those used in Ocsid.

The model driven architecture (Object Management Group Home Page, 2006) is based on model transformations. Moreover, some predefined levels of abstraction have been defined, referred to as *computation independent, platform independent,* and *platform specific* models, abbreviated as *CIM, PIM,* and *PSM*, respectively. *Transformations* are then used to alter the level of abstraction. Since pattern applications can be interpreted as transformations, it would be interesting to see whether our work could be applied in this setting for generating more detailed models or even complete implementations with verifiable behavioral properties.

Conclusion

We have presented how the experimental Ocsid language lets patterns of collective behavior be expressed and verified in an abstract form. Ocsid templates can be used to express Design patterns that have meaningful temporal properties. Patterns are used by instantiating them and subsequently composing specifications from those pattern instances in a manner that preserves temporal safety properties. Verification effort to prove template invariants is then reused across all instantiation. Templates can be composed to create larger, more comprehensive patterns for commonly occuring combinations.

While the explicit goal of our work has not been the formalization of Design patterns, there are many parallels. In a distributed system, there can be many concurrent and asynchronous activities that need to be coordinated. When decomposing activities into meaningful patterns of interactions, it is essential to be able to control the interactions of individual patterns. Thus, much of our work has concentrated on devising mechanisms that allow such interactions to take place, but in a controlled manner.

References

Abrial, J.R., Lee, M.K.O., Neilson, D.S., Scharbach, P.N., & Sørensen, I.H. (1991). The B-method. In S. Prehn & W.J. Toetenel (Eds.), *VDM'91: Formal software development methods: Vol. 2.* (LNCS 552, pp. 398-405). Springer-Verlag.

Chandy, K.M., & Misra, J. (1988). *Parallel program design: A foundation.* Addison-Wesley.

Dijkstra, E.W., & Scholten, C.S. (1980). Termination detection for diffusing computations. *Information Processing Letters, 11*(1), 1-4.

DisCo Project Home Page. (2006). Retrieved November 14, 2006, from http://disco.cs.tut.fi

Dong, J., Alencar, P., & Cowan, D. (2004). A behavioral analysis and verification approach to pattern-based design composition. *The International Journal of Software and Systems Modeling, 3*(4), 262-272.

Gamma, E., Helm, R., Johnson, R., & Vlissides, J. (1995). *Design patterns.* Reading, MA: Addison Wesley.

Hammouda, I., Koskinen, J., Pussinen, M., Katara, M., & Mikkonen, T. (2004). Adaptable concern-based framework specialization in UML. In *Proceedings of 19th IEEE International Conference on Automated Software Engineering.* IEEE Computer Society.

Helin, J., & Kellomäki, P. (2004). Concern-based specification of distributed systems using behaviourally complete views. In H.M.M. Huang & J. Zhao (Eds.), *Proceedings of the International Workshop on Aspect-Oriented Software Development (WAOSD 2004)* (pp. 74-78).

Helin, J., & Kellomäki, P. (2005). Invariants come from templates. In T. Margaria & M. Massink (Eds.), *Proceedings of the 10th International Workshop on Formal Methods for Industrial Critical Systems (FMICS 2005)* (pp. 90-97).

Herrmann, P., Graw, G., & Krumm, H. (1998). Compositional specification and structured verification of hybrid systems in cTLA. In *Proceedings of the 1st IEEE International Symposium on Object-oriented Real-time Distributed Computing (ISORC'98)* (pp. 335-340). IEEE Computer Society Press.

Järvinen, H-M., & Kurki-Suonio, R. (1991). DisCo specification language: Marriage of actions and objects. In *Proceedings of the 11th International Conference on Distributed Computing Systems* (pp. 142-151). IEEE Computer Society Press.

Järvinen, H.-M., Kurki-Suonio, R., Sakkinen, M., & Systä, K. (1990). Object-oriented specification of reactive systems. In *Proceedings of the 12th International Conference on Software Engineering* (pp. 63-71). IEEE Computer Society Press.

Lam, S.S., & Shankar, A.U. (1984). Protocol verification via projections. *IEEE Transactions on Software Engineering, 10*(4), 325-342.

Lamport, L. (1994). The temporal logic of actions. *ACM Transactions on Programming Languages and Systems, 16*(3), 872-923.

Lamport, L. (2000). Specifying concurrent systems with TLA+. In M. Broy & R. Steinbrüg-gen (Eds.), *Calculational System Design: Vol. 173* (NATO: Science Series: Computer & Systems Sciences). IOS Press.

Mikkonen, T. (1999). *Abstractions and logical layers in specifications of reactive systems.* Doctoral thesis, Tampere University of Technology.

Object Management Group Home Page (2006). Retrieved November 14, 2006, from http://www.omg.org

Owre, S., Rajan, S., Rushby, J.M., Shankar, N., & Srivas, M.K. (1996). PVS: Combining specification, proof checking, and model checking. In R. Alur & T.A. Henzinger (Eds.), *Computer-aided verification, CAV '96*: Vol. 1102 of Lecture Notes in Computer Science (pp. 411-414). New Brunswick, NJ: Springer-Verlag.

Pitkänen, R., & Selonen, P. (2004). A UML profile for executable and incremental specifica-tion-levle modeling. In *Proceedings of UML 2004—The Unified Modeling Language: Modelling Languages and Applications 7th International Conference.* Springer-Verlag. Lecture Notes in Computer Science, 3273.

Rumbaugh, J., Jacobson, I., & Booch, G. (1998). *The unified modeling language reference manual.* Addison-Wesley.

Soundarajan, N., & Hallstrom, J.O. (2004). Responsibilities and rewards: Specifying Design patterns. In *Proceedings of the 26th International Conference on Software Engineering (ICSE'04)* (pp. 666-675). IEEE.

Tarr, P., Ossher, H., Harrison, W., & Sutton, S.M. (1999). N degrees of separation: Multi-di-mensional separation of concerns. In *Proceedings of the 1999 International Conference on Software Engineering* (pp. 107-119). IEEE Computer Society Press/ACM Press.

Tarr, P., Ossher, H., & Sutton, S.M. (2002). Hyper/J: Multi-dimensional separation of concerns for Java. In *Proceedings of the 24th International Conference on Software Engineering (ICSE-02)* (pp. 689-690). New York: ACM Press.

Weiser, M. (1984). Program slicing. *IEEE Transactions on Software Engineering, 10*(4), 352-357.

Chapter V

Formal Specification and Verification of Design Patterns

Jing Dong, University of Texas at Dallas, USA

Paulo Alencar, University of Waterloo, Canada

Donald Cowan, University of Waterloo, Canada

Abstract

This chapter introduces our approaches to formal specification of the structural and behavioral aspects of Design patterns. We investigate the logic-based formalisms in our specification methods and demonstrate the applications of these methods in examples. Our formal specifications methods not only help for rigorous, precise, and unambiguous descriptions of Design patterns, but also allow us to verify the consistencies of Design pattern applications and compositions.

Introduction

A Design pattern (Gamma, Helm, Johnson, & Vlissides, 1995) documents expert solutions to a recurring problem in a particular context. Design patterns are then applied in many applications to improve the quality of the resulting software system and the productivity of the associated personnel. Thus, the specification and description of Design patterns are critical to their successful application.

Design patterns are typically described informally to facilitate understanding by software developers. However, there are several drawbacks to the informal representation of Design patterns. First, informal specifications may be ambiguous, and Design patterns may not be able to be expressed precisely in an informal language. Second, informal representation may not be amendable to rigorous analysis. Each Design pattern may have some particular properties that characterize it, and the application of a Design pattern should maintain these properties. Formal specification allows the use of automated tools to check such properties. Third, formal specifications of Design patterns also form the basis for the discovery of Design patterns in large software systems. Rigorous descriptions of Design patterns allow reverse engineering tools and techniques to be built to discover the Design patterns used in a design.

We have investigated several approaches to the formal specification of Design patterns and their composition in the past decade. In particular, we separated the structural and behavioral aspects of Design patterns and proposed specification methods based on first-order logic, temporal logic, temporal logic of action, process calculus, and Prolog. We also explored verification techniques based on theorem proving. The main objective of this chapter is to describe our investigations on formal specification techniques for Design patterns, and then demonstrate using these specifications as the methods of reasoning about Design pattern properties when they are used in software systems.

Background

The application and composition of Design patterns is still an ad-hoc process as designers struggle to discover the inconsistencies and errors in Design pattern application and composition. This discovery process is mostly based on personal experience. With the development of software tools, such as Rational Rose, which can transform an object-oriented design into implementations of different object-oriented programming languages, software developers have been partially released from tedious and error-prone work in mapping a design into an implementation. However, design errors are changed into implementation errors, which become even harder to detect because they are transformed and blended into complex implementation structures. Failure to discover the errors in software design and development may result in huge losses of money and even human lives, as demonstrated in the failed launch of the $500 million Ariane 5 (Jezequel & Meyer, 1997) in 1996 and the unsuccessful automation of the London Ambulance Service (Dalcher, 1999).

Design analysis can assist in the discovery of errors in a design early in the development phase and reduce the cost of finding and correcting them downstream. Formal specification and verification techniques are useful for design analysis in that formal specifications are more precise, clear, expressive, and unambiguous than informal representations, such as graphical and textual notations. Formal specification can be the basis for formal verifications, which can help detect errors. Thus, a number of papers on formalizing Design patterns have appeared in the literature.

A formal specification approach based on logics is presented in Eden and Hirshfeld (2001). Some graphical notations are also introduced to improve the readability of the specifications. While their approach concentrates on the visual formalism of Design patterns, our specifications of Design patterns tend to reduce the ambiguity and allow reasoning about relevant pattern-based properties.

Similar to our ideas presented in Dong, Alencar, and Cowan (2000), Taibi and Ngo David (2003) propose specifying the structural aspect of Design patterns in the first order logic (FOL) and the behavioral aspect in the temporal logic of action (TLA). Their approach using FOL and TLA differs from ours, thus resulting in different specifications of Design patterns.

The structural and behavioral aspects of Design patterns in terms of responsibilities and rewards are formally specified in Soundarajan and Hallstrom (2004). Following the ideas of the design by contract approach in Meyer (1992), the structural and behavioral specifications are captured as responsibilities, whereas the rewards capture the benefits of applying the pattern with the expected behavior in a system. Similar to our goal of avoiding over-specification, their formal specifications retain flexibility.

The composition of two Design patterns based on a specification language (DisCo) has been discussed in Mikkonen (1998). The behavior of each pattern is formalized as a layer in DisCo. The composition of Design patterns is defined as a refinement on the layers of specifications. Similar to our approach, the refinement is property-preserving, such that the refinements of one pattern by another preserves all properties of both patterns.

Formal specification of Design patterns and their composition based on the language of temporal ordering specification (LOTOS) is proposed in Saeki (2000). In particular, the behavioral aspect of the Command and Composite patterns and their combination is specified. In addition to behavior, we are interested in the structure. Our work also presents methods for reasoning about the specifications of Design patterns.

Law-governed support for realizing Design patterns has been investigated in Pal (1995). Some rules and constraints of Design patterns have been defined. However, the property checking is performed at implementation level, whereas our form of checking work is during design.

Main Thrust of the Chapter

In this section, we present the main issues related to the description of Design patterns. We then introduce our specification approaches based on first-order logic, temporal logic of action, and Prolog.

Issues, Controversies, Problems

Design patterns are a means to capture successful software development design practice within a particular context. Patterns should not be limited in what they can describe and can be used to encapsulate good design practices at both the specification and implementation levels. Thus, Design patterns can be applied at many different levels of abstraction in the software development lifecycle, and can focus on reuse within architectural design as well as detailed design and implementation. In fact, a system of patterns for software development should include patterns covering various ranges of scale, beginning with patterns for defining the basic architectural structure of an application and ending with patterns describing how to implement a particular design mechanism in a programming language.

The descriptions of Design patterns are generally informal diagrams and text, which usually make them relatively easy to understand. This informality also facilitates the flexibility of Design patterns. However, the problems with informal specification of Design patterns (or informal specification in general) are ambiguity and difficulty to reason about them. When there is ambiguity in the descriptions, the designers may make mistakes while applying a Design pattern. Such mistakes are difficult to find without proper reasoning techniques and tools.

Design patterns are typically described in terms of several aspects, such as intent, motivation, structure, behavior, sample code, and related patterns. Although not all aspects of a Design pattern can be formalized, some functional aspects (structure and behavior) are amenable to formal specification and rigorous reasoning. In this chapter, we present our formal techniques and methods for the specification and verification of the structural and behavioral aspects of Design patterns. In the rest of this chapter, for simplicity, we use the phrase "formalizing Design patterns" to mean formalizing both the structural and behavioral aspects of Design patterns.

Solutions and Recommendations

In this section, we present our formal specification techniques for Design patterns based on first-order logic, temporal logic of action and Prolog. In addition, we investigate the verification of Design patterns.

First-Order Logic

In specifying structural aspects of Design patterns, we investigated a formal specification method using general first-order logic to represent each Design pattern structure as a logic theory (Dong et al., 2000).

To illustrate the problem, let us consider the Composite pattern and the Iterator pattern from (Gamma et al., 1995) as examples. The structural aspect of the Composite and Iterator patterns is depicted in Figure 1. The Component class is an abstract class which defines the interfaces of the pattern. The Composite and the Leaf classes are concrete classes defining the attributes and operations of the concrete components. The Composite class can contain a group of children, whereas the Leaf class cannot. The Composite pattern is often used to represent part-whole hierarchies of objects. The goal of this pattern is to treat composition of objects and individual objects in the composite structure uniformly. In the Iterator pattern, the Iterator class is an abstract class which provides the interfaces of the operations, such as *First, Next, IsDone, CurrentItem,* to access the elements of an aggregate object sequentially without exposing its underlying representation. The ConcreteIterator class inherits the operation interfaces from the Iterator class and defines concrete operations which access the corresponding concrete aggregate. The Aggregate class defines a common interface for all aggregates that the Iterator accesses. The ConcreteAggregate class defines an operation to create the corresponding concrete Iterator.

The representations of the Composite pattern and the Iterator pattern contain predicates for describing classes, state variables, methods, and their relations. More precisely, the following sorts denote the first-class objects in a pattern: *class* and *object*. We also make use of sorts *bool* and *int*. The signature for the Composite pattern is:

- **Add:** class → bool
- **Remove:** class → bool
- **GetChild:** class × int → bool
- **Operation:** class → bool
- **Variable:** class × object → bool
- **Inherit**: class × class → bool

The Signature for the Iterator pattern is:

- **CreateIterator:** → bool
- **New:** class → bool
- **First:** → bool
- **Next:** → bool
- **IsDone:** → bool
- **CurrentItem:** → bool
- **Variable:** class × object → bool
- **Inherit**: class × class → bool

Table 1 contains (partial) theories associated with the two patterns. θ_C denotes the theory of the Composite pattern and θ_I denotes the theory of the Iterator pattern. The theory θ_C is divided into three class groups and one relation group. The first group defines the abstract class Component and four method interfaces. The second group corresponds to the Leaf class. The third group contains theories about the Composite class, which include the definition of a state variable and the operations applied to it. The last group defines two inheritance relations. The first class in each inheritance relation is the parent class and the second class is the

Figure 1. The Composite and Iterator patterns

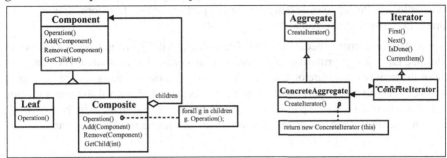

Table 1. Partial Composite pattern and Iterator pattern theories

Θ_c	Θ_I
AbstractClass(Component) Operation(Component) Add(Component) Remove(Component) GetChild(Component, int)	AbstractClass(Aggregate) CreateIterator
	Class(ConcreteAggregate) CreateIterator→New(ConcreteIterator)
Class(Leaf) Operation(Leaf)	AbstractClass(Iterator) First Next IsDone CurrentItem
Class(Composite) Variable(Component, Children) Operation(Composite)→[∀g[Children(g)→Operation(g)]] ∀v [Add(v)→Children(v)] ∀v [Children(v)→Remove(v)] ∃v [Children(v) ∧ GetChild(v, int)]	
	Class(ConcreteIterator) Variable(Aggregate, aggregates)
Inherit(Component, Leaf) Inherit(Component, Composite)	Inherit(Aggregate, ConcreteAggregate) Inherit(Iterator, ConcreteIterator)

child class. The theory θ_I is divided into five groups. The first four groups contain theories about four classes in the pattern. The last group contains two inheritance relations.

Prolog

In another approach (Alencar, Cowan, Dong, & Lucena, 1999), Design patterns are represented in Prolog (Clocksin & Mellish, 1987) and stored in a Prolog database. There are several advantages of using Prolog as a repository of design knowledge. First, the representations of these Design patterns can be reused by instantiating the corresponding Prolog rules of each pattern when they are applied to produce a concrete domain-specific pattern representation. Second, the properties and constraints of each Design pattern can be described as Prolog rules, and these rules can be used to check the consistencies of the Design patterns. Third, the addition and removal of structural facts about Design patterns can be accomplished by using the Prolog *assert* and *retract* clauses. Fourth, the transformation of the Design pattern representations in Prolog to code templates can be performed by a transformation tool such as Draco-PUC (Leite, Sant' Anna, & Freitas, 1994).

Design patterns are represented in terms of object-oriented design primitives in a predicate-like format. Each design primitive consists of two parts: *name* and *argument*. The *name* part contains the name of a feature or a relationship in object-oriented design, such as class or inheritance. The *argument* part contains general information about a feature or a relation such as the information on the participants of an inheritance relationship. In the following, we present the syntax and the meaning of the design primitives used in this chapter:

- **Class(C):** C is a class.

- **Abstractclass(C):** C is an abstract class.

- **Inherit(A, B):** B is a subclass of A.

- **Attribute(C, A, V, T):** V is the name of an attribute in class C with type T. T is optional. A describes the access right of this attribute, that is, public, private, or protected.

- **method(C, A, F, R, P_1, T_1, P_2, T_2, ...):** F is a method of a class C. A describes the access right of this method, that is, it can be public, private, or protected. R describes the return type. The method's parameters and their types are P_1, T_1, P_2, T_2, ..., respectively, and this part is optional. The return type R is also optional if the method has no parameters.

- **Return(C, F, V):** V is the return value of the method F in the class C.

- **new(C1, F, C2, P):** This predicate represents a pointer to the dynamic instantiation of class C_2 in the method F of class C_1. P is the initial value of the class C_2. P can contain zero or more parameters depending on the number of parameters for the constructor of class C_2.

- **Assign(C, F, L, R):** Right value R is assigned to left variable L in the method F of the class C.

- **Invoke(C, C_f, O, O_f, P):** A method O_f which belongs to the object O is invoked in the method C_f of the class C, where P is the parameter of the method O_f. P can contain zero or more parameters depending on the number of parameters the method O_f.

- **Member(E_1, S_1, E_2, S_2, ...):** E_1 is an element of set S_1. E_2 is an element of set S_2, and so on. When universal quantification *forall* and *member* are used together, it enumerates set S_1, S_2, ..., S_n simultaneously, that is, the first elements of all sets are enumerated first, then the second elements.

A higher level of abstraction is provided by introducing pattern primitive operators. Pattern primitive operators are represented in terms of design primitive operators and they allow general object-oriented schemas such as delegation, aggregation, and polymorphism to be defined. Pattern primitive operators can capture the subpatterns, which occur frequently in the declarative representation of Design patterns. They can also be used to change, transform, or make the declarative representation evolve. This operator can assist with the evolution of the pattern schema and also with the application of this pattern.

As an example, a pattern primitive operator called abstract coupling or *polymorph* can be represented in Prolog as follows:

```
polymorph(Interface, Imp, Binding, ConcreteImpSet, ImpOperation, Operation) :-
 assert(abstractclass(Imp)),
 assert(method(Imp, public, ImpOperation)),
 forall(member(ConcreteImp, ConcreteImpSet),
  assert(inherit(Imp, ConcreteImp)) ),
 forall(member(ConcreteImp, ConcreteImpSet),
  assert(class(ConcreteImp)) ),
 forall(member(ConcreteImp, ConcreteImpSet),
  assert(method(ConcreteImp, public, ImpOperation))),
 assert(abstractclass(Interface)),
 assert(attribute(Interface, private, Binding, Imp)),
 assert(method(Interface, public, Operation)),
 assert(invoke(Interface,Operation,Binding,ImpOperation)).


extend_polymorph(Imp,NewConcreteImpSet,ImpOperation) :-
 forall(member(ConcreteImp, NewConcreteImpSet),
  assert(inherit(Imp, ConcreteImp)) ),
 forall(member(ConcreteImp, NewConcreteImpSet),
  assert(class(ConcreteImp)) ),
 forall(member(ConcreteImp, NewConcreteImpSet),
  assert(method(ConcreteImp, public, ImpOperation))).


retract_polymorph(Imp,OldConcreteImpSet,ImpOperation) :-
 forall(member(ConcreteImp, OldConcreteImpSet),
  retract(inherit(Imp, ConcreteImp)) ),
 forall(member(ConcreteImp, OldConcreteImpSet),
  retract(class(ConcreteImp)) ),
 forall(member(ConcreteImp, OldConcreteImpSet),
  retract(method(ConcreteImp,public,ImpOperation))).
```

The Prolog rules of *polymorph* represent the structure of polymorphism. The arguments of the *polymorph* predicate denote the generic elements, for example, class, attribute, or method. *Interface* and *Imp* are abstract classes. *Binding* represents an object reference, which is a state variable of the *Interface* class. *ImpOperation* and *Operation* are two important methods. *ConcreteImpSet* defines a set of concrete classes which may include, for example, *ConcreteImpA* and *ConcreteImpB*. This Prolog representation contains more information than the UML representation, which cannot, for example, represent an undetermined number of classes. All the arguments will be instantiated by class and operation names, and these names result in specific domain knowledge.

The Prolog operators *assert* and *retract* are used to insert or remove certain facts into or from a Prolog database, respectively. The *forall* predicate represents the universal quantification operator. It can quantify over a set of class names and add the corresponding facts about each class name into the Prolog database. For instance, the Prolog rule forall(member(ConcreteImp, ConcreteImpSet), assert(inherit(Imp, ConcreteImp))), corresponds to the following first-order logic formula:

$$\forall \text{ ConcreteImp} \in \text{ConcreteImpSet} : \text{inherit(Imp, ConcreteImp)}.$$

The nondeterminism in *polymorph* leaves space for evolution, that is, for adding or removing concrete classes which inherit from the abstract class *Imp*. The addition or removal of one such class can be performed by the *extend_polymorph* or the *retract_polymorph* rules, respectively, which in turn *assert* and *retract* the corresponding facts related to the insertion or removal of this concrete class.

Notice that the primitive operators represent basic constituents of an object-oriented design and that the structural information related to Design patterns can be represented by pattern primitive operators and design primitive operators. For example, *polymorph* is used to represent the Bridge, State, and Strategy patterns. In this way, the design of an object-oriented application can be assembled by combining the design components stored in the Prolog database. In addition, the evolution (addition or removal of design components) of a software system design can be achieved by applying specific Prolog rules.

The Prolog representation of the structural aspect of the Bridge pattern is shown as follows. It uses the *polymorph* pattern primitive as a design subcomponent.

```
bridge(Abstraction,Implementor,Imp,RefinedAbstractionSet,
ConcreteImplementorSet,ImpOperation,Operation) :-
 polymorph(Abstraction, Implementor, Imp, ConcreteImplementorSet, ImpOperation,Operation),
forall(member(RefinedAbstraction,RefinedAbstractionSet),
    assert(inherit(Abstraction,RefinedAbstraction))),
forall(member(RefinedAbstraction,RefinedAbstractionSet),
    assert(class(RefinedAbstraction)) ).

extend_bridge_abstract(Abstraction,NewRefinedAbstraction):-
 assert(inherit(Abstraction, NewRefinedAbstraction)),
 assert(class(NewRefinedAbstraction)).

extend_bridge_imp(Implementor, NewConcreteImplementor, ImpOperation) :-
 extend_polymorph(Implementor, NewConcreteImplementor, ImpOperation).
```

```
retract_bridge_abstract(Abstraction, OldRefinedAbstraction):-
retract(inherit(Abstraction, OldRefinedAbstraction)),
retract(class(OldRefinedAbstraction)).


retract_bridge_imp(Implementor, OldConcreteImplementor, ImpOperation) :-
retract_polymorph(Implementor, OldConcreteImplementor, ImpOperation).
```

The main purpose of the Bridge pattern is to separate the abstraction from its implementation so that they can vary independently. The *bridge* Prolog rule is used to specify the structure facts of the Bridge pattern. It uses the *polymorph* Prolog rule to specify part of the structure facts of the Bridge pattern, including the Abstraction, Implementor, ConcreteImplementor, and their relationships. The two *forall* rules are used to specify the refined abstraction classes and their inheritance relationships to the Abstract class. Since the Bridge pattern allows extensions of both the refined abstractions and the concrete implementations, there are two rules related to *extend_bridge* and two rules related to *retract_bridge*.

When a designer chooses a Design pattern to solve a particular application problem during the actual design, he or she can save this design decision as facts in the Prolog database by applying the rules that correspond to the Design pattern and using as parameters the domain specific names required by the application. In this way, the Prolog facts which represent the structural constituents of that Design pattern will be saved in Prolog database.

There are four major tasks during instantiation. First, to improve readability and understandability, the generic element names (e.g., classes, attributes, or methods) are replaced by application domain names or domain-specific vocabulary. Each Design pattern encapsulates general design practice that is independent of the application domain. The instantiation of a Design pattern applications leads to domain-dependent designs. This replacement or renaming is achieved by instantiating the arguments of the corresponding Prolog rule of the Design pattern.

Second, according to the application requirements, a number of concrete components are created. The structural solution provided by Design patterns often involves an undefined number of concrete classes, which depends on the application. This undefined character is due to the fact that Design patterns are domain-independent abstract design solutions. We capture this Design pattern characteristic by using sets of elements in Prolog. The arguments in the Prolog rules, which represent Design patterns, can be single elements or sets of elements, that is, one argument may represent a set of elements. Arguments related to sets of elements, when instantiated, assume the value of a fixed number of elements.

Third, Design patterns are added as Prolog facts into the design knowledge base. In the representation of the Design pattern, there is a collection of *assert* statements associated with a Prolog rule. The application of the Prolog rule automatically leads to the insertion of the selected facts into the database through these *assert* statements. Through argument instantiation discussed in the previous two tasks, the free variables of the inserted facts are unified with domain-related names.

Fourth, a Design pattern can be extended or retracted if it does not violate the constraints of the pattern. It is important to have, in the documentation of the Design pattern, information about the evolution of the patterns. We also provide rules in Prolog about the evolution of

Design patterns. These rules and constraints restrict the addition and removal of elements to avoid undesired interactions among components of a single Design pattern. However, these rules do not preclude interactions among different Design patterns.

Temporal Logic of Action

In contrast to the structural aspect of Design patterns, we specify the behavioral aspect using the temporal logic of action (TLA) (Lamport, 1994). We choose TLA because it is an axiomatic style of semantic definition suitable for describing both safety and fairness properties.

In TLA, semantics is provided by assigning a meaning [F] to each syntactic object F. The semantics are defined in terms of a mapping from the set of variable names to the collection of values.

We use the following TLA notations: f denotes a list of variables in the old states, whereas f' denotes a list of variables in the new state. $\Box F$ denotes always F, and $\Diamond F$ denotes that eventually F will be true. A describes an action which relates the old state to the new state. $[A]_f$ is equivalent to $A \vee (f'=f)$, which represents that either action A is taken or there is no change on state function f. $<A>_f$ is equivalent to $A \wedge (f' \neq f)$ which represents that action A is taken and the state function f has been changed. *Enabled A* means that it is possible to take the action A. Weak fairness, $WF_f(A)$, is defined as $\Box\Diamond<A>_f \vee \Box\Diamond\neg Enabled<A>_f$. It asserts that eventually action A must either be taken or become impossible to be taken.

We define a formula Φ that represents the semantics of each Design pattern, meaning that $\sigma[\Phi]$ equals *true* if the behavior σ represents a possible application of the pattern.

For example, the semantics of the *Composite* pattern describes the behavior related to inserting or removing objects of an aggregate. All objects in the aggregate have a common type. The fairness condition is that eventually an insertion or deletion occurs unless both are impossible. Removing an object from an empty aggregate is one example of impossi-

Table 2. Semantics of the Composite pattern

$Init_\Phi$	$\equiv$	$op = $ "ready" $\wedge$ *children* = "emptybag"
S_{add}	$\equiv$	$op = $ "ready" $\wedge op' = $ "add" $\wedge child' \in$ Component $\wedge children'=children$
E_{add}	$\equiv$	$op = $ "add" $\wedge op' = $ "ready" $\wedge children'=children+child$
S_{remove}	$\equiv$	$op = $ "ready" $\wedge op'=$ "remove" $\wedge child' \in$ Component $\wedge children'=children$
E_{remove}	$\equiv$	$op = $ "remove" $\wedge op' = $ "ready" $\wedge child \in children \wedge children'=children-child$
$S_{getchild}$	$\equiv$	$op = $ "ready" $\wedge op'= $ "get" $\wedge child' \in$ Index $\wedge children'=children$
$E_{getchild}$	$\equiv$	$op = $ "get" $\wedge op' = $ "ready" $\wedge child' = children(index) \wedge children'=children$
$N_{children}$	$\equiv$	$E_{add} \vee E_{remove}$
N	$\equiv$	$N_{children} \vee S_{add} \vee S_{remove} \vee S_{getchild} \vee E_{getchild}$
U	$\equiv$	$<op,child,children,index>$
Φ	$\equiv$	$Init_\Phi \wedge \Box [N]_u \wedge WF_u(N_{children})$

Table 3. Semantics of the Iterator pattern

$Init_\psi$	$\equiv$	$position = \text{"start"}$
M_{first}	$\equiv$	$position' = \text{"start"}$
M_{next}	$\equiv$	$position' = Next(position)$
M_{isdone}	$\equiv$	$position = \text{"last"} \wedge position' = position$
$M_{current}$	$\equiv$	$val' = aggregate(position) \wedge position' = position$
M_1	$\equiv$	$M_{first} \vee M_{next}$
M	$\equiv$	$M_1 \vee M_{isdone} \vee M_{current}$
v	$\equiv$	$< position, val >$
Ψ	$\equiv$	$Init_\psi \wedge \Box [M]_v \wedge \text{WF}_v(M_1)$

bility. The semantics of the *Iterator* pattern (Gamma et al., 1995) describes the behavior of traversing an aggregate of objects. It defines the traversing methods which are independent of the structure of the aggregate which they traverse. These traversing methods require primitive behaviors, such as *first* and *next*. An internal state memorizes the current position of traversing. Multiple-traversing can be performed provided that enough state variables are available for recording the current position of each traverse. The fairness condition is that traversing steps will eventually proceed which will update the corresponding internal state variables.

Verification

The main goals of formal specification of Design patterns include precise and unambiguous descriptions of Design patterns and formal verification. In the previous section, we present several approaches to formal specification to achieve the former goal. In this section, we discuss our formal verification techniques to check consistency and prove the correctness of Design patterns and their applications, compositions, and evolutions. In particular, we describe our approaches based on theorem proving techniques.

As presented in the previous section, we specify Design patterns in logic theorems (in first-order logic, TLA, Prolog). Therefore, we can check the consistencies of Design pattern specifications by proving the theorems related to the corresponding requirements.

Consistency checking is not an easy task when graphical notations are used. It requires intuition and experience. Consistency checking is also difficult because of the informal notations. On the other hand, representing Design patterns in formal logic notation allows us to describe the properties and constraints of each Design pattern in a precise way and, thus, to check automatically whether a pattern loses some properties after it is combined with other patterns.

The formal specification of Design patterns allows clear understanding of Design patterns. In addition, it helps the application, composition, and evolutions of Design patterns since understanding of Design patterns is not the final goal of a designer. Formal specifications can also help with the applications of Design patterns. For example, our formal specification using Prolog not only provides the facts related to a Design pattern, but also describes how a designer can apply the Design pattern using the corresponding Prolog rule of the pattern. In this way, we not only specify the structure of a Design pattern, but also describe the process under which the Design pattern can be applied.

Formal specification of Design patterns may also help with the compositions of Design patterns. A large software design may consist of many Design patterns. However, there may be inconsistencies among them. There are many reasons to check the consistency of the composition of Design patterns. For example, when two patterns are combined, they may share some common parts. The part that they are sharing can play one role in one pattern, but another role in the other pattern. This situation may lead to an inconsistent combination. In addition, an existing design may be modified and gradually evolve. This may lead to a situation in which the new design no longer conforms to the properties that its Design patterns must preserve. The manual discovery of the inconsistency in design can be a difficult job without a formalism or tool support. The Design pattern representations in Prolog allow us to take advantage of the deductive facilities of Prolog to find the inconsistencies automatically.

Formal specification of Design patterns can further help with the evolutions of Design patterns. Since change is a constant theme in software development, the application of a Design pattern may evolve in some particular way. In our approach, we provide the formal specification of the evolution process of each Design pattern as a Prolog rule using *extend* or *retract*. In this way, the designers may change the applications of Design patterns in some predefined ways to reduce mistakes in the evolution process.

In order to facilitate the automation of theorem proving, we take advantage of Prolog's inference engine. More specifically, we specify Design patterns and their applications, compositions, and evolutions as Prolog clauses and rules. The properties of the Design patterns to be checked can be described as Prolog queries, which provide true/false answers. In this way, the theorems can be proved automatically. We may verify the properties of each individual Design pattern, the compositions, and evolutions of Design patterns. For example, each *ConcreteImplementor* class in the Bridge pattern should define an *OperationImp* operation. We may specify this property as a Prolog query to check whether it is satisfied in the Prolog knowledge base. This process is straightforward in our approach. After the Bridge pattern is applied, the designer may change the design by adding more *ConcreteImplementor* class(es). In this case, we may also need to check whether the new *ConcreteImplementor* class has the *OperationImp* operation. This can be checked similarly. When the Bridge pattern is applied and composed with other patterns in an application, there may be inconsistencies among these patterns. For instance, one of the main intents of the Bridge pattern is to separate the Abstraction from its Implementations so that they can vary independently. In Alencar et al. (1999), we presented a case where the Bridge pattern application has interactions with other pattern applications, such that the Abstraction and its Implementations are not independent anymore. We found this subtle problem using our formal specification and verification techniques in Prolog. More details can be found in Alencar et al. (1999).

Future Trends

In large software systems, more than one Design pattern is generally applied and composed. Although each Design pattern encapsulates good design experience, their composition may not always exhibit good design composition. There may be unexpected conflicts among the Design patterns used in a system. Such conflicts and inconsistencies may result in wrong applications of Design patterns, which are then difficult to find and correct. Formal specification and verification methods and techniques may help to find such errors.

Change is a constant theme of software design and development. Because of constant changes of user requirements, platforms, technologies, and environments, software systems need to be adapted to such changes. One of the important goals of Design patterns is design for change. Thus, most Design patterns encapsulate future changes that may only affect a limited part of a Design pattern. However, the evolution information is generally not explicitly specified in the documentation accompanying each Design pattern. One of the current challenges is to specify the possible changes in a Design pattern explicitly in terms of the evolution process so that the developer may follow such a process when changes are required.

Conclusion

In this chapter, we present our approaches to formal specification and verification of Design patterns and their application, composition, and evolution. We separate structural and behavioral aspects of Design patterns in our specification. We investigate different specification techniques, such as first-order logics, temporal logic of action, and Prolog, because different formalisms are suitable for specifying different aspects of Design patterns. For example, first-order logics and Prolog can be used to specify the structural aspect of Design patterns. First-order logics are a standard formalism that renders specifications which are easy to understand. However, it lacks the automated support for applying the theorems. Prolog, on the other hand, provides a knowledge base such that the specifications can be stored as facts and the corresponding rules can be applied automatically. It is also possible to reason about the properties using the knowledge base supported by Prolog.

In contrast to the structural aspect of Design patterns, the specification of the behavior require sthe formalisms to be able to represent event orders and action sequences. Since first-order logics and Prolog cannot represent states and timing, they are not suitable for the behavioral specifications. We investigated the specifications of the behavior of Design patterns using temporal logic of actions. As described in the previous section, we describe the behavioral semantics of the Composite and Iterator patterns and show that temporal logic of action is a suitable formalism for specifying behavioral aspects of Design patterns.

In addition to the goal of precise and unambiguous specification of Design patterns, we explore different verification techniques. In this way, we are able to reason rigorously about the application, composition, and evolution of Design patterns.

References

Alencar, P.S.C., Cowan, D.D., Dong, J., & Lucena, C.J.P. (1999). A pattern-based approach to structural design composition. In *Proceedings of the IEEE 23rd Annual International Computer Software & Applications Conference* (pp. 160-165). IEEE CS Press.

Clocksin, W.F., & Mellish, C.S. (1987). *Programming in Prolog*. Berlin: Springer-Verlag.

Dalcher, D. (1999). Disaster in London: The LAS case study. In *Proceedings of the 6th Annual IEEE International Conference and Workshop on Engineering of Computer Based Systems* (pp. 41-52). IEEE CS Press.

Dong J., Alencar, P.S.C., & Cowan, D.D. (2000). Ensuring structure and behavior correctness in design composition. In *Proceedings of the 7th Annual IEEE International Conference and Workshop on Engineering of Computer Based Systems* (pp. 279-287). IEEE CS Press.

Eden, A.H., & Hirshfeld, Y. (2001). Principles in formal specification of object-oriented architectures. In *Proceedings of the 11th CASCON*. IBM Press.

Gamma, E., Helm, R., Johnson, R., & Vlissides, J. (1995). *Design patterns: Elements of reusable object-oriented software*. Addison-Wesley.

Jezequel, J.-M., & Meyer, B. (1997). Design by contract: The lessons of Ariane. *IEEE Computer, 30*(1), 129-130.

Lamport, L. (1994). The temporal logic of actions. *ACM Transactions on Programming Languages and Systems, 16*(3), 873-923.

Leite, J.C.S.P., Sant'Anna, M., & Freitas, F.G. (1994). Draco-PUC: A technology assembly for domain oriented software development. In *Proceedings of the 3rd IEEE International Conference of Software Reuse* (pp. 94-100). IEEE CS Press.

Meyer, B. (1992). Applying design by contract. *IEEE Computer, 25*(10), 40-51.

Mikkonen, T. (1998). Formalizing Design pattern. In *Proceedings of the 20th International Conference on Software Engineering* (pp. 115-124). IEEE CS Press.

Pal, P. (1995). Law-governed support for realizing Design patterns. *Technology of object-oriented languages and systems* (pp. 25-34).

Saeki, M. (2000). Behavioral specification of GoF Design patterns with LOTOS. In *Proceedings of the Seventh Asia-Pacific Software Engineering Conference* (pp. 408-415). IEEE CS Press.

Soundarajan, N., & Hallstrom, J.O. (2004). Responsibilities and rewards: Specifying Design patterns. In *Proceedings of the 26th International Conference on Software Engineering* (pp. 666-675). IEEE CS Press.

Taibi, T., & Ngo David, C.L. (2003). Formal specification of Design pattern combination using BPSL. *International Journal of Information and Software Technology, 45*(3), 157-170.

Chapter VI

SPINE:
Language for Pattern Verification

Alex Blewitt, Edinburgh University, UK

Abstract

Patterns are often described in terms of concrete examples in specific programming languages in catalogues (Gamma, Helm, Johnson, & Vlissides, 1995). The description is worded such that a practitioner in an object-oriented programming language will be able to understand the key points of the pattern and translate it into a programming language of their choice. This abstract description of patterns is well suited for intelligent readers, but less suited for automated tasks that must process pattern information. Furthermore, the way in which the pattern information is encoded is often strongly influenced by the type of processing that is being performed on the pattern. In this chapter, the SPINE language will be presented as a way of representing Design patterns in a suitable manner for performing verification of a pattern's implementation in a particular source language. It is used by a proof engine called HEDGEHOG, which is used to verify whether a pattern is correctly implemented.

Background

Patterns are often designed into a system at an early stage, often before any code has been written. The use of patterns in systems software is well known and the architect will have an appreciation of the benefits of a particular pattern when designing a system in the first place. However, errors in realising these patterns can creep into the system by two means; either an error in transcribing the architect's design into code, or a subsequence maintenance change that violates one of the pattern's assumptions.

Given that a pattern is an abstract concept, language compilers and other verification tools do not necessarily know that a particular collection of code exhibits a pattern. Automated testing harnesses (such as JUnit and TestNG) tend to be utilised to check the behaviour of code, rather than its implementation. A pattern normally does not have a specific behaviour that can be checked directly, and indeed, two pieces of code may have identical external behaviour but be implemented in completely different ways (using different patterns, or no pattern at all). As a result, there is an opportunity for a different type of tool that can verify whether a pattern exists by analysis of the code instead of the code's behaviour.

The goal of SPINE is to provide a language that can represent a Design pattern's constraints such that they can be proven with an automated proof tool HEDGEHOG (Blewitt, 2006). This language may also be useful for reasoning about patterns in other ways; for example, the same declarative specification of a pattern could be used to instantiate a pattern, or guide a refactoring tool toward the introduction of a pattern into existing code, although these are not specifically addressed by this chapter. The section on further work discusses these ideas in more detail.

Why a New Language?

Other languages already exist that can be used to describe patterns. Catalogues often present summaries in UML (Fowler & Scott, 2003), and of course the target language (Java, C++, or Smalltalk) is often used to give an example of a pattern being implemented. Why not just use one of the existing languages to describe patterns?

The problem is that the target language is sufficiently flexible to allow a pattern to be realised in a number of ways. A *Singleton*'s instance does not need to be stored in a variable called default, nor does *Observer*'s event mechanism need to be called notify(). Thus, a specific implementation of a given Design pattern cannot be compared on a like-for-like basis between a known example in order to provide differences. Similarly, regardless of the target language used, UML cannot be used to describe an infinite set of pattern instances because the language is not designed for that purpose. If there were some higher-level metaUML, then perhaps this would be appropriate, but the UML itself does not provide this.

Other languages have been introduced in the past. Amnon Eden's LePUS (1998, 2000) provided such a metamodelling language in order to describe relationships between classes, and then relationships between those relationships as well. The modelling language was graphical—like UML—because more information can be encoded in a graphical diagram than text. As with any graphical modelling language, the notation used to represent relationships between classes, both from an object inheritance point of view, but also in terms of the abstract properties of methods (such as chains of invocation, typing, etc.). Unfortunately, this meant that the graphical language is very abstract and conveys more information about the mathematical properties of a pattern rather than any detail of its construction.

While mathematically sound, this did not present much of a mechanism amenable to automatic verification of patterns. Additionally, since it was a very abstract definition, it could be applied to multiple target languages (e.g., C++ and Java). However, this approach is not something that lends itself well to verification of an implementation, since the implementation details are by definition abstract.

Other approaches for manipulating patterns also exist. Refactoring (Folwer, 2000; Opdyke, 1992) to introduce patterns (Cinnéide, 2000; Eden, Gil, & Yehudai, 1997; Tokuda & Batory, 2001) uses various ideas of patterns broken down by specific artefacts that can be used to instantiate parts of a pattern piecemeal until a pattern has been realised completely in the target language.

It is relevant to note that a pattern cannot be defined by implementation alone. The pattern-introduction-through-refactoring underlines this point. Refactoring can be defined as, *"the process of rewriting a computer program or other material to improve its structure or readability, while explicitly preserving its meaning or behaviour."* It follows that a program P may be refactored into a program P', while the behaviour remains the same. However, P' may exhibit a pattern, while the original P may not. Thus, a behavioural specification of the pattern would (incorrectly) apply to both, even though the pattern may only be present in one of the patterns.

Refactoring to introduce a pattern may be done through metaprograms that manipulate the structure of the target program in question. This approach was taken in Eden et al. (1997) and Cinnéide (2000) with tricks or metaprograms to transform existing code (not exhibiting the pattern) into code with the pattern. One problem with this approach is there may be many ways in which a program can be refactored to introduce a pattern, so a subsequently larger refactoring library is required to allow for a number of patterns and the number of ways in which they may be reached.

Other tools have also been created for languages, such as Smalltalk, with investigation into metamodelling tools for object oriented systems and introduction of patterns (Ehms, 2000; Gruijs, 1998; Mijers, 1996). These provided refactoring tools based on the original Smalltalk refactoring browser (Opdyke, 1992) that would allow transformations or instantiations of particular code fragments to introduce the existence of a pattern.

Note that the pattern definition language is designed to be suited for a particular task. Approaches that involve code manipulation, refactoring, or other transformations are more likely to be suited to the journey (how the pattern comes into being) rather than the destination (what the pattern looks like when you get there). SPINE and HEDGEHOG are concerned about what the pattern looks like at the destination, and not the journey by which it arrived. That being said, there are a number of overlapping concepts which help to validate their existence; for example, patterns in SPINE are often broken down into smaller repeating units (mini-patterns) which is a concept replicated in other journey-based approaches (such as mini-transformations). This suggests that there may be more ways of analysing patterns rather than the ubiquitous catalogues are currently defined. There are a number of repeated characteristics that are common between patterns and could be categorised in their own light.

Representing Patterns

A realisation of a pattern can be considered to be a set of constraints on a set of classes. These constraints may be either structural (connected by inheritance, subclassing, navigable through field references, etc.) or semantic (this method has this behaviour under these circumstances). Given a rich enough vocabulary, it should be possible to represent a Design pattern realisation as a set of these constraints. Of course, these constraints need to be parameterised—for example, a *Singleton* will store a reference to the unique instance as a variable, but the variable name is not relevant. The constraints must be sufficiently flexible to allow many different realisations of the same basic idea.

Because this definition is declarative, it lends itself well to automated processing systems. A constraint checker can be used to determine whether or not a particular set of classes realises a Design pattern, and as the constraints are generally cumulative, the problem can be broken down into manageable units. It would also allow a pattern to be realised onto an existing set of classes by applying the constraints to an existing set of classes (although this has not been investigated in the scope of SPINE and HEDGEHOG).

Target Language

Verification of whether a Design pattern has been correctly implemented requires examples from a specific language in order to be able to process them. In this case, the language of choice is Java for no other reason than it is widespread, well-known, and parsers are available. Additionally, because it is Java, it can be integrated into developer tools like Eclipse.

The way a pattern is implemented in one target language may be different from another. In Objective-C, a *Proxy* is implemented using a dynamic feature of the language itself, whereas in Java a different approach must be taken. Similarly, patterns like *Observer* or *Iterator* may be realised differently in C than in Java (where standard interfaces already exist in the latter to denote those patterns).

As a result, the constraints that specify a pattern define a set of constraints for a particular target language, which in this case is chosen to be Java. This does not preclude this approach working for other target languages; but the investigation of patterns in the author's PhD thesis (Blewitt, 2006) specifically focussed on Java as a target language.

Variants

In much the same way that patterns are implemented differently between languages, patterns can also be implemented differently in the same language. Often, different tradeoffs can be made in using one particular variation of a pattern over another. For example, the *Singleton* pattern can be implemented in Java in a number of ways:

- With a public static final variable
- With a private static final variable and a public accessor
- With a private static variable and a lazy initialiser

Each of these approaches results in a valid realisation of the *Singleton* pattern, but achieves it in different ways. Other esoteric ways can be used to implement a *Singleton*; a Map (hash table) can be used to only allow a single instance with a given name, or an exclusive system resource (such as a port with a specific number) can be acquired. However, these are less common and in any case are less understandable as *Singleton* patterns to readers of the code. A proof system cannot declare that there is no pattern present; it can only declare that there is no pattern variant that it knows about presently.

In order to allow for these variations, it is necessary to accept that there is no single set of constraints that will capture all possible realisations of a particular pattern. Instead, a pattern can be defined as a disjunction of sets of constraints, with each being a specific variant of a pattern. A proof system may then optimise the constraint during verification by looking for commonality between the variants.

This also allows additional variants to be added to the pattern library over time, or indeed, other patterns. Although catalogues are finite, new patterns are discovered over time and can be added into the system as new patterns or new variants to an existing pattern.

Constraints

Given that a pattern is to be represented as a set of constraints on an implementation, what do those constraints look like? Like other pattern processing works, patterns can be broken down into constituent artefacts, such as:

- Relationships between super/subclasses;
- Method signatures;
- Instance/class variables;
- Patterns of message sending between classes;
- Class signatures (abstract, final, etc.); and
- Interfaces.

These are termed *structural constraints* because they affect the structure of the implementation and the relationship with other classes. However, they are not enough on their own to be able to define a pattern completely.

As an example, the *Observer* pattern must not only have a standard interface (to which clients can subscribe) but the *Observable* must keep a list of interested parties to which it can fire events when changes occur. This cannot be expressed in terms of a structural constraint alone, It is necessary to impose a *semantic constraint* on the implementation of the registration/notification methods. Others may include:

- Creation of a particular instance;
- Forwarding a message's arguments to another method; and
- Ensuring that a method does not return a null value.

Together, the structural and semantic constraints can be enough to define a pattern such that it can be used for verification purposes. (Note that for generation purposes, while the structural constraints can be used directly to generate required features, this is a lot more difficult to do with the semantic constraints. However, some standard templates could be used with a known code that meets those constraints when introducing a pattern for the first time.)

The SPINE Language

SPINE is loosely based on Prolog, as the HEDGEHOG proof engine uses an internal proof system similar to Prolog's execution. It also makes addition of patterns and variants easier to those who have programmed in Prolog before, rather than creating an entirely new syntax. Lastly, as the pattern definitions are declarative by nature, and as Prolog is a declarative language, the two closely match and thus is a natural choice for pattern definitions. As with Prolog, letters starting with an UpperCase are treated as variables, while those starting in lowercase are treated as terms. The single-quoted string acts as a literal identifier.

Patterns are defined in terms of a number of standard predicates that correspond to the structural and semantic constraints. For example, structural predicates include isAbstract(C) and typeOf(M). The arguments to these predicates are literals that identify the elements of the source code; for the same of simplicity, references to Java classes and methods adopt the JavaDoc notation com.Example#method(type). Thus, isAbstract('com.Example') is true when com.Example is an abstract type.

These can be joined with standard connectives, such as and, or, and implies to form logical statements over a range of classes and methods. As a result, it is possible to declaratively specific that a particular class has some combination of methods or field types. It's also possible to specify a constraint that exists over a range of classes as well. The two quantifiers forAll and exists can be used to iterate over set operators, such as methodsOf and subclassesOf (or even literal lists of classes). For example, and([isAbstract(C),forAll(subclassesOf(C),Cs. isFinal(Cs)]) declares that both C is an abstract class, and all of its subclasses (Cs) are final. At evaluation time, the forAll() is expanded into a conjunction([isFinal(Cs_1), ... ,isFinal(Cs_n)]).

Together, these statements can be used to define certain properties of classes. This technique should work for any statements about class implementation, though in the use so far this has just been used to reason about patterns. The term "realises" is used here, and throughout this document, to avoid confusion with object oriented-terminology, such as implements when discussing patterns. So realises('Singleton',[C]) is used to state that the class C is a *Singleton.*

Patterns are defined through the use of rules and these primitives, using a Prolog-like rule definition. This allows patterns to be interpreted by both engines and also end users, but most importantly, it allows the set of patterns to be extended externally to the proof engine that will process them. As long as the base set of primitives are enough, it should be possible to extend the pattern definitions to cover new variants and patterns in the future.

```
realises('AbstractOrFinal',[C]) :-
    or([isAbstract(C),isFinal(C)]).
```

This defines a rule for a (mini-)pattern *AbstractOrFinal* that is true whenever a class is either abstract or it is final. Although this is just an example (it's not a pattern defined in a pattern catalogue) it demonstrates how a rule can be defined using the predicates. Additionally, the realises() can also be used on the right-hand side, as discussed below in the section on variants.

Single Paticipant Example

Here's a larger example of a SPINE definition of the *Singleton* pattern (public variant):

```
realises('PublicSingleton',[C]) :-
  exists(constructorsOf(C),true),
  forAll(constructorsOf(C),
   Cn.isPrivate(Cn)),
  exists(fieldsOf(C),F.and([
   isStatic(F),
   isPublic(F),
   isFinal(F),
   typeOf(F,C),
   nonNull(F)
])).
```

This rule defines what it means for a class to realise a *PublicSingleton*. As well as being a declarative specification, it is also possible to read this as an English description of what it means to be a *PublicSingleton*.

The rule says that a class *C* is a *PublicSingleton*, if all of the following conditions are true:

- There is at least one constructor;
- All constructors are private; and
- There exists a field *F*, which
  - Is static
  - Is public
  - Is final
  - Is a type of *C*
  - And is assigned a non-null value during construction.

Other than the last constraint, the remainder of the definition of the *PublicSingleton* is based on structural constraints, which can easily be proven using a proof system. The last one is an example of a semantic constraint; in this case, that the field F is assigned a non-null value during construction. All of these are handled by the HEDGEHOG proof engine, which is documented in Blewitt (2006), but essentially uses static analysis of the code to determine whether or not the field is assigned a value, and if so, whether it can be shown that the value is non-null. Often, this trivially succeeds because it is assigned a value from a direct instantiation of the class itself (i.e., new C()). Here's an example of a *PublicSingleton* implemented in Java:

```
public class PublicSingleton {
 public static final PublicSingleton
  instance = new PublicSingleton();
 private PublicSingleton() {
 }
}
```

Of course, this represents a particular variant of a *Singleton*; there are others that can be defined. They can be packaged together in a single realises rule definition, which is true if any one of the children are true:

```
realises('Singleton',[C]) :-
 or([
  realises('PrivateSingleton',[C]),
  realises('PublicSingleton',[C]),
  realises('LazySingleton',[C])
 ]).
```

Here's the definition of the *LazySingleton* variant as another example:

```
realises('LazySingleton',[C]) :-
 exists(constructorsOf(C),true),
 forAll(constructorsOf(C),
  Cn.isPrivate(Cn)),
 exists(F,fieldsOf(C),
  and([
   isStatic(F),
   isPrivate(F),
   typeOf(F,C),
   exists(methodsOf(C),M.lazyInstantiates(M,F))
 ])).
```

And the associated Java example:

```
public class LazySingleton {
 private LazySingleton instance;
 private LazySingleton() { }
```

```
public LazySingleton getInstance() {
 if (instance == null)
  instance = new LazySingleton();
  return instance;
 }
}
```

In this case, the pattern definition is mostly concerned with the structural aspects of the pattern. However, it is necessary to ensure that there is a method which instantiates the instance field and returns it. This can't be done syntactically, so a special constraint lazyInstantiates() is provided which uses static code analysis to determine whether or not the method body does create an instance and returns it. As long as the proof engine can correctly detect whether the method is implemented correctly, then this will be a sufficient definition of the pattern. Note that any other pattern that needs to depend on lazy instantiation can also use this predicate. In practice, a few patterns require specialised predicates such as those for performing method analysis, but as the pattern library grows, it is expected that less new predicates will need to be added (because the set of required predicates that are not implemented will grow slower).

Mini-Patterns

The example above shows that there is a certain amount of duplication between the two variants of the single pattern. The requirement that there be at least one constructor, and that all constructors must be private, is a common idiom throughout the Java language in order to mandate that no instances of that class be created outside of the class itself. Both variants of the *Singleton* pattern have this requirement as a precursor, so this can be refactored out into its own pattern rule:

```
realises('NonInstantiable',[C]) :-
 exists(constructorsOf(C),true),
 forAll(constructorsOf(C),
  Cn.isPrivate(Cn)).
```

This rule can be used in other patterns (e.g., *Immutable* or *Flyweight*) both as a means of reducing the amount of shared definitions and as a way of documenting the composition of the patterns themselves. These so-called mini-patterns (also idioms, or mini-transformations) have been noted in other works (Gruijs, 1998; Cinnéide, 2000; Tokuda & Batory, 2001) and it is reasonable to assume that there may be other smaller building blocks of patterns, even if they are too small to be considered patterns on their own.

Further code analysis could suggest a common set of implementational constructs which would not ordinarily be recognised as a pattern in their own right, but still be detectable with the same mechanism. This is an open area for further research.

Multi-Participant Example

Many patterns are implemented with more than a single participant. For example, the *Abstract Factory* pattern is realised with a number of collaborators. For clarity, it can be split into two statements:

```
realises('AbstractFactory',[AF,AP]) :-
 forAll(subclassesOf(AF),
  CF.exists(subclassesOf(AP),
   CP.realises('AbstractFactory2',[AF,CF,AP,CP])
  )
 ).
```

The first one is the starting point of the pattern; a pair of classes *Abstract Factory* and *Abstract Product* make a pattern if for all (concrete) subclasses of *AF* and *AP*, they exhibit a particular constraint (which is refactored out for clarity):

```
realises('AbstractFactory2',[AF,CF,AP,CP]) :-
 subtypeOf(CF,AF),
 subtypeOf(CP,AP),
 exists(methodsOf(AF),
  M1.and([
   typeOf(M1,AP),
   isAbstract(M1),
   exists(methodsOf(CF),
   M2.and([
    sameSignature(M1,M2),
    typeOf(M2,AP),
    instantiates(M2,CP)
 ])])])).
```

The second constraint defines a relationship between a specific concrete factory and concrete product (as well as their abstract superclasses) such that there is a method in the abstract factory that is overridden in the concrete factory, and that the concrete factory instantiates the concrete product. (instantiates() is interpreted by the HEDGEHOG proof engine to require construction of an instance of the particular class, determined by static code analysis for example, searching for the new keyword in Java.) This definition would allow checks that, whenever a new factory is added, all necessary concrete products are returned. Note that this second relationship does not hold for all possible combinations (e.g., a MotifToolkit will not create a WindowsButton), but the first constraint is that for each concrete factory, there exists at least one concrete product that the second constraint holds. So as long as there is a MotifButton, it doesn't matter how many other buttons (or toolkits) are present. Further patterns are presented in Blewitt (2006).

The Hedgehog Proof Engine

The purpose of representing patterns in a declarative manner is to allow reasoning on those patterns to be performed; specifically, determining whether or not a collection of classes exhibits a particular Design pattern or not. This is achieved with Hedgehog, which is a proof engine designed specifically for this purpose. Its goals are:

- To parse and process Java source code
- To parse and process Spine pattern definitions
- To answer the question of whether a particular set of classes meets a Design pattern

At the same time, the creation of Hedgehog required a library of Design patterns (such as the *Singleton* and *Abstract Factory*) defined above in order to realistically test this approach with existing known source code. Additionally, since the goal was to be automated and embedded inside a tool such as Eclipse, it would have to work in a way that did not require the user's involvement for each step of the processing.

The Spine statements are parsed into logical statements about the source code, and then those statements are evaluated in the context of the source code being investigated. The evaluation of the logical statements is connected with basic connectives (such as and, or), by direct appeal to the source code (isAbstract, methodsOf), or by static analysis of the code (instantiates, nonNull). These built-in predicates are coded into the Hedgehog engine directly, and can only be extended by recompilation of the engine itself. However, the basic building blocks are there and can allow a number of patterns to be defined in Spine without having to add any more primitives. (This was a design choice because it allowed others to extend the pattern library without needing to know the internals of the engine itself.)

The execution of the proof engine is deterministic and bounded. There is no recursion, so the statements are logically unpacked and then interpreted using a boolean decision tree. In order to reason about the code itself, the built-in predicates (typeOf and so on) are derived from the syntax of the code directly. Most of the predicates are easy to interpret from the code itself, but some require a bit more analysis of the code. For example, the instantiates above in the *Abstract Factory* requires that the method create a new instance of a particular type of class. This is done by static analysis of all the possible code paths of a method and ensuring that each code path results in the instantiation of the given class type. This approach mirrors other static analysis processes such as ESC/Java (Leino, Nelson, & Saxe, 2000). The downside is that the analysis is not as powerful as a complete executable semantics of the language; however, it works well enough in the situations that it is needed to merit its use. In the case that it cannot be derived, a warning can be flagged to the user and a manual analysis can be done.

Future Work

The pattern verification has only been tested using Java as the target programming language so far. These principles should be applicable to other programming languages, although the specific pattern definitions would need to be adjusted appropriately for the specific features of the target programming language.

The constraint model used for the purposes of verification is a weak semantic model based on static analysis of code. Other constraint models may be equally applicable; for example, OCL (Clark & Warmer, 2002) or ESC/Java (Leino et al., 2000). The choice of constraint language was made for pragmatic reasons during the implementation and testing of HEDGE-HOG, because other solutions were not freely available at the time and it was necessary to implement an automated proof engine that could be queried interactively after running.

There may be some benefit in being able to instantiate Design patterns based on a declarative specification. Obviously, certain parameters (such as variable/method names) would need to be provided or inferred as part of this process, but the structural constraints would be relatively easy to translate into an implementation. The semantic constraints would be more difficult to use directly, but template code may be useful as a means to provide initial implementations of code.

As noted in Blewitt (2006), this approach does not distinguish between certain pattern pairs, such as Decorator or Adapter. Fundamentally, the difference between these two patterns is not the implementation, but in its intent of where it is being used. While the verification can be used to ensure that the implementation is as intended, it cannot know whether the designer's intent was to use a *Decorator* or *Adapter* without a larger semantic understanding of how it is being used.

Additionally, patterns like *Command* or *Inversion of Control* have a relatively small implementational footprint. These are examples of highly intent-based patterns where it is only up to the designer whether it is a *Command* or happens to be implemented in a similar way to a *Command*. Fortunately, patterns like *Command* are relatively simple, and thus it is difficult to implement them incorrectly, with the result that there is less need to be able to verify them. (Of course, there may be some benefit if this approach is being used to realise patterns in new code.)

Conclusion

It is possible to represent patterns as a set of constraints against a particular target language in order to verify whether those patterns are correctly realised in a given sets of classes. This approach works well for patterns with a well-defined structure or with well-defined semantic constraints, but fails with highly intent-based patterns.

Although this approach has been used to successfully verify patterns in Java, there are no reasons why this approach could also not be used for other languages, such as Smalltalk or C++. The pattern definitions would need to be rewritten to take into account the different ways in which patterns are realised in different languages, as well as different approaches to verifying the semantic constraints in the new language.

Most patterns may be realised in two or more ways, so it is necessary to take account of variants of patterns. A pattern is therefore defined as a disjunction of sets of constraints against a set of classes, and new variants (or entire new patterns) can be added at a later stage.

It may also be useful to use the declarative definitions of patterns as they stand in order to repair or introduce Design patterns (potentially through refactoring) by identifying the proof failures that HEDGEHOG reports.

Acknowledgment

The research presented in this chapter was supported by an EPSRC CASE studentship in conjunction with the University of Edinburgh and International Object Solutions Limited. Java is a trademark of Sun Microsystems, Inc. in the United States and other countries. Eclipse is a trademark of Eclipse Foundation, Inc. in the United States and other countries. UML is a registered trademark of Object Management Group, Inc. in the United States and other countries.

References

Blewitt, A. (2006). *HEDGEHOG: Automatic verification of Design patterns in Java.* Doctoral thesis, University of Edinburgh. Also available at http://www.bandlem.com/Alex/Papers/PhDThesis.pdf

Cinnéide, M.Ó. (2000). *Automated application of Design patterns: A refactoring approach.* Doctoral thesis, University of Dublin, Trinity College.

Clark, T., & Warmer, J. (2002). *Object modelling with OCL.* Springer.

Eden, A. (1998). *LePUS: A declarative pattern specification language* (Tech. Rep.). Tel Aviv University.

Eden, A. (2000). *Precise specification of Design patterns and tool support in their application.* Doctoral thesis, Department of Computer Science, Tel Aviv University.

Eden, A., Gil, J., & Yehudai, A. (1997). Precise specification and automatic application of Design patterns. In *Proceedings of the 12th Annual Conference of Automated Software Engineering.*

Ehms, D. (2000). *Patternbox eclipse tool.* Retrieved November 14, 2006, from http://www.patternbox.com

Fowler, M. (2000). *Refactoring: Improving the design of existing code.* Addison-Wesley.

Fowler, M., & Scott, K. (2003). *UML distilled.* Addison-Wesley Professional.

Gamma, E., Helm, R., Johnson, R., & Vlissides, J. (1995). *Design patterns: Elements of reusable object-oriented software.* Addison-Wesley.

Gruijs, D. (1998). *A framework of concepts for representing object-oriented design and Design patterns.* Doctoral thesis, Department of Computer Science, Utrecht University.

Leino, K.R.M., Nelson, G., & Saxe, J.B. (2000). *ESC/Java user's manual* (Technical Report No. 2000-002). Compaq Systems Research Center.

Mijers, M. (1996). *Tool support for object-oriented Design patterns.* Master's thesis, Utrecht University.

Opdyke, W.F. (1992). *Refactoring object-oriented frameworks.* Doctoral thesis, University of Illinois at Urbana-Champaign.

Tokuda, L., & Batory, D. (2001). Evolving object-oriented designs with refactorings. In *Automated Software Engineering.*

Chapter VII

Intent-Oriented Design Pattern Formalization Using SPQR

Jason Smith, IBM T.J. Watson Research, USA

David Stotts, University of North Carolina at Chapel Hill, USA

Abstract

This chapter introduces the system for pattern query and recognition, a collection of formalisms, definitions, and concepts that provides a means for formally describing Design patterns from the viewpoint of design intent. These descriptions enable efficient and effective searching for instances of Design patterns in source code, for purposes of discovery, documentation, validation, or refactoring. SPQR is composed of ρ-calculus, a formal denotation semantics for defining relationships between programmatic entities, elemental Design patterns, a collection of binary relationships that define the basis for software design principles, and isotopes, a flexible approach to combining formal design definitions so that they retain their conceptual integrity. It is our intent that the reader be better equipped to contemplate the hierarchical nature of the concepts of programming, and to come away from this discussion with a clearer view of how software is designed, from the small to the large.

Introduction

Software production is an exercise in the communication of intent to various audiences: the compiler, other developers, and ourselves in the future. We want to explain, accessibly, what we intend the system to do. Frequently, documentation is a supplementary material used to help clarify and convey this intent, but it is generally considered to be incomplete on most projects. We present a viewpoint based on intent, *Intent-Oriented Design*, or *IOD*, that yields simple formalisms and a conceptual basis for tools which support design and implementation from an intent-oriented perspective.

Until now, the automated extraction of intent from a system design has been considered a lost and quixotic cause. The system for pattern query and recognition, or SPQR, is a collection of formalisms and techniques which enable the analysis of software systems in the small or the large, and the detection of instances of known programming concepts in a flexible, yet formal, manner. Well defined combinations of these concepts, derived from the Design patterns literature, are the basis for SPQR's ability to automatically detect Design patterns directly from source code and other design artifacts. Our previous publications (Smith, 2005; Smith & Stotts, 2002, 2003) have described SPQR in detail, as well as its successful application to a number of software systems. We will describe the three major components of SPQR briefly, and use it to facilitate a discussion of the underlying formalizations of Design patterns with a concrete example, from source code to completed results.

Intent-Oriented Design

Design patterns, first described for object-oriented software by Gamma, Helm, Johnson, and Vlissides (1995), are a common vocabulary in which software developers discuss and communicate design and architecture ideas. Our goal is to create a process for reliable identification of instances of Design patterns in source code. An effective solution would enable software developers to produce systems which adhere to good design principles. Accurate, repeatable, and automated identification of Design patterns in source code would aid maintenance, comprehension, refactoring, and design validation during software development.

Design patterns' abstract and informal nature makes them valuable as a design vocabulary because they can succinctly encapsulate a vast number of highly variable architectures and implementations, yet this same informality makes patterns difficult to formalize for effective analysis and tool support. Our approach formalizes these concepts through two main strategies. First, we use a divide-and-conquer method in which we seek easily detectable, small, foundational patterns and use automated inference to compose them into the larger algorithm- and system-scale structures. Second, we use formalized variability to create notions of variance from ideal structure within our semantics.

Ultimately, software at any level is a realization of programmatic concepts. The structures, languages, and intricacies of application specifics are artifacts of a particular implementation of those concepts as a design. Analysis of software design is, therefore, an exercise in the analysis of concepts, and how those fundamental concepts combine to form higher abstractions. Object-oriented languages, by virtue of encapsulation principles, simplify some conceptual elements of programming, and provide an appropriate starting point for conceptual analysis based on the elements of object-oriented programming. These elements and their relationships are the mechanisms by which concepts are realized in a system, and through which an architect, designer, or programmer gives form to his or her *intent*.

Comprehension of intent is the primary requirement for system comprehension, and it is the primary focus of Design patterns. This is seen when examining a Design pattern description from the established literature. A section labeled *Intent* is the first element of most description forms, including the most common set forth in the original software Design patterns text (Gamma et al., 1995), commonly referred to as the "Gang of Four," or "GoF" book. Supporting text in the Design pattern descriptions indicates the why, the how, and the when, but only the intent describes the what. Unfortunately, most software analysis concentrates on extracting the syntax of a code base, and focusses on the *constructs* embodied in the code, while what drives our interest is the *concepts*.

The concepts found in Design patterns can be readily built up from the primitive concepts of programming, and the identification of primary relationship concepts from source code is a non-trivial, but boundable, task. There is a specific intent behind each of these concept relationships, and their combinations. Extracting intent through searching for instances of Design patterns in source code provides a deep understanding of software design.

Providing software engineers with the tools to describe, utilize, and extract conceptual intent when dealing with a software system will allow for more flexible and robust designs. We leverage the established Design patterns literature to create a description of intent. When we make designers self-consciously aware of how each piece of this design relates to the others, utilization of these intents is possible. We focus on extraction in this chapter, after extending Design patterns to provide a basis for what we term *Intent-Oriented Design*.

Divining design intent through a conceptual-analysis approach has three requirements: a formal semantics for the conceptual relationships between the elements of object-oriented programming, a catalog of conceptual elements of programming expressed in the formal semantics, and a methodology for combining concepts into more useful and higher-level abstractions in a way that allows for variances in the implementation of those concepts. SPQR satisfies these requirements through *ρ-calculus, Elemental Design Patterns*, and combinations thereof. A concrete example, named KillerWidget in our previous publications, will drive the discussion. KillerWidget was derived from a situation encountered in industry by one of the authors, and has proven to be highly illustrative to readers.

ρ-Calculus

Our *ρ*-calculus (Smith & Stotts, 2003) is an extension to ç-calculus (Abadi & Cardelli, 1996), a formal denotational semantics for object-oriented programming. It extends the calculus to encompass relationships between the four entities of object-oriented programming as defined in ç-calculus: objects, fields, methods, and types. These extensions, the *reliance operators*, define the reliances between the four conceptual entities as flexible, transitive relationships. This section contains a brief explanation of ç-calculus, and demonstrates how

ρ-calculus extends the basic principles to create the necessary basis for a robust Design pattern description technique.

Basics of ς-Calculus

Software has historically been rooted in formal notations. Formal descriptions of software most decidedly lend themselves to a pattern's formal description using a formal notation. The entire pattern does not need to be given a formal form, and it would not be improved by doing so. Formal descriptions, however, should be as formal as possible with a minimal reduction of the generality that makes patterns useful. At its root, source code is a mathematical symbolic language with well-formed reduction rules. We should, therefore, strive to find an analogue for the formal side of patterns.

There is a limit, however, to how formally we should extend this approach. A rigid formalization of static objects, methods, and fields would only be another form of source code, invariant under some transformation from the actual implementation. This defeats the purpose of patterns. We must find another aspect of patterns to encode as well in order to preserve the flexibility of patterns.

Desirable traits in an intermediate formalization language include that it be mathematically sound, consist of simple reduction rules, have enough expressive power to encode object-oriented concepts directly, and have the ability to flexibly encode relationships between code constructs.

Given these constraints, there are few options. The most obvious possible solution is lambda calculus, written as λ-calculus, or one of its variants (Stansifer, 1995), but λ-calculus cannot directly encode object-oriented constructs. Various extensions which would enable λ-calculus to do so have been proposed, but they have all produced a highly cumbersome and complex rule set in an attempt to bypass apparently fundamental problems with expressing typed objects with a typed functional calculus (Abadi & Cardelli, 1996). One final candidate, sigma calculus, written as ς-calculus, meets this requirement easily.

ς-calculus and its descendants are a fresh approach to creating a denotational semantics for object-oriented languages, and are "the first that does not require explicit reference to functions or procedures" (Abadi & Cardelli, 1996, p. v). Defined and described in *A Theory of Objects* by Martín Abadi and Luca Cardelli, ς-calculus is an analogue to the λ-calculus used in procedural theory. It concentrates on the aspects of object-oriented programming which are distinct from those of procedural programming, and makes no attempt to duplicate the efforts of the λ-calculus literature. Instead, it defines a notation which provides a rigorous mathematical foundation for further object-oriented language theory. The prime elements are objects, types, methods, and fields. Methods and fields are treated as equivalent in ς-calculus, which leads to some rather elegant solutions to some of the complex problems raised in formalizing highly dynamic languages. Classes are treated as a special case of objects, further simplifying the system.

ς-calculus also scales well from pure theory research to practical applications of software analysis not easily done otherwise, most likely with some simplifications to the calculus to more easily produce support tools. For example, many analysis techniques require reformation of their base assumptions when moved from one language to another (Basili, Briand, &

Melo, 1996; Chidamber & Kemerer, 1994). The highly theoretical nature of ς-calculus, and its ability to express current OO languages, means that a technique designed at this level of analysis will remain valid for any language that can be mapped to ς-calculus. Further, proofs of validity and completeness can more easily be shown in ς-calculus than they can be in other, less formal, approaches (Smith, 2005). These establish the techniques across a broad range of languages, disciplines, and domains, instead of needing to perform ad hoc justifications as analysis methods are used in new ways.

We will only describe the fundamentals of ς-calculus in this document, and refer the reader to Abadi and Cardelli (1996) for the formal details. In many ways, ς-calculus reads similarly to a pseudo-code notation, a style which should be at least passingly familiar to most practitioners of OO languages.

ς-calculus is broken up into 24 *fragments*, each a collection of equations concerning a particular concept of the calculus. In all, there are 78 reduction rules in ς-calculus. The various formal languages described in Abadi and Cardelli (1996) are produced by mixing and matching these fragments to express certain desired language features. A very simple first-order calculus, such as O-1 (Abadi & Cardelli, 1996, pp. 153-165) will use a small number of these fragments as its foundation, while a more expressive and complex language such as O-3 (Abadi & Cardelli, 1996, pp. 305-324) will use many more.

Objects, Methods, Fields, and Types

Everything in ς-calculus can be reduced to four elements of programming: objects, methods, fields, and types. There are no classes, templates, arrays, or generalized containers, yet all of these, and many more, can be quickly constructed from the four basic elements.

Methods and fields are treated as equivalent in ς-calculus, and no attempt is made to distinguish between them: "a field can be viewed as a method that does not use its *self parameter*" (Abadi & Cardelli, 1996, p. 52). Retrieving the value of a field is equivalent in this case to calling a method that returns a private data object. Considering the prevalence of precisely this idiom in object-oriented programming, this seems a reasonable approach. It does, however, bring up an interesting side-effect. If fields are directly assignable, then so are methods. While this may seem to be an oddity to the user of C++, Java, or other mainstream languages, other languages such as Self (Agesen, Bak, Chambers, Chang, Holze, Maloney, et al., 1993), expressly allow it. ς-calculus therefore provides the most generalized and expressive approach, allowing a broader range of languages to be quickly converted to ς-calculus notation.

Method bodies are bound to instances via the sigma-binding, written as ς. This is the source of the name ς-calculus. $\varsigma(x_i : A) b_i\{x_i\}$ takes a parameter x_i, and binds it to a free variable in b_i. This parameter is the self parameter and binds the method body b_i to a particular instance object of type A.

Types are defined by explicitly listing the elements of the type, the methods and fields, and then providing a type for each. Method types are the return value type, or the type of the reduction of the method to a single product.

Objects are similarly defined, by describing each element in turn, but also giving a proper binding of Self to the methods and fields such that they are associated with a particular instantiation.

For example, a type A and an object a may be defined as in equations (1) and (2). By convention in ς-calculus, l stands for any element (method or field) of the object or type in question, capitalized Roman letters stand for types, and b stands for element definitions, usually a method body. For instance, equation (1) states that there are n elements of type A, l_1 through l_n. These elements have types B_1 through B_n, respectively. Equation (2) states that object a has n elements denoted as in A, and that each has a corresponding definition indicated by b_1 through b_n. We can say in such a case that a has type A, or $a : A$ in ς-calculus notation. In these equations, then, l_i is of type B_i, and x_i is of type A. $\triangleq$ in ς-calculus represents "equal by definition," distinguished from the $\equiv$ for "syntactically identical" (Abadi & Cardelli, 1996, p. 59) and = for "informally equal" (Abadi & Cardelli, 1996, p. 66).

$$A \equiv [l_i : B_i^{i \in 1..n}] \tag{1}$$

$$a \equiv [l_i = \varsigma(x_i : A)b_i\{x_i\}^{i \in 1..n}] \tag{2}$$

Selection and Update

Selection is the operation that allows the naming of a subelement of an object or type. If object a has an element l_2, then $a.l_2$ names that element explicitly. This is usually read as "a dot l_2," and corresponds to the dot notation of many object-oriented languages, such as C++ and Java. It performs a similar function here. Selection of a method invokes that method, and selection of a field retrieves the object stored in that field. Invocation of a method returns an object (or none), and selection of a field always returns an object. In both cases the type of the selection operation is the type of the object returned.

The update operator, $\Leftarrow$, performs the assignment of values to fields, or method bodies to methods. As noted above, methods can be updated in ς-calculus, during which they are given a new method definition, or even converted to what would generally be considered a field.

Reduction Rules

Reduction rules are the core of ς-calculus's fragments. They stipulate a set of criteria and premises and an inference or conclusion. In these rules, E is understood to mean "the environment," a shorthand for everything currently defined and under consideration. A "judgment" is a singular criteria or conclusion, and is written $X \vdash Y$ for some X context, and some Y criteria. $E \vdash a : A$ therefore encodes "an environment E such that there is an object a of type A."

We can take these judgment definitions, equations (1), (2) and the selection operator, and define a reduction rule for evaluation of a selection in a first-order calculus (Abadi & Cardelli, 1996, p. 90):

(Eval Select)

$$E \vdash A \equiv [l_i : B_i^{i \in 1..n}], \; E \vdash a \equiv [l_i = \varsigma(x_i : A)b_i\{x_i\}^{i \in 1..n}], \; E \vdash a : A \; j \in 1..n$$
$$\overline{E \vdash a.l_j \leftrightarrow b_j\{\!\{a\}\!\} : B_j}$$

Simply put, this states that, given a type A and an object a defined as above, the type of the evaluation of the selection of an element in a will reduce to that element's proper type B_j. All of ς-calculus is defined in such rules of reduction. If a reduction path exists between a premise p and a conclusion c, it can be written $p \rightsquigarrow c$.

Notation Conventions

Now that we have described the necessary elements of ς-calculus, we can introduce our extensions which result in the ρ-calculus. For clarity, in the following discussion we will use a few standard notations. $\mathcal{O}$ and $\mathcal{P}$ stand for generalized object abstractions in ς-calculus. m and n are placeholders for any method, while f and g mean any given field. s and t can stand for either a method or a field, that is, any selected element. $\mathcal{O}.m$ is to be read as "any method m of object $\mathcal{O}$," $\mathcal{P}.f$ is "any field of object $\mathcal{P}$," and $\mathcal{O}.s$ is "any selectable element of object $\mathcal{O}$." Abadi and Cardelli use l ubiquitously to indicate any selectable item, and rarely distinguish between methods and fields. This is appropriate for their foundational work, but we require a finer granularity. In general, $\mathcal{O}$, m, f, and s are used on the left-hand side of relationships, and $\mathcal{P}$, n, g, and t on the right-hand side. Additional objects, methods, and fields will be indicated by use of one or more tick marks. $\mathcal{O}$, $\mathcal{O}'$, and $\mathcal{O}''$ are to be considered as three distinct and unique objects when seen in the same equation unless otherwise indicated. To conform with the formal notation in (Abadi and Cardelli, 1996), indices and integer ranges may contain an m or an n. It will be clear from context when this is the case, rather than representing a method.

We follow ς-calculus's subtyping operator for the notation for Δ_ρ: Given that the colon, ':', is used as a typing operator, and that <: can be read as "relies on the type of," we use the < symbol to indicate reliance in general. Reliance forms are indicated by appending an appropriate mnemonic symbol to this base.

Additionally, we introduce the concept of *method-body context*. This becomes a key point of joining of ς-calculus and λ-calculus in the analyses that ρ-calculus was designed to facilitate. Informally, context is the method body within which a selection or update occurs. Formally, attempting to denote even something simple, such as "there is an update of field f in method m of object $\mathcal{O}$" entails giving an extended definition of $\mathcal{O}$, and at least an illustrative partial definition of m to indicate the use of the update: $E \vdash \mathcal{O}, \mathcal{P}, \; \mathcal{O} \equiv [l_i = b_i^{i \in 1..n}, \; b_j = \{\ldots, \mathcal{O}.f \Leftarrow \mathcal{P}.s, \ldots\}]$. This quickly becomes tedious. Instead, the context indicator is used to illustrate that a relationship, update, or selection occurs within a specific method body, that is, within a specific context, as in equation (3). $\mathcal{S}$ stands for any relationship or valid statement that can occur in the method body. The double bars, $\|\,\|$, are the delimiter pair, the contents of the scoping are contained between them, and the method within which $\mathcal{S}$ occurs is given as a subscript to the delimiter pair.

Context $$\frac{E \vdash \mathcal{O}, \ \mathcal{O} \equiv [l_i = b_i{}^{i \in 1..n}, \ b_j = \{\ldots, \mathcal{S}, \ldots\}]}{\|\mathcal{S}\|_{\mathcal{O}.l_j}} \tag{3}$$

Reliance Operators

While ς-calculus provides a solid basis for formalizing object-oriented concepts, it does not enable conceptually tying two elements together other than object definition semantics. While method calls and field accesses are incorporated via the selection operator, ascertaining the relationship between two entities without a full scan of the system at hand is difficult. These relationships of reliance are the core of SPQR's conceptually-based analysis, and we provide a formalism here for describing and manipulating them. This formalism is defined in the manner of ς-calculus's fragments, and is described as the *rho fragment*, or Δ_ρ, with rho for "reliance." A detailed treatise on Δ_ρ is not the subject of this chapter, however, and the complete Δ_ρ definition with fully expanded definitions can be found in Smith (2005). ρ-calculus is defined as ς-calculus with the addition of Δ_ρ.

We term the relationship-defining formalizations *reliance operators*. The term "relationship" is already heavily used in the literature in various ways, and "dependency" has a strong heritage as well, but the core concept is similar: one element *relies on* another. Essentially, ρ-calculus can be seen as a single unifying formalism for the various method and data-dependency approaches that have been produced. ρ-calculus achieves this by bridging the ς-calculus and λ-calculus worlds in a well formed but precisely restricted manner. ς-calculus concerns itself only with the formalisms of objects and their typing interactions. As soon as the boundary of a method body is reached, it defers to λ-calculus for further formalism. The definitions of ρ-calculus extend ς-calculus into the method bodies, but in only a few and discrete ways that do not break the fundamentals of either established formalism. A rich environment of information on which many conceptual inferences can be based arises from this small number of rules.

As stated earlier, ς-calculus reduces the entirety of object-oriented programming to four elements: object, methods, fields, and types. ρ-calculus must provide conceptual relationships between these four elements in order to successfully model reliances.

Types that rely on one another for their definitions are already handled in the ς-calculus subtyping construct $<:$. The equation $A <: B$ can be considered to be read as "the type A relies on the type B for its base definition." Type-to-type relationships are, therefore, already a part of ς-calculus, and three elements remain to be handled: object, methods, and fields.

Objects and fields can be reduced to one conceptual element, because a field is first and foremost an object. Its enclosing object is a scoping, but this alters neither the semantics of the field object, nor its type. We will use the term "field" from this point on to refer to objects in reliance relationships for simplification. Raw objects can be considered as fields of an enclosing artificial "systemic" object conceptually, but in practice they are merely unscoped.

The remaining two elements, methods and fields, give rise to four combinations of reliance relationships: method/method, method/field, field/method, and field/field. These provide a conceptual coverage of the reliances in object-oriented programming, as they are derived directly from the core elements of ς-calculus. If there are missing reliances, then either ç-calculus is missing elements in its definition, or Δ_p is conceptually incomplete. We assume the validity of ç-calculus as an axiom in this work, and show in Smith (2005) that the remaining reliance permutations involving methods or fields and types are inconsistent with ç-calculus.

Each of the reliance operators can be defined in terms of pure ç-calculus constructs, or in terms of each other through relationships akin to transitivities. The former are those that are directly detectable in source code, so we will begin with those. In the next section, we will discuss the various interrelationships that can arise through inference. In every case, the reliance operators are defined as judgments, or inferences, not as equivalences. While the ç-calculus constructs are valid requirements for each conclusion, the conclusion reliance operator does not necessarily imply the presence of the constructs.

In the following discussions, we will group the reliance operators by their left-hand side elements. The groups are the method-body-based reliance operators, $<_\mu$ and $<_\varphi$, and the update-target-based reliance operators, $<_\sigma$ and $<_\kappa$. We provide here only the most basic forms of these operators, to establish the concepts. The reader will find the remaining definitions in Smith (2005).

Method-Body-Based Reliance Operators: $<_\mu$, $<_\varphi$

Method-body-based reliance operators are so named because they describe how a method body relies on either other methods or fields to complete its task. The left-hand side of the reliance operator is the method that forms the base of the reliance.

The right-hand side of the reliance operator is either a selected method or a selected field inclusive of raw objects. A selected method on the right-hand side defines a $<_\mu$, or *mu-form*, reliance operator, while a selected field on the right-hand side defines a $<_\varphi$, or *phi-form*, reliance operator. μ mnemonically stands for *method*, while φ stands for *field*.

For example, consider the pseudo-code in Figure 1. Two objects are defined: G is a global object that is currently blank, and O has a single method that utilizes a second object P, whose definition is not currently available. Lines 1-4 will illustrate several reliance styles.

Figure 1. Pseudo-code for $<_\mu$ and $<_\varphi$ example

```
object G {}
object O {
        method m() {
                field retval;
                P.n(G);                         // (1)
                retval = P.n2();                // (2)
                G = retval;                     // (3)
                return retval;                  // (4)
        }
}
```

Starting with line (1), O.m relies on the call to P.n, as P.n presumably performs some amount of work that O.m wishes to have done. This would be written in ρ-calculus as $\mathcal{O}.m <_\mu \mathcal{P}.n$. O.m uses the object G as a parameter to be passed to P.n. This creates a $<_\varphi$ reliance between them, $O.m <_\varphi G$, as it follows that O.m expects that G will be required by P.n for some reason. It is useful to think of $<_\mu$ as "calls" and $<_\varphi$ as "uses" in such direct cases: "method m of object O calls method n of object P" and "method m of object O uses object G." These are more commonly stated as "O dot m calls P dot n" and "O dot m uses G," mirroring not only common terminology in programming environments, but also the ρ-calculus notation. The formal definitions of these two reliances are shown in equations (4) and (5).

Mu Call
$$\frac{E \vdash \mathcal{O}, \mathcal{P},\ \|\mathcal{P}.n()\|_{\mathcal{O}.m}}{E \vdash \mathcal{O}.m <_\mu \mathcal{P}.n} \qquad (4)$$

Phi Parameter
$$\frac{E \vdash \mathcal{O},\ \|\mathcal{P}.n(\mathcal{P}'.g')\|_{\mathcal{O}.m}}{E \vdash \mathcal{O}.m <_\phi \mathcal{P}'.g'} \qquad (5)$$

Update-Target-Based Reliance Operators: $<_\sigma, <_\kappa$

The other group of reliance operators are the update-target-based operators. These have direct definitions that use the update operator of ς-calculus, and the left-hand side of the update is the left-hand side of the appropriate reliance operator. Under the most basic assumptions of programming, these could also be called field-based operators. Any ς-calculus construct that is valid on the left-hand side of an update operator, however, could theoretically be the basis for such a reliance. While methods are traditionally not allowed to be updated in most practical industry programming languages, ς-calculus specifically provides such a feature in the O-1, O-2, and O-3 languages (Abadi & Cardelli, 1996, pp. 153, 275, 307).

Consider that an object at any point in time has a state, defined by the set of the various fields contained within that object. This state is mutable by changing either the entirety of the state at one time, by replacing the object with a new "value," or by altering individual fields of the object on a per-item basis. Either results in a modified state and a new "value." Whenever the state of an object changes, there is an opportunity to create a reliance to reflect how that state was altered, where, and by what.

The first possibility is the simplest to capture. It is merely an update with a field on the left-hand side. Often, the right-hand side of the update will be a method call, returning an object that is used as the new field state. This is the most primitive form of the $<_\sigma$, or *sigma-form*, reliance operator, using σ for *state change*. The sigma in this case may seem like an odd choice given that the basis of this theory is the sigma calculus, but Abadi and Cardelli chose the lesser used variant sigma form (ς) to forestall such problems. Referring back to Figure 1, the fact $O.m.retval <_\sigma P.n$ can be created from line 2, as per equation (6), to be read as: "Object retval, local to method m of object O, relies on method n of object P for its state."

A closely related reliance operator is the most basic form of the $<_\kappa$, or *kappa-form*, reliance, with κ standing for *cohesion*, or *coupling*, depending on the context. This creates a link between two fields using a field-to-field update, as in line 3 of Figure 1, where the example code would result in $G <_\kappa O.m.retval$. This is a less common case than the $<_\sigma$ form of update, but is shown in equation (7).

Sigma Update
$$\frac{E \vdash \mathcal{O}, \mathcal{O}', \mathcal{P}, \; \|\mathcal{O}'.f' \Leftarrow \mathcal{P}.n()\|_{\mathcal{O}.m}}{E \vdash \|\mathcal{O}'.f' <_\sigma \mathcal{P}.n\|_{\mathcal{O}.m}} \quad (6)$$

Kappa Update
$$\frac{E \vdash \mathcal{O}, \mathcal{O}', \mathcal{P}, \; \|\mathcal{O}'.f' \Leftarrow \mathcal{P}.g\|_{\mathcal{O}.m}}{E \vdash \|\mathcal{O}'.f' <_\kappa \mathcal{P}.g\|_{\mathcal{O}.m}} \quad (7)$$

Transitivities

We can now discuss how relationships can relate to one another. If an element A of a system relies on another element B, and B in turn relies on C, then we can deduce that A relies on C, even if there is no direct link detectable in the original source code defining the two relationships. The deductive power of ρ-calculus comes from the ability to take disparate code bases and create new webs of reliances between them according to how the code is actually used. For example, a library designer may intend for a system to be used in a particular way, but often the users of said library will have other ideas. ρ-calculus allows the designer to find out how the library is being utilized in the field, using the code bases as direct evidence. This feedback provides a designer with a much clearer picture for how the library should be designed to meet the users' needs.

When dealing with reliances, we are much less concerned with *where* relationships are formed than most approaches that work with dependencies. Such information can be deduced when it is necessary, and not be a burden before then.

Given the four reliance operators, there are 16 potential interactions between them. If two reliance operators, indicated by $<_1$ and $<_2$, exist such that $X <_1 Y$ and $X' <_2 Y'$ then it is possible that $X < Y'$, but not guaranteed. Only if the right-hand side of the first reliance operator and the left-hand side of the second reliance operator are the same sort of element can there be a new reliance formed. For instance, if $\mathcal{O}.m <_\mu \mathcal{P}.n$ and $\mathcal{O}'.f' <_\sigma \mathcal{P}'.n'$, then no $\mathcal{P}.n$ (a method) or $\mathcal{O}'.f'$ (a field) would ever create a binding between the two reliances. Hence, a μ/σ transitivity is forbidden. Similarly, the μ/κ, φ/μ, φ/φ, σ/σ, σ/κ, κ/μ, and κ/φ transitivities are nonsensical. This leaves eight possible combinations: μ/μ, μ/φ, φ/σ, φ/κ, σ/μ, σ/φ, κ/σ, and κ/κ.

A simple example of the above informal transitivity is chaining method calls, the μ/μ interaction. If $\mathcal{O}.m$ calls $\mathcal{P}.n$ within its definition, and $\mathcal{P}.n$ in turn calls $\mathcal{P}'.n'$, then it is obvious that $\mathcal{O}.m$ relies on not only $\mathcal{P}.n$, but also $\mathcal{P}'.n'$ through a simple transitivity.

Mu Transitivity
$$\frac{E \vdash \mathcal{O}, \mathcal{P}, \mathcal{P}', \; \mathcal{O}.m <_\mu \mathcal{P}.n, \; \mathcal{P}.n <_\mu \mathcal{P}'.n'}{E \vdash \mathcal{O}.m <_\mu \mathcal{P}'.n'} \quad (8)$$

This is just one of many transitive reductions in ρ-calculus, and the reader is again referred to Smith (2005) for further details and the exhaustive discussion.

Selection Operators

In any selection as defined in ς-calculus, the two halves of the selection operator can be considered separately. Not only does selection pick an item out of an object for use, it also fulfills the basic requirements of a scoping operator in most programming languages. Selection, in this light, can be thought of as the :: operator in C++. Other languages, such as Java, have unified the scoping and selection operators as ς-calculus does.

Selection follows the same common sense rules as scoping, including nesting. Just as a piece of source code may refer to window.titlebar.title.setFont() to select a deeply nested method, ς-calculus can also perform the same nested selection: *window.titlebar.title.setFont*.

Only the rightmost item in such a nested selection chain is the current selection. The remainder provides a scoping for it. Making this distinction explicit, and allowing for easier discussion of the two halves separately, we introduce the terms *leftdot* and *dotright*, written formally as (• and •). These correspond respectively to the elements to the left of the most significant selection operator, and the final element in the chain. For example, the application of the leftdot operator to window.titlebar.title.setFont(), written as (*window.titlebar.title. setFont•*, would be window.titlebar.title and the result of dotright, or •*window.titlebar.title. setFont)*, would be setFont().

Similarity Principle

With a formal notation for selection parameters established, precise discussion of one of the most important elements of ρ-calculus, the *principle of similarity*, is possible. We define similarity to be "of a common conceptual nature," a measure of how closely related in *intent* two elements of programming are. If two methods have the same intent of function, or two objects have the same intent of state encapsulation, we can expect that they will perform similar tasks within a system. This yields strong cues to the *relative* functionality of the two elements, and provides a new aspect of the binary reliance operators, another axis of relationship alongside reliance. In the type of relationship analysis performed by SPQR, deducing the relationship between two elements in the design is more important than extracting their precise functionality at runtime.

The question then becomes how to measure similarity of intent. For an initial answer, we turn to Kent Beck's Intention Revealing Selector best practices pattern (Beck, 1997) (emphasis ours).

You have two options in naming methods. The first is to name the method after how it accomplishes its task. ... *The most important argument against this style of naming is that it doesn't communicate well.* ... The second option is to name a method after what it is supposed to accomplish and leave "how" to the various method bodies. This is hard work, especially when you only have a single implementation. Your mind is filled with how you are about to accomplish the task, so it's natural that the name follow "how". The effort of moving the names of method from "how" to "what" is worth it, both long term and short term. *The resulting code will be easier to read and more flexible.*

Beck summarizes, "Name methods after what they accomplish." This is easily extensible to fields and objects as well, and can be more generalized as, "Name elements of programming after what they accomplish or represent." Because communication of code intent and flexibility are two key components of comprehensibility and maintenance, this single principle serves as a basis for important conceptual analyses.

A first pass comparing the names of elements and looking for commonalities would seem to be reasonable. Common naming indicates common intent according to the above pattern. Examples of this can be seen in a number of practical applications. The JavaBeans architecture uses a "set*Attribute*" idiom to indicate a settor method during runtime inspection (Monson-Haefel, Burke, & Labourey, 2004). Within Apple's Cocoa framework, naming conventions are ubiquitous and standardized. Usually a method name can be guessed from the intent, without needing to look it up (Davidson and Inc., 2002).

Comparison logic is then an interesting exercise. What type of comparison is appropriate to conclude that two names are similar, and, by extension, that their corresponding elements have similar intended purpose? The most simple approach, and one initially used in SPQR, is a straight lexicographic equality check. Though simple, this worked much better than we expected. This can be explained anecdotally by noticing that, for any group of engineers, whether a group consisting of a single practitioner or many, nomenclatures will tend to standardize fairly quickly. A communal naming scheme must arise for common conceptual discussion. This allows for clean and clear code development, as well as easy and precise communication of the intents we are interested in. While SPQR does not attempt to extract *exact* intent of *individual* programmatic elements, we can leverage names to divine *relative* intents much more easily. This social engineering observation is critical, and we will revisit this when describing the current implementation of SPQR, and the KillerWidget example.

The reverse is also useful, knowing when two elements are explicitly *dissimilar*. This is not the same as not knowing the similarity relationship of two elements; this is a specific negation of the similarity principle, when it is deduced that two elements simply do not have the same intent, to a high degree of confidence. The $\sim$ operator is used to indicate similarity between two elements, and $\nsim$ an explicit dissimilarity.

With this conceptual definition in place, we can now define the similarity imbued reliance operators. Because similarity is such an important analysis principle, the reliance operators are explicitly tagged with the similarity information. A superscript is added, with the following format: $\overset{\pm}{\underset{\circ}{}}.\overset{\pm}{\underset{\circ}{}}$, two *similarity indicators* separated by a selection operator. The $\overset{\pm}{\underset{\circ}{}}$ indicates that one of $+$, $-$ or $\circ$ can be used. Similarity is indicated by a $+$, dissimilarity by a $-$, and $\circ$ is a placeholder for an unknown relationship. The two similarity indicators are separated by a selection operator, mirroring the outermost selection operator on each side of the reliance operator. The left side of the similarity information indicates the similarity relationship between the leftdot of each side, and the right side of the tag indicates the similarity between the dotright of each side.

This section forms the core of ρ-calculus, but is not an exhaustive treatise on its formalisms. For further information, consult our previous publications.

Elemental Design Patterns and Pattern Composition

Generally, the decomposition of Design patterns is not a new idea. The depth to which the decomposition is taken is the new contribution of this work. Most of the literature in the Design patterns field concentrates on expanding the Design patterns to ever-higher levels of abstraction. While this has obvious worth, we believe that, without a solid foundation, using patterns in well-formed and meaningful ways will become increasingly difficult. Tool support for engineers will simply not be able to keep up, and programmers will remain in the same morass, lacking formal support.

We defined the term "*Elemental Design Patterns*," or *EDP*s, for two reasons. First, these are the fundamental building blocks of design and programming, just as the elements are the building blocks of chemistry. Second, these are elemental in the sense that they are very simple concepts that every programmer uses, often instinctually. There is very little at this level that an experienced programmer will find new. Instinctual design is not conscious design, however, and it lacks the very traits that could make software design an actual engineering discipline, formal foundations, and methods that are reproducible, teachable, and consistent.

Self-conscious design is precisely the goal that Christopher Alexander set with his original work on Design patterns in architecture (Alexander, 1964), and we should not ignore the lowest levels when building larger abstractions. The EDPs reside in these lower levels, the very core of programming, and all design can be decomposed into them.

As shown in the discussion of reliance operators, the building blocks of object interaction in object-oriented languages can be defined as binary relationships. Object use through update and selection, method calls, and typing relations are the *only* ways that objects, methods, fields, and types can interact. Any programming feature from a language expressible in ς-calculus is reducible to some combination of those interactions. We can now quantify those interactions, and how they are used to build the conceptually rich abstractions of software design. These interactions are the EDPs, and they quickly become capable of solving rather esoteric, yet familiar, design problems.

The near-primitive simplicity of EDPs, when combined with the formal derivations of ρ-calculus, provides the opportunity for formalization of complex programming concepts. These core primitives are the basis for the construction of patterns in general. We believe that we have captured the elemental components of object-oriented languages, and the salient relationships used in the vast majority of software engineering. If patterns are the frameworks on which to create large, understandable systems, EDPs and the ρ-calculus are the nuts and bolts that comprise those frameworks.

Each EDP is unique from the others, each satisfies a different set of constraints, a different set of forces, and solves a slightly different problem. Each provides a degree of semantic context and a bit of conceptual elegance, in addition to a purely syntactical construct. In this context these are still truly patterns, and provide us with an interesting opportunity, to begin to build patterns from first principles of programming, namely formalizable denotation.

EDPs, as well as all other Design patterns, are expressed in ρ-calculus as a tuple construct of the form **PatternName**(*participant1*, *participant2*, ...), in which the ordering of the participants is fixed for each definition. They are defined formally as reduction rules with required criteria and a conclusion, just as the primary reliance operators are, and form a convenient shorthand notation for highly abstract concepts. By judiciously mixing a combination of formalized EDP instances, reliance operators, and lower-level constructs from ς-calculus and λ-calculus, an expressive and precise, yet flexible, denotation environment is created. By convention, when a pattern name is expressed as above, in bold text, it indicates a formal definition of the pattern in ρ-calculus, while standard text indicates discussion of the pattern as expressed in the literature.

Example EDPs

Types are an important component of ρ-calculus, but ρ-calculus is less concerned with particular type formalizations themselves than the relationships between types. ς-calculus handles the underlying type mechanics easily, but one more complex relationship is of particular importance to us.

Objects, together with fields, are the second major piece of ς-calculus, and require a bit of runtime handling. Object creation and object retrieval are runtime behaviors. While certain classes of these cases can be detected in a generalized manner, these EDPs require a close understanding of the target language. We will not be using these EDPs in the document.

After types and objects, only methods remain for discussion. The method-derived EDPs comprise the bulk of the EDP catalog, but we will provide only two examples here.

AbstractInterface

As stated in the discussion of ς-calculus, types create a mapping from a name to a set of defined methods and fields. There are cases where such definitions are incomplete, and rely on a later subtype to complete the definition. In the case of methods, this is called a *virtual method*, an *abstract method*, or a *deferred definition*. While most binary interactions are defined ahead of time, this one is a bit different in that it states, at the point of method declaration, that a nebulous and unknown *someone* will fulfill the promise of a method. A binary relationship still exists between the declaring type and the "someone"; the missing type will simply be filled in later. See the **FulfillMethod** pattern in the section on Pattern Composition for the definition of that missing type.

$$\frac{E \vdash C, \; C : [l_i : B_i^{i \in 1..n}]}{C \equiv [l_i = b_i^{i \in 1..m-1, m+1..n}, l_m = []]} \quad \mathbf{AbstractInterface}(C, l_m)$$

(9)

RedirectInFamily

We start with a method reliance based on dotright similarity, in which we determine that the methods have similarity of intent. For the purposes of our discussion, we can assume an equivalence of name and signature. Second, we want to have distinct objects be involved in the reliance, specifying a leftdot dissimilarity. Finally, we want to be able to make a connection between the types of those objects. Let us make it a simple inheritance, or subtyping, relationship.

To summarize, we have two objects whose types belong to the same inheritance tree, and one is an ancestor of the other. A method in the object of the subtype is calling a similar method in the object of the supertype. The method similarity and object dissimilarity can be noted by the use of $<_{\mu}^{-.+}$.

We term this method reliance style a **Redirect**, because one method is redirecting part of its workload to another, similar, method. Because the two objects are in the same family of types, we call this EDP **RedirectInFamily**. This is a very common structure, used when an object needs to hand off functionality polymorphically within a related suite of classes. It can be thought of as an open-ended recursion bounded by the type definitions instead of a computational terminal case. Figure 2 illustrates this principle in UML, while equation 10 provides the formalization.

$$
\begin{array}{l}
Redirecter <: FamilyHead, \\
r : Redirecter, \\
fh : FamilyHead, \\
r.operation <_{\mu}^{-.+} fh.operation, \\
\hline
\textbf{RedirectInFamily}(r, fh, operation)
\end{array}
\tag{10}
$$

ExtendMethod

Consider what happens in the above case if the object dissimilarity is collapsed to an object *similarity*, while maintaining the subtyping relationship. While this may seem nonsensical at first, precisely this occurs during the use of *super* in object-oriented languages. As defined in ç-calculus, *super* is a selector application that retrieves a superclass' implementation of the selected item. It is a precise way to bypass method overriding in subtyping, and most object-oriented programming languages support this directly. For example, C++ uses a statically-typed Superclass::method syntax, while Smalltalk and Objective-C define it as [super method], allowing for dynamic lookup of the proper type. In all cases, ç-calculus defines the selection of a superclass' method l from superclass c as $c^\wedge l(x)$.

Figure 2. RedirectInFamily class structure

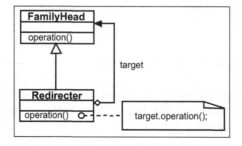

Figure 3. ExtendMethod class structure

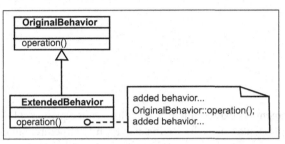

A common purpose of directly accessing a superclass' implementation of a method is to add additional behavior to that method, extending the method in some manner; it may be to fix a bug, change a default, or otherwise provide an alteration of the characteristics of the method, but in all cases it is an example of reusing existing code. Figure 3 shows a common UML notation for such a case. When a method is extended in this way, a specific interaction of object similarity, type dissimilarity, type subtyping, and method similarity create the **ExtendMethod** EDP. This is a core piece of the **Decorator** pattern, and we can formalize it as in equation 11. The **meth()** construct is simply a shorthand notation for the set of methods defined in $OriginalBehavior$.

$$\frac{\begin{array}{l} operation \in \mathbf{meth}(OriginalBehavior), \\ ExtendedBehavior <: OriginalBehavior, \\ eb : ExtendedBehavior, \\ eb.operation <_{\mu}^{+\cdot+} eb^\wedge operation \end{array}}{\mathbf{ExtendMethod}(OriginalBehavior, ExtendedBehavior, operation)} \qquad (11)$$

Isotopes

By using ρ-calculus instead of a more structural notation such as UML, an EDP can be implemented in numerous ways while still conforming to the concepts of the definition, fulfilling the encapsulation principle of isotopes. An interesting side effect of expressing the EDPs in ρ-calculus is an *increased* flexibility in expression of code while conforming to the core *concept* of a pattern. This encapsulation of concepts is related to the encapsulation of implementation at the core of object-oriented programming.

Consider the class diagram for the structure of **RedirectInFamily** from Figure 2. If we take the Participants specification of **RedirectInFamily**, as described in the pattern in Appendix B of Smith (2005), we find that:

$$FamilyHead \equiv [operation : A] \qquad (12)$$

$$Redirecter <: FamilyHead \qquad (13)$$

$$Redirecter \equiv [fh : FamilyHead,\ operation : A = \varsigma(x_i)\{fh.operation\}] \quad (14)$$

$$r : Redirecter \qquad\qquad\qquad (15)$$

$$r.fh : FamilyHead \qquad\qquad\qquad (16)$$

Each of these requirements is expressible in ς-calculus, as in equations (12) through (16). This is a concrete implementation of the **RedirectInFamily** structure, but one which fails to capture the reliance of $Redirecter.operation$ on $FamilyHead.operation$'s behavior. We, therefore, introduce the mu-form reliance operator:

$$r.operation <_{\mu}^{\circ,+} r.fh.operation \qquad\qquad (17)$$

...and produce a necessary and sufficient set of clauses at this point to represent **RedirectInFamily**, as defined in equation (10).

Consider now Figure 4, where we show what does not look much like the original specification, at first glance. We have introduced a new class to the system, the static criteria that the subclass' method invoke the method of the superclass' instance is gone, and a new calling chain has been put in place. In fact, this construction looks quite similar to the transitional state while applying Martin Fowler's *Move Method* refactoring (Fowler, 1999).

We claim that this is precisely an example of an alternative form of **RedirectInFamily**, however, when viewed as a series of formal constructs, as follows, assuming the same class definitions given in equations (12) and (14):

$$Redirection <: FamilyHead \qquad\qquad\qquad (18)$$

$$r : Redirection \qquad\qquad\qquad (19)$$

Figure 4. RedirectInFamily isotope

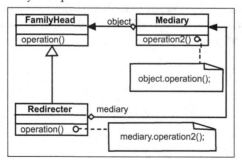

$$Mediary.object : FamilyHead \tag{20}$$

$$r.mediary : Mediary \tag{21}$$

$$r.operation <_{\mu}^{\circ.-} r.mediary.operation2 \tag{22}$$

$$Mediary.operation2 <_{\mu}^{\circ.-} Mediary.object.operation \tag{23}$$

If we start reducing this equation set, a new object-level clause can be derived from the typing for $r.mediary$ and equation (23), which results in equation (24).

$$\frac{r.mediary : Mediary, \quad Mediary.operation2 <_{\mu}^{\circ.-} Mediary.object.operation}{r.mediary.operation2 <_{\mu}^{\circ.-} r.mediary.object.operation} \tag{24}$$

A transitive operation can then be performed on equations (22) and (24):

$$\frac{r.operation <_{\mu}^{\circ.-} r.mediary.operation2, \quad r.mediary.operation2 <_{\mu}^{\circ.-} r.mediary.object.operation}{r.operation <_{\mu} r.mediary.object.operation} \tag{25}$$

This is almost the desired relationship, but it indicates a more general operation instead of the **Redirect** we initially sought. Fortunately, this is simple to fix. The dotright similarity rule suggests the creation of the more specific **Redirect** if the signatures of the operations match, from which it becomes evident that the needed form can indeed be derived:

$$\frac{r.operation <_{\mu} r.mediary.object.operation}{r.operation <_{\mu}^{\circ.+} r.mediary.object.operation} \tag{26}$$

With equations (12), (14), (18), (19), (20), and (26), satisfying the clause requirements set in the definition of **RedirectInFamily**, as per equation (10), is straightforward. This alternate structure is an example of the **RedirectInFamily** pattern, without adhering to a strict class structure. We term situations in which a variation on the original Design pattern class structure still conforms to the conceptual definition to be isotopic in general and an alternate structure such as above to be an *isotope* in particular. The concepts of *object relationships* and *reliance* are the key.

The effect of this is that there is no explicit requirement that the relationships between *Redirecter* and *Mediary* or *Mediary* and *FamilyHead* be **Redirection** EDPs. In fact, they can be explicitly non-**Redirection** expressions, as we discuss above, with no change to the meaning of **RedirectInFamily**. Only the initial and terminal function signatures are important.

More generally, this is the key to the power of analysis with SPQR: combining the formal transitivities of ρ-calculus with the recognition that *Design patterns are the encapsulation of concepts*, and allowing the implementation of those concepts to vary within well-formed guidelines. This takes the same fundamentally important principles of encapsulation from object-oriented programming that have resulted in better designed systems, and brings them to the abstract level of programming concepts. Without the formalizations of ρ-calculus, this approach would be extremely difficult to validate or provide guidance on. Without conceptual encapsulations, Design patterns become mere structural recipes and lose much of their expressiveness and importance. The two together provide the strong foundation of a reproducible, formalized science of design principles for software engineering.

It is worth noting that, while this may superficially seem to be equivalent to the common definition of *variant*, as defined by Buschmann, Meunier, Rohnert, Sommerlad, and Stal (1996), there is a key difference. Buschmann's variants are defined such that, "From a general perspective a pattern and its variants describe solutions to very similar problems." (Buschmann et al., 1996, p. 16) Isotopes solve the *same* problem, but in a slightly different manner, perhaps due to forces from an existing architecture. Variants solve *similar* problems, and in similar ways.

The distinction is that of the above-mentioned encapsulation. Isotopes may differ from the strict pattern structure in their implementation, but they provide fulfillment of the various roles required by the pattern, and the relationships between those roles are kept intact. From the view of an external calling body, the pattern is precisely the same no matter which isotope is used. In the above example, Figure 4 still shows *FamilyHead* and *Redirecter* fulfilling their assigned roles in the **RedirectInFamily** EDP. *Redirecter.operation* still performs the required conceptual task. How it implements it is immaterial, as per the principles of encapsulation.

Variants are not interchangeable without retooling the surrounding code, but isotopes are. This is an essential requirement of isotopes, and precisely why the term was chosen. Isotopes, in the EDP realm, are analogous to isotopes in chemistry, where they are externally identical when interacting in chemical processes. Only an inspection of their nuclei provides a clue as to their differing nature.

This flexible internal representation allows the implementer a great degree of latitude in system design, while still conforming to the abstractions given by Design patterns.

Pattern Composition

These EDPs are combined by cross-referencing the constituent elements with other EDPs to form larger conceptual entities, such as Design patterns from the existing literature, adding new ρ-calculus reliances as needed for necessary tying. This compositional approach allows high-level Design patterns to be represented in a conceptual form that can be mapped to a number of isotopic implementations, all within ρ-calculus. In this manner, a reader can focus on how the concepts, not the constructs of programming, interact, and think more purely about the intent of each sub-concept.

Figure 5. FulfillMethod intermediate pattern

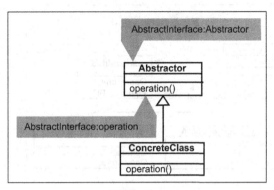

FulfillMethod

As mentioned earlier, and defined in equation 9, **AbstractInterface** sets up a relationship between a supertype and an unnamed subtype. The **FullfillMethod** pattern names that subtype explicitly, providing the other conceptual half of this relationship. As with **AbstractInterface**, this pattern involves types exclusively. The addition of the new annotations to UML, following the example of Vlissides (1998), is designed to show which subpattern and role each element of the new structure satisfies. For instance, the *Abstractor* type in **FulfillMethod** appears in the *Abstractor* role of the *AbstractInterface* subpattern.

$$\frac{\begin{array}{l} \textbf{AbstractInterface}(\mathit{Abstractor}, \mathit{operation}_n), \\ \mathit{ConcreteClass} <: \mathit{Abstractor}, \\ \mathit{ConcreteClass} \equiv [\mathit{operation}_i \Leftarrow b_i{}^{i \in 1..n-1,n+1..m}, \mathit{operation}_n \Leftarrow b_n] \end{array}}{\textbf{FulfillMethod}(\mathit{Abstractor}, \mathit{ConcreteClass}, \mathit{operation}_n)} \qquad (27)$$

Objectifier

The Objectifier pattern (Zimmer, 1995) is one such example of a core piece of structure and behavior that is shared between many more complex patterns. Its Intent section states:

Objectify similar behavior in additional classes, so that clients can vary such behavior independently from other behavior, thus supporting variation-oriented design. Instances from those classes represent behavior or properties, but not concrete objects from the real world (similar to reification).

Zimmer uses the Objectifier as a "basic pattern" in the construction of several other GoF patterns, such as Builder, Observer, Bridge, Strategy, State, Command, and Iterator. Objectifier is a simple, yet elegantly powerful, structural concept that is used repeatedly in other patterns.

Figure 6. Objectifier pattern with annotation

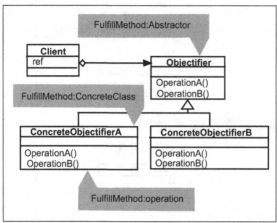

It is now clear that Objectifier is simply a class structure applying the **FulfillMethod** pattern to all methods in a class pair. The core concept is to create a family of subclasses with a common abstract ancestor, as shown annotated in Figure 6. This is expressed in ρ-calculus for one such subclass as in equation (28).

$$ObjectifierBase : [l_i : B_i^{i \in 1...n}],$$
$$Client : [ref : Objectifier],$$
$$Client.someMethod <_\mu Client.ref.l_i,$$
$$\textbf{FulfillMethod}(ObjectifierBase, ConcreteObjectifier, l_i)^{i \in 1...n},$$
$$\textbf{Objectifier}(ObjectifierBase, ConcreteObjectifier, Client) \qquad (28)$$

Object Recursion

Woolf takes Objectifier one step further, adding a behavioral component, and naming it Object Recursion (Woolf, 1998). The class diagram in Figure 7 is extremely similar to Objectifer, with an important difference, namely the behavior in the leaf subclasses of *Handler*. Exclusive of this method behavior, however, it appears to be an application of Objectifer in a more specific use. Note that Woolf compares Object Recursion to the relevant GoF patterns and deduces that Iterator, Composite, and Decorator can, in many instances, be seen as containing an instance of Object Recursion, while Chain of Responsibility and Interpreter do contain Object Recursion as a primary component. Object Recursion, in turn, contains **Objectifier** and **RedirectInFamily**. A formal ρ-calculus representation is:

Figure 7. Object Recursion, annotated to show roles

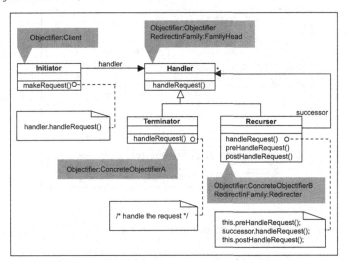

$$\textbf{Objectifier}(Handler, Recurser_i^{i \in 1...m}, Initiator),$$
$$\textbf{Objectifier}(Handler, Terminator_j^{j \in 1...n}, Initiator),$$
$$init.someMethod <_\mu obj.handleRequest,$$
$$init : Initiator,$$
$$obj : Handler,$$
$$\textbf{RedirectInFamily}(Recurser, Handler, handleRequest),$$
$$\underline{!\textbf{RedirectInFamily}(Terminator, Handler, handleRequest)}$$
$$\textbf{ObjectRecursion}(obj, Recurser_i^{i \in 1...m}, Terminator_j^{j \in 1...n}, init) \qquad (29)$$

Decorator

We can now produce a pattern directly from the Gang of Four text, the Decorator pattern (Gamma et al., 1995, p. 175). It is simple enough to be defined from the ground up, illustrating our technique of using fully formal methods entrenched in ρ-calculus coupled with the EDP catalog to create rich and conceptually true formal descriptions of useful Design patterns. Decorator is complex enough, however, to present a challenge by adding a bit of behavioral elegance to a primarily structural pattern.

Figure 8 is the standard class diagram for **Decorator**. Figure 9 shows the same diagram, annotated with our *Pattern Instance Notation* (PIN) to show how the single **ObjectRecursion** and the two **ExtendMethod** patterns interact. PIN was developed to provide clarity when multiple instances of a single pattern occur in a system. The pattern:role notation used in previous diagrams is sufficient for very simple illustrations, but becomes difficult to trace when patterns begin relating to each other.

Again, we provide a formal definition, where the keyword any indicates that any object of **any** class may take this role, as long as it conforms to the definition of **ObjectRecursion**.:

Figure 8. Decorator class structure

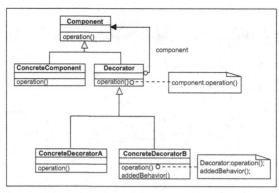

Figure 9. Decorator definition pattern instance diagram

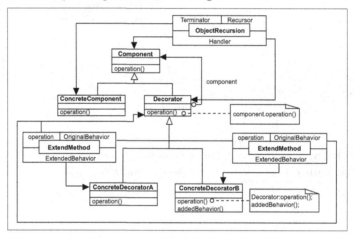

The above creates a formally sound definition of a description of how to solve a problem of software architecture design, but it does so from first principles of the relationships between fundamental elements of programming. This definition is now subject to formal analysis, discovery, and metrics, and, following these examples of pattern composition, can be used as a building block for larger, more-intricate patterns that are *incrementally comprehensible.* At the same time, this approach retains the flexibility of implementation, as demonstrated with the **RedirectInFamily** isotope, that patterns demand. Also, the conceptual semantics of the pattern remain intact, by making precise choices at each stage of the composition.

SPQR and KillerWidget

The approach described above works in the reverse as well, allowing any number of implementations, expressed in source code, UML diagrams, or other notations, to be mapped to a particular pattern definition. This mapping process results in a representation in ρ-calculus of an existing or proposed design that is formally defined, and therefore formally manipulable. The pattern/object markup language XML schema, or POML (Smith, 2004), provides a common format for expressing ρ-calculus, and therefore a concrete expression of the requirements of intent, in a more easily parsed and read form. Any object-oriented language or design document, expressible in ρ-calculus can be expressed in POML, and, therefore, can be analyzed by SPQR. The automated analysis involves feeding the POML-expressed design, the formal ρ-calculus inference rules, and POML-defined patterns into an inference engine for searching. The engine used by SPQR at this time is the automated theorem prover OTTER (McCune, 1990).

SPQR currently implements a front end, gcctree2poml, that produces POML representations of existing C++ code bases. POML is also used to report the instances of found patterns in the code. Since POML is both the input and output format of SPQR, there is a unique opportunity to train SPQR using canonical examples of concepts. Any appropriate source material that can be converted to POML will do, whether it is source code, UML diagrams, or higher-level architectural designs. The training mode of SPQR initiates an exhaustive search of all known conceptual patterns within the input. An engineer then manually inspects the output and the salient concepts are saved into a new POML definition for that concept. SPQR can then search for that new concept in any input. This training approach was used to bootstrap SPQR for the ability to search for the Gang of Four Design patterns (Gamma et al., 1995), among others. There is no reason to assume that it must stop at this level of abstraction, and we are investigating training SPQR to identify a number of other higher-level patterns from the literature.

The KillerWidget example is a real-world design issue that illustrates how automated analysis can capture emergent designs, and provide an opportunity for engineers to make them *intentional*, not accidental, behavior. It involves three libraries, as shown in Figure 10, each of which contains only a portion of a Decorator pattern. In the corporate environment in which this example was first seen, the Decorator behavior did not become apparent until all three libraries were used in a single application. It is an excellent example of how non-local design features can become intertwined in known, but unexpected, ways to form new design cues.

Figure 10. KillerWidget as UML

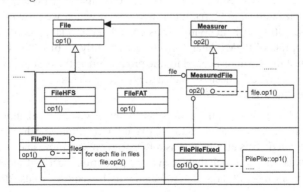

Using SPQR as the example of implementation lets us follow the analysis method with concrete examples at each stage, and show precisely how elements from the source code map to the elements of ρ-calculus, how those features combine into the required basic concepts of programming intent (as defined in the EDPs), and how those basic concepts can be quickly connected into the more-familiar Design patterns literature. In this manner, we can extract the intent of the original designer or programmer at various levels of abstraction, as desired, and understand the system more thoroughly.

In many ways, KillerWidget has been the driving example for SPQR. Based on a real-world example that one of us encountered in industry in 1996, it inspired the research that led to SPQR. Three libraries were developed and maintained by three separate developer groups within a corporation. Each was well-documented, and the behavior was well understood by each group, but a fourth group that used all three libraries reported an unexpected behavior. Though a welcome and useful functionality, the documentation for the three libraries did not describe it.

One of the authors was in one of the library development groups. Members of the other two groups and the author were intrigued by this behavior that seemed to have developed on its own, quite accidentally, and we decided to research and document the situation. We expected to spend a few hours on it, because we were quite familiar with the system in general, and our libraries in particular.

Instead, we spent approximately 120 man-hours on the problem over the course of a few weeks. Eventually, we were able to deduce that the unique and unexpected behavior arose from an instance of a Decorator Design pattern that formed only when all three libraries were brought together. Components of the pattern were scattered among the libraries, and, to make things more complex, the pattern did not exactly conform to the structure given in the defining text. It was indeed a Decorator, but one that had a method-calling chain through only vaguely related objects; in other words, an isotope. Ultimately, the uncovered functionality was refactored into an explicit intent in the design, officially documented, and supported.

We will use KillerWidget as an example of the production of an SPQR run, from beginning to end. It is large enough to be interesting, while small enough to be manually verified.

The code here is derived from the original notes on the project and is not the original source, as we no longer have access to it. We have distilled it down to the basics required to illustrate the isotopic principle. A UML diagram for the design is given in Figure 10, and the code is shown in Figure 11.

Analyzing the example using SPQR converts the code first to a POML representation, then, using the poml2ottertool, to OTTER input, portions of which we provide in Figure 12. The POML representation of KillerWidget was considered too large for this text, but we provide a short example of POML later. Shown here are only 35 of 239 lines of the OTTER file, but these are just the portions needed for the production of the proof. The comments in the figure are autogenerated by gcctree2poml and poml2otter. This aids in debugging and in providing examples such as this.

OTTER is given the above file as input, as well as the entire body of ρ-calculus's definitions, reduction rules, and transitivity sets. Additionally, an OTTER input for the pattern we wish to search for is provided. This also begins as a POML representation, and is automatically generated. SPQR was designed such that the average practitioner using it should never need to know the inner workings of OTTER. They should only be required to use the language of

Figure 11. C++ code for KillerWidget

```
// Component
class File {
        public:
        virtual void op1()=0;
        virtual void op2()=0;
};


// ConcreteComponent
class FileFAT : public File {
        public:
        void op1() {};
        void op2() {};
};


// Helper (Sits between Decorator and Component)
class MeasuredFile {//: public File {
        public:
        File* file;
        MeasuredFile() { file = new FileFAT(); };
        // void op1() { file->op1(); };
        void op2() { file->op1(); };
};


// Decorator
class FilePile : public File {
        public:
        MeasuredFile* mfile;
        FilePile() { mfile = new MeasuredFile(); };
        void op1() { mfile->op2(); };
        void op2() {};
};


// ConcreteDecorator
class FilePileFixed : public FilePile {
public:
        void op1() { FilePile::op1(); fixTheProblem(); };
        void op2() {};
        void fixTheProblem() {};
};
```

continued on following page

Figure 11. continued

```
// Initiator
int
main(int, char**) {
            File* fpf = new FilePileFixed();
            fpf->op1();
};
```

their choice, and be perhaps familiar with POML. For those interested in a more thorough description of the practical workings of the current SPQR system, we refer you to Smith (2005) for the complete treatise, as it is far too large for the scope of this chapter.

OTTER produces the proof in Figure 13 as part of its output. Here we see that this instance of **Decorator** was created from the instances of **ExtendMethod** and **ObjectRecursion** shown as clauses #41 and #47, respectively. Similar proofs exist for the production of those clauses, although we do not include them here. By parsing these proofs, a hierarchy of pattern instances can be built to facilitate reporting of results to an engineer. At this time, SPQR does not perform this massaging of output, but the opportunity remains.

Figure 12. Portions of KillerWidget as OTTER input

```
%----- Class File file=KillerWidget.cpp line=2
            %----- Method File dot op1 file=KillerWidget.cpp line=4 AbstractInterface( File, op1 ).
            %----- Method File dot op2 file=KillerWidget.cpp line=5
AbstractInterface( File, op2 ).
%----- Class FileFAT file=KillerWidget.cpp line=9
FileFAT inh File.
%----- Class MeasuredFile file=KillerWidget.cpp line=16
            %----- Method MeasuredFile dot op2 file=KillerWidget.cpp line=21
MeasuredFile defines op2.
( MeasuredFile dot op2 ) mu
                            ( MeasuredFile dot op2 dot this dot file dot op1 ).
            %----- Field MeasuredFile dot file file=KillerWidget.cpp line=18
MeasuredFile dot file : File.
%----- Class FilePile file=KillerWidget.cpp line=25
FilePile inh File.
            %----- Method FilePile dot op1 file=KillerWidget.cpp line=29
FilePile defines op1.
( FilePile dot op1 ) mu ( FilePile dot op1 dot this dot mfile dot op2 ).
```

continued on following page

Figure 12. continued

```
            %----- Field FilePile dot mfile file=KillerWidget.cpp line=27
FilePile dot mfile : MeasuredFile.
%----- Class FilePileFixed file=KillerWidget.cpp line=35
FilePileFixed inh FilePile.
directcallfrom_to_as( FilePileFixed, FilePile dot op1, FilePile_op1 ).
            %----- Method FilePileFixed dot op1 file=KillerWidget.cpp line=37
FilePileFixed defines op1.
( FilePileFixed dot op1 ) mu
                        ( FilePileFixed dot op1 dot this dot FilePile_op1 ).
( FilePileFixed dot op1 ) mu
                        ( FilePileFixed dot op1 dot this dot fixTheProblem ).
%----- Object __GLOBAL__ file=__internal__ line=0
            %----- Method __GLOBAL__ dot main file=KillerWidget.cpp line=45
__GLOBAL__ defines main.
            %----- Field __GLOBAL__ dot main dot fpf file=KillerWidget.cpp line=46
__GLOBAL__ dot main dot fpf : File.
__GLOBAL__ dot main iscontextfor updatebycall( __GLOBAL__ dot main dot fpf,
                        FilePileFixed__ClassObj dot __comp_ctor_overload_3 ).
( __GLOBAL__ dot main ) mu ( __GLOBAL__ dot main dot fpf dot op1 ).
CreateObject( __GLOBAL__ dot main, FilePileFixed,
                        __GLOBAL__ dot main dot main_anonvar_0 ).
```

Figure 13. Otter output for Decorator instance in KillerWidget

```
---------------- PROOF ----------------
41 []
ExtendMethod(FilePile,FilePileFixed,op1).
47 []
ObjectRecursion(File,FilePile,FilePileFixed,__GLOBAL__).
57 []
-ObjectRecursion(x30,x31,x32,x33) |
-ExtendMethod(x31,x34,x35) | Decorator(x30,x31,x32,x34,x35). 58 []
-Decorator(
        xComponent,
        xDecoratorBase,
        xConcreteComponent,
        xConcreteDecorator,
        xoperation
).
```

continued on following page

Figure 13. continued

```
1434 [hyper,57,47,41,eval]
Decorator(File,FilePile,FilePileFixed,FilePileFixed,op1).
1435 [binary,1434.1,58.1]

.

------------ end of proof -------------
```

Figure 14. Recovered Decorator in KillerWidget as POML

```
<poml:pattern>
        <poml:name>Decorator</poml:name>
        <poml:role>
                <poml:name>Component</poml:name>
                <poml:fulfilledBy>File</poml:fulfilledBy>
        </poml:role>
        <poml:role>
                <poml:name>Decorator</poml:name>
                <poml:fulfilledBy>FilePile</poml:fulfilledBy>
        </poml:role>
        <poml:role>
                <poml:name>ConcreteComponent</poml:name>
                <poml:fulfilledBy>FileFAT</poml:fulfilledBy>
        </poml:role>
        <poml:role>
                <poml:name>ConcreteDecorator</poml:name>
                <poml:fulfilledBy>FilePileFixed</poml:fulfilledBy>
        </poml:role>
        <poml:role>
                <poml:name>operation</poml:name>
                <poml:fulfilledBy>op1</poml:fulfilledBy>
        </poml:role>
</poml:pattern>
```

Figure 15. Recovered Decorator pattern in KillerWidget as UML

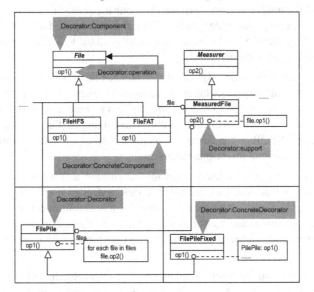

The POML output for the discovered pattern is shown in Figure 14, and the UML diagram in Figure 15 shows the mapping of the **Decorator** instance with the original design. Note that the intermediate class has been tagged as **Decorator : support**. This is a cue to developers that there are additional constructs they need to comprehend to fully capture the expected intent of the pattern in this particular system. As a comparison to the original 120 manhours, the current implementation of SPQR, running on a medium-performance laptop, was able to uncover the above instance of **Decorator** in under 20 seconds, without manual assistance or intervention.

An interesting incident occurred when initially performing this analysis. After both a substantial upgrade to SPQR and a simultaneous rewriting of KillerWidget to C++ from the hand-rolled OTTER input used in previous publications, the example stopped passing the test. In our haste, we assumed that SPQR was to blame, and invested a great deal of time verifying the tools and definitions of the EDPs, the mapping of ρ-calculus to OTTER, and every aspect of the tool chain. Instead, there was a simple typographical error in the C++ code for KillerWidget. SPQR was correct, the expected patterns were *not* in the code, despite appearing to exist on quick review. Once we thought to check the output from OTTER more closely, it became obvious where the bug was. Once fixed, the test ran successfully. This illustrates the utility of SPQR as a design validation tool for existing code.

Conclusion

In this chapter we have presented a novel view on software production and design, using and expanding on a core element of Design patterns, intent. The need for the communication of intent in design led to the production of the patterns literature, and this need has not disappeared. Instead, it is increasingly moving to the fore of software engineering, and we believe that it should be made even more explicit. Through the ability to describe the intention of each relationship in a system, a designer or programmer can produce a more-thorough conceptual map of the design, and provide a clearer guiding vision in implementation, validation, and refactoring considerations.

Our EDPs provide a conceptual description of the intent of the most fundamental relationships of programming, and the ρ-calculus creates a formal framework for the composition of those relationships into higher-level Design patterns. This formalism allows for automated analysis and manipulation of those concepts, without destroying the flexibility that has made patterns so successful. SPQR is our current implementation of one analysis approach, but there are many other potential directions for research.

We hope that the reader will take away from this discussion a new appreciation for the complexities of software design, and also retain a new understanding of the simplicity of the underlying concepts. Software, as with any other form of communication, requires clarity of purpose and execution, and comprehending the role of intent in the field of Design patterns is a light we can each bring to illuminate the unexplored crevasses of the systems we all produce.

The work described here has been supported in whole or in part by the U.S. Environmental Protection Agency's Science to Achieve Results (STAR) program, grant #R-82795901. Although the research described here has been funded by the EPA, it has not been subjected to any EPA review and therefore does not necessarily reflect the views of the agency, and no official endorsement should be inferred.

References

Abadi, M., & Cardelli, L. (1996). *A theory of objects*. New York: Springer-Verlag.

Agesen, O., Bak, L., Chambers, C., Chang, B.-W., Hölze, U., Maloney, J., et al. (1993). *The self 3.0 programmer's reference manual*. Sun Microsystems.

Alexander, C.W. (1964). *Notes on the synthesis of form (15th printing, 1999)*. Oxford University Press.

Basili, V.R., Briand, L.C., & Melo, W.L. (1996). A validation of object-oriented design metrics as quality indicators. *IEEE Transactions on Software Engineering, 22*(10), 751-761.

Beck, K. (1997). *Smalltalk best practice patterns*. Prentice Hall.

Buschmann, F., Meunier, R., Rohnert, H., Sommerlad, P., & Stal, M. (1996). *Pattern-oriented system architecture: A system of patterns* (vol. 1). Wiley series in software Design patterns. John Wiley & Sons.

Chidamber, S.R., & Kemerer, C.F. (1994). A metrics suite for object oriented design. *IEEE Transactions on Software Engineering, 20*(6), 476-493.

Davidson, J.D., & Inc., A.C. (2002). *Learning cocoa with objective-C* (2nd ed.). O'Reilly & Associates.

Fowler, M. (1999). *Refactoring: Improving the design of existing code.* Addison-Wesley.

Gamma, E., Helm, R., Johnson, R., & Vlissides, J. (1995). *Design patterns.* Addison-Wesley.

McCune, W. (1990). Otter 2.0 (theorem prover). In M.E. Stickel (Ed.), In *Proceedings of the 10th International Conference on Automated Deduction* (pp. 663-664).

Monson-Haefel, R., Burke, B., & Labourey, S. (2004). *Enterprise JavaBeans* (4th ed.). O'Reilly & Associates.

Smith, J.McC. (2004). *Pattern/Object markup language (POML): A simple XML schema for object oriented code description* (Tech. Rep. No. TR04-010). University of North Carolina at Chapel Hill.

Smith, J.McC. (2005). SPQR: *Formal foundations and practical support for the automated detection of Design patterns from source code.* Doctoral thesis, University of North Carolina at Chapel Hill.

Smith, J.McC., & Stotts, D. (2002). Elemental Design patterns: A formal semantics for composition of OO software architecture. In *Proceedings of the 27th Annual IEEE/NASA Software Engineering Workshop* (pp. 183-190).

Smith, J.McC., & Stotts, D. (2003). SPQR: Flexible automated Design pattern extraction from source code. In *Proceedings of the 18th IEEE International Conference on Automated Software Engineering* (pp. 215-224).

Stansifer, R. (1995). *The study of programming languages.* Prentice Hall.

Vlissides, J.M. (1998). *Notation, notation, notation. C++ Report* (pp. 48-51).

Woolf, B. (1998). *The object recursion pattern.* In N. Harrison, B. Foote, & H. Rohnert (Eds.), Pattern languages of program design 4. Addison-Wesley.

Zimmer, W. (1995). *Relationships between Design patterns.* In J.O. Coplien & D.C. Schmidt (Eds.), Pattern languages of program design (pp. 345-364). Addison-Wesley.

Chapter VIII

Formalising Design Patterns as Model Transformations

Kevin Lano, King's College, UK

Abstract

This chapter describes techniques for the verification of refactorings or transformations of UML models which introduce Design patterns. The techniques use a semantics of object-oriented systems defined by the object calculus (Fiadeiro & Maibaum, 1991; Lano, 1998), and the pattern transformations are proved to be refinements using this semantics.

Introduction

Design patterns are characteristic structures of classes or objects which can be reused to achieve particular design goals in an elegant manner. An example is the "State" Design pattern, which replaces local attributes of a class that record its state (in the sense of a finite state machine) by an object which provides polymorphic functionality in place of conditionals depending upon the state.

An application of a pattern should be a functionally-correct refinement step, that is, all the required properties of the original model should still remain valid in the restructured model. We will consider Design patterns applied to models in UML (OMG, 2005), with detailed behaviour of classes defined using VDM++ syntax (Durr & Dusink, 1993).

The semantics of object-oriented systems has been given in a logical axiomatic framework termed the Object Calculus (Fiadeiro & Maibaum, 1994). The chapter (Lano, 1998) gives a semantics for the UML and VDM++ notation which we use here. The application of a Design pattern will be shown to yield a theory interpretation of the semantics of the original model into the semantics of the new model, so ensuring that the functional properties of the original model still remain true in the new model.

Model specialisation using such theory interpretation is distinct from instantiation of a metamodel to a model. Metamodel instantiation is more powerful and flexible than model specialisation, in general. For example, in the case of many Design patterns, such as Template Method, the pattern is based on the existence of certain methods without any restriction on the input and output parameters of these methods. In a generic model we must be specific about such parameters. This means that the pattern is described by an unbounded collection of generic models instead of a single metamodel.

However, the power of metamodelling also has a cost, which is the requirement for developers to have more advanced UML skills and detailed knowledge of the UML metamodel. Therefore we prefer an approach using configurable generic models to define model transformations, domain models, and patterns.

The object calculus is a more appropriate formalism for reasoning about patterns than OCL, because the object calculus deals directly with actions and operations as first-class elements, and (in our extension) to timing properties and properties of system states at general time points.

The introduction of a Design pattern is one example of model transformation. Other kinds of transformation are quality improvement transformations (e.g., factoring out common elements of a number of classes into a superclass) and refinement to a platform specific model (e.g., replacing many-one associations by foreign keys). The transformation verification approach described here can also be applied to these other forms of transformations.

Section 1 introduces the object calculus, and the syntax of VDM++, which we will use to illustrate Design patterns. Section 4 addresses creational patterns, Section 5 addresses structural patterns, and Section 6 addresses Behavioral patterns. In each section we consider some typical patterns from Gamma, Helm, Johnson, and Vlissides (1994) and other sources.

The Object Calculus

An object calculus theory consists of a collection of type and constant symbols, attribute symbols (denoting time-varying data), action symbols (denoting atomic operations), and a set of axioms describing the types of the attributes and the effects, permission constraints, and other dynamic properties of the actions. The axioms are specified using linear temporal logic operators: **X** (in the next state), **P** (in the previous state), **U** (strong until), **S** (strong since), **G** (always in the future), and **F** (sometime in the future). There is assumed to be a first moment. The predicate BEG is true exactly at this time point.

X and **P** are also expression constructors. If e is an expression, **X**e denotes the value of e in the next time interval, while **P**e denotes the value of e in the previous time interval.

The version used here is that defined in Lano (1998) in order to give a semantics to VDM++. In this version actions *act* are potentially durative and overlapping, with associated times ->(*act*,i), $\wedge$(*act*,i), and $\vee$(*act*,i) denoting respectively the times at which the *i*-th invocation of *act* is requested, activates, and terminates (where i : NAT1, the positive natural numbers).

Modal operators "holds at a time" and "value at a time" are added: $P@t$ asserts that P holds at time t, while $e@t$ is the value of e at time t.

In order to give a semantics to a class C, in, for example, UML (OMG, 2005), Java or VDM++, we define a theory Th(C) which has a type symbol C representing all possible instances of C, attribute symbol C representing all the existing objects of C, and creation action *new_C(c: C)* and deletion action *kill_C(c: C)*, which respectively add and remove an object c from this set.

Each attribute *att* of C is formally represented by an attribute *att(c: C)* of Th(C) (applications of this attribute are written as *c.att* for conformance with standard OO notation) and each operation *act(x: X)* is represented by an action symbol *act(c: C, x: X)*, with invocations written as *c!act(x)*. Output parameters and local variables of methods are also represented as attribute symbols.

An additional attribute *now* is included to represent the current global time.

We can define the effect of methods by means of the "calling" operator ‹ between actions:

act1 ‹ act2 <=>

   forall i: NAT1 •

   exists j: NAT1 • $\wedge$(act2,j) = $\wedge$(act1,i) & $\vee$(act2,j) = $\vee$(act1,i)

In other words, every invocation interval of act1 is also one of act2. This generalises the Object Calculus formula act1 => act2.

Composite actions are defined to represent specification statements and executable code:

Prepost{G} {P} names an action *act* with the following properties:

   forall i: NAT1 • G@$\wedge$(act,i) => P[att@$\wedge$(act,i)/att@pre]@$\vee$(act,i)

In other words, if G is true at each activation time of act, P, with each prestate attribute att@ pre interpreted as the value att@/\(act,i) of att at initiation of act, holds at the corresponding termination time. This action corresponds to pre-post specifications of operations in OCL.

A frame axiom, termed the *locality* assumption, asserts that attributes of an object a of class C can only be changed over intervals in which at least one of the operations of a executes. Likewise, C can only change as a result of new_C or kill_C invocations.

Assignment t_1 := t_2 can be defined as the action Prepost{true}{t_1 = t_2@pre} where t_1 is an attribute symbol. Similarly, sequential composition ";" and parallel composition "||" of actions can be expressed as derived combinators.

The modal action logic (Ryan, Fiadeiro, & Maibaum, 1991) operator [act]*P* "act establishes *P*" is defined as:

[act]P <=>
 forall i: NAT1 • P[att@/\(act,i)/att@pre]@\/(act,i),

where each pre-state attribute att@pre is replaced by the value att@/\(act,i) of att at initiation of act.

The definition of ; yields the usual axiom that:

[act1;act2]P <=> [act1][act2]P.

Conditionals have the expected properties:

E => (if E then S_1 else S_2 ‹ S_1)
not(E) => (if E then S_1 else S_2 ‹ S_2)

Similarly, loops can be defined recursively. Some important properties of ‹ which will be used in the chapter are that it is transitive:

(act1 ‹ act2) & (act2 ‹ act3) => (act1 ‹ act3),

and that constructs such as ; and if-then-else are monotonic with respect to it:

 (act1 ‹ act2) & (act3 ‹ act4) => (act1; act3 ‹ act2; act4),

and:

(act1 ‹ act2) & (act3 ‹ act4) =>

   if E then act1 else act3 ‹ if E then act2 else act4

Theories representing subsystems can be composed from the theories of the classes in these subsystems by theory union and renaming. Thus, we can compare the functionality of a system (with no distinguished "main" class) with that of another system, via their theories rather than forcing all comparisons to be made between particular classes. This is useful in the case of Design patterns, which usually concern sets of classes.

Interpretations and Refinement

The most important relationship between theories is that of theory interpretation. There is a theory interpretation morphism sigma from a theory Th(C) to a theory Th(D) if every theorem P of Th(C) is provable, under the interpretation sigma, in Th(D):

Th(C) |- P => Th(D) |- sigma(P),

where sigma interprets the symbols of Th(C) as suitable combinations of symbols of Th(D). Actions are interpreted by actions (basic or composed), and attributes by terms. For example, a single action act of Th(C) could be interpreted by a sequential combination of actions of Th(D). Sigma is lifted to a map on formulae in the usual manner.

A system D *refines* a system C if there is a theory interpretation from the theory Th(C) of C to the theory Th(D) of D. In the object calculus such interpretations are usually split into two parts (Figure 1), consisting of a conservative extension and a theory interpretation. The extension S typically introduces new symbols which are defined by axioms of S as being equal to some combination of symbols of Th(D). These symbols then directly interpret the symbols of Th(C). In this chapter S and Th(D) are combined.

Figure 1. Refinement in object calculus

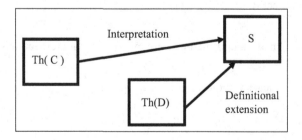

VDM++ Specifications

A VDM++ specification consists of a set of class definitions, which are close in their main elements to UML classes, but with specific notations for structural and behavioural features. VDM++ class definitions have the form:

```
class C
types T = TDef
values
 const: T = val
functions
 f: A -> B
 f(a) == Defn_f
instance variables
 v: T;
inv objectstate == Inv_C;
init objectstate == Init_C
methods
 m(x: X) value y: Y
  pre Pre(x,v) == Defn_C;
 ...
end C
```

The types, values, and functions components define types, constants, and functions as in conventional VDM (although class reference sets @D for classes D can be used as types in these items. Such classes D are termed *suppliers* to C, as are instances of these classes. C is then a *client* of D). The instance variables component defines the attributes of the class, and the inv defines an invariant over a list of these variables. objectstate is used to include all the attributes. The init component defines a set of initial states in which an object of the class may be at object creation. Object creation is achieved via an invocation of the operation C!new, which returns a reference to a new object of type C as its result. In the semantics this operation is interpreted as the action *new_C(c)* for the created object c reference.

The operations of C are listed in the methods clause. The list of method names of C, including inherited methods, is referred to as methods(C). The subset of methods(C) which may be used by external clients of C is extmethods(C), while the subset that can be only used internally is intmethods(C). The union of extmethods(C) and intmethods(C) is methods(C).

Methods can be defined in an abstract declarative way, using specification statements, or by using a hybrid of specification statements, method calls, and procedural code. They therefore span all levels of abstraction between UML-style pre/post specifications of operations, and Java-like executable code. Input parameters are indicated within the brackets of the method header, and result parameters after a value keyword. Preconditions of a method are given in the pre clause.

Other clauses of a class definition control how C inherits from other classes. The optional is subclass of clause in the class header lists classes which are being extended by the present class—that is, all their methods become exportable facilities of C.

If we have a method definition in class C of the form:

m(x: X) value y: Y
  pre Pre_m == Code_m;

then the action a!m(e) that interprets m for object a of C has the property:

a.Pre_m[e/x] & a : $\underline{C}$ & e : X   =>   a!m(e) ‹ a.Code_m[e/x]

where each attribute att of C occurring in Pre_m is renamed to a.att in a.Pre_m and similarly for Code_m. v := D!new is interpreted as new_D(a.v), self!n(f) as a!n(a.f), and so forth.

The initialisation of a class C can be regarded as an operation init_C, which is called automatically when an object c is created by the action new_C:

new_C(c) ‹ c!init_C

new_C itself has the properties:

new_C(c) => c /: $\underline{C}$

and

[new_C(c)]($\underline{C}$ = $\underline{C}$@pre union { c })

Other axioms derived from a class description are given in Lano (1998).

In the following sections, we generally characterise patterns as a transformation from a "before" system consisting of a set of classes (often a single unstructured class) into an "after" system consisting of a collection of classes organised by the pattern. We then prove that the theory of the "after" system is an extension, via a suitable interpretation, of the theory of the "before" system. Usually we will only prove interpretation for selected axioms for the effect of actions, as many of the other axioms (e.g., axioms that give the typing of attributes or actions) are trivially preserved.

Creational Patterns

Creational patterns aim to make the way objects and systems are instantiated and constructed more general and flexible. For example, "hard-coded" object creation operations are replaced with more logical and declarative operations in the following pattern. In the following examples we will use the names of classes given in Gamma et al. (1994).

Abstract Factory

This pattern allows a decrease in the level of coupling between classes in a system by enabling a client class to create objects of a general kind without needing to know what particular implementation subtype they belong to. The before and after structures of a system to which this pattern has been applied are given in Figure 2. The notation of Gamma et al. (1994) has been used. A dashed arrow indicates a creation dependency, while a solid arrow indicates clientship.

In the initial description of a system, we could have the following form of code:

```
class Client
instance variables
 productA: @AbstractProductA;
 productB: @AbstractProductB;
 implementation_kind: <type1> | <type2>
methods
 setup() ==
  if implementation_kind = <type1>
  then
  (productA := ProductA1!new;
  productB := ProductB1!new)
  else
  (productA := ProductA2!new;
  productB := ProductB2!new)
end Client
```

The disadvantage of the first approach is the necessity for a case statement and knowledge in Client of the names of the implementation classes ProductA1, ProductA2, and so forth.

The theory Th(Client) of Client is the union (formally, the *colimit*) of the theories of AbstractProductA, AbstractProductB and of their subtypes, together with the axioms and symbols derived from the attributes and methods of Client itself.

Figure 2. Application of abstract factory pattern

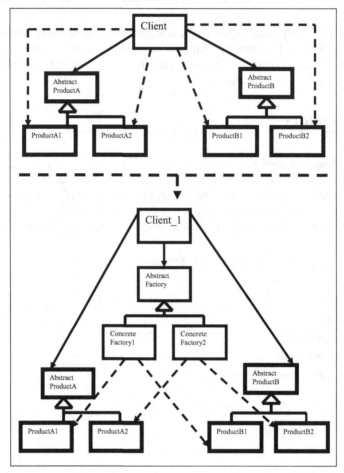

In the revised version, we can factor out the implementation dependence into the factory objects:

```
class Client_1
instance variables
 factory: @AbstractFactory;
 productA: @AbstractProductA;
 productB: @AbstractProductB
methods
 settup() ==
    (productA := factory!CreateProductA();
```

```
   productB := factory!CreateProductB())
end Client_1
```

An initialisation action to set implementation_kind in Client will become an action creating the factory object in Client_1. The concrete subtypes of Factory are:

```
class ConcreteFactory1
 is subclass of Factory
methods
 CreateProductA() value prod: @ProductA1 ==
   (prod := ProductA1!new;
   return prod);

 CreateProductB() value prod: @ProductB1 ==
   (prod := ProductB1!new;
   return prod)
end ConcreteFactory1
```

Similarly for ConcreteFactory2. The implementation_kind attribute has been replaced by polymorphic behaviour depending upon which subclass ConcreteFactory1 or ConcreteFactory2 of AbstractFactory the factory object belongs to.

The interpretation sigma of the theory of Client into the theory of Client_1 is therefore as shown in Table 1. Symbols of ProductA1, and so forth, are unchanged in the translation.

In the theory of Client we have the axiom:

```
oo : Client =>
 oo!settup ‹
   if oo.implementation_kind = <type1>
   then
    (new_ProductA1(oo.productA);
    new_ProductB1(oo.productB))
   else
    (new_ProductA2(oo.productA);
    new_ProductB2(oo.productB))
```

There is a similar axiom for settup in the theory of Client_1:

```
oo : Client_1 =>
 oo!settup ‹
```

Table 1. Interpretation of Client into Client_1

Symbol of Client	Term of Client_1
@Client	@Client_1
Client new_Client	Client_1 new_Client_1
kill_Client	kill_Client_1
obj.implementation_kind	if obj.factory : ConcreteFactory1 then <type1> else <type2>

(oo.productA := factory!CreateProductA;

oo.productB := factory!CreateProductB)

The interpretation of the Client axiom under sigma is:

oo : Client_1 =>
  oo!setup ‹
    if oo.factory : ConcreteFactory1
    then
    (new_ProductA1(oo.productA);
    new_ProductB1(oo.productB))
    else
    (new_ProductA2(oo.productA);
    new_ProductB2(oo.productB))

This must be valid in the theory of System_1. It is proved by using the definition of CreateProductA and CreateProductB in the respective ConcreteFactory classes. For example, using the definition of CreateProductA we have:

obj : ConcreteFactory1 =>
  res := obj!CreateProductA ‹ new_ProductA1(res)

Using oo.factory for obj and oo.productA for res, and the similar axiom for CreateProductB in the theory of ConcreteFactory1, we then have from the Client_1 axiom of setup:

oo : Client_1 & oo.factory : ConcreteFactory1 =>
  oo!setup ‹
    (new_ProductA1(oo.productA);
    new_ProductB1(oo.productB))

The other case of the interpretation of the axiom of settup in Client follows by consideration of oo.factory : ConcreteFactory2.

The application and justification of the pattern shown above generalises directly in the case that there are more than two types of factory or two types of product. An important correctness property which must be true for any pattern which introduces an intermediate class such as Factory to implement attributes of a client class, is that objects of this intermediate class should not be shared between distinct clients.

For example, if another object had access to the factory of a Client object obj, then it could delete or change the class of factory during the execution of obj!settup, so invalidating the above reasoning.

The locality axiom of a class C requires that if there is an interval $[t\_1, t\_2]$ over which no method of oo: C executes, then all the attributes oo.att of oo should have the same value at t_2 as at t_1: oo.att@t_1 = oo.att@t_2.

If, however, some intermediate object obj is used to implement these attributes: oo.att being implemented by oo.obj.att1, say, then methods could execute on oo.obj in the interval $[t\_1, t\_2]$ without any action of oo executing because some distinct client oo2 /= oo has oo2.obj = oo.obj and calls methods of oo.obj in this interval. Thus, it would be possible for oo.obj. att1 to change in value over such intervals.

Structural Design Patterns

Structural patterns address ways of combining classes via inheritance or class composition to form larger structures useful in design. Before application of the pattern, the functionality of the initial version of the system is typically carried out via a direct but inflexible combination of objects. The new version introduces more objects and indirection, but provides a more adaptable and reusable architecture.

Proof of correctness of these patterns is usually based on the observation that ‹ is transitive. If we implement a method m() == Def by defining an intermediate method n() == Def and redefining m to call n, then the resulting functional semantics is unchanged.

Adapter Pattern

In this pattern the interface of an existing class is adapted for use in a new system by placing an intermediate object or class between it and the system, which translates requests from the system into a form appropriate to the reused class.

An example of this transformation in VDM++ could look as follows. The original unrefined specification attempts to do the adaption directly within a client:

class Client

instance variables

```
  adaptee: @Adaptee;
methods
 m(x: X) ==
   (C1; adaptee!specific_request(f(x)); C2)
end Client
```

Client_1 instead uses an intermediate object target:

```
class Client_1
instance variables
 target: @Target;
methods
 m(x: X) ==
   (C1; target!request(g(x)); C2)
end Client_1
```

target should be in the following subtype of Target when target!request(g(x)) is executed:

```
class Adapter is subclass of Target
instance variables
 adaptee: @Adaptee;
methods
 request(t: T) ==
   adaptee!specific_request(h(t))
end Adapter
```

where $h(g(x)) = f(x)$ for x: X.

The theory Th(Client) of Client incorporates the theory of Adaptee, and has action symbols obj!m(x: X) with the axiom:

```
obj : Client =>
 obj!m(x) ‹ (obj.C1; (obj.adaptee)!specific_request(f(x)); obj.C2)
```

The theory Th(Client_1) of Client_1 also incorporates the theory of Adaptee, and additionally that of Target and its subclasses including Adapter. It has the local attributes of Client except that adaptee is replaced by target: @Target. It has the same local action symbols as Client, but the axiom for m is replaced by:

Table 2. Interpretation sigma for Adapter pattern

Symbol of Client	Symbol of Client_1
obj.adaptee	obj.target.adaptee
Client	Client_1

obj : <u>Client_1</u> =>

  obj!m(x) ‹ (obj.C1; obj.target!request(g(x))); obj.C2)

where we know that target : <u>Adapter</u> at commencement of m(x):

  forall i: NAT1 • (target : <u>Adapter</u>)@Λ(m(x),i),

and that C1 does not change this property:

  target : <u>Adapter</u> => [C1](target : <u>Adapter</u>)

Part of the sigma map for this interpretation is shown in Table 2. *new* and *kill* actions are also mapped from Client to Client_1. Other symbols are left unchanged by sigma.

The interpretation of the axiom of m in Client is then:

obj : <u>Client_1</u> =>

  obj!m(x) ‹ (obj.C1; (obj.target.adaptee)!specific_request(f(x)); obj.C2)

From the theory of Adapter we know that

  target : <u>Adapter</u> =>

  target!request(t) ‹ (target.adaptee)!specific_request(h(t))

Hence, we can derive the axiom for Client from that of Client_1, by using the transitivity of ‹ and the monotonicity of ; with respect to ‹.

Other cases of the Adapter pattern can be treated in a similar way. The key requirement for correctness is that the intermediate target exists and is in the correct subtype at the point in the client code where the interface call is made.

Facade

The Facade pattern aims at bundling up a group of objects which are used together by client subsystems, via a few high-level operations. It replaces direct interfaces to these objects by a single simplified interface in a "facade" object (Figure 3).

Figure 3. Application of Facade pattern

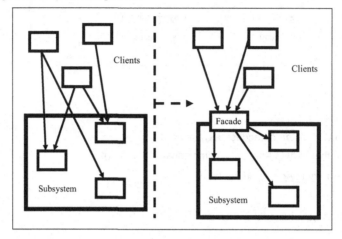

This pattern has a similar structure to the previous pattern. The difference is that the facade object must interpret calls to a number of objects contained within the subsystem for which it serves as an interface.

Thus a direct call obj1!m1(e) in a client of the subsystem could be replaced with a call facade!method1(e) where method1(e) simply calls obj1!m1(e). The interpretation sigma interprets obj1 by facade.obj1, and similarly for each of the contained objects.

A more interesting case is where the external services offered by the facade are some combination of calls on the contained objects. For example, if an external service of the subsystem was usually achieved by two successive calls:

obj1!m1(e1);

obj2!m2(e2)

then it would be sensible to package this sequence up as a single external method of the facade:

m(e: T) ==

(obj1!m1(e1);

obj2!m2(e2))

Proving that an invocation facade!m(e) refines the original combination of calls is direct. The theory of the new version of the system contains the additional Facade class and attributes and actions for it (its attributes include an attribute for each object obj that was originally in the system). For each client, the old version of its functionality has to be rewritten in terms of calls to a supplier facade object. The refinement relation is that each original object obj is now implemented by facade.obj. Again, we must be able to guarantee that the facade object exists at the points where invocations of its methods are made. In addition, the object references obj of the facade must be *constant* after its creation.

Behavioural Patterns

Behavioural patterns are more complex than Structural patterns, as they concern algorithm definition and distribution between objects, and the patterns of communication between objects. The interpretation mappings are thus more complex than in the previous cases, and resemble more the type of data refinement transformations used in languages such as Z and VDM.

The State Pattern

This pattern replaces a variable state, CState, which records the current state of an object (where CState is an enumerated type), and tests on this state, with a new subordinate object which implements the state-dependent behaviour of the object via polymorphism. The aim is to avoid excessive case-considerations within the method definitions of the object, and to factor out state-independent functionality. It is similar in some respects to the Factory pattern, but involves more general behaviour than object creation.

Thus transformation of the Context class from Gamma et al. (1994) could be from:

```
class Context
types
 CState = <state1> | <state2> | ...
instance variables
 state: CState;
 ...
init objectstate ==
 (state := <state1>; ...)
methods
 request() ==
  if state = <state1>
  then Code1
  else Code2
end Context
```

into:

```
class Context_1
instance variables
 stateobj: @State;
  ...
init objectstate ==
 (stateobj := ConcreteState1!new; ...)
methods
 request() ==
   stateobj!handle()
end Context_1
```

The attribute state is replaced by stateobj. Other attributes of Context remain in Context_1. handle has definition Code1 in ConcreteState1 and Code2 in ConcreteState2 and likewise in other subclasses of State representing concrete states. In general any number of states can be defined in the same manner.

Likewise, transitions from one state to another are implemented in Context_1 by object deletion and creation: state := <statei> becomes:

```
 stateobj!kill;
 stateobj := ConcreteStatei!new
in Context_1.
```

state is interpreted by the term:

```
 if stateobj : ConcreteState1
 then <state1>
 else
  if ...
```

Other attributes att in Context are interpreted by att in Context_1 if att is not mentioned in Code1 or Code2. Attributes att used in either of these codes need to be moved into State and are interpreted by stateobj.att.

@Context is interpreted by @Context_1 and Context by Context_1. It is similar for the creation and deletion actions of these classes.

The theory of Context contains attributes and actions for its attributes and methods, and the axiom:

```
 obj : Context => (obj!request ⟨ if ... )
```

The theory of Context_1 has additionally the theory of State and its subclasses, and state is replaced by stateobj: @State, with the axiom for request changed to:

```
obj : Context_1 => (obj!request ‹ (obj.stateobj)!handle)
```

The axiom for request in Context is then interpreted by:

```
obj : Context_1 =>
 (obj!request ‹
  if obj.stateobj : ConcreteState1
  then obj.Code1'
  else obj.Code2')
```

where Code1' is Code1 with each attribute att in its text replaced by stateobj.att, and similarly for Code2'.

But this is implied by the axiom for request in Context_1 because obj.stateobj!handle has the semantics of the above conditional in this class.

Likewise, the combination stateobj!kill; stateobj := ConcreteStatei!new has the following effect:

```
stateobj : ConcreteState0 =>
 [kill_ConcreteState0(stateobj); new_ConcreteStatei(stateobj)](
        ConcreteState0 = ConcreteState0@pre - { stateobj } &
        ConcreteStatei = ConcreteStatei@pre union { stateobj })
```

assuming that ConcreteState0 is different to ConcreteStatei, and that no other creations or deletions for these two subclasses occur during execution of this combination. This effect is the interpretation of the assignment state := <statei> from Context.

Mediator

The Mediator pattern aims to decouple direct interaction between two objects. A typical example is the representation of a one-many association via buried pointers:

```
class A
instance variables
 b: Set(@B)
methods
 ...
end A
```

```
class B
instance variables
 a: @A
methods
 met1() == a!m()
 ...
end B
```

An overall invariant linking the two parts of the association is present (*1*):

forall x: <u>A</u>; y: <u>B</u> • y : x.b <=> x = y.a

This is stated in the theory of this specification, that is, in the union of the two class theories.

The transformation of this system into a version which avoids direct reference between A and B involves the following mediator:

```
class Mediator
instance variables
 r_table: map @B1 to @A1;
 ...
methods
 met1(b: @B1)
  pre b : dom(r_table) ==
      r_table(b)!m()
end Mediator
```

where B1 and A1 are B and A without the embedded pointers or method met1 (or other methods which modify or access the pointers).

Table 3. Interpretation sigma for Mediator

Symbol of A or B	Symbol of Mediator
@A	@A1
@B	@B1
<u>A</u> <u>B</u>	<u>A1</u> <u>B1</u>
y!met1	oo!met1(y)
x.b	{ y | y : <u>B1</u> & x = oo.r_table(y) }
y.a	oo.r_table(y)

The theory of the new system is as for the old system but with the new attributes and axioms for Mediator, and without the attributes a of B and b of A. A specific object oo : <u>Mediator</u> is defined such that oo.r_table contains exactly the pairs in the original relationship, and such that dom(oo.r_table) = <u>B1</u>. The creation of an instance b of B1 must be carried out by this oo via an operation that also sets a link from b to some existing A1 object.

The axiom defining met1 is replaced by the definition of met1(a) in the new system. The definition of sigma is given in Table 3.

y: @B and x: @A in the last three definitions. Creation and deletion actions of A and B are likewise interpreted as the corresponding actions of A1 and B1.

Suitable new actions are needed in Mediator in order to add new pairs or delete pairs from the relation, and to maintain this invariant, in particular, to ensure that every link recorded in r_table is between existing objects.

Given these interpretations of the symbols of A and B, we can show that all the axioms of the original version of the system are still true in the new system. The requirement that the attributes a and b are mutually inverse follows directly from their derivation from r_table: *(1)* is interpreted as:

```
forall x : A1; y : B1 •
  y : { y | y : B1 & x = oo.r_table(y) } <=>
  x = oo.r_table(y)
```

which is clearly true. Similarly, the proof of the interpretation of the axiom for met1 is direct.

Observer

The intent of this pattern is to separate out aspects of an object which are conceptually distinct, and to maintain consistency between the states of the factored objects. A classic example is a system that displays data in several different formats. The presentation of the data (in windows, etc.) should be separate from the storage of that data.

An abstract, unstructured version of such a system could look like:

```
class System
instance variables
 subjectstate: SState;
 observerstate: OState
methods
 Setstate(x: SState) ==
  subjectstate := x;
```

```
Notify() ==
  observerstate := f(subjectstate)
end System
```

Here subjectstate is the basic data of the system, and observerstate represents some presentation of this data. There can be many different observers in general. Usually Setstate will lead immediately to a call of Notify.

A refined version using the Observer pattern would have the form:

```
class Subject
instance variables
 observers: seq of @Observer;
methods
 Setstate(x: SState)
  is subclass responsibility;

 Notify() ==
  for all obs : elems(observers)
  do obs!Update();

 Getstate() value SState
  is subclass responsibility
end Subject
```

where:

```
class ConcreteSubject is subclass of Subject
instance variables
 subjectstate: SState;
methods
 Setstate(x: SState) ==
  subjectstate := x;

 Getstate() value SState ==
  return subjectstate
end ConcreteSubject

class Observer
instance variables
 observerstate: OState;
```

```
subject: @Subject
methods
Update() ==
  (dcl v := subject!Getstate();
  observerstate := f(v))
end Observer
```

There can be a number of subclasses of Observer, each with their own definition of Update. This means that knowledge of how to convert data for presentation is held only in the presentation classes, and Subject does not need to be modified to cope with new presentation formats.

The theory of System thus consists of attribute symbols for subjectstate and observerstate, type symbols for SState and OState, and so forth, and action symbols for Setstate and Notify.

The new version of the system consists of linked Observer and Subject objects:

```
class System_1
instance variables
 subject: @Subject;
 observer: @Observer
invariant
 subject.observers = [observer] & observer.subject = subject
end System_1
```

So, its theory contains that of Subject and Observer, together with the appropriate attribute, type, and action symbols from these theories and subclass theories. We need to additionally assume that subject : ConcreteSubject.

Table 4. Theory interpretation for Observer pattern

Symbol of System	Term of System_1
obj.subjectstate	obj.subject.subjectstate
obj.observerstate	obj.observer.observerstate
obj!Setstate	obj.subject!Setstate
obj!Notify	obj.subject!Notify
@System	@System_1
System	System_1

Sigma for the interpretation of Th(System) into Th(System_1) is shown in Table 4.
In System the axiom for Setstate(x) is:

oo : <u>System</u> => oo!Setstate(x) ‹ oo.subjectstate := x

which is clearly implied under translation by the corresponding axiom of System_1 (inherited
from ConcreteSubject):

obj : <u>ConcreteSubject</u> =>
  obj!Setstate(x) ‹ obj.subjectstate := x
by taking obj = oo.subject where oo : <u>System_1</u>.

This holds, because the interpretation of the System axiom is:

oo : <u>System_1</u> =>
  oo.subject!Setstate(x) ‹ oo.subject.subjectstate := x

Likewise, the axiom for oo!Notify in System:

oo : <u>System</u> =>
  oo!Notify ‹ oo.observerstate := f(oo.subjectstate)
is satisfied by the implementation
for all obs : elems(oo.subject.observers)
do
  obs!Update()

as this reduces to a call: (oo.observer)!Update() because oo.subject.observers = [oo.observer]
from the invariant of System_1.

This calls oo.observer.observerstate := f(oo.subject.subjectstate) by definition of Update
and Getstate.

Classifying Design Patterns

The above patterns can be decomposed into a number of smaller transformations:

- **Annealing:** The introduction of object-valued attributes for nonobject valued attributes. This can be used to (1) protect a system from over-dependence on the form of this attribute; (2) to introduce concurrency; and (3) to share common values.

- **Indirection:** Introducing an intermediary object in place of an original object-valued attribute. This is used, particularly in combination with Generalisation to create greater flexibility in a system.

- **Generalisation:** Extending a class by a superclass to allow alternative specialisations of behaviour or meaning.

- **Replacing conditional behaviour by polymorphism:** Replacing explicit conditionals in a code segment by polymorphic behaviour of supplier objects. Often involves an annealing or generalisation.

Figure 4. Basic Design patterns

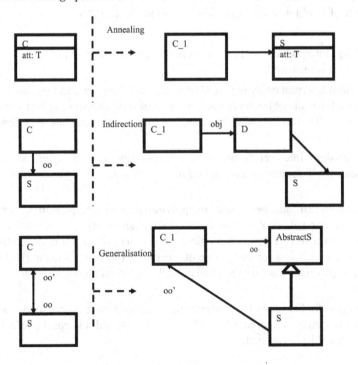

Figure 4 shows the structure of the first three of these basic patterns. In the Generalisation pattern either one of the directions of access between C and S may be missing.

The patterns described in the chapter can now be decomposed into these basic patterns:

- **Factory** is an example of the fourth basic pattern. It is more specialised than *State* because it is assumed that the object whose polymorphic behaviour will be used to replace conditional behaviour will be of a constant type once it is created. In contrast, the State pattern allows this object to change type after creation.

- **Adapter** is a combination of indirection plus generalisation;

- **Facade** is an example of bundling;

- **State** is an example of the fourth basic pattern.

- **Mediator** is an application of generalisation twice (once to the domain class A and once to the range class B).

- **Observer** is an application of annealing to obtain separate Observer and Subject classes from the original system, and then a double application of generalisation, as with the Mediator pattern.

The proof techniques associated with each of the basic patterns are as follows, where oo denotes any object-valued attribute of C which is being transformed, and att any non-object valued attribute of C. obj denotes an introduced intermediate object.

- **Annealing:** Interpret att by obj.att. Ensure that obj exists when reference is made to it, and that it is unshared.

- **Indirection:** Interpret oo by obj.oo. Correctness conditions are as for annealing. The requirement that the obj is unshared can be weakened to requiring that each of the obj.oo is constant throughout its lifetime, if these object references were constant in the original system.

- **Generalisation:** Interpret oo by itself, but correctness proof against the original functionality will require an assumption that oo : $\underline{S}$ where C_1 just expects oo : $\underline{AbstractS}$.

- **Replacing conditional behaviour by polymorphism:** Interpret att by if obj : $\underline{ConcreteS1}$ then value1 else ..., where we have a new subtype ConcreteSi of a new supplier class S of C_1 for each possible value valuei of att. More generally, there may be a new subclass for each value of a certain expression in the attributes of C, rather than just the values of a particular attribute. Correctness conditions are as for annealing.

- **Bundling:** As for Facade pattern, the intermediate object must exist as soon as accesses to the subsystem are required, but can be shared, provided it keeps the references to the enclosed objects constant.

This set of basic proof techniques and interpretations allows us to compose proofs of correctness and refinement steps when we build a pattern out of these basic steps.

Conclusion

This chapter has provided a formal justification for a number of widely-used Design patterns, in a way which connects them with formal refinement and annealing steps in object-oriented specification languages. Other examples of structural transformation and refinement in VDM++ are given in the papers Lano (1995a), Lano and Goldsack (1996), and the book Lano (1995b). We have also applied this approach to proving correct some of the subtyping steps for statecharts defined in Cook and Daniels (1994). The semantic approach shown above applies to all forms of transformation on UML models, not just those based on Design patterns.

Modelling transformations in UML using OCL (Clark, Evans, Girish, Sammut, & Willans, 2003) is a satisfactory approach for coarse-grain transformations on the structure of a model, such as the elimination of multiple inheritance. However, for Design patterns, normally a more fine-grain approach, considering the details of operation definitions, is necessary. We find the use of a language such as VDM++, with the object calculus as a semantic framework, more convenient in this respect. Our work is related to that of Kosiuczenko (2001). However, our concept of theory interpretation is more general than the algebraic interpretations used there, and hence can be applied to verify a wider range of transformations.

Some Design patterns and other model transformations have been implemented in the UML-RSDS tools (Lano, 2005), in particular the Facade, Singleton, and Observer patterns have been incorporated.

References

Clark, T., Evans, A., Girish, M., Sammut, P., & Willans, J. (2003). Modelling language transformations. *L'Objet, 9*(4), 31-51.

Cook, S., & Daniels, J. (1994). *Designing object systems: Object-oriented modelling with Syntropy*. Prentice Hall.

Durr, E., & Dusink, E. (1993). The role of VDM++ in the development of a real-time tracking and tracing system. In J. Woodcock & P. Larsen (Eds.), *FME '93* (LNCS). Springer-Verlag.

Fiadeiro, J., & Maibaum, T. (1991). Describing, structuring and implementing objects. In de Bakker et al. (Eds.), *Foundations of object oriented languages* (LNCS 489). Springer-Verlag.

Fiadeiro, J., & Maibaum, T. (1994). Sometimes "Tomorrow" is "Sometime". *Temporal logic* (LNAI 827, pp. 48-66). Springer Verlag.

Gamma, E., Helm, R., Johnson, R., & Vlissides, J. (1994). *Design patterns: Elements of reusable object-oriented software.* Addison-Wesley.

Kosiuczenko, P. (2001). Redesign of UML class diagrams: A formal approach. In *Proceedings of the PUML 2001*, Canada.

Lano, K. (1995a). Specification of distributed systems in VDM++. In *Proceedings of the FORTE '95.* Chapman and Hall.

Lano, K. (1995b). *Formal object-oriented development* (FACIT Series). Springer-Verlag.

Lano, K. (1998). Logical specification of reactive and real-time systems. *Journal of Logic and Computation, 8*(5), 679-711.

Lano, K. (2005). *Advanced system design with Java, UML and MDA.* Elsevier.

Lano, K., & Goldsack, S. (1996). Integrated formal and object-oriented methods: The VDM++ approach. In *Proceedings of the 2nd Methods Integration Workshop* (EWIC Series). Springer-Verlag.

OMG. (2005). *UML 2.0 specification.* Retrieved November 16, 2006, from http://www.omg.org/uml

Ryan, M., Fiadeiro, J., & Maibaum, T.S.E. (1991). Sharing actions and attributes in modal action logic. In T. Ito & A. Mayer (Eds.), *Proceedings of the International Conference on Theoretical Aspects of Computer Science (TACS'91).* Springer-Verlag.

Chapter IX

The Role-Based Metamodeling Language for Specifying Design Patterns

Dae-Kyoo Kim, Oakland University, USA

Abstract

This chapter describes a UML-based pattern specification language called the role-based metamodeling language (RBML), which defines the solution domain of a Design pattern in terms of roles at the metamodel level. The goal of the RBML is to support the development of precise pattern specifications that can be used for the development of pattern tools. The author describes the approach and benefits of the RBML, and demonstrates the notation for capturing various perspectives of pattern properties using the Observer, Interpreter, and Iterator patterns. The author also discusses tool support for the RBML and the future trends in pattern specification.

Introduction

A major goal of software development is to develop high quality software in less time. Systematic reuse of software artifacts that encapsulate high quality development experience can help developers reduce the development time (Mili, Mili, Yacoub, & Addy, 2002; Pressman, 2005). A common form of such reusable software artifacts is Design patterns. A Design pattern describes a family of solutions for a class of recurring design problems. Prevalent descriptions of Design pattern (e.g., Buschmann, Meunier, Rohnert, Sommerlad, & Stal,1996; Gamma, Helm, Johnson, & Vlissides, 1995; Grand, 1999; Pree, 1995; Schmidt, Stal, Ronhert, & Buschmann, 2000) describe the pattern solution domain using a combination of diagrams and text. Such informal descriptions are useful for communicating Design patterns. However, the nature of informal descriptions inhibits their use as a base for systematic use of patterns (e.g., tool development) in software development.

There have been many efforts to address this problem. These efforts can be categorized into two formal methods-based approaches and UML-based approaches. Formal methods-based approaches (e.g., Eden, 1999; Lano, Bicarregui, & Goldsack, 1996; Mikkonen, 1998; Taibi & Ngo, 2003) make use of formal specification techniques to specify Design patterns. While these techniques have, by virtue of formalism, strong support for reasoning and verifying pattern properties, it is difficult for users who are not familiar with the formal techniques to use them. This contributes to the absence of widely accepted formal techniques. There have been recent efforts (e.g., Guennec, Sunye, & Jezequel, 2000; Lauder & Kent, 1998, Maplesden, Hosking, & Grundy, 2002) to specify Design patterns using the unified modeling language (UML) (OMG, 2005), a widely accepted modeling language. A major benefit of these approaches is that because of the wide acceptance of the UML, these approaches can be easily adopted. However, these approaches exhibit several limitations, such as high complexity in representation.

In this chapter, we present a UML-based pattern specification notation called role-based metamodeling language (RBML) (France, Kim, Ghosh, & Song, 2004; France, Kim, Song, & Ghosh, 2003; Kim, 2004) that specifies a Design pattern in a precise and concise manner. The RBML describes a Design pattern in terms of roles that define a specialization of the UML metamodel. The benefits of the RBML include:

- The support for the model-level use of Design patterns,
- The capability to capture various perspectives of a Design pattern,
- The adoptability supported by the UML,
- The precise and concise representation of pattern properties,
- The rigorous notion of pattern conformance for UML models, and
- Its tool support that facilitates the systematic use of patterns in the development of UML models.

The rest of the chapter is organized as follows. Section 2 describes the role-based metamodeling approach and the notion of pattern roles. Section 3 describes the metamodel of the

RBML and the notation of the RBML. Section 4 discusses tool support for the RBML, and Section 6 concludes the chapter.

A Role-Based Metamodeling Approach

The RBML is a UML-based pattern specification language that specifies the pattern solutions as a specialization of the UML metamodel. An RBML specification of the solution domain of a pattern is obtained by specializing the UML metamodel so that it defines only the models belonging to the solution domain. This is illustrated in Figure 1. M1 and M2 in the figure denote the model-level and metamodel-level, respectively, in the UML infrastructure. UML models are defined at the M1 level and the UML metamodel is defined at the M2 level.

The RBML specifies a pattern in terms of pattern roles where a role is played by UML model elements (e.g., classes, associations). A pattern role defines two types of constraints, *metamodel- level constraints and constraint templates*. Metamodel-level constraints are well-formedness rules that specialize the UML metamodel to restrict the type of model elements that can play the role. They can be represented either graphically or textually in the object constraint language (OCL) (Warmer & Kleppe, 2003). Constraint templates are parameterized OCL expressions that define model-level constraints (e.g., invariants, pre- and postconditions). They are instantiated when model elements are bound to pattern roles. A model is said to conform to a pattern specification if the model has elements that can play the roles defined in the pattern specification.

Pattern Roles

The UML infrastructure is defined as a four-layer metamodel architecture: Level M3 defines a language for specifying metamodels, level M2 defines the UML metamodel, level M1

Figure 1. An overview of the approach

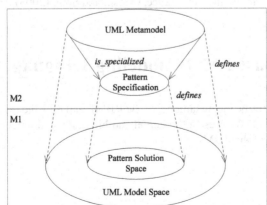

Figure 2. Relationship between model role and UML infrastructure

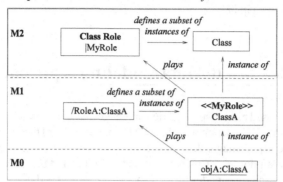

consists of UML models specified by the M2 metamodel, and level M0 consists of object configurations specified by the models at level M1. Pattern roles are defined at level M2 as a specialization of a UML metaclass.

Figure 2 shows relationships between a pattern role and the UML infrastructure (OMG, 2005) where pattern roles are denoted by "|" symbol. Every pattern role has its base metaclass in the UML metamodel. For example, in the diagram the pattern role |*MyRole* has the Class metaclass as its base as indicated by the bold text label above the role name. The |*MyRole* defines a subset of instances of the *Class* metaclass by constraining the metaclass with metamodel-level constraints and constraint templates. For example, the following metamodel-level constraint *self.isAbstract = true* on the |*MyRole* role defines the subset of instances of the *Class* whose members are only abstract classes. In the figure, the *ClassA* plays the |*MyRole* role. This means that the *ClassA* is a member of the subset defined by |*MyRole*, satisfying the constraints defined on the |*MyRole* role. Pattern roles should not be confused with collaboration roles in the UML, which are played by objects. A collaboration role defines a subset of instances of a class at M1 level, and the member objects of the set at M0 can play the role. In the figure, |*RoleA* is a collaboration role that defines a subset of instances of *ClassA*, and it is played by an object *objA* that is an instance of the *ClassA*. The complete characteristics of pattern roles can be found in Kim, France, Ghosh, and Song (2003).

The Role-Based Metamodeling Language (RBML)

In this section, we describe the metamodel of the RBML and how the metamodel is related to the UML metamodel. We present the kernel and binding metamodel of the RBML and describe the notation of the RBML.

RBML Metamodel

Every RBML specification is an instance of the RBML metamodel shown in Figure 3, which defines the abstract syntax for RBML specifications. The metamodel stipulates that every pattern role must have a name, the base metaclass, and a realization multiplicity. A realization multiplicity is defined by the lowerbound and upperbound of the role. The default is 1 for the lowerbound and many (*) for the upperbound if not defined. A pattern role must have at least one metamodel-level constraint, and may have constraint templates. In the figure, the subclasses of the *PatternRole* class are the types of structural pattern roles that define specializations of their base in the UML metamodel. The instances (roles) of the RBML metaclasses are expressed in the UML notation, and thus observe the syntax of the UML. For example, an association role which is an instance of the *AssociationRole* class is expressed using the association notation in the UML, and is connected to two or more association end roles (OMG, 2001).

An exception in the notation is generalization roles and realization roles. These roles are expressed using the association notation to specify the reflectiveness of generalization and realization roles (Kim, 2004) which cannot be expressed using the generalization and realization notation in the UML. More will be discussed in Section 3.2 with an example.

A major benefit of the RBML is precision. The precision of RBML specifications allows them to be used as compliance-check points in evaluating pattern conformance of UML models defines the binding semantics between the RBML and metamodel and the UML metamodel.

In the metamodel, the *PatternRole* class from the RBML kernel is used to access the RBML metamodel from the UML metamodel, and the *Element* class from the UML kernel is used to access the UML metamodel from the RBML metamodel. The *BoundInstance* class is a metaclass whose instances are UML model elements bound to RBML roles. That is, bound

Figure 3. A partial RBML kernel

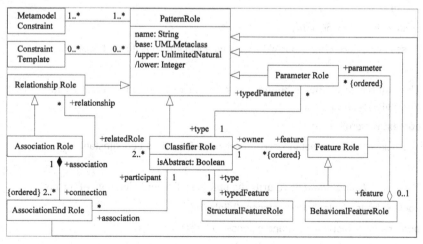

Figure 4. RBML binding metamodel

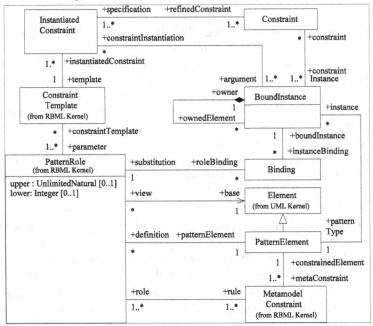

elements are instances of the base UML metaclass of the roles. The *Binding* class defines binding instances between RBML roles and bound UML elements. An instance of the *PatternElement* class is a specialization of a UML metaclass constrained by the metamodel-level constraints of a role whose base is the UML metaclass. The followings are some of the well-formedness rules for the binding metamodel:

- A bound element must be an instance of the base metaclass of the role to which it was bound:

  context BoundInstance **inv**:

    self.instanceBinding → forAll(b|self.isInstanceOf(b.substitution.base))

- The number of elements bound to a role must satisfy the realization multiplicities associated with the role:

  context PatternRole *inv*:

    self.lower ≥ boundInstances() and self.upperBound() ≤ boundInstances()

  The query *boundInstances* returns the number of bound elements of a role:

  context PatternRole::boundInstances():[Integer];

  post: result = roleBinding.boundInstance → size()

- If a bound element is a classifier, the classifier must possess features that can play the feature roles defined in the classifier role to which it was bound:

  context BoundInstance **inv**:

    self.oclIsTypeOf(Classifier) **implies** self.allFeatures()

    → exists(f|self.instanceBinding → forAll(b|b.substitution.ownedRole

    → forAll(r|f.isInstanceOf(r)))

- If a bound element is an association, the association must have association ends that can play the association end roles of the association role to which it was bound:

  context BoundInstance **inv**:

    self.oclIsTypeOf(Association) **implies** self.patternType.memberEnd

    → exists (e|self.instanceBinding → forAll(b|b.substitution.memberEndRole

    → forAll(r|e.isInstanceOf(r)))

- If a bound element is a generalization, the generalization must have the general and specific classifiers that can play the general and specific classifier roles of the generalization role to which it was bound:

  context BoundInstance **inv**:

    self.oclIsTypeOf(Generalization) **implies** self.instanceBinding

    → forAll(b|self.patternType.general.isInstanceOf (b.substitution.generalRole) and

    self.patternType.special.isInstanceOf (b.substitution.specialRole))

These rules are enforced when evaluating the conformance of UML models to RBML pattern specifications. The RBML provides three types of pattern specifications to capture various perspectives of pattern properties:

- **Static pattern specifications (SPSs):** An SPS captures the structure of pattern participants and their properties in a class diagram view.
- **Interaction pattern specifications (IPSs):** An IPS captures the interaction behaviors of pattern participants in a sequence diagram view, specifying how they collaborate to implement the solutions. IPS participants are a subset of SPS participants, making IPSs dependent on the SPS. IPSs are useful for behavioral patterns (e.g., Visitor, Observer).
- **StateMachine pattern specifications (SMPSs):** An SMPS captures the state-based behaviors of a pattern participant in a statechart diagram view. SMPSs complement the capability of specifying local behaviors of pattern participants.

In the following subsections, we describe the notation of each of these.

Static Pattern Specifications (SPSs)

An SPS characterizes class diagram views of pattern solutions, specifying the structure of pattern participants. An SPS consists of structural roles (e.g., classifier role, relationship role) whose base is a structural metaclass (e.g., Classifier, Relationship) in the UML metamodel. SPS roles are associated with other roles in observation of the syntax of their base metaclass in the UML metamodel. For example, a classifier role is associated with other classifier roles by relationship roles.

Figure 5(a) shows an SPS that specifies the class diagrams belonging to the solution domain of a simplified Observer pattern. It should be noted that the SPS is based on a simplified Observer pattern for the sake of demonstration, and thus it does not necessarily conform to the Observer pattern in Gamma et al. book (1995). The SPS characterizes class diagrams in which subjects are associated with one or more observers. Each subject can have one or more structural features (i.e., attributes) that play the |SubjectState role (specified by the realization multiplicity 1..* next to the role name), and one or more behavioral features (i.e., operations) that play the |Attach() and |Notify() roles. Each observer must have only one structural feature that plays the |ObserverState role, and one behavioral feature that plays the |Update() role. The roles in the SPS define subtypes (specializations) of their base class in the UML metamodel as shown in Figure 5(b). The following are some of the OCL metamodel constraints defined on the SPS.

Figure 5. An SPS for a simplified Observer pattern and the UML metamodel specialized by the SPS

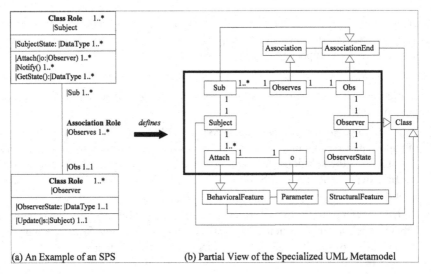

(a) An Example of an SPS   (b) Partial View of the Specialized UML Metamodel

- A class playing the |*Subject* role must be concrete:

  context |Subject **inv**:

    self.isAbstract = false

- An association-end playing the |*Sub* role must have a multiplicity of 1..1:

  context |Sub **inv**:

    self.lowerBound() = 1 and self.upperBound() = 1

  This constraint should not be confused with the realization multiplicity shown next to the |*Sub* role in the diagram constraining how many association-ends can play the role.

- An association-end playing the |*Obs* role must have a multiplicity of *:

  context |Obs **inv**:

  self.lowerBound() = 0 and self.upperBound() = *

The SPS also has the following constraint templates defined:

- An operation playing the |*Attach* role attaches an observer object to the subject object:

  context |Subject::|Attach(|obsv:|Observer)

    pre: self.|Obs → excludes(|obsv)

    post: self.|Obs = self.|Obs@pre → including(|obsv)

- An operation playing the |*Notify* role invokes a Update operation call:

  context |Subject:: |Notify()

    post: |Observer^^|Update()→ notEmpty()

- An operation playing the |*GetState* role returns the current value of a *SubjectState* attribute:

  context |Subject::|GetState():|SubjStateType

    pre: true

    post: result=|SubjectState

- An operation playing the |*Update* role changes the value of an *ObserverState* attribute to the value obtained from the *Subject* class, and invokes a *GetState* operation call:

  context |Observer::|Update(|subj:|ConcreteSubject)

    pre: true

    post: let observerMessage: OclMessage =

|ConcreteSubject^^|GetState()→ notEmpty()

in

observerMessage.hasReturned() and message.result() = st

|ObserverState = st

These templates are instantiated when the mapping between the model elements and the roles that are played by the model elements is determined.

By enforcing the well-formedness rules defined on the binding metamodel in Figure 4, the Observer SPS in Figure 5(a) can be used as a checkpoint to evaluate the conformance of a class diagram to the structure of the Observer pattern. Figure 6 shows an example of a conforming class diagram to the Observer SPS. The class diagram in Figure 6(b) describes a part of an enrollment system for the statistics of the enrollment in pie chart and bar chart.

In the figure, the dashed arrows show the mapping between model elements and the roles that they play. Given the mapping, the following are notable points in conformance.

- The operation attach *PieChart()* can play the |*Attach()* behavioral role because the operation has a parameter *p* whose type is *PieChart* that plays the |*Observer* role. Similarly, *attachBarChart()* operation can play the |*Attach()* role. The two operations satisfy the realization multiplicity constraint 1..* of the |Attach() role that there must be one or more operations playing the role. notify the *Chart()* operation which has no parameter and return can only play the |*Notify* role since other behavioral roles (|*Attach*, |*GetState*) require a parameter or return. *getNumOfStud()* operation can play the |*GetState* role because the operation returns a value whose type is integer that can play the return type role |*DataType* of the |*GetState* role. *getSemester()* operation is interpreted similarly.

Figure 6. A conforming class diagram

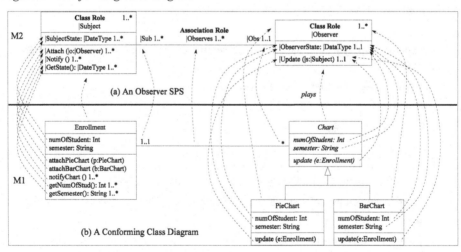

Figure 7. An Interpreter pattern SPS

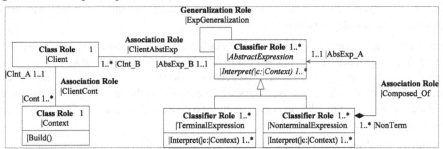

- The association end on Enrollment class can play the |*Sub* role because its object multiplicity * satisfies the OCL metamodel-level constraint of the role that association ends playing the role must have an object multiplicity of 1..1. The association end on *Chart* class playing the |*Obs* role is interpreted similarly.

- The three classes *Chart*, *PieChart*, and *BarChart* can play the |*Observer* role because they have features playing the feature roles (|*ObserverState*, |*Update*) of the |*Observer* role. The three classes satisfy the realization multiplicity 1..* of the |*Observer* role.

The mapping between model elements and roles can be determined by the developer or found automatically with tool support. In our previous work (Kim & Lu, 2006), we used logic programming to find mappings of UML class diagrams to SPSs.

Figure 7 shows another example of an SPS for the Interpreter pattern (Gamma et al., 1995). The Interpreter pattern is used to interpret expressions described in a simple language using a representation of the grammar of the language. A notable property in the SPS is the |*ExpGeneralization* role on the |*AbstractExpression* role, expressed in the association notation. The |*ExpGeneralization* role characterizes the hierarchies of the abstract expression classes playing the |*AbstractExpression* role.

For example, Figure 8 shows a conforming generalization structure to the |*ExpGeneralization* and |*AbstractExpression* roles. In the figure, the two abstract classes *RegularExpression* and *LiteralExpression* play the |*AbstractExpression* role and the generalization relationship

Figure 8. A conforming generalization structure

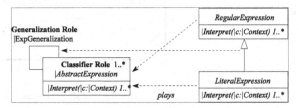

between the classes play the |*ExpGeneralization* role. The |*ExpGeneralization* role is inherited to the |*TerminalExpression* and |*NonTerminalExpression* roles to capture the generalization structures of classes playing these roles.

From this example, one might think that we could have a generalization role on the *Observer* role in the Observer SPS in Figure 6 to characterize the generalization structures of observer classes. That is true. If we have the generalization role specified, the generalization relationships in the conforming class diagram in Figure 6 play the role. For the limitation of the space, the OCL metamodel-level constraints and constraint templates of the Interpreter SPS are not presented.

The Interpreter SPS is based on our interpretation of the description of the Interpreter pattern in Gamma et al., and thus a different SPS likely results from a different interpretation. It is not our intent in this work to develop complete or correct pattern specifications.

For structural patterns (e.g., Composite, Bridge), SPSs might be sufficient to capture the pattern properties. However, some patterns involve behavioral properties to be specified. In the following section, we describe how interaction behaviors of pattern participants can be specified using IPSs.

Interaction Pattern Specifications (IPSs)

An IPS characterizes sequence diagram views of pattern solutions, specifying the interaction behaviors between pattern participants. An IPS consists of interaction roles (e.g., lifeline role, message role) whose base is an interaction metaclass (e.g., Lifeline, Message) in the UML metamodel. Roles in an IPS may be related to the roles in the SPS on which the IPS is based. That is, roles in the IPS have corresponding roles in the SPS. For example, a lifeline role is associated with a classifier role in the base SPS where a lifeline playing the lifeline role is an instance of a classifier playing the corresponding classifier role in

Figure 9. An IPS for the Observer pattern and the UML metamodel specialized by the IPS

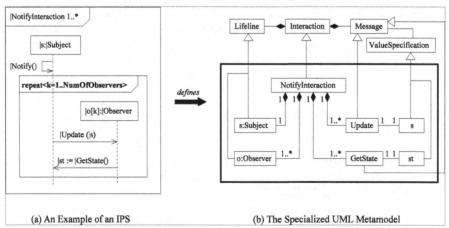

| (a) An Example of an IPS | (b) The Specialized UML Metamodel |

the SPS. Similarly, a message role is associated with a behavioral feature role in the base SPS. For example, a message playing a message role specifies a call to an operation that plays the corresponding behavioral feature role in the SPS. We use the UML 2.0 sequence diagram notation for IPSs for a richer set of constructs, including constructs for packaging and referencing interactions.

Figure 9(a) shows an IPS that describes the interaction between a subject and its observers that takes place as a result of invoking the subject's notify operation. The notify behavior results in calls to update operations for each observer associated with the subject. Each observer then calls a *GetState* operation in the subject to obtain the update. The |*Update* message role in the SPS characterizes asynchronous calls to the operations that play the |*Update* behavioral role in the Observer SPS in Figure 5(a). The |s:|*Subject* lifeline role characterizes instances of a subject class that plays the |Subject role in the Observer SPS.

The fragment and parameterized lifeline notation in UML 2.0 are used to capture the repetition of the calls to each observer. The *repeat* operator in the fragment is an RBML operator constraining the number of occurrences of the fragment to appear in a conforming sequence diagram. It should not be confused with the *loop* operator in the UML. Use of the *loop* operator in the IPS constrains that a conforming sequence diagram must have the *loop* operator. *NumOfObservers* is a function that returns the number of observers linked to the subject lifeline playing the |s:|*Subject* role. In this example, all the metamodel-level constraints are represented graphically in the diagram, and there are no constraint templates defined.

Formally, an IPS defines a specialized UML metamodel that specifies a family of sequence diagrams as shown in Figure 9(b). For example, the interaction role |NotifyInteraction defines a specialization of the *Interaction* metaclass in the UML metamodel, and the lifeline role labeled |s:|*Subject* defines a specialization of the *Lifeline* metaclass.

A sequence diagram is said to conform to an IPS if the relative sequence of the messages playing the message roles in the IPS is the same as the message role sequence in the IPS.

Figure 10. A conforming sequence diagram

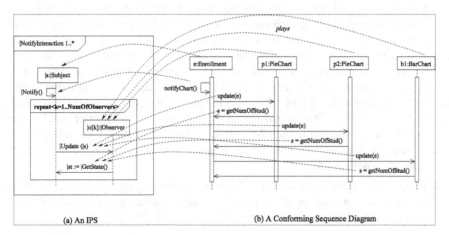

(a) An IPS   (b) A Conforming Sequence Diagram

Figure 11. An interpreter IPS for interpret scenario

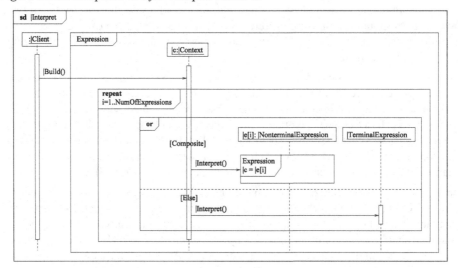

Figure 10(b) shows a conforming sequence diagram to the Observer IPS. The sequence diagram describes the notify scenario for the enrollment application in Figure 6(b).

In the sequence diagram, the :Enrollment lifeline plays the |s:|*Subject* role, and the other lifelines play the |o[i]:|*Observer* role. There are three repetitions of the *update* and *getNum-Stud* message pair in the sequence diagram between the enrollment subject and the chart observers. These repetitions are captured by the repeat fragment in the Observer IPS as indicated by dashed arrows.

Figure 11 shows an IPS for the Interpreter pattern based on the SPS in Figure 7. The IPS captures the behavior of interpreting an expression by interpreting each terminal and non-terminal subexpressions in the expression.

The IPS describes that a client requests a build operation on the context that contains the abstract tree of the expression being interpreted, and the context carries out the request by calling the interpret operation to each expression in the tree. If the expression is non-terminal, the expression itself plays the role of the context of its subexpressions and delegates the request to the subexpressions repeatedly until it reaches a terminal expression. This is specified by the *repeat* fragment in the figure. If the expression is terminal, then the request is carried out on the expression. The determination of non-terminal and terminal expressions is specified by *or* fragment which is an RBML operator constraining that a conforming sequence diagram must have either of the alternatives in the fragment. The *or* operator should not be confused with the *alt* operator in the UML 2.0. Use of the *alt* in the IPS requires presence of the *alt* operator in a conforming sequence diagram. The default multiplicity 1..* of the roles in the IPS is not shown.

While IPSs enables specifying interaction behaviors of pattern participants, some patterns (e.g., Iterator) involve participants that have local behaviors to be specified. In the following section, we describe how such local behaviors can be specified using SMPSs.

StateMachine Pattern Specifications (SMPSs)

An SMPS characterizes statechart diagram views of pattern solutions, specifying the state-based behavior of pattern participants. An SMPS consists of statemachine roles (e.g., state role, transition role) whose base is a statemachine metaclass (e.g., State, Transition) in the UML metamodel. SMPS roles may be related to the roles in the SPS on which the SMPS is based. For example, invoking an operation playing a behavioral feature role in the base SPS may cause a call event that triggers a state transition.

Figure 12(a) shows an example of an SMPS for turnstyle systems, such as subway and library turnstyles. The SMPS describes the following:

- A turnstyle object enters a closed state when the object is created.

- The object in a closed state changes its state to an open state when the object receives a call event caused by an invocation of an operation that plays the |*MakePayment* behavioral role in the base SPS (not shown). This is specified in the following OCL metamodel-level constraint:

  context |Pay **inv**: self.operation.oclIsKindOf(|MakePayment)

  A similar constraint template is defined for Pass role.

- The object in an open state changes its state to a closed state when a pay event is received.

- *TransConforming* transitions of the T1 role must be extensible:

  context |T1 **inv**: self.isFinal = false

Figure 12. An SMPS and a partial view of the UML metamodel specialized by the SMPS

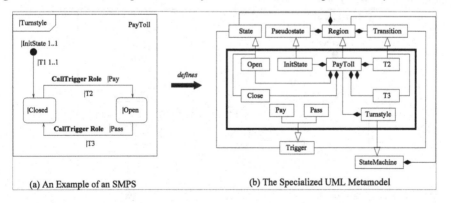

(a) An Example of an SMPS   (b) The Specialized UML Metamodel

Figure 13. A conforming statechart diagram

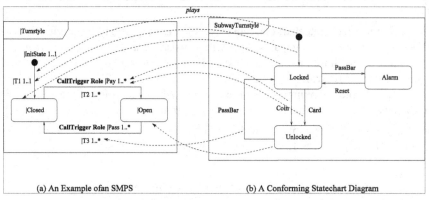

A similar constraint is defined for the T2 and T3 roles.

• States playing *Closed* and *Open* must be simple and extensible:

context |Closed **inv**: isSimple = true and self.isFinal = false

Similar constraints are defined for Open role.

The specialization of the UML metamodel defined by the *Turnstyle* SMPS is shown in Figure 12(b). In the diagram, the state roles |*Closed* and |*Open* define specializations of the *State* metaclass, and the transition roles |T1 and |T2 define specializations of the *Transition* metaclass.

A statechart diagram is said to conform to an SMPS if the statechart diagram has the relative sequence of the transitions playing the transition roles in the SMPS is the same as the

Figure 14. An Iterator pattern SMPS

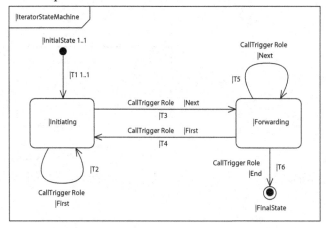

transition role sequence in the SMPS. Figure 13(b) shows a conforming statechart diagram to the Turnstyle SMPS. In the diagram, the *Locked* state plays the |Closed role, the *Unlocked* state plays the Open role, and the *Coin* and *Card* triggers play the |Pay role. Those elements (e.g., |*Alarm*, |*PassBar*, |*Reset*) that are not mapped to any role are application-specific elements not participating in the pattern.

Figure 14 presents another example of an SMPS for specifying the local behavior of the iterator in the Iterator pattern (Gamma et al., 1995). The SMPS is based on the Iterator SPS (Kim, France, Ghosh, & Song, 2003b). The SMPS depicts the following behaviors:

- **Initiating:** When an iterator object is created, it enters to an initiating state. From this state, the object has two possible transitions depending on the event received: (1) staying at the current state when a call event triggering a T2 transition is received, or (2) changing to a forwarding state when a call event triggering a T3 is received.

- **Forwarding:** An iterator object in a forwarding state has three possible transitions: (1) changing back to an initiating state when a call event triggering a T4 transition is received, or (2) staying at the current state when a call event triggering a T5 transition is received, or (3) changing to the final state, terminating the lifetime of the object, when a call event triggering a T6 transition is received.

The full specification of the Iterator SMPS including the OCL metamodel-level constraints, can be found in Kim, France, Ghosh, and Song (2003).

Tool Support

As an expression pattern language based on UML, the RBML has the advantage that it can be implemented in existing UML-based CASE tools. We have developed two RBML prototype tools, RBML-Pattern Instantiator (RBML-PI) (Kim & Whittle, 2005) and RBML-Conformance Checker (RBML-CC) (Kim, 2005b), based on Rational Rose, a popular UML modeling tool from IBM. These tools are developed in C++ as add-ins to Rose.

RBML-PI generates a UML model from an RBML pattern specification as an instance of the pattern. It takes an SPS and a set of IPSs as input and generates an initial class diagram and sequence diagrams for an application. Developer may customize the pattern specification to generate a model that has a structure specific to the application being developed. For example, realization multiplicities of classifier roles can be constrained to generate a particular class structure in the model. The generated model is populated by naming the generated model elements specific to the application and defining other application-specific elements for the requirements. The current version of RBML-PI supports the repeat operator in IPSs. For example, if the repeat operator is defined in an IPS, RBML-PI instantiates the messages the number of times specified in condition of the repeat fragment until the condition is met. From a practical point of view, RBML-PI is especially useful in the domain of product line engineering. RBML-PI can be used to generate an initial design of a system in a product family by instantiating a product family specification capturing the commonalties of the family members. The generated model is then detailed with application-specific properties for the system being developed. Such a process will result in significant development time in modeling. The tool has been used in a case study to develop models of a library system and car rental system using the checkin-checkout (CICO) pattern [26] in the domain where items are checked in and out. Some properties (called variation points) of the RBML specification of the CICO pattern were customized for implementation of the pattern specific to the application domains. The two generated models had noticeably different structures with high complexity resulting from the variations given in the variation points. We felt that developing such models manually would be very complex and time consuming. The current version of RBML-PI requires users to have the minimal knowledge of the RBML to set variations. This limitation can be removed by proving a front-end interface to RBML specifications.

RBML-CC evaluates pattern conformance of a class diagram to an SPS. The SPS is decomposed into role blocks, where a role block consists of two classifier roles and one relationship role connecting the classifier roles. For example, an association role block consists of two classifier roles associated with an association role. Similarly, the class diagram is decomposed into model blocks consisting of two classifiers and one relationship. Every model block in the class diagram is evaluated for conformance to each role block in the SPS. A model block is said to conform to a role block if the model elements in the model block satisfy the metamodel-level constraints and constraint-templates defined on the roles in the role block. After all the role blocks have been evaluated to be conformed, the dependencies between role blocks are evaluated. An example of such dependencies is classifier roles that are shared by role blocks. If two role blocks share a classifier role, the model blocks conforming to these role blocks must have a shared class that plays the shared classifier role. After the role block dependencies are checked, the realization multiplicities of classifier roles are checked over the class diagram. When all the role blocks in the SPS are evaluated to be conformed, and the role block dependencies and the realization multiplicities of classifier roles are satisfied, the model is said to conform to the SPS. In development, RBML-CC can be used for checking the existence of a pattern in a model in the efforts to improve the model quality (e.g., model refactoring), or verifying the correct application of a pattern during model development. In general, such tasks are done manually, which is time consuming and error prone, and because of this, they are often not practiced. Tool support for these tasks will promote practice of the tasks, which consequently contributes to the improvement of the system quality. The tool has been used in a small case study using the Visitor pattern and a model of a toy system to verify the correct application of the Visitor pattern in the model. While this study was successful, the scalability of the tool was left as future work.

The development of the tools benefited from the UML syntax used as a base of the RBML in utilizing Rose for which:

- Rose is used to build RBML pattern specifications,

- the API provided by Rose is used to process RBML pattern specifications, and

- Rose maintains the consistency between generated diagrams from RBML-PI, for example, changes (e.g., adding a class) made to a generated class diagram are automatically reflected to related sequence diagrams (e.g., adding a corresponding lifeline).

Future Trends

Specifying Design patterns has been an active research area since the introduction of the popular Design patterns by Gamma et al. (1995). By the notion of Design patterns, they can be specified from two domains—pattern's problem domain and pattern's solution domain. Specifying the problem domain of pattern focuses on capturing the properties of the problems addressed by the pattern, while specifying the solution domain of pattern focuses on capturing the properties of the solutions provided by the pattern.

There has been considerable work done on specifying the pattern solution domain. There are two mainstreams in this work. One is based on formal methods, and the other one is based on the UML. Formal-method based approaches use formal notations to specify the solution properties. A major advantage of these approaches is that the formal representation of pattern facilitates verification of and reasoning about pattern properties in pattern implementation. This is especially important when using patterns for the development of safety-critical or secure systems that requires high assurance. However, the downside is that the mathematical notation can make the tasks of creating and evolving the pattern specifications difficult for pattern authors, especially those who are not familiar with formalism. While, by virtue of formalism, there is strong tool support for the formal methods, there are only a few tools available that support the use of patterns.

UML-based approaches make use of the UML as a base. The earlier work in these approaches specified patterns at the model-level where a pattern is defined as a model that describes a typical solution of the pattern. Later work pointed out that, by the notion of Design patterns, a pattern specification should describe not just a single solution, but a family of solutions belonging to the solution domain. Some researchers (e.g., France, Kim, Ghosh, & Song, 2004; Guennec, Sunye, & Jezequel, 2000) have proposed metamodeling approaches, where a pattern is defined as a metamodel, defining a set of models. Major advantages of the UML-based approaches are the high adoptability and the strong tool support from the popularity of the UML. In fact, many commercial UML tools (e.g., Rational Rose) support the use of Design patterns in some ways, though they are limited. The downside is that by the inherent informal nature from the UML, these approaches cannot support formal verification or reasoning about the pattern properties.

In future research, we believe that combining approaches of the two mainstreams are viable. In the approaches, the UML can be used at the front-end and formal methods can be used as underlying representations of the UML front-end. This will promote the adoptability and reliability of the approaches, while hiding the details of complicated formal notations from the user. Also, the pattern features supported by commercial UML tools can be utilized. Another point to make is that most of the pattern specification work focus on mainly the static structural aspect of patterns. The future research should investigate more on how other aspects (e.g., behavioral aspect) of patterns can be specified.

The problem domain of a Design pattern describes the problem context of the pattern where the pattern can be applied. While there has been much work on specifying the pattern solution domain, the same is not true for the pattern problem domain. The reason for this would be that the use of the pattern problem specification has not been paid much attention. One intuitive use of pattern problem specifications is to use them as compliance-check points to evaluate the pattern applicability of a model. In general, determining the pattern applicability of a model heavily relies on the designer's pattern knowledge and experience. Codified pattern specifications enable systematic evaluation of pattern conformance. A model that conforms to the problem specification of a pattern is a problem model that can be addressed by the pattern. Another use is to refactor models using Design patterns, which is called pattern-based model refactoring (France, Ghosh, Song, & Kim, 2003). In pattern-based model refactoring, a pattern specification consists of three components; a problem specification, a solution specification, a set of refactoring rules. The refactoring rules describe how the elements in the problem specification can be refactored to the elements in the solution specification. Models that conform to the problem specification can automatically be refactored by applying the rules. These uses of problem specifications require a rigorous notion of pattern conformance to be defined beforehand.

Conclusion

We have presented the RBML that specifies Design patterns in a precise and concise manner to support systematic use of Design pattern in the development of UML models. The RBML has been used to specify the solution domain of the Abstract Factory, Abstract Method, Singleton, Adapter, Bridge, Composite, Decorator, Interpreter, Iterator, Observer, State, and Visitor pattern (France, Kim, Song, & Ghosh, 2003; Kim, France, Ghosh, & Song, 2002; Kim, France, Ghosh, & Song, 2003a; Kim, France, Ghosh, & Song, 2003b; France, Kim, Ghosh, & Song, 2004, Kim, 2004) and the problem domain of the Visitor, Abstract Factory, and Observer pattern (Khawand, 2005) from Gamma et al. (1995) and Design patterns in the security domain (Kim & Gokhale, 2006) and a checkin-checkout (CICO) domain (Kim, France, & Ghosh, 2004).

We found the three types (SPSs, IPSs, SMPSs) of pattern specifications are sufficient to specify the Design patterns that have been studied in our work. We will investigate other types of pattern specifications as we encounter patterns that have properties that cannot be specified with these three types.

We have developed techniques for evaluating the conformance of a class diagram to a solution SPS of pattern using graph decomposition (Kim, 2005a, 2005b) and for finding pattern instances in a class diagram using a solution SPS of pattern by representing a class diagram as a logic program and a solution SPS as a query in Prolog (Kim & Lu, 2006). These techniques support automatic finding of mappings from model elements to pattern roles.

Given an RBML pattern specification, one can loosen the constraints to include more models in the set of models characterized by the specification (generalization of an RBML specification) or tighten the constraints to exclude some models from the model set (specialization of an RBML specification). An RBML specification is a specialization (child) of another (parent) RBML specification if it further restricts the properties specified in the parent specification. A specialization of an RBML specification characterizes a subset of conforming models of its parent.

Specifying patterns at the UML metamodel level allows tool developers to build support for creating patterns and checking conformance to pattern specifications. This can be accomplished through interfaces that allow developers to access and specialize a tool's internal representation of the UML metamodel. This does not have to require direct modification of the internal metamodel. The specializations can be created and managed by a layer that sits on top of the UML metamodel layer in the tool. New generation of UML tools that allow software developers to specialize the UML metamodel in limited ways are emerging (e.g., Rational XDE). These tools are expected to mature to the point where users can define a pattern by specializing the metamodel, as described in the RBML.

The popularity of the UML and the heightened interest in model-driven approaches for software development has raised interest in model transformations. Techniques and tools that support systematic and rigorous application of Design patterns through model transformations can ease to access and reuse design experience during software development. We are currently working on pattern-based model transformations using the RBML.

Acknowledgment

This work is supported in part by NSF Grant CCF-0523101.

References

Buschmann, F., Meunier, R., Rohnert, H., Sommerlad, P., & Stal, M. (1996). *A system of patterns: Pattern-oriented software architecture.* NY: John Wiley & Sons.

Eden, A. (1999). *Precise specification of Design patterns and tool support in their application.* Doctoral thesis, University of Tel Aviv, Israel.

France, R., Ghosh, S., Song, E., & Kim, D. (2003). A metamodeling approach to pattern-based model refactoring. *IEEE Software, Special Issue on Model Driven Development, 20*(5), 52-58.

France, R., Kim, D., Ghosh, S., & Song, E. (2004). A UML-based pattern specification technique. *IEEE Transactions on Software Engineering, 30*(3), 193-206.

France, R., Kim, D., Song, E., & Ghosh, S. (2003). Using roles to characterize model families. In H. Kilov & K. Baclawski (Eds.), *Practical foundations of business and system specifications* (pp. 179-195). Dordrecht, The Netherlands: Kluwer Academic Publishers.

Gamma, E., Helm, R., Johnson, R., & Vlissides, J. (1995). *Design patterns: Elements of reusable object-oriented software.* Indianapolis, IN: Addison Wesley.

Grand, M. (1999). *Patterns in Java-A catalog of reusable Design patterns illustrated with UML: Vol. 1* (2nd ed.). Indianapolis, IN: Wiley.

Guennec, A.L., Sunye, G., & Jezequel, J. (2000). Precise modeling of Design patterns. In *Proceedings of the 3rd International Conference on the Unified Modeling Language (UML),* volume 1241 (LNCS 1241, pp. 482-496). York, UK: Springer Verlag.

Khawand, C.E. (2005). *Specifying problem domain of Design patterns.* Master's thesis, Oakland University, Department of Computer Science and Engineering, Rochester, Michigan.

Kim, D. (2004). *A meta-modeling approach to specifying patterns.* Doctoral thesis, Colorado State University, Fort Collins.

Kim, D. (2005a). Evaluating conformance of UML models to Design patterns. In *Proceedings of 10th IEEE International Conference on Engineering of Complex Computer Systems (ICECCS)*, Shanghai, China (pp. 30-31). IEEE Computer Society Press.

Kim, D. (2005b). Evaluating pattern conformance of UML models. In *Submission to the 18th International Conference on Software Engineering and Knowledge Engineering (SEKE)*, San Francisco.

Kim, D., France, R., & Ghosh, S. (2004). A UML-based language for specifying domain-specific patterns. *Journal of Visual Languages and Computing, Special Issue on Domain Modeling with Visual Languages, 15*(3-4), 265-289.

Kim, D., France, R., Ghosh, S., & Song, E. (2002). Using role-based modeling language (RBML) as precise characterizations of model families. In *Proceedings of the 8th IEEE International Conference on Engineering of Complex Computer Systems (ICECCS)*, Greenbelt, Maryland (pp. 107- 116). IEEE Computer Society Press.

Kim, D., France, R., Ghosh, S., & Song, E. (2003a). A role-based metamodeling approach to specifying Design patterns. In *Proceedings of the 27th IEEE Annual International Computer Software and Applications Conference (COMPSAC)*, Dallas, Texas (pp. 452-457). IEEE Computer Society Press.

Kim, D., France, R., Ghosh, S., & Song, E. (2003b). A UML-based metamodeling language to specify Design patterns. In *Proceedings of the Workshop on Software Model Engineering (WiSME) at UML 2003*, San Francisco.

Kim, D., & Gokhale, P. (2006). A pattern-based technique for developing UML models of access control systems. In *Submission to the 30th Annual International Computer Software and Applications Conference (COMPSAC)*, Chigaco.

Kim, D., & Lu, L. (2006). Inference of Design pattern instances in UML models via logic programming. In *Submission to the 11th IEEE International Conference on Engineering of Complex Computer Systems (ICECCS)*, Stanford, California.

Kim, D., & Whittle, J. (2005). Generating UML models from pattern specifications. In *Proceedings of 3rd ACIS International Conference on Software Engineering Research, Management & Applications (SERA2005)*, Mount Pleasant, Michigan (pp. 166-173). IEEE Computer Society Press.

Lano, K., Bicarregui, J., & Goldsack, S. (1996). Formalising Design patterns. In *Proceedings of the 1st BCS-FACS Northern Formal Methods Workshop, Electronic Workshops in Computer Science*, Ilkley, UK. Springer-Verlag.

Lauder, A., & Kent, S. (1998). Precise visual specification of Design patterns. In *Proceedings of the 12th European Conference on Object-Oriented Programming (ECOOP)* (LNCS 1445, pp. 114-136). Brussels, Belgium: Springer-Verlag.

Maplesden, D., Hosking, J., & Grundy, J. (2002). Design pattern modelling and instantiation using DPML. In *Proceedings of the 40th International Conference on Technology of Object-Oriented Languages and Systems (TOOLS)*, Sydney, Australia (pp. 3-11). ACS.

Mikkonen, T. (1998). Formalizing Design patterns. In *Proceedings of the 20th International Conference on Software Engineering (ICSE)*, Kyoto, Japan (pp. 115-124). IEEE Computer Society Press.

Mili, H., Mili, A., Yacoub, S., & Addy, E. (2002). *Reuse-based software engineering: Techniques, organization, and controls*. NY: Wiley InterScience.

The Object Management Group (OMG) (2001). *Unified modeling language*. Version 1.4, OMG. Retrieved November 16, 2006, from http://www.omg.org

The Object Management Group (OMG) (2005). *Unified modeling language: Superstructure*. Version 2.0 Formal/05-07-04, OMG. Retrieved November 16, 2006, from http://www.omg.org

Pree, W. (1995). *Design patterns for object-oriented software development*. Wokingham, UK: Addison-Wesley.

Pressman, R.S. (2005). *Software engineering, A practitioner's approach* (6th ed.). NY: McGraw-Hill.

Schmidt, D., Stal, M., Rohnert, H., & Buschmann, F. (2000). *Pattern-oriented software architecture, vol. 2: Patterns for concurrent and networked objects*. NY: John Wiley & Sons.

Taibi, T., & Ngo, D.C.L. (2003). Formal specification of Design patterns: A balanced approach. *Journal of Object Technology, 2*(4), 127-140.

Warmer, J., & Kleppe, A. (2003). *The object constraint language: Getting your models ready for MDA* (2nd ed.). Boston: Addison-Wesley.

Chapter X

Modeling and Reasoning about Design Patterns in SLAM-SL

Angel Herranz, Universidad Politécnica de Madrid, Spain

Juan José Moreno-Navarro, IMDEA Software, Spain

Abstract

In this chapter, a formal model for Design patterns is studied. The formal specification of a Design pattern is given as a class operator that transforms a design given as a set of classes into a new design that takes into account the description and properties of the Design pattern. The operator is specified in the SLAM-SL specification language, in terms of pre and postconditions. Precondition collects properties required to apply the pattern and postcondition relates input classes and result classes encompassing most of the intent and consequences sections of the pattern. Formalization is mandatory for reasoning about Design patterns and for implementing assistant tools.

Introduction

Design patterns (Gamma, Helm, Johnson, & Vlissides, 1995) and refactoring (Fowler, 1999) are two sides of the same coin. The aim of the application of both concepts is creating software with an underlying high quality architecture. Design patterns are *"descriptions of communicating objects and classes that are customized to solve a general design problem in a particular context"* (see Gamma et al., 1995). Theoretically, the domain of application of Design patterns is the set of problems. Refactoring is *"the process of changing a software system in such a way that it does not alter the external behavior of the code yet improves its internal structure"* (Fowler, 1999). Its application domain is the set of solutions. In practice, Design patterns are not directly applied to problems but to incomplete solutions, to conceptual solutions, or to concrete solutions. In many cases Design patterns are *model refactoring descriptions*.

According to Tokuda (1999) and Cinnéide (2001), automating the application of Design patterns to an existing program in a behavior preserving way is feasible. In other words, refactoring processes can be automatically guided by Design patterns. In this work, we describe our pattern design formalization technique and its relation with design and refactoring automation (as well as other useful applications).

The first unavoidable step is to introduce a formal specification of Design patterns. This will be done in terms of *class operators*. Then, some practical applications will be presented, including how to use the formalism to reason about Design patterns and how to incorporate this model into design tools and software development environments.

Let us provide an informal and intuitive description of our proposal. A given (preliminary) design is the input of a Design pattern. This design is modeled as a collection of classes. The result of the operation is another design obtained by modifying the input classes or by creating new ones, taking into account the description of the Design pattern.

For instance, consider you have an interface Target that could be implemented by an existing class Adaptee but its interface does not match the target one. The Design pattern ADAPTER, considered as an operator, accepts classes Target and Adaptee as input, and returns a new class Adapter that allows for connecting common functionality. Similarly, when a client needs different variants of an algorithm, it is possible to put each variant of the method in different classes and abstract them, automatically "introducing" the abstract class that configures the STRATEGY pattern.

A function that models the Design pattern is specified in terms of pre and postconditions. A precondition collects the logical conditions required to apply the function with success. In our case, it allows specifying some aspects of the Design pattern description in an unambiguous way. Talking in terms of the sections used to describe a pattern, the pattern function precondition establishes the applicability of the pattern. For instance, in the pattern STRATEGY, the precondition needs to ensure that all the *input* classes (concrete strategy) define a method with the same signature. A postcondition relates input arguments and the result. In the Adapter function, the postcondition establishes that input classes (Target and Adaptee) are not modified, and that a new class (Adapter) is introduced, inheriting from the input classes. The Adapter's methods are described by adequate calls to the corresponding Adaptee methods. The postcondition encompasses most of the elements of the intent and consequences sections of the pattern description.

In order to define Design patterns as operations between collections of classes, we use formal specification languages. Examples are *Z* (Spivey, 1992), *VDM* (Jones, 1996), *OBJ* (Goguen, Winkler, Meseguer, Futatsugi, & Jouannaud, 1993), *Maude* (Clavel, Duran, Eker, Lincoln, Marti-Oliet, & Quesada, 2000), *Larch* (http://www.sds.lcs.mit.edu/Larch/index.html), or SLAM-SL (http://babel.ls.fi.upm.es/slam). Specification languages are used as the working framework. These languages have a well-established semantics and provide elements to describe formal software components. Among the wide variety of mentioned specification languages, we will use our own language, SLAM-SL, in the chapter for practical reasons, basically, because we have a complete model of object oriented aspects in the language itself by the use of reflection, and a firm knowledge of the tools around it. It will be clear to the reader that any other language can be used instead. One key point of SLAM-SL is the powerful reflection capabilities described in Herranz, Moreno-Navarro, and Maya (2002), that is, the ability of the language for representing and reasoning on aspects of itself (classes, methods, pre and postconditions, etc.).

Formalization is one of the main advantages of our approach because it allows for rigorous reasoning about Design patterns. The purpose of formalization is to resolve questions of relationships between patterns (when a pattern is a particular case of another) or validation (when a piece of program implements a pattern). Formalization is mandatory for tool support. Additionally, the view of Design patterns as class operators allows for a straightforward incorporation into object oriented design and development environments, It can be used to modify an existing set of classes to adapt them to fulfill a Design pattern, which is an example of refactoring.

This chapter is organized as follows: section *Background* provides a brief presentation about our specification language SLAM-SL. The next section is devoted to the main subject of the chapter, how Design patterns can be described as class operations. Additionally, we describe two possible applications: how to reason about Design patterns, and how a design can be automatically refactored using Design patterns. Related work and future and emerging trends are included in a dedicated section. Finally, we provide some concluding remarks.

Background

This section focuses on our approach to modeling object oriented specifications. As we have mentioned, we use object oriented specification languages, in particular SLAM-SL.

Modeling Object Oriented Specifications

Object oriented concepts must be modeled in order to formalize Design patterns and refactoring. There are two options, either to model all these characteristics in some specification language (as an additional theory, or a library), or to use a reflective object oriented specification language. For this chapter, we have decided to use SLAM-SL, an object oriented formal specification language that fulfils the second option (see Herranz et al., 2002).

Data Modeling

The two fundamental means of modeling in the object-oriented approach are composition and inheritance. The abstract syntax to specify composition and inheritance in SLAM-SL is virtually identical to those found in widespread object-oriented programming languages like Java and C++ and design notations like UML. So, an ordinary developer should feel comfortable with the notation.

Class Declaration

A class is declared with the following construction:

class C

where the symbol C represents a valid class name. Once a class is declared, the user can add properties for that class. We use the term *property* to name every characteristic of instances of the class, including methods. Composition and inheritance relationships allow the user to model data.

Generics

SLAM-SL also supports generic classes by using *bounded parametric polymorphism* (see Cardelli & Wegner, 1985). Syntax for generics is similar to Java 1.5 and C++ templates. The declaration of a generic class in SLAM-SL follows this syntax:

class B <X **inherits** A>

X is a class variable. It can be used in the specification of B and must be instantiated when B is used. The syntax for instantiation is B<D>, where D is a subclass of A.

Composition

In class-based object oriented languages, a class is a template that defines the structure of the information of class instances. Usually, the data are modeled through a set of fields containing the information. The construction:

state s $(l_1 : C_1, ..., l_n : C_n)$

in a class specification establishes that instances have n fields ($1..i$). Each one is an instance of the class C_i.

The syntax designed to access to property p of an instance o is the infix *send* operator $o \leftarrow p$ (in other object oriented languages the *dot* notation $o.p$ is used instead.) Fields are instance properties, so in the example above, if o is an instance of the class C, then $o \leftarrow l_i$ is an instance of the class C_i. Formally l_i is a function from C in C_i.

SLAM-SL has a *toolkit* with predefined classes like Boolean, Integer, Float, String, Seq (generic sequences), Tup2 (generic tuples of two components), and so forth.

Let us show a concrete simple class specification of a telephone database.

class PhoneDB

state phoneDB (members : **Seq**<Person>, phones : **Seq**<**Tup2**<Person,Phone>>)

Every instance db of PhoneDB has two properties.

-     members is a finite sequence of instances of Person, and
-     phones is a finite sequence of pairs of instances of Person and Phone.

The syntax to *access* the information of fields members and phones is db←members and db←phones.

The name given after the keyword **state** is a constructor of instances of the class. This allows us to write an expression that represents an instance of PhoneDB:

phoneDB([mary, jones], [(mary,7254)]),

assuming that the names mary and jones are persons and 7254 is a telephone number, and that the syntax [x1, ..., xn] represents sequences.

A sugared syntax for sequences and tuples has been introduced in SLAM-SL. [X] is shorthand for Seq<X>. Similarly, (X,Y) denotes Tup2<X,Y>.

Invariants

In order to constraint the domain, the use of *invariants* is allowed. In the example of the database, a reasonable constraint could be that every person in an entry of the collection of phones was in the collection of members:

invariant forall e:(Person, Phone) (e ∈ phones **implies** e←fst ∈ members),

where fst is a method that returns the first component of a tuple and ∈ is a method that decides if an instance belongs to a sequence of instances.

Figure 1. Additional SLAM-SL class examples

```
class Point                          class Color
  state cart (x : Float, y : Float)    state red
                                       state blue
                                       state green
```

Invariants establish which expressions are really *valid* instances. The expression:

phoneDB([mary, jones], [(jim,7254)]),

would not be valid because jim is not in the collection [mary, jones]. These invariants can be understood as preconditions of the state constructor.

Two additional examples are shown in Figure 1. Data representation of the class Point is specified by mean of two fields that represent Cartesian coordinates. In the case of the class Color we can see more than one state, that is, alternative representations are used.

For the moment, observable properties of any instance of Point are x and y, and points can be represented by expressions cart(a,b) where *a* and *b* are **Floats**. On the other hand, when more than one representation is used, the conditions (Boolean functions) is_red, is_blue, is_green are automatically generated by SLAM-SL.

Inheritance

The construct to specify that a class is a subclass of other classes is the following:

class C **inherits** C_1 C_2 ... C_n.

The informal meaning of the declaration above is that class C is a subclass of C_1, C_2, ..., C_n (with $n \geq 0$) and *inherits* properties from them. Its actual meaning in SLAM-SL is similar to that in most of object-oriented languages.

- An instance of a subclass can be *used* in every place in which an instance of the superclass is allowed (*subtyping*), and
- Properties in superclasses are directly inherited by subclasses (*inheritance*).

A very important property, unfortunately not so extended in object-oriented languages, is the following one: *the behavior of subclasses is consistent with the behavior of the superclasses.*

For the moment, let us show a pair of paradigmatic examples.

class ColoredPoint **inherits** Point, Color

As expected from the declared inheritance relationship, ColoredPoint instances must inherit properties from Point and Color, properties like x in Point or is_red in Color.

The user can specify a condition that every instance of a subclass must fulfill in order to be considered a *valid* instance. This invariant condition is given over public properties of the superclasses. For instance, in the specification:

class NoRedColoredPoint **inherits** Point, Color
invariant not self←is_red,

the invariant establishes that for every instance of NoRedColoredPoint, its property is_red is false.

Predefined Collections

Class Collection plays an important role in SLAM-SL. All predefined containers classes in SLAM-SL inherit from the class Collection and all instances of Collection can be quantified. SLAM-SL introduces several predefined quantifiers like universal and existential quantifiers, counters, maximisers, and so forth. The most important predefined classes that inherit from Collection are sequences and sets.

Visibility

Reserved words **public, private,** and **protected** have been introduced in SLAM-SL with the usual meaning in object oriented notations for design and programming. By default, state names and fields are private, while the methods are public.

Behavior Modeling

The SLAM-SL notation allows the user to distinguish among several kinds of methods:

*   **Constructors:** Constructors are *class members* that build *new* instances of the class.
*   **Observers:** Observers are *instance members* that *observe* instance properties.
*   **Modifiers:** Modifiers are *instance members* that *modify* the state of an instance.
*   **Functions:** Functions are *class members* that *observe* properties of the class.

The SLAM-SL semantics is *stateless*. This means that the classification above, from the semantics point of view, is artificial, because methods will be interpreted as functions. From a methodological and pragmatic point of view, the classification given by the designer is used in static analysis and code generation stages.

Methods are specified by giving a precondition and a postcondition. Preconditions and postconditions are SLAM-SL formulas involving explicitly declared formal parameters. There are also two implicit formal parameters: self and result. self represents the state of the instance *before* the message is received. result represents the result of the method (the state of the instance after the *execution* of the method if the method is a modifier). Obviously, when constructors or functions are being specified, the formal parameter self is not accessible.

The syntax of SLAM-SL formulas is similar to first-order logic formulas. In fact, SLAM-SL specifications are axiomatized into first-order logic.

The *reserved* word *method* represents any reserved word for the different kind of methods: constructor, observer, modifier, or function. The specification of a method in SLAM-SL has the following scheme:

class *A*

...

method *m* $(T_1, ..., T_n)$: R
pre *P*(**self**, $x_1, ..., x_n$)
call *m* $(x_1, ..., x_n)$
post *Q*(**self**, $x_1, ..., x_n$, **result**)
sol *S* (**self**, $x_1, ..., x_n$, **result**)

A method specification involves a *guard* or *precondition*, the formula $P(\textbf{self}, x_1, ..., x_n)$, that indicates if the rule can be triggered, an *operation call scheme* $m(x_1, ..., x_n)$, and a *postcondition*, given by the formula $Q(\textbf{self}, x_1, ..., x_n, \textbf{result})$ that relates input and output states. The informal meaning of this specification is given by the following formula:

$$\forall \ s, x_1, ..., x_n \ (s \leftarrow pre\_m(x_1, ..., x_n) \Rightarrow s \leftarrow post\_m(x_1, ..., x_n, s \leftarrow m(x_1, ..., x_n))),$$

where:

$$s \leftarrow pre\_m(x_1, ..., x_n) \equiv P(s, x_1, ..., x_n) \wedge inv(s)$$
$$s \leftarrow post\_m(x_1, ..., x_n, r) \equiv Q(s, x_1, ..., x_n, r) \wedge inv(r),$$

being inv(o) the invariant of the object o's class.

Precondition, call scheme, and postcondition must be considered the specification of the method. The *procedure* to calculate the result of the method is called a *solution* in SLAM-SL terminology. It has been indicated by the reserved word **sol** followed by the formula *S*(**self**,

$x_1, ..., x_n$, **result**). Notice that the formula is written in the same SLAM-SL notation, but must be an *executable expression* (a condition that can be syntactically checked). The objective is that the SLAM-SL compiler to synthesize efficient and readable imperative code from solutions. Solutions must be considered as a *refinement* of the postcondition and the user, with the help of the system, must prove that every solution entails its postcondition post_m (i.e., invariant included).

Some shortcuts help the user write formulas concisely and readably: **self** identifier can be omitted for accessing attributes, explicit function definitions, as in VDM, are allowed, and unconditionally true preconditions can be skipped.

Let us show an example of specification of a *sortable sequence*. A sortable sequence is a generic class and its type argument must inherit from the predefined class Ordered (that introduces a partial order relation).

class SortableSeq <X **inherits** Ordered> **inherits Seq<X>**

Constructor empty creates instances with the property length inherited from **Seq** equal to 0.

constructor empty
call empty
post result←length = 0

The distinction between postconditions and solutions is crucial for code generation. A *proof obligation* establishes that the solution entails the postcondition. Code is obtained from solutions. The fact that both formulas are written in the same language has a number of advantages: (1) it is a very abstract way of defining operational specifications from the user point of view, (2) it is easier to manipulate for optimization of generated code, and (3) ensuring correctness is easier.

The following example is the specification of a sorting method for sortable sequences where the postcondition and a solution are offered:

modifier sort
call sort
post result←isPermutation(**self**) **and result**←isSorted
sol result = **self if self**←length < 2 **and**
        result = **self**←tail←sort←insertSort(**self**←head) **if self**←length > 1

Methods isPermutation, isSorted, and insertSort are specified bellow. Methods length, tail, and head are inherited from class **Seq**.

The mentioned proof obligation in the SLAM-SL underlying logic is:

(length(l) < 2 → sort(l) = l) ∧
(length(l) ≥ 2 → sort(l) = insertSort(sort(tail(l)),head(l))) →

$\qquad\qquad\qquad$ isPermutation(sort(l),l) ∧ isSorted(sort(l))

The above specification of method sort used the following specification of methods:

observer isSorted : Boolean
call isSorted = (**self**←length < 2 **or**
$\qquad\qquad$ (**self**←elementAt(1) ≤ **self**←elementAt(2) **and self**←tail←isSorted)),

given as an explicit (functional) definition,

observer count (X) : Integer
call count(x) = **countQ quantifies** x = y **with** y **in self**,

by using the predefined quantifier that counts elements in a collection with a given property,

observer isPermutation(**Seq**<X>) : Boolean
call isPermutation
post forallQ quantifies self←count(x) = **result**←count(x) **with** x **in self and**
$\qquad$ **forallQ quantifies self**←count(x) = **result**←count(x) **with** x **in result,**

by using the universal quantifier, and:

modifier insertSort(X)
pre self←isSorted
call insertSort(x) = **if self**←length = 0 **then self**←cons(x)
$\qquad\qquad\qquad$ **else if self**←head ≤ x **then self**←insertSort(x)←cons(x)
$\qquad\qquad\qquad\qquad\qquad$ **else self**←cons(x).

Quantification

In SLAM-SL some constructs have been added in order to make writing of executable specification easier. One of those constructs consists of the generalization of the quantifier concept.

In standard logic, the meaning of a quantified expression $\forall\ x \in C.\ P(x)$ is the conjunction $true \wedge P(x_1) \wedge P(x_2) \wedge \dots$ with each x_i in C. The quantifier $\forall$ determines the *base value* (*true*) and the binary operation $\wedge$. In SLAM-SL we have extended quantified expressions with the following syntax:

q quantifies *e(x)* **with** *x* **in** *d*

where q is a *quantifier* that indicates the meaning of the quantification by a binary operation (let us call it $\otimes$) and a starting value (let us call it b), d is an object of a special predefined class Collection, x is the variable the quantifier ranges over, and e represents the function applied to elements in the collection previous to computation. The informal meaning of the expression above is:

$$b \otimes e(x_1) \otimes e(x_2) \otimes e(x_3) \otimes \dots \qquad x_i \in d$$

The abstract class Collection in SLAM-SL has the following interface:

class Collection <T>
observer traversal : Seq<T>

In SLAM-SL the user can specify the way in which a collection is traversed by inheriting from Collection and by specifying the way in which it is traversed. For instance, if the collection is a tree, it can be traversed in three different depth-first ways: preorder, inorder, and postorder.

The abstract base class for quantifiers has the following interface:

class Quantifier<Element, Result>
state quantifier (**public** accumulated : Result)
modifier next (Element)

Figure 2. Some SLAM-SL quantifiers

class Forall **inherits** Quantifier<Boolean,Boolean>	**class** Count **inherits** Quantifier<Boolean,Integer>
constructor forallQ **post** accumulated = true	**constructor** countQ **post** accumulated = 0
modifier next (Boolean) **call** next(c) **post** result←accumulated = accumulated **and** c	**modifier** next (Integer) **call** next(c) **post** result←accumulated = accumulated + **if** c **then** 1 **else** 0

and a pair of concrete quantifier specifications are displayed in Figure 2.

Other predefined SLAM-SL quantifiers are existsQ (existential), searchQ (searching), orallQ (all true in a Boolean sequence), andallQ, mapQ (traversing a sequence), maxQ (maximum), minQ, maximQ (maximizer), minimQ, filterQ (filtering those that fulfill a condition), and so forth.

Reflection

A SLAM-SL program is a collection of specifications that defines classes and their properties: name, relationships with other classes, and methods. Relationships with other classes are the inheritance relationship, and aggregation, or composition among classes, the last defined in state specification.

In this section the specification of SLAM-SL classes, properties, expressions, and so forth, are presented. The reader should understand that the specification of any construct needs the specification of the others, so we will need to refer to constructs that have not been specified yet.

class Class
public state mkClass (name : String, inheritance : {Class},   inv : Formula,
                              states : {State}, methods : {Method})
invariant
  forallQ quantifies s←noCycle({}) **with** s **in** inheritance **and**
  forallQ quantifies m1←differ(m2) if m1 ≠ m2 **with** m1 **in** methods, m2 **in** methods

observer noCycle ({Class}) : Boolean
call noCycle(c) = **not self** in c **and**
                    forallQ quantifies s←noCycle(c←add(**self**)) **with** s **in self**←inheritance

For modeling classes, we have made a natural reading of "what a class is": a name, an inheritance relationship, an invariant, and its properties (states and methods), respectively: a string, a collection of instances of Class, an instance of Formula, a collection of instances of State and a collection of instances of Method. The syntax {X} or [X] is used to denote sets (respectively, sequences) of type X.

The invariant in Class establishes that:

- There is no cycle in the inheritance relationship.

- Properties are correctly specialized: method overloading is allowed, but there must be an argument of different type. Notice that thanks to this declarative specification, SLAM-SL is able to identify those properties that a class must fulfill. It is much more expressive and powerful than the reflective features of Java or C# that are merely syntactic.

Among the interesting methods of classes, let us show a couple of them. Whether a class is just an interface is detected by checking if among the properties there are no states or constructors defined and if all the methods are undefined. Finally, a class is a subtype of another one if the latter can be found in the inheritance sequence of the former.

public observer isInterface : Boolean

call isInterface = (states = {} **and forallQ quantifies** m←undefined **with** m **in** methods)

public observer isSubtype (Class) : Boolean

call isSubtype(c) = (c = **self or existQ quantifies** cl←isSubtype(c) **with** cl **in** inheritance)

Formulas

SLAM-SL formulas and expressions are the heart of SLAM-SL specifications. Therefore, we discuss reflective features related to *formula* management, which, at the same time, gives us an idea about what a SLAM-SL formula is. The SLAM runtime environment can manage formulas in the same way the compiler does. This means that formulas can be created and compiled at runtime, so the user can specify programs that manage classes and class behaviors. The following specification of formulas reflects its abstract syntax in SLAM-SL:

class Formula
  public state mkVar (name : String)
  public state mkTrue
  public state mkFalse
  public state mkNot (f : Formula)
  public state mkAnd (left : Formula, right : Formula)
  public state mkOr (left : Formula, right : Formula)
  public state mkImpl (left : Formula, right : Formula)
  public state mkEquiv (left : Formula, right : Formula)
  public state mkForall (var : String, type : Class, qf : Formula)
  public state mkExists (var : String, type : Class, qf : Formula)
  public state mkEq (lexpr : Expr, rexpr : Expr, type : Class)
  public state mkPred (name : String, args : [Expr])

  public observer wellTyped (ValEnv) : Boolean
  call wellTyped(env) =
   (is_mkTrue **or** is_mkFalse) **or**
   ((is_mkAnd **or** is_mkOr **or** is_mkImpl **or** is_mkEquiv)
         and left←wellTyped(env) **and** right←wellTyped(env)) **or**
   is_mkNot **and** f←wellTyped(env) **or**
   is_mkEq **and** lexpr←type←isSubtype(type) **and** rexpr←type←isSubtype(type) **or**

(is_mkForall **or** is_mkExists) **and** qf←wellTyped(env←put(var,type)) **or**

ismkPred **and forallQ quantifies** env←get(name)←argSig(i)←isSubtype(args←type(env))

> **with** i **in** [1..args←length]

public modifier substitute (String, Expression)

call substitute (var, expr)

post result= self if is_mkTrue **or** is_mkFalse **and**

> **result**= mkNot(f←substitute(var,expr) **if** is_mkNot **and**

>> **result**= mkAnd(left←substitute(var,expr),right←substitute(var,expr)) **if self**←is_mkAnd **and**

>> **result**= mkOr(left←substitute(var,expr), right←substitute(var,expr)) **if self**←is_mkAOr

> …

public observer isExecutable: Boolean

call isExecutable = (is_mkEq **and** lexpr = mkVar("result") **and** rexpr←isExecutable) **or**

> is_mkTrue **or** is_mkFalse **or** (is_mkNot **and** f←isExecutable) **or**

>> …

Class Formula represents the abstract syntax of S<small>LAM</small>-S<small>L</small> formulas that are those in the underlying logic plus the introduction of meta names for formulas. Methods have been added for checking if a formula is well typed, for substituting variables with expressions, and for checking if a formula is executable. Counterpart class Expression follows a similar pattern.

Properties

The classes modeling properties are called State and Method. Its models are the following:

class State

state mkState (name : String, attributes : {Attribute}, inv : Maybe<Formula>)

invariant forallQ quantifies a1←differ(a2) **if** a1 ≠ a2 **with** a1 **in** attributes, a2 **in** attributes

In S<small>LAM</small>-S<small>L</small>, a composition relationship among classes is defined by the *state* specification. A state defines attributes that are the internal representation of the class instances. A state can have an invariant that establishes properties of the attributes or relationships between them.

class Method

public state mkMethod (kind : MethodKind,   visibility : Visibility,

>> name : String,   signature : Signature,

precondition : Formula   postcondition : Formula,
solution: Maybe<Formula>)

public observer typeSig : [Class]
call typeSig = **mapQ quantifies** d←type **with** d **in** sig

observer invokation : [String]

call invokation = **mapQ quantifies** d←name **with** d **in** signature

In the class Method, we have also introduced a couple of useful operations, constructing a method, abstracting the type signature just using the argument types (the names are almost irrelevant except for the pre and postconditions), and composing a method call with the argument names.

On top of them, we can describe a number of interesting operations on methods. The first one (isCompatible) indicates when two methods are equivalent (same name, types, and equivalent pre and postconditions). The second one (canInherit) specifies when a method can override another definition. They must have a coherent definition (same name and arguments/return type) and the inheritance property must hold.

public observer isCompatible (Method) : Boolean
call isCompatible (m) = kind = m←kind **and** name = m←name **and**
                    typeSig = m←typeSig **and return** = m←**return and**
                    (prec1 **implies** prec2) **and** (post2 **implies** post1)
where
  prec1 = **orallQ quantifies** r←get_prec **with** r **in** rules;
  post1 = **andallQ quantifies** r←get_prec **implies** r←get_postc **with** r **in** rules;
  prec2 = **orallQ quantifies** r←get_prec **with** r **in** m←rules;
  post2 = **andallQ quantifies** r←get_prec **implies** r←get_postc **with** r **in** m←rules

public observer canInherit (Method) : Boolean
call canInherit (m) =
      kind = m←kind **and** name = m←name **and**
      sig←length = m←sig←length **and**
      (**forallQ quantifies** sig(i)←isSubclassOf(m←sig (i)) **with** i **in** sig←dom) **and**
      return = m←**return and** (prec1 **implies** prec2) **and** (post2 **implies** post1)
where *prec1, post1, prec2, post2 as before*

Finally, we specify operations to decide when two methods are really different (up to argument names) and when a method implements an interface method (i.e., precondition false):

public observer differ (Method) : Boolean

call differ (m) = name ≠ m←name **or** sig←length ≠ m←sig←length **or**

  existsQ quantifies sig(i)←type ≠ m←sig(i)←type **with** i **in** sig←dom

public observer doNothing : Boolean

call doNothing = **existsQ quantifies** (r←get_prec = false **and** r←get_postc = true)

  with r **in** rules

For the sake of simplicity, we assume that all record components of classes Class, Method, and State are public. In fact, good object oriented methodologies recommend to make them private and to declare adequate methods to access them. We omit such definitions to avoid an overloaded specification.

Notice that what we have presented is only a subset of the full SLAM-SL specification, just selected to show the main elements of the language as well as to make Design pattern description easy to follow. The full reflective specification is included in the reflect.sl module of the SLAM-SL distribution. More details can be found in the SLAM Web site and Herranz et al. (2002).

SLAM-SL Sentences and Substitution

An instance of the class Class represents a SLAM-SL class, an instance of the class Method represents a SLAM-SL method, and an instance of the class Formula represents a SLAM-SL formula. Instead of using expressions based on constructors and methods, the user can write those instances by using SLAM-SL sentences directly. This makes the specification much more concise. Let us show an example for representing the class Point by using constructors and methods:

mkClass ("Point", {}, mkTrue, {mkState("cart",[mkField("x","Float"), mkField("y","Float")])}, {})

SLAM-SL introduces a syntax that allows the user to give the class by using the SLAM-SL own syntax for classes:

```
<scode>
class Point
state cart (x : Float, y : Float)
</scode>
```

Both expressions are equivalent.

Every SLAM-SL (sub)sentence representing any object oriented concepts can be given between <scode> and </scode> and its meaning is an instance of the class that models such a concept.

Substitution has been added to SLAM-SL as a metalanguage capability. Its syntax is $S[x := e]$ where S is an instance that represent a SLAM-SL (sub)sentence, x is a string to be substituted, and e is an instance that represent other SLAM-SL (sub)sentence. The SLAM-SL compiler checks that substitutions are well typed.

Let us show an example of substitution. The following expression:

```
<scode>
class Point
state cart (x : Float, y : Float)
</scode>["Float" := <scode>Integer</scode>],
```

is equivalent to this one:

```
<scode>
class Point
state cart (x : Integer, y : Integer)
</scode>
```

Design Patterns as Class Operations

A Design pattern consists of the description of a valuable design that solves a general problem. Strictly speaking, Design patterns cannot be formalized because their domain of application is *problems*. Nevertheless, relevant parts of Design patterns are susceptible of formalization: *structure, participants* and, more difficultly, *collaborations*. Our proposal is to *view* Design patterns as class (set of) operators that receive a collection of classes that will be instances of (some) participants and return a collection of classes that represents a new design.

In our model, a given (preliminary) design is the input of a Design pattern. This design is modeled as a collection of classes. The result of the operation is another design obtained by (possibly) modifying the old classes, and potentially creating new ones, according to the description of the Design pattern.

For instance, consider you have a collection of classes *leafs* (e.g., Line, Circle, Rectangle, ...) that share some operations (e.g., draw, rotate, resize, ...) and you want to compose all of them in a wider object that has all of them as particular cases and also can collect some of them inside (e.g., a Figure). The COMPOSITE pattern, considered as an operator, accepts classes (*leafs*) as input and returns two new classes:

- Component (merely an interface), and
- Composite (for the collection of components) with the common operations as methods.

Moreover, the pattern operator modifies classes in *leafs* to inherit from Component.

More specifically, a Design pattern is modeled as a class with a single method apply that is a class operator. The precondition for this function collects the logical conditions required to use the pattern with success. Basically, this means that the pattern precondition establishes the *applicability* of the pattern (talking in terms of the sections in the pattern description). For instance, in the Composite pattern we mentioned above, the precondition needs to ensure that all the classes in *leafs* define the common methods with the same signature.

On the other hand, the postcondition encompasses most of the elements of the *intent* and *consequences* sections of the pattern description. In the Composite pattern, the postcondition establishes that:

- Input classes *leafs* now inherit from Component,
- Composite and Component classes are introduced, the first one inheriting from the second one, and,
- Composite's state is a collection of Components and its methods are described by iterative calls to the corresponding *leafs* methods.

In order to describe all these elements, the reflective features play a significant role because they allow inspecting argument classes and describing new classes as a result (Herranz et al., 2002). Design patterns can be described by a (polymorphic) class DPattern. The method apply describes the behavior of the pattern by accepting a collection of classes as arguments (the previous design) and returning a new collection of classes. This method can describe a general behavior of the pattern, or can describe different *applications* of the pattern with different *consequences*, each one in a different rule. The class argument <Arg> (coming from the generic definition) is occasionally needed to instruct the pattern about the selection of classes, methods, and so forth, that take part in the pattern. This argument is stored in the internal state of the class DPattern.

class DPattern <Arg>

private state dp (**protected** arg : Arg)

public observer apply ([Class]) : [Class]

Inheritance is used to derive concrete Design patterns. It is also needed to instantiate the type argument and supplying a value for the state. Notice that Design patterns variants are easily supported in our model through further use of inheritance.

Let us describe in detail the method by using a couple of examples taken from Gamma et al. (1995). UML class diagrams complement the formal definition. A preliminary version of these ideas can be found in Herranz and Moreno-Navarro (2001), where a good number of examples (Decorator, Abstract Factory, Bridge, Strategy, Adapter, Observer, Template Method, ...) are described. This collection clearly shows the feasibility of our approach.

Figure 3. Composite arguments and results respectively

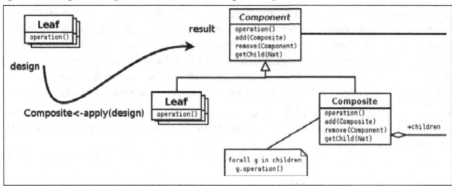

COMPOSITE **Pattern**

The COMPOSITE pattern is part of the object structural patterns. It is used to compose objects into three structures to represent whole-part hierarchies. Using the pattern, the clients treat individual objects and compositions of object uniformly.

When we treat it as a class operator, we have the collection of basic objects as argument (called the *leafs*), as depicted in Figure 3. The SLAM-SL specification is depicted in Figure 4 and Figure 5 (note that line numbers are not part of the SLAM-SL specification, and are included for referencing in the informal description.) The precondition (on line 7) has been already discussed. The collection of base classes and common methods are non-empty. The result introduces two new classes, Component and Composite (line 9). Component (lines 11..15) is just an interface. For instance, the state is empty as can be seen in the use of the empty set as the fourth argument of mkClass in line 12. The methods are all the common methods in all the leaf classes (line 13, 14) plus some methods to add, remove, and consult internal objects (line 15).

Composite (lines 16..18) inherits from Component (second argument of mkClass in line 17). The state stores the collection of components (fourth argument of mkClass in line 17). The result also collects all the classes in *leafs* that are modified by inheriting from Component (line 10). The methods in Composite can be grouped in two parts. On one hand, we have methods to add and remove a component, and also to consult the ith element in the component collection (getChild). On the other hand, we have all the common methods of the *leafs* that have a very simple specification by iterative calling the same operation in all the components (lines 19, by means of function gen from lines 39..43). The description of methods create (lines 21..26), add (lines 27..31) remove (line 32, skipped for similarity with the others), and getChild (lines 33..38) are also included.

Figure 4. Slam specification of the COMPOSITE pattern

```
1:      class Composite inherits DPattern <Unit>

2:      public constructor composite (Unit)
3:      call composite (unit)
4:      post result←arg = unit

5:      public observer apply ([Class]): [Class]
6:      let common_meths = {m with cl in leafs | m in cl←methods} with m in cl.methods)
7:      pre  (not leafs←isEmpty ) and (not common_meths←isEmpty)
8:      call apply (leafs)
9:      post result = [component, composite]
10:                        + [c\inheritance←insert(component) with c in leafs]
        -- additional definitions in a separate figure
```

Figure 5. Additional definitions

```
11:     component =
12:     mkClass("Component", {},true,{},
13:                 {m \ prec = (postc = true </scode>[q := postc]
14 :                                                        | m in commonMethods}
15:                     + {create, add, remove, getChild})
16:     composite =
17:     mkClass ("Composite", {Component}, true, {children},
18:                 {create, add, remove, getChild}
19:                     + {gen(m) | m in commonMethods})

20:     children = <scode>state mkComposite (children : [component])</scode>

21:     create = <scode>
22:                 public constructor create
23:                 pre true
24:                 call create
25:                 post result = {}
26:             </scode>

27:     add = <scode>
27:                 public modifier add (C)
28:                 pre true
29:                 call add(c)
30:                 post result = children<-insert(c)
31:             </scode>

32:     remove = ...

33:     getChild = <scode>
34:             public modifier getChild (Nat)
35:             pre true
36:             call getChild(i)
37:             post result = self<-children(i)
38:                 </scode>

39:     function gen (Property) : Property
40:     call gen(p) =
41:         p \ prec = <scode>forall p in children</scode> [p := m<-prec [self := c]]
42:             \ postc = <scode>result = [mkCall(n,[c] + i) | c in children]</scode>
43:                                 [n := m<-name, i := m<-invokation]
```

Different Modeling Possibilities

For several patterns, such as FACTORY METHOD, the most general case specification is a difficult issue. Nevertheless, one can specify in a simpler way different situations in which the pattern could be *applied* with different *consequences*. It can be made, as we already said, by generating a different SLAM-SL rule for each situation you want to manage, that is, a different *precondition-postcondition* pair.

For example, you can find the situation in which several classes in a hierarchy implement a common method similarly except for an object creation step, so you can apply a refactoring by the FACTORY METHOD. This example, "Introduce Polymorphic Creation with Factory Method", has been taken from Kerievsky (2004). The *precondition* specifies this situation in an easy way. The *postcondition* indicates that a new Abstract class will be created with the following characteristics:

* The *inheritance* relation will be established between initial classes and the new one,
* Two methods will be added:
* A new abstract *factory method,* and,
* The common method in which the object creation step will be replaced by a call to the former. Additionally, in the initial classes the common method will be removed as long as the *factory method* will be added with a call to the concrete object constructor.

Now, if the designers find a new *application* of the FACTORY METHOD pattern, they will only have to add a new rule to describe this *application* and its *consequences*.

Application: Reasoning with Design Patterns

An immediate application of the formalization of Design patterns is to reason about certain properties. In this section, some properties that can be stated with our formalism are presented. Remember that SLAM-SL formulas are in fact first order formulas. Therefore, for reasoning about SLAM-SL formulas about Design patterns FOL is enough.

Commuting Patterns

Proving that the application of two patterns commutes is less relevant for the user at least at the design level, but it is useful for a software team to know that these tasks are interchangeable in time if recommended by the project planning.

Additionally, a design can look messy after the application of a pattern. In this case, it can be desirable to postpone its application to the end of a commutative sequence of pattern applications.

So, given two Design patterns *dp1* and *dp2*, we say that they commute if the following property written in SLAM-SL holds:

forallQ quantifies $(dp2\leftarrow\text{apply}(dp1\leftarrow\text{apply}(\text{design})) = dp1\leftarrow\text{apply}(dp2\leftarrow\text{apply}(\text{design}))$
if $(dp1\leftarrow\text{pre\_apply}(\text{design})$ **and** $dp2\leftarrow\text{pre\_apply}(\text{design})$
with design **in** [Class]

ADAPTER and DECORATOR form an example of two patterns that commute. We omit the proof to save space, but it is straightforward. Let us discuss the influence of this fact. Consider the example of a drawing editor, as in Chapter IV of Gamma et al. (1995), which lets you draw and manipulate graphical elements (lines, polygons, text, etc.). The interface for graphical objects is defined by an abstract Shape class. Each elementary geometric Shape's subclass is able to implement a draw method, but not the TextShape one. Meanwhile, an off-the-shelf user interface toolkit provides a sophisticated TextView class for displaying and editing text. Besides, this toolkit should let you add properties like borders or scrolling to any user interface component. In this example, we can apply two Design patterns: the ADAPTER in order to define TextShape so that it adapts the TextView interface to Shape's, and the DECORATOR in order to attach "decorating" responsibilities to individual objects (scroll, border, etc.) dynamically.

In the previous example, the application of the ADAPTER Design pattern only adds an association relation between TextView and TextShape classes, whereas the application of DECORATOR Design pattern transforms the design in a more complicated one. So in order to obtain simpler intermediate designs, DECORATOR would be applied last.

In general, it is not a usual case that two patterns directly commute. But it is more frequently the case that they commute after some trivial modifications (i.e., permutation of arguments, renaming of operations, etc.). As this modification can be specified in SLAM-SL itself, more general properties can be proved.

More General Patterns

Another interesting property might be to detect that a Design pattern is an instance of a more general one. In the *Pattern Languages of Program Design* conferences, it is usual that a pattern proposal is rejected with the argumentation that it is an instance of an existing one. We offer the basis for formally proving (or disagreeing with) such statements. However, this does not mean that the less general pattern is useless. Firstly, because we are not specifying all the components of a pattern, and two operationally similar patterns can differ in the suggestions of usage. This difference could be crucial for a software engineer. Secondly, because the general pattern could be complicated enough, or rarely used in full, and the simpler version could be more adequate for being part of the expertise of the practitioner. Nevertheless, a tool can detect that storing the concrete Design pattern is not needed because it is an instance of the other pattern that can be used instead.

A Design pattern *cdp* of type CDP<CArgs> is an instance of a more general Design pattern *gdp* of type GDP<GArgs> (where CArgs is a subtype of GArgs) can be characterized through the following SLAM-SL formula:

forallQ quantifies (*cdp*←apply(design)=*gdp*←apply(design) **if** *cdp*←pre_apply(design)
with design **in** [Class]

Our specification of the Design pattern COMPOSITE is an instance of the Design pattern COMPOSITE presented in Chapter IV of Gamma et al. (1995). The general version allows several Composite classes, each one with its own behaviour. We can specify it in the following way:

class CompositeGOF
 inherits DPattern<[Class]>

public constructor compositeGOF ([Class])
pre ...
call compositeGOF(composites)
post result←arg = composites

public apply ([Class])
pre ...
call apply(leafs)
post ...

and formally prove that composite is an instance of compositeGOF. Again we omit the proof.

Other Properties

Other interesting examples of properties that can be easily stated for reasoning about Design patterns and systems are:

- **Pattern composition:** To find out that a pattern is the composition of two patterns can be interesting. This does not preclude excluding the composed pattern from the catalogue, but an implementation can take advantage of this feature. A Design pattern *dp* is the composition of two Design patterns *dp$_1$* and *dp$_2$* if:

    forallQ quantifies (*dp*←apply(design) = *dp$_2$*←apply(*dp$_1$*←apply(design))
    if *dp*←pre_apply(design)
    with design **in** [Class]

- **Pattern implementation:** An additional usage, out of the scope of this work, is to prove that a concrete piece of software really implements a pattern. A *design* is the result of the application of a Design pattern *dp* if:

    existsQ quantifies (*dp*←post_apply(original,*design*)) **with** original **in** [Class]

- **Refactoring:** Given a system design we can explore if a subsystem can be refactored by the application of any Design patterns in a collection of previously specified Design patterns:

    filterQ quantifies *dp*←pre_apply(subsystem) **with** subsystem **in**
    design←subSequencies

- **Pattern's portion:** There are designs in which we can find that a portion of a Design pattern has been applied but not the whole one. So the design can be refactored applying only the remaining part. In these cases, we can find out if a Design pattern *cdp* is a component (or a piece) of another Design pattern *wdp*:

    forallQ quantifies (*wdp*←pre_apply(design) **and**
    existsQ quantifies

Figure 6. A tool for using Design patterns

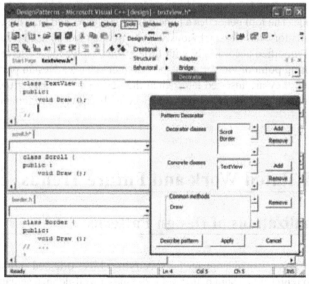

$$(sub\_design \leftarrow \text{is\_in}(design) \textbf{ and}$$
$$dp \leftarrow \text{pre\_apply}(design) \textbf{ implies } cdp \leftarrow \text{pre\_apply}(sub\_design) \textbf{ and}$$
$$dp \leftarrow \text{apply}(design) \textbf{ implies } cdp \leftarrow \text{apply}(sub\_design)))$$

with *sub_design* **in** [Class]

with design **in** [Class]

In the same way we look for a pattern implementation, we can find out if a piece of a pattern has been applied to a design and find the remaining part to be applied.

Application: Incorporating Design Patterns into Design and Development Environment

Once we have the modelling of Design patterns as class operation, it is relatively easy to incorporate them as a refactoring tool into design and development environments. Let us describe how to achieve this goal. An additional feature of a CASE development environment (Visual Studio, Visual Age, Rational Rose) can allow the user to select a Design pattern and to provide arguments to it. Figure 6 shows an example in C++, where the DECORATOR pattern has been chosen to organize the responsibilities in a flexible way of three existing display classes: Border, Scroll, and TextView. The first two are selected as "decorators" (they just allow the display of things in different ways), while the third one is classified as a concrete component (this is just a concrete way to display something, in this case a text).

Once the pattern is applied, the existing code is automatically modified and the new classes (if any) are generated as depicted in Figure 7. The pattern preconditions are checked and, in case of failure, a message explaining the reason is displayed.

Tools for incorporating Design patterns into a project have already been developed. However, they depart from the idea that the designer has in mind the pattern to be used before generating any code. The tool generates a code/design skeleton, and then the user provides the particular details for each class. Obviously, our approach can be used also for this purpose (and the tool modified accordingly with little effort). However, we have preferred to focus on a refactoring point of view. Rarely the designer selects a Design pattern from the very beginning, but they are inserted later when the design complexity grows. Additionally, our ideas reinforce the reusability of existing code, because the argument classes can be part of a library.

Related Work and Future Trends

Other Formalizations of Design Patterns

LePUS (Eden, 2001) is a formal language for specifying object-oriented architecture that is abstract enough to represent Design patterns. LePUS has a well-defined semantics based in

Figure 7. Result of the application of the pattern

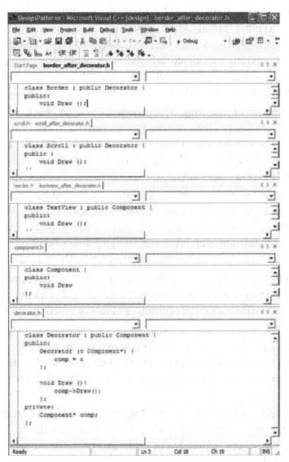

mathematical logic that allows for capturing static and dynamic properties of Design patterns. Specifications of Design patterns have two parts, a representation of the participants and constraints on the relationships among those participants that reflect collaborations. Some LePUS specifications are semantically equivalent to visual diagrams.

The DisCo method (Mikkonen, 1998) introduce notation to formalize behaviours of Design patterns with special attention to the composition of specifications of complex systems. The notation is textual and it is based on the participants and collaborations parts of Design patterns.

Probably Taibi and Ngo (2003) have one of the most interesting approaches, proposing the use of BPSL. In BPLS, the structural description of the pattern is described in first order logic, while TLA (Lamport, 2002) is used for the behavioral one. The most remarkable point of the approach is the introduction of a very high abstraction layer in the description of the behaviours of Design patterns. They introduced temporal relations (predicates) between instances, and the behaviour is specified as temporal actions defined on those predicates.

The domain of application of LePUS, DisCo Method, and BPSL is object oriented architecture. Our notation, as other formal specification languages, is powerful in describing any particular system. To apply SLAM-SL to the formalization of Design patterns the universe of discourse has been previously modeled in SLAM-SL by using refactoring. A comparation between our approach and LePUS, DisCo, or BPSL is not directly easy because they focus on different aspects of pattern description.

We claim that our approach of modeling Design patterns as class operators in SLAM-SL is as expressive as LePUS, DisCo, or BPSL for the Design patterns formalization. However, to our knowledge, our approach to model Design patterns as class operators is novel. While it could be a bit more restrictive than the other approaches, it has clear advantages for practical uses, for instance in applying refactoring.

Other papers also tackle the problem of formalization of Design patterns. However, they differ in their goals and are more interested in describing temporal behavior and relations between Design patterns, by using variations of temporal logic. Alencar, Cowan, and Lucena (1996) focus on the formalization of architectural Design patterns based on an object oriented model integrated with a process oriented method to describe Design patterns.

Tokuda and Batory (1995), and Tokuda (1999) already pointed out that some Design patterns can be expressed as a series of program transformations applied to an initial software state, where these program transformations are primitive object oriented transformations.

In Cinnéide (2001) the author points out that Design patterns can guide the refactoring process. A methodology for the construction of automated transformation, that introduces Design patterns to an existing program preserving its behavior, is presented. The main difference between this approach and our proposal is that we can detect the patterns to apply in a given design.

Le Guennec, Sunye, and Jezequel (2000) use UML and OCL as specification languages for Design patterns. While the paper contains some useful ideas in order to develop a tool, it also honestly shows the severe limitations of UML and OCL for this goal, and particular extensions are proposed.

Lastly, Blazy, Gervais, and Laleau (2003) describe how Design patterns that are expressed in a formal specification language can be reused by instantiating it or composing it with other Design patterns. This approach used a model of object oriented concepts in B Abrial (1996).

Future Trends

Although we consider our approach very promising, some additional work can be done. Our future work will address the following issues:

- Obviously, it is important to provide a formalization of a more significant collection of patterns (even if we have already described a good number of them). We also plan to reformulate the descriptions in other specification languages, more widely used, like Z or Maude. Notice that this is a simple translation (except that the reflective features need to be modelled either from scratch - Z - or augmenting the already existing - Maude). New formulations can make it easier to include Design patterns in existing tools for these languages.

- One of the most promising applications is related to the development of tools. We plan to fully develop efficiently the tools described, exploring in concrete applications the real impact of our approach.

  Although we have displayed how to incorporate Design patterns into a development tool, it can be done in a similar way in a design tool, like Rational Rose for UML. In this case, the system generates new diagrams and OCL specifications.

  In fact, we have only shown the easiest tool possible, and many extensions are possible. In particular, an additional feature could be to select some classes and then leave the system to find the pattern that can be applied to them (i.e., the preconditions are fulfilled).

- Although the reflexive features of SLAM-SL allow for many semantical treatments of specifications, it is true that it is possible to go deeper on this approach. Many interesting issues of SLAM-SL (for instance, proving that solutions imply the postconditions) needs for "hard" reasoning on formulas. This means that some non trivial mathematical proofs are needed. Either we leave them to those responsible for the specification (human), or we use some automatic theorem proving tools (computer, or mixed). We want to explore this second approach in the future. This allows us to include more semantical conditions in our modeling of object oriented aspects. For instance, the doNothing method just checks syntactically that the postcondition is exactly the atom false, while it can be checked that the postcondition is logically equivalent to false.

Conclusion

We have proposed a formalization of Design patterns by viewing them as operators between classes.

The idea is not new and has circulated in the Design patterns community for some time (for instance, John Vlissides mentioned it in a panel at the ACM Conference on Principles of Programming Languages, 2000). However, to our best knowledge, we have not found a development of the technique.

The precise definition of Design patterns is a prerequisite for allowing tool support in their implementation. Thus, coherent specifications of patterns are essential not only to improve their comprehension and to reason about their properties, but also to support and automate their use.

One possibility for evaluating our proposal is trying to follow the criteria of A.H. Eden in his FAQ page on *Formal and precise software pattern representation languages* (see http://www.cs.concordia.ca/%7efaculty/eden/precise_and_formal/faq.htm). Following them, our approach seems to be *expressive* enough, because it conveys the abstraction observed in patterns, (relatively) *concise*, at least more than other descriptions, *compact* because it is heavily focused on relevant aspects of patterns, and *descriptive* in the sense that we can apply our model to any pattern(although for some patterns, if you model the most general pattern it may lead to a less *concise* formalization than if you formalize the specific ones).

It is worth mentioning that we are not claiming our approach is the "unique" or "the most appropriate" way to formalize Design patterns. In fact, different formalizations focused on a particular aspect yield to different tools, properties to prove, aspects to understand, and so forth.

Our formal understanding of patterns gives support for tools that interleave with existing object oriented environments. The main difference between our tool and some others (Eden, Yehudai, & Gil, 1997, 1998; Taibi & Ngo, 2003, etc.) is that our method could be adapted to "everyday" existing CASE environments, instead of a totally new application, so the user of existing tools can benefit from Design patterns almost for free. Our tool can be applied to existing code, even to code stored in libraries. However, other proposed tools are not alternative but complementary.

In summary, our work tries to add some value to Design pattern modeling, including the possibility of reasoning about them, understanding, refactoring, and so forth.

Acknowledgment

This work is partially supported by research project TIC2003-01036, funded by the Spanish Ministry of Education and Science.

References

Abrial, J.-R. (1996). *The B-book: Assigning programs to meanings*. Cambridge University Press.

Alencar, P.S.C., Cowan, D.D., & Lucena, C.J.P. (1996). A formal approach to architectural Design patterns. In M.C. Gaudel & J. Woodcock (Eds.), *FME'96: Industrial benefit and advances in formal methods* (pp. 576-594). Springer-Verlag.

Blazy, S., Gervais, F., & Laleau, R. (2003, June 4-6). Reuse of specification patterns with the B method. ZB 2003: Formal Specification and Development in Z and B. In D. Bert, J.P. Bowen, S. King, & M. Waldén (Eds.), In *Proceedings of the Third International Conference of B and Z Users*, Turku, Finland (LNCS 2651, pp. 40-57).

Cardelli, L., & Wegner, P. (1985). On understanding types, data abstraction and polymorphism. *ACM Computing Surveys, 17*(4), 471-522.

Cinnéide, M. (2001). *Automated application of Design patterns: A refactoring approach*. Unpublished Doctoral dissertation, University of Dublin, Trinity College. Retrieved November 16, 2006, from http://www.cs.ucd.ie/staff/meloc/home/papers/thesis/thesis.htm

Clavel, M., Durán, F., Eker, S., Lincoln, P., Martí-Oliet, N., Meseguer, J., & Quesada, J. (2000). *A Maude tutorial* (Tech. Rep. CSL). Menlo Park, CA: SRI International.

Eden, A.H. (2001, November 21-22). Formal specification of object oriented design. In *Proceedings of the International Conference on Multidisciplinary Design in Engineering CSME-MDE 2001*, Montreal, Canada.

Eden, A.H., Yehudai, A., & Gil, J. (1997). Precise specification and automatic application of Design patterns. In *Proceedings of the 12th Annual Conference on Automated Software Engineering*.

Eden, A.H., Yehudai, A., & Gil, J. (1998). *LePUs - A declarative pattern specification language* (Tech. Rep. No. 326/98). Department of Computer Science, Tel Aviv University, Israel.

Fowler, M. (1999). *Refactoring: Improving the design of existing code.* Addison-Wesley.

Gamma, E., Helm, R., Johnson, R., & Vlissides, J. (1995). *Design patterns - Elements of reusable object oriented software.* Addison-Wesley.

Goguen, J.A., Winkler, T., Meseguer, J., Futatsugi, K., & Jouannaud, J.P. (1993). Introducing OBJ (Tech. Rep. SRI). Menlo Park, CA.

Herranz, A., & Moreno-Navarro, J.J. (2001). Design patterns as class operator. In *Proceedings of theWorkshop on High Integrity Software Development at V Spanish Conference on Software Engineering, JISBD'01*.

Herranz, A., Moreno-Navarro, J.J., & Maya, N. (2002). Declarative reflection and its application as a pattern language. *Electronic Notes in Theoretical Computer Science, 76.* Elsevier Science Publishers.

Jones, C.B. (1996). *Systematic software development using VDM.* Prentice Hall.

Kerievsky, K. (2004). *Refactoring to patterns.* Addison-Wesley.

Lamport, L. (2002). *Specifying systems: The TLA+ language and tools for hardware and software engineers.* Addison-Wesley.

Le Guennec, A., Sunyé, G., & Jezequel, J.M. (2000). Precise modelling of Design patterns. In *Proceedings of the Third International Conference on the Unified Modelling Language (UML2000)*. University of York.

Mikkonen, T. (1998). Formalizing Design patterns. In *Proceedings of the International Conference on Software Engineering* (pp. 115-124). IEEE Computer Society Press.

Spivey, J.M. (1992). *The Z notation: A reference manual* (2nd ed.). Prentice Hall International Series in Computer Science.

Taibi, T., & Ngo, D.C.L. (2003). Formal specification of Design patterns - A balanced approach. *Journal of Object Technology, 2*(4), 127-140.

Tokuda, L. (1999). *Evolving object-oriented designs with refactorings.* Unpublished doctoral dissertation, University of Texas.

Tokuda, L., & Batory, D. (1995). Automated software evolution via Design pattern transformations. In *Proceedings of the 3rd International Symposium on Applied Corporate Computing*, Monterrey, Mexico.

Chapter XI

The Applications and Enhancement of LePUS for Specifying Design Patterns

Rajeev R. Raje, Indiana University-Purdue University Indianapolis, USA

Sivakumar Chinnasamy, Verizon Information Services, USA

Andew M. Olson, Indiana University-Purdue University Indianapolis, USA

William Hidgon, University of Indianapolis, USA

Abstract

Standardized pattern representations have become a popular way to capture, classify, and communicate the essential characteristics of software designs. Both books and large Web sites serve as pattern repositories for use by software design engineers. Because they are usually expressed in verbal and diagrammatic form using, say, UML, they are susceptible to ambiguities and the consequent misinterpretation. The goal of this chapter is to illustrate how to represent rigorously Design patterns, in order to avoid this problem, and to analyze the capabilities of this technique. It describes a more formal, logic-based language for representing pattern structure and an extension that can also represent other aspects of patterns, such as intent, applicability, and collaboration. This mathematical basis serves to eliminate ambiguities. The chapter explains the concepts underlying the languages and shows their utility by representing two classical patterns, some concurrent patterns, and various aspects of a few other patterns.

Introduction

Software *Design patterns*, such as described in Gamma, Helm, Johnson, and Vlissides, (1995), Buschmann, Meunier, Rohnert, Sommerlad, and Stal (1996), and Schmidt, Stal, Rohnert, and Buschmann (2000), indicate efficient solutions to common recurring problems in software engineering that have been cataloged for reuse and other related benefits. The growth in popularity and acceptance of Design patterns has reached a state that may result in a phenomenal increase in the application of Design patterns. However, being a nascent field, Design patterns also have shortcomings: (a) patterns do not have formal mechanisms for validation of their correct use, (b) usage of patterns is almost entirely done based upon experience rather than formal rules, and c) commonly agreed upon guidelines for specification or rules to regulate and maintain a repository of patterns are lacking. These present possible hindrances to the widespread usage of patterns. These deficiencies result from the lack of a proper framework for the rigorous mathematical analysis of patterns.

Typically, *patterns* are specified in an informal manner, which includes the specification of the four standard components of a pattern: name, problem description, solution and consequences, and side effects, along with other information, such as implementation tips or a detailed account of participating objects and their collaborations or interrelationships with other patterns. *Pattern catalogs*, such as Coplien and Schmidt (1995) and those mentioned above use, informal, text-based descriptions and diagrams based on popular object notations, such as UML. Informal specifications are easy to understand and the principles of patterns can be elaborated by many examples. However, because a pattern is expressed through natural languages in these informal methods, it is prone to ambiguity. Thus, the wide dissemination of patterns, in such cases, depends upon the expressive ability of the pattern writer. An ambiguous specification can lead to incorrect usages of the pattern. The limitations of informal specification methods have been widely reported (Agerbo & Cornils, 1998; Eden, 1998). These include a *lack of precision* and *inherent limitations of the object notations for specifying patterns*. Also, informal specifications make it difficult to detect duplication, refinement, and distinctness between different patterns. These are important factors that have a strong effect on one's ability to disseminate and use Design patterns. The absence of these factors, in addition to impeding the designer in the correct usage or selection of patterns, also is a drawback in automatic pattern discovery and pattern-assisted software development. Hence, there is a need for a framework that can formally specify all aspects of Design patterns and assist in pattern-oriented software development.

One promising approach for formally describing Design patterns is the LePUS (LanguagE for Pattern UniForm Specification) (Eden, 2000; Eden & Hirshfeld, 1999). The LePUS has been used to describe the *structure* of the Design patterns of the so-called "Gang of Four" (GoF), Gamma, Helm, Johnson, and Vlissides (1995). However, it does not attempt to describe other aspects (such as *intent, applicability,* and *collaboration*) of patterns. This chapter presents a discussion of applying the LePUS to specify the structure of concurrent patterns from Schmidt et al. (2000) and enhancing the LePUS to describe these other aspects of the GoF patterns.

Background

There have been many attempts at formally specifying software designs. A majority of these are generic in nature, and so are not particularly suited for describing Design patterns. For example, languages such as Z (Davies & Woodcock, 1996), Larch (Guttag & Horning, 1993), and VDM (Durr & van Katwijk, 1992) are too comprehensive for Design patterns. These languages are also limited in their support of object-orientation. Although a version of Z, called Object Z, has been proposed, it is also too comprehensive for describing Design patterns. Architectural description languages, such as Intercol (Tichy, 1980) or Rapide (Luckham & Vera, 1995), are intended to describe properties and interactions between different constituents of a software system, and so are not particularly suited for patterns, which cut across modular boundaries (Eden, 2000). The language, Contracts (Helm, Holland, & Gangopadhyay, 1990), is an extension of first order logic for describing behavior and obligations of interacting objects. It captures dependencies between cooperating objects and includes necessary preconditions required for the communication between participants. DisCo (Jarvinen & Suonio, 1991) is a framework for specifying reactive systems. It is a textual language based on first order predicate calculus. It can model object interactions and represent temporal behavior of patterns. Constraint Diagram Notation (Lauder & Kent, 1998) provides an approach for visually specifying Design patterns. It separates the specification of patterns into three models (role, type, and class). It also provides textual supplements to resolve any ambiguities. The LePUS (Eden, 2000) is a declarative language that specifies Design patterns as a set of variables and relationships among them. It has a strong underlying theory based on higher order monadic logic.

Chinnasamy (2000) carried out a study to assess the applicability of some of these approaches (GoF representation, Contracts, the LePUS, & Constraint Diagrams) for specifying Design patterns. The result of this study suggested that, although other approaches are aimed at specifying Design patterns, they tend to be less rigorous and less comprehensive than the LePUS. Hence, the LePUS formed a basis for creating eLePUS, whose suitability he studied for specifying other aspects of GoF patterns. As the LePUS is the basis of the content of this chapter, it is described briefly below. A detailed description of the LePUS is available in Eden (2000).

The LePUS

Eden (2000) specially designed the LePUS as a language for specifications concerning object-oriented design and architecture. It overcomes ambiguities of natural languages and incompleteness of visual representations. A mathematical formula and a complementing visual notation specify patterns in the LePUS. Hence, it transcribes patterns to formulae. It also suggests an approach, based on its underlying mathematical model, for tackling various management issues related to creating and maintaining a repository of Design patterns.

Given integer sets M and N, a well-formed binary-valued expression in the LePUS has the form:

$$\exists_{k \in M} X_k : \wedge_{j \in N} R_j(S_j),$$

where the collection of arguments $S_j \subseteq \{X_k\}_{k \in M} \, \forall j \in N$, each X_k is a variable with some type and each R_j is a predicate, which defines an association, or relation, among its arguments S_j according to its semantics.

A variable's type defines its dimension. Its membership in a specific collection determines its type. Variables of type *ground*, defined as those that are atomic for the purposes of a given context, have dimension 0. In the context of object-oriented patterns, examples are elements in the collection F of functions (or methods) and in the collection C of classes. Identifiers beginning in lowercase represent functions and numerical variables. Those that begin in uppercase letters represent predicate relations or variables of other types, such as classes.

In the LePUS, a predicate relation's meaning frequently can be determined from its name and arguments. It is read left to right, and, if its truth implies an activity, the first argument is the actor. In other cases, its meaning will be defined explicitly. The set of relations may be extended by providing appropriate definitions. They can be ground relations (defined over ground entities), or *generalized* relations (e.g., unary, ternary) or *commutativity* relations (to indicate commutative properties of relations). The LePUS also provides a few auxiliary relations (e.g., *Clan, Tribe,* applying to functions, and *inheritance, abstraction* applying to classes in hierarchies). Some of the common relations defined in the LePUS include *Assignment, creation, invocation,* and *forwarding.* The remainder of this section expands upon the explanations of the notation that Eden and Hirshfeld (1999) give.

Definition 1: Letting $exp_b()$ be exponentiation base b, the power collection $exp_2(X)$ consists of all subsets of elements of the collection X, including the empty subset. If X is a collection of elements of a single type with dimension d, then the elements of $exp_2(X)$ will be sets of this type, except that, by definition, their dimension will be said to be $d+1$ because they belong to a much larger space. That is, a variable of type $exp_2(X)$ has dimension $d+1$ if X is a collection of elements of a single type with dimension d. In particular, a variable of type $exp_2(F)$ has dimension 1, as does one of type $exp_2(C)$. Let $X_1 = exp_2(X)$, where variables of type X have dimension 0, and $X_2 = exp_2(X_1)$, so that variables of types X_1 and X_2 have dimensions 1 and 2, respectively. Recursively, if $X_{n+1} = exp_2(X_n)$, then variables of type X_{n+1} have dimension $n+1$. This defines variables of types F_n and C_n.

Definition 2: Let $B \in C$ and $S \in C_1$ be a class and a set of classes. The relation *Inheritance$^{+\rightarrow}$* (S,B) is true if and only if each class in S is a derived class inheriting from the base class B. This chapter will use the common shorthand *iff* in place of *if and only if.*

The notation here requires some additional amplification.

Definition 3: + as an adornment on a relation implies that the relation is transitive, that is, $R^+(X,Y) \wedge R^+(Y,Z)$ implies $R^+(X,Z)$

Definition 4: Predicate relations whose arguments are sets S, Y conform to:

- **Unary:** $R(S)$ means $R(X) \; \forall \; X \in S$
- **Total:** $R^{\rightarrow}(S,Y)$ means $\forall \; X \in S \; \exists \; Z \in Y$ for which $R(X,Z)$ is the value. This says that there is at least one function f from S into Y for which $R(X,f(X)) \; \forall \; X \in S$ defines the values of $R^{\rightarrow}(S,Y)$. $R^{\leftarrow}(S,Y)$ says that the mapping is in the reverse order.
- **Isomorphic:** $R^{\leftrightarrow}(S,Y)$ means $\exists$ an invertible, onto function $f: S \leftrightarrow Y$ for which $R(X,f(X))$ $\forall \; X \in S$ [or $R(f^{-1}(Z),Z) \; \forall \; Z \in Y$] defines the values of $R^{\leftrightarrow}(S,Y)$.

Thus, Inheritance is a transitive, Total relation.

An element H of type H_1 is a set of entities of a given type organized hierarchically with respect to a single member entity called the root of H. The root acts as a surrogate for the set, with the constituent entities lending their characteristics to the properties of H. A variable of type H_1 has dimension 1 by definition. Thus, variables of type $H_2 = exp_2(H_1)$ have dimension 2, and of type H_n have dimension n. An example of a variable of type H_1 is an inheritance hierarchy of classes. Inheritance is the only kind of hierarchy this chapter considers. The explicit definition of H_1 for this case is:

Definition 5: A variable is of type *inheritance hierarchy* H_1 if it has a set of "derived" classes $\{D_i\}$ in C_1 in addition to a root R in C, that satisfy the conditions:

Abstraction(R)

Inheritance$^{+\rightarrow}(\{D\},R)$

The unary relation *Abstraction* applied to a class is true iff its argument is an abstract class.

Definition 6: Let $H \in H_1$, *root(H)* be its root, *nodes(H)* be its set of derived classes, S be a set. A binary relation R applied to H is a *Total hierarchical* relation, written as follows, with its meaning dependent upon its arguments:

$R^{\rightarrow H}(S, H) = R(S,root(H))$

$R^{\rightarrow H}(H, S) = R(nodes(H),S)$

$R^{\rightarrow H}(G,H) = R(nodes(G),root(H))$, if $G \in H_1$.

Definition 7: *Defined-In(y,K) for y∈F, K∈C* is true iff *y* is a method defined in class *K*. Let *y∈F_d, K∈C_d*, for *d>0*, be generalized function sets and class sets, respectively. *Defined-In↔ (y,K)* implies that there is an invertible correspondence between the sets of *y* and the sets of *K*; furthermore, the relation is true iff each member of *y* is defined in its corresponding member of *K*.

Definition 8: For *y,z∈F*, *Same-Signature(y,z)* means that *y* and *z* have the same signature. *Same-Signature⁻(y,z)*, in which y,z∈*F_d* are function-variables with dimension *d*, implies that each member *y'* of *y* corresponds to some member *z'* of *z*, and that the relation's value for the pair *(y',z')* is determined by *Same-Signature⁻(y',z')*. But, *y',z'∈F_{d-1}*, so recursive reduction leads to a set of *Same-Signature* relations between pairs of functions of *y* and *z* that collectively define the values of *Same-Signature⁻(y, z)*.

Definition 9: For *y∈F*, K∈C, *Clan(y,K)* = *Defined-In(y,K)*. If *d>0*, for *y∈F_d* and *K∈C_d*, *Clan(y,K)* = *Defined-In↔(y,K)* ∧ *[Same-Signature⁻(z, g) ∀ z,g∈F_{d-1}]*.

Definition 10: Let *d>=0*. For *y∈F_{d+1}* and *K∈C_d*, *Tribe(y,K)* = ∧_{x∈y}*Clan(x,K)*.

Two patterns that illustrate using the LePUS are described below. Higdon (2003) considered the first, modeling the description in Schmidt et al. (2000).

The Wrapper Facade Pattern

The *Wrapper-Facade* pattern, as Schmidt et al. (2000) define it, encapsulates the functions and data provided by an existing nonobject-oriented API within more concise, robust, portable, maintainable, and cohesive object-oriented interfaces. Each method in these interfaces is implemented through inheritance, so that it invokes one or more of the API functions.

This example illustrates two of the LePUS' relations and the general format stated previously. Here, *Wrapper-Façade* is a class variable (specifically, a ground variable), whereas *M* and *S_m* are variables that are sets of functions. *Tribe* here simply means the association of a set of methods with the class in which they are defined. Suppose that *S* is a given subset in *F_1* *=exp_2(F)* of functions. The relation *Invocation⁻(m,S)* is true iff the method *m* invokes each function in *S*. Below, *M* indicates the set of methods in the *Wrapper-Facade* class that correspond to *S,* the set of methods in the nonobject version in the API. The pattern's structure, normally shown by UML, or similar, diagrams, appears elegantly using the LePUS:

∃ *Wrapper-Façade∈C, M∈F_1, S_m∈F_1* ∀ *m∈M :*

Tribe(M,Wrapper-Façade)

∧ _{m∈M} *Invocation⁻(m,S_m)*

Eden and Hirshfeld (1999) employed the *State* pattern to illustrate the LePUS.

The State Pattern

In this pattern, *Context* is a variable representing a class that can handle a number of requests with its set of methods *handle-Requests*. The variables *handle-Requests* and *execute-Request* are function sets of dimension one and two, respectively. *Context* determines the current context of the system the pattern models. *States* is an inheritance hierarchy consisting of a root class *State* and a number of distinct *Concrete State* classes, which represent the various possible states the pattern can adopt, depending upon the current context. *Context* maintains a reference to a single concrete state in *States*, which it obtains using *Reference-To-Single*, a hierarchy Total relation, in this case. When *Context* receives a particular request, its method set, *handleRequests*, forwards it to the currently appropriate *Concrete State* class, which responds by executing its own set of methods (an element in *executeRequest*). *Forwarding* is a predefined relation on function types. Here it is applied to function-sets. *Forwarding* implies the possible inclusion of the sender's ID in the information passed. A constraint on the pattern is that the relation between the elements of *handle-Requests* and *execute-Request* must be one-to-one and onto during the forwarding process, as the double arrow shows.

∃ *Context* ∈*C, States* ∈*H*$_1$, *handle-Requests* ∈*F*$_1$, *execute-Request* ∈*F*$_2$:

Tribe(handle-Requests, Context) ∧

Tribe(execute-Request, States) ∧

Reference-To-Single$^{\rightarrow H}$ *(Context, States)* ∧

Forwarding$^{\leftrightarrow}$ *(handle-Requests, execute-Request)*

The preceding two examples illustrate the LePUS notation necessary for this chapter. The following ones show its usefulness in representing the structure of a range of concurrent patterns.

Eden (2000) used the LePUS successfully to describe the structure of all GoF patterns, validate architectural specifications, reason about and prove relations between specifications and patterns, implement patterns by support tools, and document concrete architectures of class libraries and of application frameworks.

Applying the LePUS to Concurrent Patterns

An obvious extension of the applicability of the LePUS is to assess its effectiveness by using it to describe concurrent patterns from Schmidt et al. (2000). Higdon (2003) studied this question in detail. He considered all patterns from this catalog, except for the synchronization patterns, as candidates for using the LePUS to describe their structures. The synchronization patterns are locking mechanisms intended to enhance the implementation of the concurrency patterns. Thus, they cannot be described without an explicit notation for representing threads. As the LePUS does not contain such a notion, he did not consider these patterns. A few of the concurrent patterns that Higdon (2003) specified using the LePUS are described below.

Although the LePUS provides a visual representation of patterns along with its formulae, the present chapter does not analyze this aspect.

The Component Configurator Pattern

As Schmidt et al. (2000) indicate, this pattern allows dynamically changing an application without recompiling or statically relinking it. It consists of a number of components, each of whose implementation can change dynamically. It is quite similar to the *State* pattern, except that *States* is replaced by a set of *Components*, each of which is represented dynamically by a hierarchy. The *Aggregation* relation is the standard design concept of assembling a set of classes so that they are shareable with others. The class *Component-Configurator* possesses a method *manage-Links* capable of linking and unlinking component implementations at runtime by selecting a reference to a single set of components from *Component-Repository*. The implementation of each component may change dynamically, so it is represented by an inheritance hierarchy. *Request-Config* represents selecting these components. The truth of the relation *Manage-Links$^{\to H}$* represents the events of unlinking/linking these hierarchical components via their roots. The forwarding shown in the *State* pattern does not appear here because it models application behavior rather than dynamic structural modification of an application, which is the focus of the present pattern.

$\exists$ *Component-Configurator, Component-Repository* $\in C$*, Components* $\in H_2$*,*

  manage-Links, specify-Implementation, link $\in F$ *:*

Tribe(manage-Links, Component-Configurator) $\wedge$

Tribe(specify-Implementation, Component-Configurator) $\wedge$

Tribe(link, Components) $\wedge$

Aggregation$^{\to}$(Component-Repository, Components) $\wedge$

Request-Config (Component-Configurator, Component-Repository) $\wedge$

Manage-Links$^{\to H}$(Component-Configurator, Components)

The Extension Interface Pattern

According to Schmidt et al. (2000), this pattern is used when a component needs to export multiple interfaces in order to prevent interface bloating and client code breaking when developers extend or modify the functionality of the component. In the LePUS formula for this pattern, *Invocation* is a relation similar to *Forwarding*, except that it does not involve passing the first argument's ID. The purpose of an interface is to decouple the *Component* from its *Client*. The function *node(H)* returns a specified node of a hierarchy variable *H*. The *Composition* relation is the standard design concept of assembling a set of classes so that they cannot be shared with others. Note that this formula uses the *Component Factory* pattern from the GoF catalog. This technique is similar to functional composition. The relation *Creation* is predefined in the LePUS to indicate generation (of classes in this case).

This representation of the pattern includes the role of the client also. Its final invocation is of a class of the composition formed by Component.

$\exists$ *Component-Factory, Component, Client* $\in C$, *Extension-Interface* $\in H_1$:

Invocation(Client, Component-Factory) $\wedge$

Creation(Component-Factory, Component) $\wedge$

Composition$^{\rightarrow}$(Component, nodes(Extension-Interface)) $\wedge$

Invocation(Client, node(Extension-Interface))

The Acceptor-Connector Pattern

This pattern decouples the connection and initialization of cooperating services from the subsequent processing performed by these services (Schmidt et al., 2000). It is a rather complex pattern, but the LePUS notation clearly reveals its basic structure. The three key roles, *Connector, Acceptor*, and *Dispatcher*, in the pattern are clearly visible in the specification. Although *Connector, Acceptor, Service-Handler* are inheritance structures, this pattern assumes that their roots have certain responsibilities, so they are not abstract. For this reason, the *Inheritance* relation represents them rather than variables in H_1. The notation references explicitly *Acceptor's* components to show their roles. The meanings of the relations *Uses* and *Owns* follow standard software design practice, and the latter implies that an entity has one owner. Therefore, the ownerships referencing the set *Transport-Handle* are for distinct elements. The same holds for the activations referencing the set *Concrete-Service-Handler*.

$\exists$ *Connector, Acceptor, Service-Handler, Dispatcher* $\in C$, *Transport-Handle* $\in C_1$,

Concrete-Connector, Concrete-Acceptor, Concrete-Service-Handler $\in C_1$:

Inheritance$^{+\rightarrow}$(Concrete-Connector, Connector) $\wedge$

Inheritance$^{+\rightarrow}$(Concrete-Acceptor, Acceptor) $\wedge$

Inheritance$^{+\rightarrow}$(Concrete-Service-Handler, Service-Handler) $\wedge$

Creation$^{\rightarrow}$(Acceptor, Transport-Handle) $\wedge$

Owns$^{\rightarrow}$(Concrete-Service-Handler, Transport-Handle) $\wedge$

Owns$^{\rightarrow}$(Acceptor, Transport-Handle) $\wedge$

Uses$^{\rightarrow}$(Dispatcher, Transport-Handle) $\wedge$

Uses$^{\rightarrow}$(Connector, Transport-Handle) $\wedge$

Notification(Dispatcher, Service-Handler) $\wedge$

Notification(Dispatcher, Acceptor) $\wedge$

Notification(Dispatcher, Connector) $\wedge$

Activation$^{\rightarrow}$(Acceptor, Concrete-Service-Handler) $\wedge$

Activation$^{\rightarrow}$(Connector, Concrete-Service-Handler)

The Monitor Object Pattern

The *Monitor Object* pattern (Schmidt et al., 2000) is used to indicate the concepts of synchronization and mutual exclusion needed to ensure that only one method at a time runs within an object's critical section. Clients invoke functions defined by a monitor object through methods marked as synchronized. These properties of synchronization and mutual exclusion are evident from the LePUS specification. The simple nature of the LePUS specification emphasizes its expressive power.

Definition 11: The relation *Isomorphic* is true iff $\exists$ an isomorphism between its two set arguments that is available for use by other pattern activities to associate their elements.

For example, the values of the two *Uses* relations require a shared isomorphism in this pattern. *Isomorphic* is similar to the $\leftrightarrow$ on predicates, except that it holds globally, whereas the arrow applies just to arguments in that relation.

$\exists$ *Client* $\in C$, *Monitor-Object* $\in C_1$, *Condition*, *Lock* $\in C_2$:

Composition$^\rightarrow$*(Monitor-Object, Condition)* $\wedge$

Composition$^\rightarrow$*(Monitor-Object, Lock)* $\wedge$

Isomorphic(Condition, Lock) $\wedge$

Invocation$^\rightarrow$*(Client, Monitor-Object)* $\wedge$

Uses$^\rightarrow$*(Monitor-Object, Condition)* $\wedge$

Uses$^\rightarrow$*(Monitor-Object, Lock)*

Limitations of the LePUS

Higdon (2003) found the LePUS to be expressive enough to describe the structure of a majority of patterns from Schmidt et al. (2000). However, he observed two limitations from the perspective of specifying concurrent patterns. First, the LePUS specifications do not explicitly provide any information related to the sequencing of operations that may take place in a distributed system. Such a specification is necessary to indicate temporal dependencies between various constituents of concurrent patterns. Second, it is difficult to represent explicitly the existence of multiple threads in patterns like *Leader-Follower*. A possible solution to both these issues would be to extend the ground variables and relations to support temporal activities.

eLePUS

Although the LePUS is comprehensive and has been validated in the context of different patterns, it describes only the structure of Design patterns. As critical as the structure of a pattern is, its specification does not fully convey the semantics underlying the pattern. Thus, specifying just the structure captures only one aspect, resulting in an incomplete description. Other aspects, such as Intent, Applicability, and Collaboration, need to be specified formally as well to provide a comprehensive description of patterns and facilitate automatic tool support of the selection and comparison of different patterns. An analysis of GoF patterns reveals that some patterns share a similar structure, but differ mainly in their Intents, Applicabilities, or Collaborations. For example, Gamma et al. (1995) state that the *Adapter* and *Bridge* patterns have common attributes, but the key difference between them lies in their Intents. Similarly, the *Composite* and *Decorator* patterns also differ mainly in their Intents. eLePUS (Chinnasamy, 2000; Raje & Chinnasamy, 2001) provides for the formalization of these three additional aspects, augmenting the structural specification the LePUS supplies, thereby capturing all important aspects of Design patterns in a formula-based representation. This section presents a comprehensive overview of that work, more detailed than in Raje and Chinnasamy (2001). In order to support the specification of Intent, Applicability, and Collaboration of a Design pattern, eLePUS provides the following enhancements to the LePUS:

1.   Amendments to basic abstractions

2.   Addition of new constructs

3.   Modifications to the representation of patterns

The quotes accompanying the following examples in this section are all from Gamma et al. (1995), with the page numbers in parentheses.

Enhancements to the LePUS

eLePUS extends LePUS by adding entries to its variable and relation sets. It adds the following two variable types to the LePUS's variable set:

Object Variables

Gamma et al. (1995) argue that descriptions of communicating objects and classes, object compositions, and relationships are critical concepts in patterns. Hence, eLePUS incorporates objects as ground variables (or first class citizens) by adding the type O to the types F and C in the LePUS. Their identifiers begin in lowercase letters, the same as functions. Analogous to higher dimensional variables of type like C_n, O_n represents the type of an n-dimensional collection of objects. Providing object variables facilitates the representation of state information and object dynamics.

Definition 12: The *Instantiation* relation is true iff its first argument, of type C_n or H_n, creates an instance of object type O_m indicated in its second argument. The *instantiation* function returns an instance of its argument. *Public-Access* is true iff its first argument, of type C_n or H_n, defines as being publicly available the object of type O_m indicated in its second argument.

For example, consider the Intent specification of the *Singleton* pattern – *"Ensure a class has only one instance, and provide a global point of access to it"* (p. 127). Using object variables, this intent can be specified as:

$\exists$ *aSingleton* $\in O$, *Singleton* $\in C$:

Instantiation(Singleton, aSingleton) $\wedge$

Public-Access(Singleton, aSingleton) $\wedge$

Cardinality(aSingleton, 1)

Here *aSingleton* indicates a single instance of an object of the type defined by the *Singleton* class. The subsection below labeled *Other Predicates* describes the *Cardinality* relation, which constrains aSingleton to one instance here.

Environment Variables

These represent the domains of influence of pattern participants. They are required to specify the relationship between a participant and the system or the constraints the system places on a participant. *Env* denotes variables of this type, and Env_n represents an *n*-dimensional collection of such variables, analogous to C_n. For example, consider the Applicability of the *Prototype* pattern—"Use the *Prototype* when a system should be independent of how its products are created, composed, and represented and ... to avoid building a class hierarchy of factories that parallels the class hierarchy of products" (p. 118). Environment variables permit describing this as:

$\exists$ *Factories, Products* $\in H_2$, *SYSTEM* $\in Env$:

Decouple(SYSTEM, Creation(Products)) $\wedge$

NOT Equivalence(cardinality(Factories), cardinality(Products))

The subsection labeled *Other Predicates* also describes the *Decouple* and *Equivalence* relations.

In addition to augmenting the variable set, eLePUS extends the relation set by adding the following ones:

Attribute Qualifiers

There are unary relations defined on an eLePUS variable. These are qualifiers because their definitions on a variable map/qualify the variable to a well defined set of elements. These are classified into further subcategories: (a) predicates for object-orientation, (b) predicates for access specification, and (c) additional predicates for structural aspects. These include those briefly described below.

- **For object-orientation:** The LePUS already defines predicates, such as A*bstraction* and *Inheritance*, whose meanings can be extended to objects. eLePUS adds two additional functions: *Encapsulation* and *algorithm-Abstraction*. For example, an *Encapsulation* relation on a class indicates the concept of hiding the internal details of that class. This is useful in defining the Intent of a pattern like *Strategy*. The function *algorithm-Abstraction*, defined on a class or function variable, returns a representation of the algorithm(s) the class or function utilizes. This is useful in indicating the Intent specification of patterns like *Builder*.

- **For access specification:** eLePUS introduces two types of access specifiers: (a) *Public-Access* and (b) *Restricted-Access*. These two correspond to the access control mechanisms in the object-oriented domain. The relation *Public-Access* is defined for class variables of dimension >=0. *Restricted-Access* is a relation defined on a class or a function variable.

- **For structural aspects:** Two additional predicates were introduced into eLePUS based on their occurrence in the informal description of Design patterns. These were *List* and *Tree*. They are unary relations that apply to a class variable to indicate whether or not the objects of that class are to be composed as a list or a tree, respectively. These predicates are useful in defining patterns like *Iterator* and *Composite*.

Predicates for Temporal Relations

Temporal relations are crucial for describing the collaborations among pattern constituents. Many of the LePUS relations could be annotated by incorporating a time aspect. For example, the LePUS relation *Invocation* could be converted into its timed-version, which places an additional constraint requiring the invocation of a function to occur within a certain time interval. However, during the design of eLePUS, it was observed that such annotations were not necessary because the addition of three temporal concepts was found to be sufficient to specify the temporal aspects. These three are:

- **State-Change:** This predicate becomes true iff an object variable changes state during a specific time interval. This is useful in describing patterns like *Observer*.

- **State:** This is a unary function that, when applied to an object variable, returns its state. It is used in conjunction with the *Roll-Back* relation.

- **Roll-Back:** This is a binary relation defined on the state of an object variable and the instant of time to which the state should revert back. It is useful in specifying patterns like *Memento*.

Other Predicates

eLePUS also adds a few additional predicates that are used neither for indicating access properties nor for describing temporal aspects. These include:

- **Cardinality:** This acts on an object, function, class, or a hierarchy variable to indicate its argument's cardinality.

Definition 13: The relation *Cardinality(S, n)*, where *S* is a set variable and *n* is an integer, is true iff *S* has *n* members. The function *cardinality(S)* returns the number of elements in the set variable *S*, that is,

Cardinality(S, cardinality(S)) is always true.

As seen above, the constraint that the *Singleton* pattern places on the instantiation is specified using this relation.

- **Couple:** Coupling refers to the degree of interconnectivity between entities. This property is characteristic in Design patterns. It is defined between class variables to indicate their dependency by holding references to one another. It is useful in patterns like *Abstract Factory*.
- **Decouple:** This is a complement of the *Couple* relation.

Definition 14: *Decouple(X, Y)* is true iff its arguments, of class type, are independent of each other, that is, change in one does not affect the other. This includes their possible disengagement during execution as well as structural (static) independence.

This appeared earlier in the Applicability of the *Prototype* pattern.

- **Delegation:** This is a ternary relation between two participating entities (such as classes or objects) and a function.

Definition 15: *Delegation(X, f, Y)*, where *X* and *Y* are object, class, or hierarchy variables, and *f* has a function type, is true iff the first argument yields its responsibility for executing *f* to the third argument. *Delegation** indicates a recursive version of this relation.

- **Dynamic-Binding:** One of the major failures of the LePUS is attempting to specify dynamic properties with static observations. *Dynamic-Binding* is eLePUS's construct (in conjunction with the temporal predicates mentioned earlier) for describing dynamic interactions (such as configuration) between two objects.

Definition 16: *Dynamic-Binding(X, Y)*, where *X* and *Y* have type object, class, or hierearchy, is true iff instances of objects *X* and *Y* (or of their variables of object type if they are of class or hierarchy type) can be bound together during execution.

The Intent of Factory Method requires this relation.

- **Equivalence:** This relation acts as a comparator between two entities of the same type, such as enumerable relationships, like cardinality, or syntactically equitable entities, like interface or function signatures. Equivalence between two entities implies equality of the entities. The specification of the *Iterator* pattern uses this predicate.

- **Interface-Compatibility:** This relation indicates compatibility between the interfaces of two classes. This, in a way, describes the type compatibility between the function signatures of the two interfaces. The *Adapter* pattern is an example where this relation is used.

Redefinition of the LePUS Relations

eLePUS also redefines a few of the LePUS constructs to be more consistent with the introduction of the explicit object variables and its focus on more aspects than merely Design pattern Structure. These are briefly described below.

Define

- **Definition 17:** *Define(K,f)*, where K is a variable of class type and f is a variable of function type, is true iff its first argument must provide a definition of the function in its second argument (eventually).

This serves as a variation of Defined-In in the LePUS for use when K may not physically exist yet. The Intent aspect of the *Observer* pattern employs it.

- **Invocation:** The *Invocation* relation of the LePUS is redefined to incorporate the invocation of a function by an instance of a class variable. The *Prototype* pattern needs this variation of the original *Invocation* relation.
- **Creation:** eLePUS assumes the *Creation* relation to be polymorphic to indicate, for example, the creation of an object by a function or the creation of an object instance by a class (implicitly representing a function defined in that class). The specification of the Collaboration aspect of the *Builder* pattern utilizes this extended meaning.

This section provides an informal and a brief overview of the enhancements that eLePUS has incorporated into the LePUS. Chinnasamy (2000) presents the formal definitions and a BNF grammar for their syntax (pp. 77-84), along with an elaborate discussion of the extended language.

Utility of eLePUS

Inasmuch as eLePUS includes the LePUS, their utilities in representing pattern structures are essentially the same. To study eLePUS's utility with respect to other aspects of Design patterns, it was applied to many patterns from the GoF catalog. This section provides a few samples to indicate its utility. Again, the quotes are from Gamma et al. (1995), with the page numbers in parentheses.

Specification of Intent

The informal descriptions of the Intents of a few GoF patterns appear below, along with their eLePUS equivalents. The Intent specification of other GoF patterns is described in Chinnasamy (2000).

Abstract Factory Pattern

"Provide an interface for creating families of related or dependent objects without specifying their concrete classes" (p. 87). The *Production* predicate is primarily used in Factory patterns. It is true iff its first argument is to generate instances of the second one.

$\exists$ *Creators* $\in H$, *Product-Family*$\in H_2$, *factory-methods* $\in F_2$:

Define$^{\rightarrow H}$*(Creators, factory-methods)* $\wedge$

Production$^{\rightarrow H}$*(factory-methods, Product-Family)*

Factory Method Pattern

"Define an interface for creating an object, but let subclasses decide which class to instantiate. Factory Method lets a class defer instantiations to subclasses" (p. 107). Here, the purpose of the function *instantiate* is to return the results of invoking the chosen *factory-methods*. A major difference between the *Abstract Factory* pattern and the present pattern is that the former allows for greater variety in the products that it creates. This is clearly manifested by eLePUS here through the differences in dimensionality of the corresponding variables, which models the mention of families that appears in the Intent of the *Abstract Factory* but not in *Factory Method's* Intent.

$\exists$ *Creators, Product* $\in H_1$, *factory-methods* $\in F_1$:

Production$^{\rightarrow H}$*(factory-methods, Product)* $\wedge$

Delegation(root(Creators), instantiate(Product), nodes(Creators))

Adapter Pattern

The Intent of this pattern is to *"convert the interface of a class into another interface clients expect. Adapter lets classes work together that could not otherwise because of incompatible interfaces"* (p. 139). The model below states the simple condition that the clients' interface, *Adapter*, makes that of *Adaptee* functionally accessible.

$\exists$ *Adapter, Adaptee* $\in C$:

Interface-Compatible(Adapter, Adaptee)

Bridge Pattern

"*Decouple an abstraction from its implementation so that the two can vary independently*" (p. 151). The eLePUS formula below is a clear restatement of this condition on the Intent. Also, the GoF catalog states that the real difference between the *Adapter* and *Bridge* patterns lies in their Intents. This is clearly emphasized in the eLePUS specification of these two patterns.

∃ *Abstract-Item, Implementation-Item* ∈C :

Dynamic-Binding(Abstract-Item, Implementation-Item) ∧

Decouple(Abstract-Item, Implementation-Item)

Specification of Applicability

This subsection illustrates the eLePUS specifications of the Applicability aspect of the GoF Design patterns considered in the previous subsections. Chinnasamy (2000) provides them for the remaining GoF patterns. Normally, the verbal statement of the Applicability aspect consists of a number of illustrations where the pattern might be useful. For brevity, only a sample will be quoted here. Nevertheless, the eLePUS formula attempts to capture the bulk of the illustrations.

Abstract Factory Pattern

"*A system should be independent of how its products are created, composed, and represented. A system should be configured with one of multiple families of products*" (p. 88). The function *member* returns a subset of dimension d-1 of its d-dimensional argument. Compare this with the pattern's Intent specified in the previous subsection. There appear families of related *Products*, each set of related products organized in a hierarchy. Here appears a family of such hierarchies represented by a member of H_2.

∃ *Product-Families* ∈H_2, *SYSTEM* ∈*Env* :

Decouple(SYSTEM, Creation(Product-Families)) ∧

Couple(nodes(member(Product-Families)))

Factory Method Pattern

This pattern is applicable when "*a class can't anticipate the class of objects it must create. Classes delegate responsibility to several helper classes, and you want to localize the knowledge of which helper subclass is the delegate*" (p. 108). A comparison of this specification with that of the pattern's Intent shows that the granularity of attention here is much finer than for the Intent. This reflects the differences in the two verbal statements.

∃ *Client* ∈*C, Product-Object* ∈*O, Creators* ∈*H₁* :

Dynamic-Binding(Client, Product-Object) ∧

Delegation(root(Creators), instantiate(Product-Object), nodes(Creators))

Adapter Pattern

Use this pattern *"when you want to use an existing class, and its interface does not match the one you need"* (p. 140) This eLePUS specification states that the Client (your interface) and the available interface (Adpatee) are not compatible, but that the Client can be chained together with the Adapter to access the features of the Adaptee. This is a relatively straight-forward restatement of the verbal form of the Applicability.

∃ *Client, Adapter, Adaptee* ∈*C* :

NOT Interface-Compatible(Client, Adaptee) ∧

Interface-Compatible(Client, Adapter) ∧

Interface-Compatible(Adapter, Adaptee)

Bridge Pattern

This has a number of suggested applications, so only two are cited here. *"You want to avoid permanent binding between an abstraction and its implementation … . You want to share an implementation among multiple objects … and this fact should be hidden from the client"* (p. 153)

In this eLePUS specification, note that *NOT Couple* is not the same as the condition *Decouple* employed earlier. This is because not referencing is not the only way two entities can be independent. In the specification below, the condition implies that *Abstract-Item* cannot reference *Implementation-Item*. The inheritance predicate states that the reverse linkage must be true. Each client class obtains a reference to *Implementation-Item* via the interface *Abstract-Item*. Note also that this specification is significantly different from that for the Adapter pattern, just as for Intent.

∃ *Abstract-Item, Implementation-Item* ∈*C, Clients* ∈*C₁* :

Abstraction(Abstract-Item) ∧

NOT Couple(Abstract-Item, Implementation-Item) ∧

Inheritance⁺⁻(Implementation-Item, Abstract-Item) ∧

Reference-To-Single⁻(Clients, Implementation-Item)

Specification of Collaboration

The eLePUS specifications of the Collaboration aspect of only two of the preceding GoF patterns are given below because of space considerations. Chinnasamy (2000) describes the specifications for the remaining GoF patterns.

Abstract Factory Pattern

A statement of the Collaborations for this pattern is *"Normally, a single instance of a ConcreteFactory class is created at run-time. This concrete factory creates product objects having a particular implementation. To create different product objects, clients should use a different concrete factory. AbstractFactory defers creation of product objects to its ConcreteFactory subclass"* (p. 89). The term "subclass" here implies that *ConcreteFactory* inherits from *AbstractFactory* to form a structure of type H_1. *Creators* plays this role in the eLePUS specification below. The *Tribe* relation states that the functions to produce the instances of the product objects must be defined in the various hierarchies that define the product families. *Products* represents this set of product families and *production* represents these functions. The abstract factory, or root, node of *Creators* defers the actual invocation of the production functions to its concrete factories, indicated by the *nodes* function. The arrow on *Delegation* indicates that the *production* should be assigned in a one-to-one fashion to *Creators'* nodes. Finally, the last predicate imposes the constraint mentioned above that only a single instantiation of a concrete factory be active at a time.

$\exists$ *Creators* $\in H_1$, *Products* $\in H_2$, *production* $\in F_2$:

Tribe(production, Products) $\wedge$

Delegation$\leftrightarrow$(root(Creators), production(Products), nodes(Creators)) $\wedge$

Cardinality(Instantiation(node(Creators)), 1)

Bridge Pattern

The statement, *"Abstraction forwards client requests to its Implementor object"* (p. 154), expresses the Collaborations of this pattern. This is specified below by the two *Invocation* predicates, in which the abstraction *Abstract-Item* provides an interface for the operations and *Implementors* provides their implementations. *Tribe* again serves to state where these functions are defined.

$\exists$ *Abstract-Item* $\in C$, *Clients* $\in C_1$, *Implementors* $\in H$,

operations $\in F_1$, *operation-Imp* $\in F_2$:

Tribe(operations, Abstract-Item) $\wedge$

Tribe(operation-Imp, Implementors) $\wedge$

Invocation$\rightarrow$(Clients, operations) $\wedge$

Invocation$\rightarrow$(operations, operation-Imp)

Validation and Experience Using eLePUS

It was possible to specify the comprehensive Intent of more than 70% of the patterns from the GoF catalog and to capture the essential characteristics of the remaining patterns using eLePUS (Chinnasamy, 2000). A 67% success rate for completely specifying the Applicability aspect of patterns and a substantial specification of this aspect of the remaining patterns were achievable using eLePUS. The limitations (the inability to specify Intent and Applicability of all GoF patterns) arise mainly due to the plethora of scenarios where patterns are applicable, which may need domain specific vocabulary for complete specification. For example, to specify the Intent and the Applicability of the *Iterator* pattern, it is necessary to introduce relations that depict the interpretation or compilation process. Applying eLePUS to specify the GoF patterns' Collaboration aspect resulted in a greater success of about 90%.

Although some knowledge of sets and logic are required in addition to the special notation, such as $\stackrel{+}{\rightarrow}$, in order to write design specifications using eLePUS, the task does not seem as taxing as writing them in a language such as *Z* (Davies & Woodcock, 1996).

Beyond questions of eLePUS's ability to represent various aspects of patterns, there is also the question of how useful such representations are for analyzing them. To treat the problem of deciding which of two patterns is better for use with a specified architecture, one approach would be to represent each pattern in eLePUS and compare them to the architectural specifications. For example, the *State* and *Component Configurator* patterns are quite similar in basic structure. However, the 2-dimensional inheritance hierarchy variable in the latter exhibits its emphasis on mutability of complex architecture. The *Reference-To-Single* predicate in *State* implies a simpler, more static environment in which the *Forwarding* relation with function arguments emphasizes the activity of the application. It is clear from these two eLePUS formulations what the objectives of the two patterns are and that they are distinct, and therefore, which, if any, is more appropriate for the given architecture.

If one deems that two patterns meet the requirements of the given specification, it would be wiser to choose the less complex. To resolve this issue, one could write the patterns in eLePUS. For analysis, one could replace each identifier by text of a fixed length, say b, except for variables of dimension>0, which are replaced by text of length like $exp_b(dimension+1)$. Count the number of characters in the resulting representations. Although this example measure is very simple and omits semantic complexity, it provides estimates of the patterns' relative structural complexities. The one with the smaller measure is likely to be the simpler. For example with $b=2$, the *State* pattern has a measure of 122, while the *Component Configurator* pattern measures 138, indicating that the former is simpler. This type of measure has been employed in other domains, such as human/computer interaction (Payne & Green, 1986), but no study of its efficacy was done for this domain as part of the eLePUS project. A somewhat more sophisticated approach would be to parse the patterns' eLePUS expressions according to the BNF grammar and count the depth and breadth of the parse trees, again assigning weights to the variables according to their dimensions. This would require a parser implementation to assist in the computation, so it remains as a project for future investigation.

Future Trends

There are many alternatives for applying and enhancing the LePUS in the context of Design patterns during the future. An obvious approach is to apply eLePUS, just like the LePUS effort described in this chapter, to concurrent patterns in order to assess its effectiveness in specifying their aspects in addition to structure. Exploration of formalizing pattern languages and pattern-oriented design and analysis are two other avenues for further investigation. Further research on methods of comparing and analyzing patterns using eLePUS for their specifications, such as the two suggested at the end of the previous section, may also be fruitful.

Conclusion

This chapter has described the experiences learned in applying and enhancing the LePUS language to the field of Design patterns. The LePUS is a promising alternative for specifying the structure of Design patterns due to its rigorous formal model and validation by its application to GoF patterns and concurrent patterns. Here, the scope of the LePUS is broadened and its associated limitations are reduced by augmenting it with additional features to adapt it for specifying additional aspects of Design patterns. eLePUS, the resulting enhancement, is capable of describing the Intent, Applicability, and the Collaboration aspects of Design patterns, as well as their Structure. The development of the LePUS and eLePUS are initial, yet promising and concrete, steps in the direction of formal specification of patterns and associated tool support and their proliferation in the efforts of designing software.

References

Agerbo, E., & Cornils, A. (1998). How to preserve the benefits of Design patterns. In *Proceedings of the 13th ACM OOPSLA'98* (pp. 134-143). New York: ACM Press.

Buschmann, F., Meunier, R., Rohernert, H., Sommerlad, P., & Stal, M. (1996). *A system of patterns*. New York: John Wiley & Sons.

Chinnasamy, S. (2000). *eLePUS: Extended language for pattern uniform specification*. Unpublished master's thesis, Department of Computer and Information Science, Indiana University, Purdue University, Indianapolis. Retrieved November 16, 2006, from http://www.cs.iupui.edu/~rraje/pub/elepus.pdf

Coplien, J., & Schmidt, D. (1995). *Pattern languages in program design*. Reading, MA: Addison-Wesley.

Davies, J., & Woodcock, J. (1996). *Using Z: Specification, refinement and proof*. International Series in Computer Science. Englewood Cliffs, NJ: Prentice Hall.

Durr, E., & van Katwijk, J. (1992). VDM++ —A formal specification language for object-oriented design. In *Proceedings of CompEuro'92* (pp. 214-219). Los Alamitos, CA: IEEE Press.

Eden, A. (1998, June). Giving "the quality" a name (Guest column). *Journal of Object-Oriented Programming, 3*(11), 5-11.

Eden, A. (2000). *Precise specification of Design patterns and tool support in their application*. Unpublished doctoral dissertation, Department of Computer Science, Tel Aviv University, Israel.

Eden, A., & Hirshfeld, Y. (1999). LePUS—Symbolic logic modeling of object-oriented architecture: A case study. In *Proceedings of the 2nd Nordic Workshop on Software Architecture—NOSA*, Ronneby, Sweden. Retrieved November 16, 2006, from http:// www.eden-study.org/articles/1999/nosa99.pdf

Gamma, E., Helm, R., Johnson, R., & Vlissides, J. (1995). *Design patterns: Elements of reusable object-oriented software*. Reading, MA: Addison-Wesley.

Guttag, J., & Horning, J. (1993). *Larch: Languages and tools for formal specification*. Heidelberg, Germany: Springer-Verlag.

Helm, R., Holland, I., & Gangopadhyay, D. (1990). Contracts: Specifying behavioral compositions in object-oriented systems. In *Proceedings of OOPSLA/ECOOP'90* (pp. 169-180). Heidelberg, Germany: Springer Verlag.

Higdon, W. (2003). *Formal representation of distributed computing Design patterns with LePUS*. Unpublished master's project (TR-CIS-2904-03), Department of Computer and Information Science, Indiana University, Purdue University, Indianapolis. Retrieved November 16, 2006, from http://pages.uindy.edu/~whigdon/HigdonW_DP.pdf

Jarvinen, H., & Suonio, R. (1991). DisCo specification language: Marriage of actions and objects. In *Proceedings of the 11th International Conference on Distributed Computing Systems* (pp. 142-151). Los Alamitos, CA: IEEE Press.

Lauder, A., & Kent, S. (1998). Precise visual specification of Design patterns. In *Proceedings of ECOOP'98* (LNCS 1445, pp. 114-134). Heidelberg, Germany: Springer Verlag.

Luckham, D., & Vera, J. (1995). An event-based architecture definition language. *IEEE Transactions on Software Engineering, 21*(9), 717-734.

Payne, S., & Green, T. (1986). Task-action grammars: A model of mental-representation of task languages. In *Human-Computer Interaction* (vol. 2, pp. 93-133). Mahwah, NJ: Lawrence Earlbaum Associates.

Raje, R., & Chinnasamy, S. (2001). eLePUS—A language for specification of software Design patterns. In *Proceedings of the ACM SAC2001* (pp. 600-604). New York: ACM Press.

Schmidt, D., Stal, M., Rohnert, H., & Buschmann, F. (2000). *Pattern-oriented software architecture (vol. 2): Patterns for concurrent and networked objects*. New York: John Wiley & Sons.

Tichy, F. (1980). *Software development control based on system structure description*. Unpublished doctoral dissertation, Carnegie Mellon University, Pittsburgh, PA.

Chapter XII

An Ontology Based Representation of Software Design Patterns

Jens Dietrich, Massey University, New Zealand

Chris Elgar, SolNet Solutions Limited, New Zealand

Abstract

This chapter introduces an approach to define Design patterns using semantic Web technologies. For this purpose, a vocabulary based on the Web ontology language OWL is developed. Design patterns can be defined as RDF documents instantiating this vocabulary, and can be published as resources on standard Web servers. This facilitates the use of patterns as knowledge artefacts shared by the software engineering community. The instantiation of patterns in programs is discussed, and the design of a tool is presented that can x-ray programs for pattern instances based on their formal definitions.

Introduction

Design patterns are artefacts used to share knowledge across particular communities. Software Design patterns (Gamma, Helm, Johnson, & Vlissides, 1995) describe structural and behavioural properties of software, and are used by the software engineering community in order to exchange knowledge about software design. Currently, this is done the old-fashioned way: patterns are published in books or on Web sites, and consumed by people reading and applying them. This includes recognising pattern instances in programs in order to comprehend the structure of complex programs, and using patterns as design blueprints in order to address a specific design problem.

The main limitation with this modus operandi is the lack of tool support—patterns have to be found, and good and appropriate patterns have to be selected manually. A more effective, tool supported way of processing patterns (in particular instantiation and recognition) requires a formal representation of the patterns that supports reasoning about patterns. There are some obvious contenders of modeling frameworks and languages that could be used for this purpose. This includes first order predicate logic, higher order logic, and UML based modeling languages (either profiles or separate, MOF based modeling languages). In recent years, several approaches to Design pattern formalisation have been proposed based on these choices. While these representations allow us to reason about the internal structure of a pattern, there is limited support for reasoning about the patterns themselves, their metadata, and relationships to other patterns. Moreover, logic based and UML based approaches usually lead to monolithic, static models. While this has advantages (for instance, to ensure the consistency of the models) it does not support the sharing of patterns in an open environment like the Internet. Here, knowledge is distributed and inherently inconsistent, and additional means are needed to deal with inconsistency. This is one of the key issues addressed by the Semantic Web initiative endorsed by the W3C (Berners-Lee, Hendler, & Lassila, 2001). The Semantic Web is based on the idea of a distributed, open knowledge base where everybody can publish knowledge in the form of simple subject-predicate-object assertions. This leads necessarily to inconsistencies that must be resolved. The key to solving this problem is the prioritisation of knowledge based on metadata annotations—knowledge is selected based on the author, the time of creation, and other explicit and harvested metadata.

Another issue is whether it is realistic to hope that the software engineering community will adopt one particular model or vocabulary to represent patterns. It seems more likely that there will be multiple models, each supported by a particular community, standard body, or vendor group. Mappings defining transformations between instances of the respective models will have to be developed. In the case of formal logic, this is only possible with higher order constructs describing the relationship between different predicates, functions, and types. For UML based models, standards to transform instances of different meta models are only emerging now in the realm of model driven architecture (MDA), in particular QVT ("MOF QVT Final Adopted Specification," 2005). On the other hand, modern ontology languages like OWL have built-in support to express the relationship between different ontologies.

We claim that a modeling language suitable to publish Design patterns on the Web should meet the following requirements:

1.   A formal semantics is needed in order to safeguard reasoning about the patterns.

2.   Pattern definitions must be easy to process by tools. In particular, this is the case if an XML based serialization format is supported.

3.   There must be facilities to describe the relationships with alternative models, languages, or pattern vocabularies.

4.   The physical distribution of pattern definitions and the separation of schema and instances must be supported. The pattern definition language itself should be deployed as a network resource and single pattern definitions should reference this resource. In particular, it should be possible to validate the pattern definitions against such a central schema. This is similar to the validation of XML documents against their XML schema or DTD. Furthermore, patterns refining other patterns can also refer to them as network resources, and clients can easily resolve these references using standard network clients.

It appears that a pattern deifntion language based on the Web ontology language OWL (McGuinness & Harmelen, 2004) meets these requirements. Firstly, OWL has a formal semantics (Patel-Schneider, Hayes, & Horrocks, 2004) and built-in derivation rules which support safe reasoning about patterns. This can be used to infer additional knowledge from models or to check them for consistency. Secondly, OWL ontologies (both schemas and instances) can be serialised as XML using the RDF/XML syntax, and a growing number of tools are available to facilitate the work with OWL knowledge bases, including editors like Protégé (Knublauch, Musen, & Rector, 2004), APIs like Jena ("Jena – A Semantic Web Framework for Java," 2006), documentation tools like OWLDoc ("OWLDoc," 2006) and reasoners such as Fact (Horrocks, 1999), Pellet (Sirin, Parsia, Grau, Kalyanpur, & Katz, 2006) and Racer (Haarslev & Moeller, 2001). Thirdly, OWL has built-in constructs that can be used to describe the relationship between different vocabularies. Fourthly, OWL has a simple yet powerful import facility (owl:imports[1]) that can be used to reference the assertions made in external knowledge bases. In particular, this feature can be used to link ontology instances with a central ontology schema.

For this reason we believe that OWL is a suitable language to formalise Design patterns. In this chapter, we will present an ontology that can be used to define patterns. We discuss how metadata can be used to reason about patterns, and sketch how tools can process these definitions. This leads to a discussion on Design pattern instances. The results presented here are mainly based on Dietrich and Elgar (2005a, 2005b).

Background

The Semantic Web initiative aims at turning the Web currently focusing on human end users into a Web that also contains content that can be processed by machines (Berners-Lee et al., 2001). The basic infrastructure is provided by the resource description framework RDF (Klyne & Carroll, 2004)—a simple language that uses subject-predicate-object constructs to describe resources. This strongly resembles the structure of the Web for humans consisting of node-link-node triples with Web pages being the nodes and the hyper links connecting them being the edges.

Meaning is added to RDF by using an ontology language such as RDFS, DAML-OIL, or OWL. We focus on OWL as it is the most expressive of these languages, and has been standardised by the W3C. Using OWL, resources can be associated with resource types (classes), and predicates[2] can be defined for associating instances of certain classes. Furthermore, several constraints can be expressed restricting properties, and rules can be added to allow the assertion of new, additional properties. The formal semantics of OWL defines the precise meaning of these language constructs, and forms the sound base for OWL reasoners (Patel-Schneider et al., 2004). By describing how concepts are used in context, ontologies are defined—shared terminologies or "specifications of a conceptualization" (Gruber, 1993).

In Dietrich and Elgar (2005a), we have developed a terminology expressive enough to define basic Design patterns, and open enough to be extended whenever more expressiveness is required. This openness is important to define patterns that have a limited scope. Traditional pattern catalogues like the GangOf4 catalogue aim at programming language independent patterns, and their scope is object-oriented programming in general. However, it does make sense to publish patterns that refer to features not present in all languages, such as inner classes and annotations (Java) or class instance variables (Smalltalk). The scope of these patterns is a certain programming language, and they are shared within their respective communities. While the core ontology presented here does not directly support such PL specific patterns, it can be easily extended in various ways to do so.

Using OWL (or RDF for that matter) has another advantage: patterns are identified by uniform resource identifiers (URIs). These URIs are usually composed from the pattern name and a name space. This allows distinguishing between several flavours of one pattern all using the same name. A good example is Iterator. The definitions presented in Gamma et al. (1995) and Grand (1998) differ—the GangOf4 definition has an additional first() method. The Iterator pattern used in Java is again different—there is an additional, optional remove() method. Adding a name space and referencing the pattern with the full URI immediately removes the ambiguity from the pattern definitions.

An Ontology for Software Design Patterns

Metamodeling Architecture

The formal definition of Design patterns, their participants, and the properties of and relationships between the participants proposed here is based on an OWL ontology, that is, on a system of OWL classes, their properties, and relationships. These classes are instantiated in Design pattern definitions. Design patterns themselves do not contain classes, methods, and similar programming artefacts, but only placeholders or role names for such artefacts. In other words, Design pattern definitions contain typed variables that are instantiated by a particular pattern instance found in a concrete program. It has been pointed out by Eden

Figure 1. Metamodeling architecture

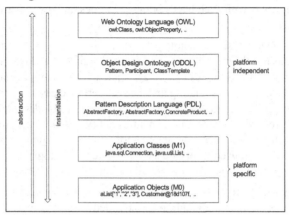

(2002a) that for this reason UML class models are not suitable to represent Design patterns. The same applies to other M1 models—they contain concrete classes, not variables. In Dietrich and Elgar (2005a) we have proposed a meta model architecture to tackle this problem (Figure 1). The lower layers correspond to MOF M0 (application objects) and M1 (application classes, members, and associations). M1 artefacts instantiate pattern participants defined using the pattern description language (PDL). These are the variables found in pattern definitions like the AbstractFactory and the AbstractProduct in the AbstractFactory (Gamma et al., 1995) pattern. These variables are typed. The types are constraints restricting the kind of (M1) artefact that can instantiate these variables. These types are modeled in the object design ontology layer (ODOL). In ODOL, the (OWL) ontology defined is the base for the pattern definitions. It contains classes such as ClassTemplate and MethodTemplate and their relationships, as well as the Pattern class representing patterns themselves. The meta model of ODOL is OWL– ODOL contains instances of OWL classes (for instance, owl:Class and owl:ObjectProperty).

The Ontology Schema

The ODOL ontology presented here is a revised version of the ontology presented in Dietrich and Elgar (2005a), adding pattern refinement and aligning it with the refactoring meta model proposed in Tichelaar, Ducasse, Demeyer, and Nierstrasz (2000). This adds significant expressiveness to the ontology, as it makes it possible to attribute relationships between participants such as Access, Association, and Invocation. Figure 2 does not show the full ontology, and in particular the data type properties (owl:DatatypeProperty) are omitted for space reasons. This includes the abstractness of class templates, access modifiers for member templates, cardinalities for associations, and similar properties. For the complete ontology, the reader is referred to "The ODOL OWL Ontology" (2006). The graph syntax used in Figure 2 and Figure 3 should not be confused with the RDF instantiation syntax. While

Figure 2. The ODOL ontology: Class hierarchy

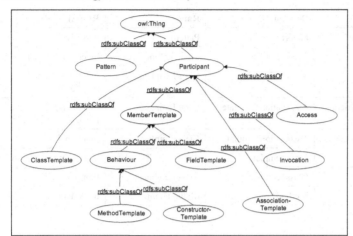

Figure 3. The ODOL ontology: Object properties

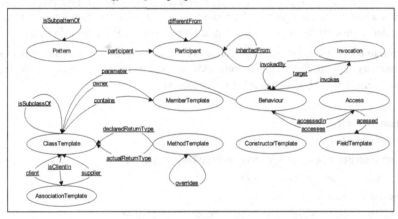

the nodes do represent RDF resources (the OWL classes that are part of ODOL), the edges are object properties (owl:ObjectProperty) having the start node as the domain (rdfs:domain) and the end node as the range (rdfs:range). This is different from standard RDF graphs. We emphasise this difference by underlining the property names.

Built-In Rules

The model has a number of constraints describing its intended meaning. In particular, object properties are associated with OWL property types. For these types, the OWL semantics defines rules that can be used by reasoners to check the consistency of the model, and to infer

Table 1. ODOL rules (selection)

Property	Domain	Range	Rule(s)
isSubPatternOf	Pattern	Pattern	transitive
contains	ClassTemplate	MemberTemplate	inverseOf "owner"
owner	MemberTemplate	ClassTemplate	inverseOf "contains", functional
associationClient	AssociationTemplate	ClassTemplate	functional, inverseOf "isClientIn"
associationSupplier	AssociationTemplate	ClassTemplate	functional
isClientIn	ClassTemplate	AssociationTemplate	inverseOf "associationClient"
isSubclassOf	ClassTemplate	ClassTemplate	transitive
overrides	MethodTemplate	MethodTemplate	transitive

additional assertions. This implies that pattern definitions do not have to include assertions that are redundant according to those rules. However, it is useful to have these redundant statements when processing pattern definitions, as this results in a better connected graph that is easier to process by applications. Table 1 shows some of the built-in rules.

In addition to these rules, the ontology contains references to *informal* definitions of some of the concepts defined. For instance, the (XML version of the) ontology contains the following references to Web sites intended for end users:

```
<owl:Class rdf:ID="Pattern">
    <owl:sameAs
     rdf:resource="http://en.wikipedia.org/wiki/Design_pattern_
        %28computer_science%29"/>
    <owl:sameAs
     rdf:resource="http://hillside.net/patterns/definition.html"/>
</owl:Class>
```

Code Snippet 1: Informal definition of pattern in ODOL.

While the formal rules listed in Table 1 can be used directly by tools to process pattern definitions, these statements are intended for human end users like application programmers in order to help them to write correct applications consuming the patterns defined using this ontology. Using the terminology proposed by Uschold (2003), ODOL contains *formal* semantics intended for machine processing as well as *informal* semantics intended for human processing.

Defining Patterns

While the Design pattern ontology resembles the classical UML meta model, it contains some features that add additional expressiveness needed to represent Design patterns. For instance, the AbstractFactory pattern (Gamma et al., 1995) contains a ConcreteFactory method that overrides an AbstractFactory method and returns an instance of a ConcreteProduct class. The declared return type of the ConcreteFactory method instantiation equals the declared return type of the abstract method instantiation. Therefore, we must be able to distinguish between declared return type and the actual return type. In Code Snippet 2, the declared return type of the create method is the Connection class, while the actual return type is the ConnectionImpl class.

```
1. public Connection create () {
2.     return new ConnentionImpl () ;
3. }
```

Code Snippet 2: A concrete factory method.

Figure 4. The AbstractFactory pattern (participants and their types)

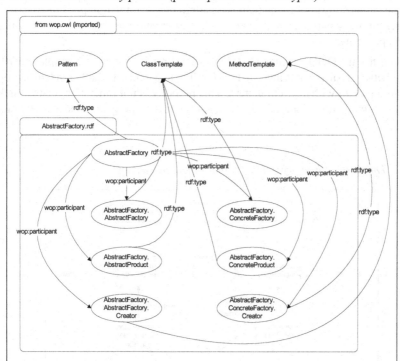

To address this problem, the ontology has two object properties associating method templates with return types (class templates): declaredReturnType and actualReturnType. There is an implicit constraint relating these two properties that can be expressed as a rule:

actualReturnType(m,t$_1$) & declaredReturnType(m,t$_2$) $\Rightarrow$isSubclassOf(t$_1$,t$_2$)

Currently, this kind of rule is not part of the ontology. Languages like OWL do not support custom derivation rules, although this area is an active area of research with emerging standards such as RuleML (Boley, Tabet, & Wagner, 2001) and SWRL (Patel-Schneider et al., 2004). Therefore, the isSubclassOf property cannot be inferred and has to be added explicitly to the pattern definition, and it remains the responsibility of the client to check the constraint. On the instance level, this would usually be done by a compiler.

The definition of AbstractFactory (without data type properties) is depicted in Figure 4 and Figure 5. The types are defined in the central ontology deployed at a certain URL. This resource is explicitly imported using an owl:imports directive. This allows maintaining a central ontology that can be referenced by different patterns.

Pattern Refinement

Pattern refinement defines an inheritance relationship between patterns. Using refinement, patterns inherit participants from parent patterns, and add new participants or new relationships. The simplest form of refinement is a pattern definition that imports another pattern, references all of the participants using the wop:participant property, and adds new participants and properties.

In addition to this, ODOL contains additional constructs to support multiple inheritance and joins between participants inherited from different parents. The isSubPatternOf property associates a pattern with a parent pattern. This property is not functional, that is, multiple inheritance is explicitly permitted. The semantics of this property is that all participants and

Figure 5. The AbstractFactory pattern (other object properties)

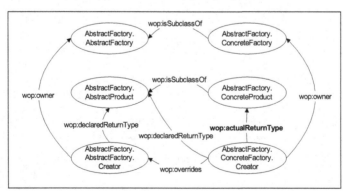

their properties of the parent pattern are appended to the definition of the importing pattern. Using a derivation rule, this can be expressed as follows:

isSubPatternOf(pat_1,pat_2) & participant(pat_2,part) $\Rightarrow$ participant(pat_1,part)

The inheritedFrom relationship identifies participants with participants inherited from parents. The semantics is simple, the bindings for these participants must be the same. This property is also not functional, that is, a "local" participant can be associated with more than one imported/inherited participant. This allows joining inherited participants, as depicted in Figure 6. In this example, the CompositeVisitor is a Visitor (Gamma et al., 1995) visiting a Composite (Gamma et al., 1995) structure. It refines both the Visitor and the Composite-Visitor pattern.

Multiple inheritance can lead to conflicts, for instance if participants with contradicting properties are defined. It is again part of the informal semantics of ODOL to require that inheritedFrom can only associate properties with no conflicting ODOL properties. That means that:

1.   If two joined participants have an ODOL data type property, then the values of these participants must be the same.
2.   The graph containing participants and ODOL object properties obtained by replacing the participants referenced using the inheritedFrom predicate by the referencing participants must be consistent.

Figure 6. Definition of CompositeVisitor using pattern refinement (imported participants are represented by the shapes with a darker colour)

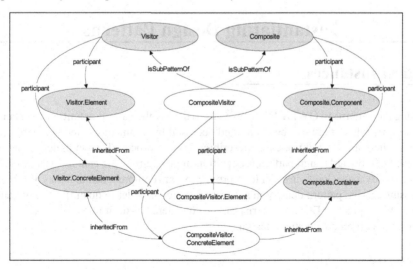

An example for how condition 2 could be violated is the following situation: let R be a functional property in ODOL, and let R(a,b) and R(c,d) be statements in two pattern definitions P1 and P2 (written in relational syntax). If P is a sub pattern of both P1 and P2 with conditions joining a and c, but no condition joining b and d, the "functional" condition for R would be violated.

Note that both integrity conditions are explicitly referring to the ODOL vocabulary. Conflicts in other vocabularies might not be as critical. In particular, conflicts concerning metadata (such as dc:Description or dc:Creator) are acceptable.

Attaching Meta Information

Reasoning about patterns becomes important if patterns are published in an open, essentially uncontrolled and unmoderated environment like the Internet. In particular, this reasoning will facilitate the selection of trustworthy knowledge. There are no special constructs in ODOL to support metadata, instead standard vocabularies are used. In particular, the Dublin Core ("The Dublin Core Metadata Initiative," 2006) properties can be used to annotate the pattern instances in pattern definitions. Using these annotations, derivation rules can be used to select all GangOf4 patterns (using an assertion like "dc:Creator=GangOf4"). Often, additional predicates have to be used in these rules, either based on explicit meta information, or on harvested meta information such as:

1.   **isSecure:** Has an HTTPS connection been used to download patterns?

2.   **isKnownBy:** Is the pattern resource referenced by the Web sites of pattern communities such as hillside.net or on vendor Web sites like ibm.com.

3.   **isWellknown:** Is the pattern definition known as well referenced by Google? That is, does the Google query link:<aPatternURL> return more than 42 results?

Instantiating Design Patterns

Pattern Instances

Defining the patterns in OWL/RDF enables us to deploy the pattern definitions on standard Web servers, where they can be found and accessed by applications and standard search engines. There are several use cases describing how to process Design patterns, the most important one being Design pattern recognition in programs. This enables users to X-Ray complex software packages in order to improve program comprehension. It may also be used to measure Design pattern density in software package in order to quantify design quality: the use of best practise Design patterns can be considered as desirable as it makes it easier for teams to communicate about design.

The Design pattern definitions can be easily translated into derivation rules in typed first order logic with the pattern itself as the predicate in the head of the respective rule, and the pattern participants as free variables. The precise definition is presented in Dietrich and Elgar (2005b), and we use the AbstractFactory pattern to explain the transformation. The pattern has the following participants: AbstractFactory (af), AbstractProduct (ap), ConcreteFactory (cf), ConcreteProduct (cp), AbstractFactory.Creator (afc), ConcreteFactory.Creator (cfc). These participants are associated with typed variables, and the types are the respective ODOL classes. The head of the rule is AbstractFactory(af,ap,cf,cp,afc,cfc). The prerequisites of the rule are:

1.   isSubclassOf(cf, af)

2.   isSubclassOf(cp, ap)

3.   contains(af, afc)

4.   contains(cf.cfc)

5.   declaredReturnType(afc,ap)

6.   declaredReturnType(cfc,ap)

7.   actualReturnType(cfc, cp)

8.   overrides(cfc, afc)

9.   isAbstract(af,"abstract")

10.   isAbstract(afc, "abstract")

11.   isAbstract(ap,"abstract")

12.   ..

That is, object properties are translated into binary constraints associating participants with other participants (or more precisely, the respective variables), while data type properties are transformed into binary predicates associating participants with string literals. The typing imposes additional constraints that can be seen as unary predicates. In the AbstractFactory example, this would lead to additional prerequisites such as isClass(af), isMethod(afc), and so forth. Similar to the mechanisms proposed by other authors (Beyer, Noack, & Lewerentz, 2003; Eden, 2002a; Kraemer & Prechelt, 1996), Design pattern detection becomes a matter of instantiating the variables in these rules. The values binding the variables are artefacts from the program to be analysed. Artefacts include classes and their members, but also associations, method invocations, and field accesses. If Var(P) denotes the set of participants in a pattern P and A(Progr) the set of artefacts in a program Progr, then a pattern instance is a function instance:Var(P)→A(Progr).

Instantiation requires a universe of artefacts to be extracted from the analysed program, and a set of ground facts for the predicates used in the rules instantiated using these artefacts. Because the rules are structurally fairly simple (datalog without negation), the only challenge is to find the appropriate fact base. The universe itself must contain representations of the artefacts found in the program. These could either be names, instances of classes of the programming language representing artefacts (such as reflection frameworks), or instances of classes from separate object models describing the structure of programs. As far as the fact base is concerned, there are some fundamentally different approaches that can be used to instantiate predicates. This includes:

1.   Using the reflective features of the programming language itself. Most modern PLs offer such a feature, and relationships such as membership, return type, and inheritance can be easily instantiated.

2.   Source code analysis. Reflection based analysis is usually not suitable to instantiate associations and invocations. This often requires source code analysis. The respective concepts have been studied comprehensively in the realm of compiler technology. Source code is usually represented by abstract syntax trees (AST), and analysis is done using AST visitors. Using visitors, symbol tables are compiled to resolve the references between artefacts.

3.   Naming pattern analysis. Often naming patterns do have meaning, and they can be used for program analysis as well. A good example for meaningful naming patterns is the java bean specification ("The JavaBeans Spec," 2006).The use of certain prefixes for method names and parameter signatures indicates that there are certain properties of and relationships between objects. An example is the one to many relationship between event sources and event listeners. Tools such as GUI builders use these semantics.

4.   Behavioural analysis. Based on the run and observe approach, behavioural analysis can detect relationships not accessible by any of the above methods. This includes the analysis of code that uses reflection, for instance the interpretation of strings as methods. Behavioural analysis requires that the program can be executed "completely," that is, that each code branch is visited during code execution. In some cases, complete execution is provided by test suites, particularly if test-case driven methodologies like extreme programming (Beck, 1999) are used in conjunction with tools measuring test coverage. Technically, behavioural analysis can take advantage of debugging APIs or newer approaches used to instrument code (for instance, aspect-oriented programming).

Client Architecture

The WebOfPatterns (WOP) project ("The WebOfPatterns Project," 2006) is a client that consumes and produces pattern definitions based on ODOL. Technically, the client is an Eclipse plugin. It interprets the pattern definitions in Java, and features the following functionality: a *pattern scanner* with a built-in HTTP client that downloads patterns from a given URL, detects pattern instances in Eclipse Java projects and compiles JavaDoc style (HTML and XML) reports from the findings. The client also supports several pattern aggregations (see page 15). A *pattern browser* generates a graph from pattern definitions that can be navigated in a browser-like manner. A *pattern publishing wizard* allows users to select artefacts, their properties and relationships from projects, give those artefacts abstract role names, and generate the pattern definition as a RDF file. This file can then be deployed on a standard Web server.

The WOP client serves as a reference application for the ontology. It contains guidelines on how to consume the ontology based pattern definitions. This makes it part of the "formal semantics for human processing" (Uschold, 2003). This is similar to software specifications—many specs consist mainly of interfaces (UML, IDL, Java interfaces). The semantics of these interfaces is defined by documents, formal constraints (like OCL), and test suites. Often, a reference implementation is provided that can be considered as part of the semantics—software engineers are referred to the reference implementation if the other parts of the specification leave questions open.

The pattern scanner is the most important part of the WOP client, as it has to map the structures defined in the ontology to the structures found in the Java programming language. This is rather simple for some elements, as there is an obvious homomorphism (structure preserving mapping) between the ontology and the grammar of the programming language—classes have methods, methods have return types, and so forth. It is less obvious for participants that have no direct counterparts in Java, such as Association.

The WOP Client has the following structure:

- Participants are represented by Java classes in the nz.ac.massey.cs.wop package. Example: AssociationTemplate, ClassTemplate, Participant, Pattern.

- Artefacts instantiating the participants are represented by Java classes in the nz.ac.massey.cs.wop.reflect package. Example: Association, JClass, JMethod, and so forth.

- Object properties are represented by classes implementing the interface nz.ac.massey.cs.wop.BinaryConstraint<SOURCE,TARGET> in the nz.ac.massey.cs.wop.constraints package. Example: IS_SUBCLASS_OF, OVERRIDES.

- Data type properties are represented by subclasses of nz.ac.massey.cs.wop.UnaryConstraint<TYPE> in the nz.ac.massey.cs.wop.constraints package. Examples: IS_ABSTRACT_CLASS, IS_PUBLIC_MEMBER.

The type parameters of the generic constraint classes represent the types associated by the respective constraints. This must be consistent with the domain and the range types of the associated object property. The constraints contain methods defining the extension of the respective (unary or binary) predicate in the context of the program investigated. The Eclipse project analysed is represented by an instance of Workspace. This contains a reference to a class loader, the byte code location(s), the source code location(s), and entry points for behavioural analysis. In particular, the BinaryConstraint interface defines the following three methods (SOURCE and TARGET are the generic type parameters):

1. boolean check(SOURCE,TARGET,Workspace)

2. Iterator<SOURCE> getPossibleSourceInstances(Workspace,TARGET)

3. Iterator<TARGET> getPossibleTargetInstances(Workspace,SOURCE)

Code Snippet 3: Methods in BinaryConstraint defining the semantics of an object property in Java

These methods precisely define the semantics of the associated object property. The first method allows verifying whether two given instances instantiate the predicate. The other two methods return an iterator over possible instances if one instance is known. This supports the "navigation" of the predicates. There is no method that computes the entire extension of the predicate (i.e., an iterator over SOURCE-TARGET pairs). This is highly inefficient and can generally be avoided by choosing appropriate algorithms to resolve the constraints.

For instance, the IS_SUBCLASS_OF class implements BinaryConstraint as follows:

1.   Both SOURCE and TARGET are JClass, JClass.

2.   If instances of both source and target are given, reflection (isAssignableFrom in java.lang.Class) is used to check whether class 1 is a subclass of class 2.

3.   If only the source is known, the reflection methods getSuperclass() and getInterfaces() are recursively called, the results are collected in a collection and an iterator over this collection is returned.

4.   If only the target is known, all classes in the workspace are scanned to find all subclasses of the target, and the respective iterator is returned.

In general, classes implementing the interface nz.ac.massey.cs.wop.reflect.Analyser provide the structural information needed by the constraint classes. Analysers are organised as a chain, and if an analyser cannot provide the information requested the next analyser is called (ChainOfResponsibility pattern (Gamma et al., 1995)). The analysers currently implemented are based on reflection, (Eclipse) AST analysis, and naming pattern analysis.

The pattern scanner itself uses cost-based scheduling to arrange the constraint in an optimal order. It always attempts to solve "cheap" constraints (like those that can be verified using reflection) first, and arranges constraints so that at least one of the participants is already known. This is facilitated by having redundant constraints (the deductive closure according to the rules encoded in the ontology in Table 1), as this results in a better connected graph consisting of participants as nodes and binary constraints as edges. The ontology itself is accessed using the Jena ("Jena – A Semantic Web Framework for Java," 2006) framework that includes an OWL reasoner.

The constraint resolution process uses a simplified version of SLD (Robinson, 1965). The unification can be simplified as there are no complex terms in the pattern rule.

Validation

The question arises whether the formal pattern definitions and the tool processing them (the pattern scanner) capture the meaning of the respective pattern. This includes two aspects: firstly, correctness, that is, are all pattern instances detected *intended* instances? Secondly, completeness, that is, are all intended instances found by the scanner? In other terms, are there false positives (correctness) and are there false negatives (completeness)?

The WebOfPatterns client has been validated using test cases based on code that is part of two text books on patterns in Java (Grand, 1998; Stelting & Maassen, 2001). While this validation is successful in the sense that all test cases succeed, it has some obvious weaknesses. Firstly, the code examples used in these text books are (on purpose) very simple, and more complex language features such as inner classes and reflection, are avoided. The current version of the WebOfPatterns source code analyser does not support inner classes, and therefore certain instances of predicates like actualReturnType and invokedBy are not detected. That is, the fact base built by the client is incomplete. Therefore, certain pattern instances are not found—there are false negatives. But as this is mainly due to limitations of the current implementation of the analysers, the problem should be solved as the client is improved. If behavioural analysis is used, the completeness of the fact base still depends on whether the analyser is able to cover the entire program. This would be the case for programs with unit test cases and 100% test coverage.

An interesting approach to validation would be the comparison of scan results with the results produced by other tools such as CrocoPat (Beyer, Noack, & Lewerentz, 2003) and Fujaba (Niere, Schafer, Wadsack, Wendehals, & Welsh, 2002).

The question whether there are false positives is more difficult to answer and requires the analysis of some scan results. This leads to the introduction of some new concepts related to pattern instantiation.

Normal and Aggregated Instances

The analysis of pattern instances found in non trivial programs reveals a number of "unintended instances." Most of them feature different participants instantiated by one artefact. For instance, consider the following code snippet:

```
1. public abstract class A {
2.    public abstract A copy ( ) ;
3. }
4. public class AImpl extends A {
5.    public A copy ( ) {
6.       A clone = new AImpl ( ) ;
7.       / / configure, set instance variables
8.       return clone;
9.    }
10. }
```

This program instantiates AbstractFactory in a trivial way: A is both the AbstractFactory (role) and the AbstractProduct, while AImpl is the ConcreteFactory and the ConcreteProduct. In this program, a cloneable structure is defined, with A representing the specification of the structure and AImpl being an implementor. The question arises whether there is an implicit constraint in AbstractFactory that requires that the factory and the product must be different. The ontology does contain the respective language feature, the wop:differentFrom property[3]. For some patterns, there is clearly a need for such a constraint. For example, in the Proxy (Gamma et al., 1995) pattern, the Proxy (wrapper) and the RealSubject (the wrapped

Table 2. Scan results

Package	Time[d] (s)	Abstract-Factory	Adapter	Bridge	Composite	Proxy	Template-Method
Mandarax 3.4	35	166	91	0	3	2	495
MySQL Con-nectorJ 3.1.12	134	56	289	28	0	0	0

class) must be different. For other patterns the situation is less clear. In this case we opt for not having such an explicit constraint. This leaves two options open: to use the refinement mechanism to add such an explicit constraint in a sub pattern, or make it a feature of the client to add the wop:differentFrom constraints on demand. Conceptually, we call instances of patterns where different participants are mapped to different artefacts *normal*. In other terms, normal pattern instances are injective.

The number of "good" instances found is surprisingly high. Often it is useful to identify some instances by abstracting from certain details. For instance, two AbstractFactory instances might be considered equal if all abstract participants are mapped to the same artefacts. Two instances of Bridge (Gamma et al., 1995) could be considered variants of the same instance if they have the same abstraction and the same implementor. In general, pattern aggregation is used to identify certain patterns. Instead of considering pattern instances as defined above, classes of instances modulo an equivalence relation $\sim$. This relation meets the following three conditions:

1. **Reflexivity:** $\forall$ instance: instance $\sim$ instance
2. **Symmetry:** $\forall$ instance$_1$,instance$_2$: instance$_1 \sim$ instance$_2 \Rightarrow$ instance$_2 \sim$ instance$_1$
3. **Transitivity:** $\forall$ instance$_1$,instance$_2$,instance$_3$: instance$_1 \sim$ instance$_2$ & instance$_2 \sim$ instance$_3$ $\Rightarrow$ instance$_1 \sim$ instance$_3$

Such a relation can be defined as projection with respect to a subset of participants **S** that are part of a pattern as follows:

instance$_1 \sim_S$ instance$_2$ iff $\forall p \in S$:instance$_1$(p) = instance$_2$(p)

There are a number of possible aggregations, each defining a separate view on the structure of the program investigated.

1. Identify instances if they map all marked participants to the same artefacts. This allows a default aggregation to be built into the ontology, making this aggregation part of the pattern itself. For this purpose, the ontology has a built-in data type property isAggregationPoint that allows tagging participants explicitly.

Table 3. Pattern instance aggregation

Package/ Pattern	No Aggregation	Built-in Aggregation	Group by abstract participants	Group by abstract classes
Mandarax 3.4 / AbstractFactory	166	48	48	29
MySQL ConnectorJ 3.1.12 / AbstractFactory	56	46	46	16
MySQL ConnectorJ 3.1.12 / Bridge	28	1	8	1

2.   Identify instances if they map abstract participants to the same artefacts.

3.   Identify instances if they map abstract classes to the same artefacts.

4.   Identify instances mapping abstract class templates to the same classes, and method templates to methods sharing the same name and the same owner class. This allows the identification of instances containing overloaded methods.

5.   No aggregation ("null aggregator").

Aggregation of instances is an alternative to using higher order logic constructs like Eden's higher dimension entities (Eden, 2002b) to describe patterns. By adding default aggregation support to the pattern definition itself but also allowing tools to override it by applying no or alternative aggregations we gain greater flexibility in supporting alternative views on the system design.

Limitations of our Approach and Future Trends

There are some known limitations with the approach presented here. ODOL is not expressive enough to describe constraints referencing instances (and not classes). An example of a pattern that uses this kind of constraint is Prototype (Gamma et al., 1995). The Prototype participant contains a clone() method. The semantics of this method is to provide a copy of the Prototype *object*. In Java style syntax, this can be written as follows: "prototype. clone()!=prototype". This cannot be expressed directly using the current version of ODOL. To address this problem, a data type property isClone is defined in ODOL. The semantics of this method is mainly informal, and the responsibility to interpret it correctly is delegated to applications. Obviously, there is a trade-off here between ontological reductionism (having a small number of modeling primitives with a clear semantics) on the one side, and how simple and convenient it is for software engineers to use the ontology on the other side. In the long term, the solution is to have more expressive vocabularies and to define more derived concepts by means of explicit rules.

There are entire families of patterns for which the ontology presented here is not appropriate. Architectural patterns (Buschmann, Meunier, Rohnert, Sommerlad, Stal, Sommerlad, et al.,

1996) use concepts such as tier and layer. On the other hand, code level patterns like lazy initialisation refer to concepts used in PL grammars like blocks and error handlers.

A very promising direction for further research is the adoption of the approach presented by Fowler (1999) and Opdyke (1992) for refactoring. A formal, ontology based refactoring language would enable software engineers to find solutions to design problems on the Web, and to perform them in the context of the programming language used. The design problems themselves can be described using an ontology similar to the one presented here as antipatterns. By means of additional derivation rules similarity between patterns can be defined, further increasing the chances of finding a solution to problems encountered.

The relationship between the platform independent ontology layer and the interpretation of these concepts in a particular programming language is an interesting area for further research. We have argued that a client is more than just an implementation. The client has to interpret the concepts found in the ontology correctly. This warrants a closer integration of ontology and client. In particular, for languages like Java where components can be deployed as Web resources,[5] RDF statements can be used to associate object properties and their correct interpretation in a context given by a programming language (Java) and a client application (WOP).

The pattern scanner presented here is far from being mature. Despite the gaps in the AST analyser mentioned, there are other issues related to scalability. The main benefit of having a scalable pattern scanner in the standard toolbox of software engineers (in the form of ANT tasks, or Eclipse plugins) is that this will enable researchers to gather vast amounts of empirical data about software design, and how this design evolves. This may lead to new research on pattern based metrics, and investigations into quantifying the correlation between patterns and software quality.

Conclusion

In this chapter, we have shown how techniques developed in the realm of the semantic Web can be used to formalise software Design patterns. We have elaborated an ontology based on the Web ontology language OWL and have shown how this fits into a meta modeling framework that extends the meta modeling architecture used by the OMG. Several aspects related to pattern instantiation discussed are not only relevant to our approach, but should be addressed whenever Design patterns are formalised. In particular, this concerns validation and pattern instance aggregation.

The semantic Web offers tremendous opportunities for the software engineering community. This community is most likely to adapt the semantic Web as it is already accustomed to share much of the knowledge it produces on the Web. It has pioneered the use of Wikis and Blogs, and has found solutions for how to deal with inconsistencies in open environments. A good example is open source repositories like SourceForge using source control systems such as Subversion or CVS. Participating programmers produce inconsistencies that are resolved with merge and diff tools based on metadata (version tags, commit time, committer). Giving this community better tools to share their knowledge will significantly improve the way software engineering is done. It could eventually lead to an open eco system of patterns (and antipatterns, and refactoring, and ...) where Darwinian forces lead to the survival of the fittest.

Critical for the semantic Web to succeed in software engineering as well as in general is the availability of tools to manage the knowledge produced. Of particular importance is search engine support, for example, to be able to query Google for RDF resources containing instances of the ODOL ontology. Furthermore, modules that allow reasoning about knowledge based on customisable rules and mainly harvested metadata are needed.

Once the community accepts this approach, it is likely that domain specific ontologies will emerge serving the needs of particular communities. These communities are not necessarily organised around programming languages or vendors, but also application areas (desktop, server, embedded), industries (financial, e-commerce) or programming paradigms (Aspect-Oriented Programming). We will have to deal with a multidimensional space of ontologies. This poses new challenges for describing the relationships between these ontologies.

References

Beck, K. (1999). *Extreme programming explained: Embrace change*. Addison-Wesley Professional.

Berners-Lee, T., Hendler, J., & Lassila, O. (2001, May). The Semantic Web. *Scientific American*, 34-43.

Beyer, D., Noack, A., & Lewerentz, C. (2003). Simple and efficient relational querying of software structures. In *Paper presented at the 10th Working Conference on Reverse Engineering (WCRE 2003)*.

Boley, H., Tabet, S., & Wagner, G. (2001). Design rationale of RuleML: A markup language for Semantic Web rules. *Paper presented at the International Semantic Web Working Symposium (SWWS)*.

Buschmann, F., Meunier, R., Rohnert, H., Sommerlad, P., Stal, M., Sommerlad, P., et al. (1996). *Pattern-oriented software architecture, vol. 1: A system of patterns* (1st ed.). John Wiley & Sons.

Dietrich, J., & Elgar, C. (2005a). *A formal description of Design patterns using OWL*. Paper presented at the Australian Software Engineering Conference (ASWEC), 2005.

Dietrich, J., & Elgar, C. (2005b). *Towards a Web of patterns*. Paper presented at the Workshop on Semantic Web Enabled Software Engineering (SWESE), Galway.

The Dublin Core Metadata Initiative. (2006). Retrieved November 16, 2006, from http://dublincore.org/

Eden, A. (2002a). LePUS, A visual formalism for object-oriented architectures. *Paper presented at the 6th* World Conference on Integrated Design and Process Technology, Pasadena, California.

Eden, A. (2002b). A theory of object-oriented design. *Information Systems Frontiers, 4*(4), 379-391.

Fowler, M. (1999). *Refactoring: Improving the design of existing code*. Reading, MA: Addison-Wesley.

Gamma, E., Helm, R., Johnson, R., & Vlissides, J. (1995). *Design patterns: Elements of reusable object-oriented software*: Addison-Wesley.

Grand, M. (1998). *Patterns in Java: A catalog of reusable Design patterns illustrated with UML*. Wiley.

Gruber, T.R. (1993). A translation approach to portable ontologies. *Knowledge Acquisition, 5*(2), 199-220.

Haarslev, V., & Moeller, R. (2001). Description of the RACER system and its applications. *Paper presented at the 2001 International Workshop on Description Logics (DL2001)*, Stanford.

Horrocks, I. (1999). *FaCT and iFaCT*. Paper presented at the 1999 International Workshop on Description Logics (DL'99).

The JavaBeans Spec. (2006). Retrieved November 16, 2006, from http://java.sun.com/products/javabeans/docs/spec.html

Jena – A Semantic Web Framework for Java. (2006). Retrieved November 16, 2006, from http://jena.sourceforge.net/

Klyne, G., & Carroll, J.J. (2004). *Resource description framework (RDF): Concepts and abstract syntax*. W3C recommendation. Retrieved November 16. 2006, from http://www.w3.org/TR/rdf-concepts/

Knublauch, H., Musen, M., & Rector, A. (2004). Editing description logics ontologies with the Protégé OWL plugin. *Paper presented at the International Workshop on Description Logics*, Whistler, British Columbia.

Kraemer, C., & Prechelt, L. (1996). Design recovery by automated search for structural Design patterns in object-oriented software. *Paper presented at the 3rd Working Conference on Reverse Engineering (WCRE ,96)*.

McGuinness, D.L., & Harmelen, F.V. (2004). *OWL Web ontology language overview*. W3C recommendation. Retrieved November 16,2006, from *http://www.w3.org/TR/owl-features/*

MOF QVT Final Adopted Specification. (2005). Retrieved November 16, 2006, from http://www.omg.org/docs/ptc/05-11-01.pdf

Niere, J., Schafer, W., Wadsack, J.P., Wendehals, L., & Welsh, J. (2002). Towards pattern-based design recovery. *Paper presented at the 24th International Conference on Software Engineering (ICSE 2002)*.

The ODOL OWL Ontology. (2006). Retrieved November 16, 2006, from http://www-ist.massey.ac.nz/wop/20060324/wop.owl

Opdyke, W.F. (1992). *Refactoring object-oriented frameworks*. University of Illinois at Urbana-Champaign, IL.

OWLDoc. (2006). Retrieved November 16, 2006, from http://co-ode.man.ac.uk/downloads/owldoc/co-ode-index.php

Patel-Schneider, P.F., Hayes, P., & Horrocks, I. (2004). *OWL Web ontology language semantics and abstract syntax, W3C recommendation.* Retrieved November 16, 2006, from http://www.w3.org/TR/owl-semantics/

Robinson, J.A. (1965). A machine-oriented logic based on the resolution principle. *Journal of the ACM, 12*(1), 23-41.

Sirin, E., Parsia, B., Grau, B.C., Kalyanpur, A., & Katz, Y. (2006). Pellet: A practical OWL-DL reasoner. *Journal of Web Semantics (To Appear).*

Stelting, S., & Maassen, O. (2001). *Applied Java patterns.* Prentice Hall PTR.

Tichelaar, S., Ducasse, S., Demeyer, S., & Nierstrasz, O. (2000). *A meta-model for language-independent refactoring.* Paper presented at the International Symposium on Principles of Software Evolution.

Uschold, M. (2003). Where are the semantics in the semantic Web? *AI Magazine, 24*(3), 25-36.

The WebOfPatterns Project. (2006). Retrieved November 16, 2006, from http://www-ist.massey.ac.nz/wop/

Endnotes

[1]   Name space prefixes used in this chapter are defined as follows:

xmlns:wop="http://www.massey.ac.nz/iist/cs/pattern/ontology#"

xmlns:rdf="http://www.w3.org/1999/02/22-rdf-syntax-ns#"

xmlns:xsd="http://www.w3.org/2001/XMLSchema#"

xmlns:rdfs="http://www.w3.org/2000/01/rdf-schema#"

xmlns:owl="http://www.w3.org/2002/07/owl#"

xmlns:dc="http://purl.org/dc/elements/1.1/"

[2]   In OWL, properties are called *data type properties* and relationships/predicates associating resources are called *object properties*.

[3]   This property is different from owl:differentFrom that states that two individuals are different. The semantics of wop:differentFrom is that the respective participants have to be instantiated by different artefacts.

[4]   These results have been obtained using the following configuration: Pentium 4 CPU 3.20 GHz, 1GB RAM, Windows XP Pro, Java 1.5.0_06, Eclipse 3.1.0

[5]   Jar files can be deployed on Web servers and accessed using a special URL class loader.

Chapter XIII

Precision, Flexibility, and Tool Support:
Essential Elements of Pattern Formalization

Neelam Soundarajan, The Ohio State University, USA

Jason O. Hallstrom, Clemson Universtiy, USA

Abstract

There are two important requirements that any approach to formalizing Design patterns must meet. First, the approach must enable the precise specification of the implementation requirements and behavioral guarantees associated with a wide range of patterns. Second, the formalization of each pattern must retain the pattern's inherent flexibility. In this chapter, we present a novel approach to formalizing Design patterns that satisfies these seemingly conflicting requirements. For the formalism to be of practical value, we also need tools that can assist practitioners in determining whether the patterns used in designing their systems have been implemented correctly. Such tools are especially important during system maintenance and evolution to ensure that the design integrity of a system is not compromised. We show how our approach lends itself to the construction of such tools.

Introduction

Any pattern formalization approach must satisfy two seemingly conflicting requirements. First, the approach must enable the *precise* specification of the implementation requirements that must be satisfied by any system built using a particular pattern, and the resulting system behaviors that should be expected as a result. Second, the formalism must retain the pattern's inherent *flexibility*. It is this flexibility that is the hallmark of Design patterns, and one of the most important factors contributing to their success. Precise pattern formalization would seem to reduce this flexibility almost by definition. As we will see, however, this conflict can be resolved. The formalization approach that we describe in this chapter enables pattern specifications that are both *precise* and *flexible*. Indeed, somewhat surprisingly, our approach often helps to identify new dimensions of pattern flexibility.

If pattern formalizations are to be of practical value to developers, appropriate validation tools must be made available. Such tools are especially important during system maintenance and evolution when system design integrity is subject to erosion. We show how our approach lends itself to the construction of such tools.

Consider the conflict between precision and flexibility in the context of the classic *Observer* pattern. According to the informal description (Buschmann, Meunier, Rohnert, Sommerlad, & Stal, 1996; Gamma, Helm, Johnson, & Vlissides, 1995), there are two *roles* in this pattern, Subject and Observer. The pattern is intended to be used when one or more observer objects are interested in the state of a subject object. The informal description indicates that when the state of the subject changes, it must invoke notify(), which must in turn invoke update() on each of the subject's observers. The update() invocations must *update* the states of these observers to be *consistent* with the new state of the subject.

While this description may seem clear, there are a number of interesting subtleties that arise. What is meant, for example, when referring to the point at which "the state of the subject *changes*"? There are certainly systems in which some portions of a subject's state are irrelevant to its observers. *Significant* changes are what is of interest here. But what *precisely* constitutes a "*significant change*"? Further questions arise in the standard informal description: "subject notifies its observers whenever a change occurs that could make its observers' state inconsistent with its own" (Gamma et al., 1995, p. 295) But what *exactly* does it mean for an observer to be *consistent* with the state of a subject?

To put these questions differently, what if design team members have different interpretations of when notify() should be invoked? The system may exhibit subtle defects, or even defects that are not subtle at all, depending on the degree of variation across the team members' interpretations. The problem will be amplified as the system evolves, especially if the membership of the team changes. All members of the software team—both present and future—must have a clear and common understanding of the relevant pattern implementation requirements. This includes a precise understanding of when notify() must be invoked, and what it means for the state of an observer to be *consistent* with that of a subject.

The goal of pattern formalization is to facilitate this understanding. But this brings us face-to-face with the tension between precision and flexibility. If, for example, we were to adopt a single notion of *consistency* in our formalization of Observer, how could the pattern be applied in systems that require a different notion of this concept? Indeed, the conflict appears even more serious. Suppose that a particular subject has two different observers, each interested in a different portion of the subject's state. This is the scenario that we will consider in our running *Hospital* system example. The system implements a basic hospital simulation constructed using the Observer pattern. Instances of the Patient class play the role of Subject, and instances of Nurse *and* Doctor play the role of Observer – and what it means for a nurse to be consistent with a patient is different from what it means for a doctor to be consistent with a patient. So the notion of consistency varies *within the same system*! While the formalization of *Observer* would provide precise answers to the questions raised above, it would also seem to limit the pattern's applicability.

But as we will see, our approach resolves this apparent conflict. The aspects of a pattern that are common across all of its potential applications are formalized in a *pattern contract*. Each contract is specified in terms of relations between the states of its constituent roles; these relations are referred to as *auxiliary concepts*. The Observer pattern contract, for example, declares two auxiliary concepts. The first, *Consistent()*, is a relation between the state of an observer and the state of a subject, corresponding to the notion of *consistency* between the two. The second, *Modified()*, is a relation between two states of a subject, corresponding to the notion of whether the second state represents a *significant change* from the first. While the concepts are used throughout the contract, the definitions are provided separately as part of the *subcontract* corresponding to a particular application of the pattern. Thus, while the contract captures the precise implementation requirements and behavioral guarantees associated with the pattern, the auxiliary concepts provide the flexibility to tailor the contract to the needs of particular applications. Indeed, as we will see, the formalism allows multiple definitions of a given concept for a given application, to accommodate variation across the participating objects within the same system. The subcontract for the Observer pattern as used in the Hospital system, for example, provides definitions of the *Consistent()* concept corresponding to both the Nurse and Doctor classes. Members of the associated design and maintenance teams will be able to rely on the subcontract documentation to understand how the pattern has been applied, ensuring that any implementation changes respect the system's *design integrity*.

Pattern contracts and subcontracts can be used to support a variety of tools to aid software developers. In the case of *safety-critical* systems, for example, it may be appropriate to *verify* the correctness of a system's underlying pattern implementations based on the corresponding contracts and subcontracts. Existing theorem provers (Abrial, 1996; Owre, Rushby, Shankar, & Srivas, 1996) and model checkers (Holzmann, 1997) could be used to assist in this process. In cases where formal verification is inappropriate, *runtime monitoring* tools can be used to check that pattern contracts are respected – as in the *Eiffel* approach (Meyer, 1997). We have explored this possibility, and in fact shown that it is possible to *automatically generate* such monitors from the relevant pattern contracts and subcontracts. We will present highlights of our monitoring approach later in the chapter. These monitoring tools can also be extended to *log* runtime state information about the objects participating in various pattern instances. The information can then be *"played back"* in the form of a visualization to provide *pattern-centric* views of a system's runtime behavior. Such tools would allow new design team members to explore these pattern-centric views, and to more quickly come to an understanding of how the system is structured, and why it behaves in particular ways. Due to space limitations, we will only briefly consider runtime monitoring tools.

Chapter Organization. In the next section, we present key aspects of the Hospital system. We then present our formalization approach, and apply the approach in the context of the

Figure 1. Patient *class (partial)*

```
 1  public class Patient {
 2    private String name;
 3    private Integer temp, hrtRt, medLvl;
 4    private Set<Nurse> nurses;
 5    private Doctor doctor;
 6    ...constructors...
 7    ...field accessor methods...
 8    ...addNurse(n), removeNurse(n)...
 9    ...setDoctor(d), unsetDoctor()...
10    public void adjustMeds(int newLvl) {
11      medLvl = newLvl; }
12    public void changePatientCondition() {
13      temp=...; hrtRt=...; notify(); }
14    private void notify() {
15      ...call update() on nurses and doctor... }
16    ...
```

Hospital system. In the section following, we discuss tool support for runtime monitoring of pattern contracts and subcontracts. We then compare our approach to existing formalization approaches discussed in the literature. Finally, we summarize our contributions and discuss their integration in a pattern-centric software lifecycle.

The Hospital System

Consider developing a basic *hospital* simulation. The system will include Patient, Nurse, and Doctor classes that model their respective real-world counterparts. The system will simulate the assignment of nurses and doctors to patients, and their continuous observation of each patient's vital signs. The design calls for a standard application of the Observer pattern with patient objects playing the Subject role, and nurse and doctor objects playing the Observer role.

A silhouette of the Patient class is shown in Figure 1. A patient object includes a number of fields that store patient characteristics (lines 2-3), including temp and hrtRt, corresponding to the patient's temperature and heart rate, respectively. The remaining fields, nurses and doctor (lines 4-5), maintain references to the nurse and doctor objects assigned to the patient. (We assume that zero or more nurses and zero or one doctor may be assigned to each patient.) notify() (lines 14-15) invokes update() on each nurse and doctor to which there is a reference in nurses and doctor. changePatientCondition() (lines 12-13) simulates a change in the patient's vitals and then invokes notify() to signal the change. The appropriate *"getter"* methods are invoked by the update() methods of the signaled nurse and doctor objects to retrieve information about their patients. This allows nurse and doctor objects to be brought up-to-date in response to a change in a patient's state. The constructors and field accessor methods are written in the standard fashion and are omitted in the figure.

We have also omitted the bodies of the methods used to assign and unassign doctors and nurses – that is, addNurse(), setDoctor(), removeNurse(), and unsetDoctor(). According to the standard description of the Observer pattern, addNurse() must simply add the attaching ob-

Figure 2. Nurse, Doctor *classes (partial)*

```
1  public class Nurse {
2    private Map<Patient,Integer> vitals;
3    ...constructors...
4    public void update(Patient p) {
5      vital.put(p, p.getTemp()); }
6    public String getStatus(Patient p) {
7      int t = vitals.get(p);
8      if((t>95)&&(t<103)) return("normal");
9        else return("emergency"); } ... }
10
11 public class Doctor {
12   private Map<Patient,Integer> vitals;
13   ...constructors...
14   public void update(Patient p) {
15     vitals.put(p, p.getHrtRt()); }
16   public String getStatus(Patient p) {
17     int t = vitals.get(p);
18     if(t>0) return("alive");
19       else return("deceased"); } ... }
```

server to the set of observers maintained by the subject (i.e., the nurses Set). setDoctor() must be defined analogously. As we will see when we consider the pattern contract for Observer, there is a subtle problem that this directive ignores. Indeed, if updating the set was the only action performed, the intent of the pattern would be violated.

Key portions of the Nurse and Doctor classes are shown in Figure 2. Consider the Nurse class. Since a nurse can be assigned to multiple patients, each nurse maintains multiple heart rate readings. This is implemented using the vitals field, an instance of Map. When update() (lines 4-5) is invoked on a nurse, the object retrieves the patient's current temperature (i.e., temp), and updates its map accordingly. The getStatus() method (lines 6-9) returns an appropriate message about a given patient based on this information. The Doctor class is defined analogously, but monitors heart rate information (i.e., hrtRt).

Consider a variation of the Hospital system that might be introduced during system maintenance and evolution. Suppose the Nurse class is required to keep track not only of the temperature of each assigned patient, but also the patient's current medication level. This information is stored in the medLvl field of the Patient class. This change would first require the introduction of a new field in the Nurse class to store the additional information. Second, the update() method of the Nurse class would need to be modified to retrieve and store the value of the medLvl field. Finally, the getStatus() method might be revised to account for the patient's medication level.

But if these are the only changes, the system may exhibit a defect. To see this, suppose that the adjustMeds() method is invoked on a particular patient, changing the patient's medication level. Since there is no call to notify() in adjustMeds(), the nurse objects assigned to the patient will not update their information about the patient's medication level until changePatient-Condition() is called. As a result, if getStatus() is invoked, a nurse may, on occasion, return incorrect patient status information.

So where is the bug? From a pattern-centric view, one could argue that the bug was actually present *before* the system evolved since the designer of the Patient class should have included a call to notify() in adjustMeds(). The change in the system did not introduce the bug—it only resulted in its manifestation. Whether it is the system designers or the system maintainers that are at fault, the question remains: How could the defect have been avoided? Would it be possible for a software tool to identify the bug—preferably at an early stage? Or even better, is there a software methodology that would prevent its introduction in the first place? As we will see, the answer to both of these questions is *yes*.

Pattern Formalization

Pattern Instances, Role Players

During the execution of the Hospital system, there will be multiple *instances* of the Observer pattern coexisting simultaneously. In effect, each patient object plays the Subject role in a distinct instance of the pattern from the point of its creation. Each nurse and each doctor play the role of Observer in zero or more instances of the pattern, and their *enrollment* status varies over time. Following a call to addNurse() on a given patient, the nurse passed as argument is enrolled in the instance defined by the patient. The nurse remains enrolled in the instance until the corresponding call to removeNurse(). The scenario for doctor objects is analogous. Thus, in formalizing a pattern, we must characterize not only the required method behaviors, but also the corresponding *instantiation action*, the method or constructor call invoked to create a new pattern instance. The contract must similarly specify the *enrollment* and *disenrollment actions* associated with each role. As we will see, a pattern

Figure 3. Grammar of pattern contracts (partial)

```
1  ⟨contract⟩        →  pattern contract ⟨pId⟩
2                        ⟨conceptBlock⟩ ⟨roleContracts⟩
3                        ⟨instantiation⟩ ⟨invariant⟩
4  ⟨conceptBlock⟩    →  concepts: ⟨concepts⟩ ⟨constraints⟩
5  ⟨concept⟩         →  ⟨coId⟩ (⟨rIds⟩);
6  ⟨constraints⟩     →  constraints: ...predicate on auxiliary concepts...
7  ⟨roleContract⟩    →  [lead] role contract ⟨rId⟩
8                        ⟨fields⟩ ⟨methods⟩ ⟨others⟩
9                        ⟨enrollment⟩ ⟨disenrollment⟩
10 ...⟨fields⟩, ⟨methods⟩, ⟨others⟩...
11 ⟨enrollment⟩      →  enrollment: ⟨rId⟩.⟨mId⟩(⟨args⟩)
12                        lead: (target|source|⟨arg⟩|...code...)
13                        enrollee: (target|source|⟨arg⟩|...code...)
14                        post: ...enrollment post-condition...
15                      | enrollment: new ⟨rId⟩(⟨args⟩)
16                        lead: (source|⟨arg⟩|...code...)
17                        enrollee: (newOb|source|⟨arg⟩|...code...)
18                        post: ...enrollment post-condition...
19 ⟨disenrollment⟩   →  ...similar to enrollment...
20 ⟨instantiation⟩   →  ...similar to enrollment...
21 ⟨invariant⟩       →  invariant: ...assertion on roles and concepts...
```

contract specifies the actions, and the subcontract corresponding to a particular application maps the actions to the *player class* methods that implement the pattern.

The contract for a pattern P designates one of P's roles as the *lead role*. The instantiation action will be a method or constructor call involving an object that plays this role. When the action is performed, a new pattern instance is created, with only the *lead object* enrolled in the instance. The object will be used as a handle to refer to the instance throughout the pattern contract. (Hence, only one object may enroll in the lead role per pattern instance.)

In the contract for P, we will need to refer to the objects playing roles in an instance of P. For this purpose, we introduce the players keyword, which denotes a vector of the enrolled objects in the order that they enrolled. The vector contains an ordered pair for each enrollee, consisting of a reference to the enrolled object and the name of its corresponding role. If an object disenrolls, the corresponding pair will be removed from the vector, shifting the remaining pairs over one position. Elements of players can be referenced using standard indexing notation.

Many patterns require specific methods to be invoked in particular sequences under various conditions. The notify() method, for example, is required to invoke update() on each of the subject's attached observers. These requirements will be captured in the form of *call sequence* conditions. Each invocation of a method m() will have an associated trace variable τ that records the sequence of calls that m() makes during its execution. The specification of m() may include conditions that τ must satisfy as part of its postcondition. Both players and τ are "*auxiliary*" or "*ghost*" variables (Jones, 1990). As we will see, however, tools that assist software designers in validating the pattern-centric aspects of their systems will be required to keep track of information about the various pattern instances active in a system, the objects enrolled in each instance, and so forth.

Pattern Contracts

The partial grammar for specifying pattern contracts appears in Figure 3. The contract for a pattern specifies (1) the name of the pattern, (2) an auxiliary concept block, (3) a contract for each role, (4) an instantiation clause that specifies how a new instance of the pattern is created, and (5) an invariant for the pattern. We use <pId> to emphasize that this nonterminal represents a pattern name; similarly, <rId> will be used for role names, and so forth.

The <conceptBlock> declares the auxiliary concepts used throughout the pattern contract. Note that we have omitted some simple productions. <concepts> represents any number of repetitions of <concept>, <roleContracts> represents repetitions of <roleContract>, and so forth. For each auxiliary concept, we specify its name (<cId>) and the list of role names over which the concept is defined (<rIds>). The same role name may appear multiple times in this list. We will see an example of this in the contract for the Observer pattern. Each auxiliary concept is a boolean function over its arguments. The various auxiliary concepts will be used throughout the specification, including (1) in specifying the method contracts for each role, (2) in specifying the enrollment and disenrollment clauses, (3) in specifying the instantiation clause for the pattern, and finally, (4) in specifying the pattern invariant.

As we noted earlier, auxiliary concepts are not defined as part of a pattern contract. Instead, they are defined as part of the subcontracts corresponding to particular applications of a pattern. However, as we will see in the contract for Observer, although the definitions may be tailored to meet the needs of individual applications, if these definitions do not satisfy certain constraints, the intent of the pattern may be violated, even if the system satisfies all of the other requirements specified in the corresponding contract. The constraints that must be satisfied by concept definitions are referred to as *concept constraints*, and are expressed as predicates over the relevant auxiliary concepts (<constraints>).

Next consider the role contracts corresponding to the individual roles of a pattern (<roleContract>). Each role contract specifies the name of the role (<rId>); one role is labeled as the *lead role* of the pattern. The first part of the role contract specifies the *role fields* (<fields>), a list of typed field declarations corresponding to the state components required to implement the pattern. The syntax is the same as for standard field declarations, and we omit the details. Note that the fields listed in the role state need not be explicitly present in the class that ultimately plays the role in a given application. Instead, as we will see, the subcontract for the specialization will include a map that specifies how each of the role fields is represented by the actual variables of participating classes.

Following the role field declarations are the specifications of the *role methods*. These are the methods that an object must provide to support its role in the pattern. For example, the Observer role of the Observer pattern must provide an update() method, and the Subject role must provide an attach() method. Suppose, as specified in a subcontract of a given pattern P, instances of class C play the role R. C will then be required to provide each of the role methods listed in the role contract of R. More precisely, as in the case of role fields, the subcontract will map each of the role methods of R to the appropriate methods of C. These methods will be required to satisfy the corresponding role method specifications under the subcontract mappings. The specifications are similar to standard pre- and post-conditional specifications; we omit the detailed productions.

A class will typically provide additional methods beyond those required to support its role; these non-role methods are the *other methods* of the class. If these methods are not suitably designed, the intent of the pattern may be compromised. For example, if the class playing the Subject role in an application of the Observer pattern includes a method that destroys the set of attached observers, the system will violate the pattern's intent if the method is invoked, even if the role methods are implemented correctly. The *others specification* (<others>) imposes conditions to prevent such problems, and these conditions must be met by all nonrole methods.

A pattern contract additionally includes *enrollment conditions* (<enrollment>) that specify the actions that must be performed for objects to enroll in each role. The first production alternative corresponds to the case when enrollment is associated with the invocation of a particular role method. <rId> is the name of the role, <mId> is the name of the method, and <args> is the list of arguments. The lead clause specifies the lead object that identifies the pattern instance into which the player object is enrolling. The lead object may be specified as the target of the call, the source of the call, one of the arguments to the call, or an object specified using a code fragment. The target object might, for example, maintain a reference to the lead object of interest. The enrollee clause specifies the enrolling object and is defined in the same manner; of course, lead and enrollee must specify different objects in this case. The post clause specifies any state conditions that must be satisfied at the termination of the enrollment action. The second production alternative corresponds to the case when enrollment is associated with the creation of a new object via a call to a suitable constructor, and is defined analogously. The enrollment clause is omitted in the case of the lead role because, as we will see, the lead object enrolls at the point of pattern instantiation.

A role contract similarly defines the actions that must be performed for an object to *disenroll* from a pattern instance (<disenrollment>). The production is similar to the <enrollment> production, but specifies the *disenrollee*; we omit the details. The clause is optional; when omitted from a role contract, a player object remains enrolled until the object or the pattern instance is destroyed.

Next consider the <instantiation> clause of a pattern contract, which is defined in a similar manner as the <enrollment> clause. An invocation of the specified action defines the point at which a new instance of the pattern is created. In this case, there is no enrollee clause because the lead object is automatically enrolled at the point of pattern instantiation.

The final element of a pattern contract is the *pattern invariant* (<invariant>), which captures the behavioral guarantees afforded by virtue of satisfying contract requirements. The invariant is expressed in terms of auxiliary concepts as a predicate over the states of participating objects, and is guaranteed to be satisfied whenever control is outside of these objects. This is of course true only if the requirements specified in the role contracts, concept constraints, and so forth, are satisfied. In effect, the invariant is the formal version of the "*defined properties*" described in Buschmann et al. (1996, p. 24) that the correct use of the pattern ensures.

Pattern Subcontracts

The grammar for specifying pattern subcontracts appears in Figure 4. A subcontract specifies (1) the name of the subcontract (<sId>), (2) the name of the pattern contract that it specializes (<pId>), (3) a set of role maps corresponding to participating player classes, and (4) definitions for the required auxiliary concepts.

A *role map* (<roleMap>) is specified for each class (<cId>) whose instances may play a role (<rId>) in an instance of the pattern. In effect, a role map serves as a lens that specifies how an object playing the role can be viewed as an instance of its role type.

First consider the *state map* portion of the role map (<stateMap>), which consists of a set of *field maps*. Each field map (<fieldMap>) corresponds to a role field specified in the role's role

Figure 4. Grammar of pattern subcontracts (partial)

```
1  ⟨subcontract⟩   →  subcontract ⟨sId⟩ specializes ⟨pId⟩
2                       ⟨roleMaps⟩ ⟨concDefBlock⟩
3  ⟨roleMap⟩       →  rolemap ⟨cId⟩ as ⟨rId⟩
4                       ⟨leadObjRel⟩ ⟨stateMap⟩ ⟨interfaceMap⟩
5  ⟨leadObjRel⟩    →  lead relation: ...relation on lead object and role object...
6  ⟨stateMap⟩      →  state: ⟨fieldMaps⟩
7  ⟨fieldMap⟩      →  ⟨rfId⟩ = ...code...
8  ⟨interfaceMap⟩  →  methods: ⟨methodMaps⟩
9  ⟨methodMap⟩     →  ⟨rmId⟩(⟨rmArgs⟩):⟨cmId⟩(⟨cmArgs⟩)[⟨argMaps⟩]
10 ⟨argMap⟩        →  ...see discussion...
11 ⟨concDefBlock⟩  →  concepts: ⟨concDefs⟩
12 ⟨concDef⟩       →  ⟨coId⟩(⟨coArgs⟩) ...code...
```

contract. A field map identifies the role field (*<rfld>*), and a *code fragment* that computes, based on the state of the *<cld>* instance, the value of the field when the object is viewed as an instance of *<rld>*. In the simplest case, there is a corresponding field in the class for each role field, and the code fragment simply returns the appropriate field. In general, however, more complex mappings can be expressed in our formalism. We chose to express the mappings as code fragments, and to use code fragments elsewhere in our formalism, to ensure practitioner accessibility. The speculation is that practitioners are likely to prefer expressing the required elements in the form of code fragments rather than in terms of mathematical notations. However, this is relevant only to pattern *subcontracts*, because these specifications correspond to *particular* systems, and will hence have to be developed by the system design team. By contrast, developing a pattern contract is a one-time effort shared by the community. Note that the code fragments are intended to substitute for mathematical expressions, and must not modify any of the objects in the system.

The *interface map* (*<interfaceMap>*) defined by a role map specifies the mapping between the role methods required of the role and the corresponding class methods. For each role method (*<rmld>*), its *method map* (*<methodMap>*) specifies the class method (*<cmld>*) that serves as the role method. The method map may also provide *argument maps* (*<argMaps>*) that specify how the class method's arguments (*<cmArgs>*) map to the role method arguments (*<rmArgs>*). For example, in some cases a class method may provide fewer arguments than the role method to which it corresponds. In such cases, the designer may specify a mapping from the state of the player object to the relevant role method argument. We will see an example of this in our case study. The production for *<argMap>* is similar to that for *<fieldMap>*, and we omit it. We will later see that a role method can be mapped to more than one class method. Again, some of the production details have been omitted.

In general, an object may be simultaneously enrolled in multiple instances of a pattern. For example, in the Hospital system, a nurse object may be assigned to observe multiple patient objects. To handle such cases, the lead object corresponding to each instance will be used as an index into the state of the player object, to project out those portions relevant to each instance. To ensure the correctness of the indexing, the state of the object in question must contain information relevant to the lead object. This requirement is captured by the

Figure 5. Observer *contract (partial)*

```
 1  pattern contract Observer
 2    concepts:
 3      Consistent(Subject,Observer)
 4      Modified(Subject,Subject)
 5    constraints:
 6      ∀s1,s2,o1:::(¬Modified(s1,s2) ∧ Consistent(s1,o1))
 7        ⇒ Consistent(s2,o1)
 8    instantiation:
 9      new Subject()
10      lead: newOb
11      post: newOb.obs=∅
12    invariant:
13      ... ∧ ∀ob:ob ∈ players[1:]::Consistent(players[0],ob)
```

lead-object relation (*<leadObjRel>*) clause. We omit the production for this clause but will see its use in the case study.

Finally, each subcontract provides auxiliary concept definitions (*<concDefBlock>*, *<concDefs>*) appropriate to its particular pattern specialization. For each auxiliary concept identified in the pattern contract (*<cold>*), and each combination of classes that play the various roles that appear as its parameters, a corresponding definition must be provided. As in the case of field maps and method maps, the definitions are provided in the form of suitable code fragments. Each code fragment performs the appropriate comparisons across objects playing the relevant roles, and returns true or false to indicate whether the corresponding relation is satisfied. The definitions must satisfy the concept constraints specified in the pattern contract.

To summarize our approach, a pattern contract is a *parameterized* pattern formalization. Each contract includes parameterized (1) specifications of the individual role methods, (2) enrollment and disenrollment clauses, (3) a pattern instantiation clause, and (4) a pattern invariant. The auxiliary concepts declared by the contract serve as the primary parameters, and the field and method maps serve as additional parameters. For a particular pattern application, the corresponding subcontract defines the actual parameters via the definitions of the auxiliary concepts, field maps, and method maps. Thus, while the pattern contract specifies the pattern precisely, the parameterization structure ensures that pattern flexibility is not compromised.

Applying Contracts and Subcontracts in the Hospital System

Key portions of the Observer pattern contract appear in Figures 5, 6, and 7. Figure 5 includes the "*pattern-level*" portions of the contract, Figure 6 includes the Subject role contract, and Figure 7 includes the Observer role contract. For the sake of presentation, the instantiation and invariant clauses appear in Figure 5 instead of after the role contracts, as required by the contract grammar.

Consider the portion of the contract shown in Figure 5. The contract specifies two auxiliary concepts (lines 2-4). The first, *Consistent*(), captures the notion of whether a given subject state is *consistent* with a given observer state. The second, *Modified*(), captures what it means for a given subject state to be *significantly changed* from another state of the subject. The specified constraint (lines 5-7) expresses an important requirement that must be satisfied

Figure 6. Subject *role contract (partial)*

```
ı  lead role contract Subject
ı  Set<Observer> obs;
ı  void attach(Observer ob):
ı     pre: ob ∉ obs
ı     post: ¬Modified(#this,this) ∧ (obs=(#obs∪{ob}))
ı           ∧ (|τ|=1) ∧ (|τ.ob.update|=1)
ı  ...detach(ob)...
ı  void notify():
ı     post: (obs=#obs) ∧ ¬Modified(#this,this) ∧ (|τ|=|obs|) ∧
ı           ∀ob:ob ∈ obs::(|τ.ob.update|=1)
ı  others:
ı     post: (obs=#obs) ∧ ((¬Modified(#this,this) ∧ (|τ|=0)) ∨
ı           ((|τ|=1) ∧ (|τ.this.notify|=1)))
```

by definitions of these concepts; we will return to this point after discussing the rest of the contract.

The instantiation clause (lines 8-11) specifies that a new instance of the pattern is created when an instance of the class playing the Subject role is created. The new object is identified as the *lead* object of the pattern instance. Following instantiation, the subject's observers set (obs) must be empty because no observers have yet enrolled to observe the subject.

The key portion of the invariant clause shown in the figure (lines 12-13) captures the intent of the pattern. The clause specifies that each object enrolled after the lead object (players[0]) will remain consistent with the lead object throughout the pattern's lifetime. The elided portions of the clause specify that (1) the lead object plays the Subject role, (2) the remaining objects play the Observer role, and (3) instances of Observer maintain a reference to their corresponding subject.

Next consider the Subject role contract shown in Figure 6. The contract specifies that the state of the role consists of a single field, obs (line 2), which is used to store references to the set of attached observers. The contract specifies three role methods: attach(), detach(), and notify(). As specified in the precondition of attach() (line 4), this method may only be called if the attaching observer (ob) is not already attached, and by consequence, not already enrolled in the pattern instance. The first conjunct of the postcondition (lines 5-6) requires that attach() not *modify* the state of the subject. (The "#" prefix denotes the preconditional value of a variable.) The second conjunct requires that the enrolling object be added to obs. While this may seem contradictory given the previous constraint on subject modification, this is not a *significant change*, and it is not the kind of change observers are interested in.

The condition captured by the last two conjuncts of the postcondition (line 6) is often overlooked in informal descriptions of the pattern. As specified by the pattern invariant, the intent of the pattern is to keep the set of attached observers *consistent* with the state of the subject. The attach() method must therefore invoke the attaching observer's update() method, because it might be *inconsistent* with the state of the subject at the point of attachment. The first of these two conjuncts requires the method call to include only one role method invocation. The second conjunct states that this call must be to the update() method of the attaching object. The detach() method is specified analogously, but does not impose the update() call sequence requirement.

The postcondition of notify() (lines 9-10) requires that obs not be changed, and that notify() not make any *significant changes* to the subject. The last two conjuncts require that update() be invoked on each attached observer. This corresponds directly to the standard informal descriptions of notify(), except that the requirement concerning the obs field is often missed in these descriptions.

Figure 7. Observer *role contract (partial)*

```
1  role contract Observer
2    Subject sub;
3    void update():
4      post: (sub=#sub) ∧ Consistent(sub,this)
5    others:
6      post: (sub=#sub) ∧
7              ∀ss:::Consistent(ss,#this) ⇒ Consistent(ss,this)
8    ...enrollment and disenrollment clauses...
```

Figure 8. Hospital *subcontract (partial)*

```
 1  subcontract Hospital specializes Observer {
 2    rolemap Patient as Subject
 3      lead relation: lead = this
 4      state: obs = { Set<Observer> obs =
 5                       new HashSet<Observer>(nurses);
 6                       if(doc!=null) obs.add(doc);
 7                       return(obs); }
 8      methods:
 9        attach(Observer ob): addNurse(ob),setDoctor(ob)
10        detach(Observer ob): removeNurse(ob),unsetDoctor(){ob=doc}
11        notify(): notify()
12
13    rolemap Nurse as Observer
14      lead relation: lead ∈ vitals.keySet
15      state: sub = { return(lead); }
16      methods:
17        update(): update(lead)
18
19    rolemap Doctor as Observer ...similarly defined...
```

Recall that the others clause imposes conditions on the *nonrole* methods provided by a player class. According to the specified conditions (lines 11-13), nonrole methods are required to preserve the set of attached observers. Further, they must either not *modify* the state of the subject, or they must invoke the notify() method. As discussed above, notify() is in turn required to invoke update() on each attached observer.

Next consider the Observer role contract shown in Figure 7. The contract specifies that the state of the role consists of a single field, sub (line 2). As specified in the omitted portion of the pattern invariant, this field maintains a reference to the observer's subject. The only required role method is update(). Its specification (lines 3-4) requires that the method preserve the observer's subject reference, and of course, that it leave the observer in a state that is *consistent* with the state of its subject.

The others clause (lines 5-7) requires that the observer's subject reference be preserved. Further, if the state of the observer is *consistent* with **ss**, a possible state of its subject, at the start of an invocation, it must be *consistent* with that same state at the termination of the call. This clause captures a critical aspect of the Observer role's behavior. It allows nonrole methods to modify the state of an observer as long as the modifications do not affect the consistency of the observer with respect to its subject. Standard descriptions of the pattern suggest that an observer should *not* be changed except during the execution of update(), but this is unnecessarily restrictive. Suppose, for example, that the observer in question is a graphical object that displays information about the state of its subject in the form of a pie-chart. Suppose also that this observer provides methods for switching between *iconified* and *de-iconified* images of the pie-chart. In going from one view to another, there is no information lost about the subject. Hence, such a change should be permitted. Our formalism allows this type of flexibility given an appropriate definition of the *Consistent()* concept in the corresponding subcontract. By contrast, standard informal descriptions of the pattern seem to disallow such changes.

The omitted enrollment clause specifies that observer enrollment is associated with a call to attach(). Similarly, the omitted disenrollment clause specifies that observer disenrollment is associated with a call to detach().

Figure 9. Hospital *concept definitions*

```
1 auxiliary concepts:
2   Modified(Patient p1, Patient p2) {
3     return((p1.temp!=p2.temp) || (p1.hrtRt!=p2.hrtRt)); }
4   Consistent(Patient p, Nurse n) {
5     return(p.temp == n.vitals.get(lead)); }
6   Consistent(Patient p, Doctor d) {
7     return(p.hrtRt == d.vitals.get(lead)); }
```

Recall the auxiliary concept constraint specified as part of the pattern contract (Figure 5, lines 5-7). To understand the motivation for this constraint, suppose that a given subject state s1 is *consistent* with a given observer state o1 according to the definition of *Consistent()* provided by an appropriate subcontract. Now suppose the state of the subject changes to s2, and that *Modified*(s1, s2) evaluates to false according to the definition of *Modified()* provided in the same subcontract. Finally, suppose that the new state s2 is *not consistent* with the observer state o1 according to the same definition of *Consistent()*. At this point, the intent of the pattern will be violated. The subject will not update its observers because, in its view, a *significant change* has not occurred. According to the definition of *Consistent()*, however, the observer's state o1 is not consistent with the new state of the subject. The problem arises here not because of the failure of the subject or the observers to interact in a manner intended by the pattern, but rather because of incompatible notions of *consistency* and *significant change*. The concept constraints in our contract formalism serve to eliminate such incompatibilities. Thus, while the definitions of a pattern's auxiliary concepts may be tailored to the needs of particular systems, the concept constraints ensure that this flexibility is not used in a way that would violate the intent of the pattern.

Next consider the subcontract corresponding to the hospital simulation, shown in Figure 8. The subcontract begins with the role map for Subject (lines 2-11), which is played by the Patient class. The lead relation clause (line 3) states that each patient object is itself the lead object that identifies the pattern instance in which it participates. The field map (lines 4-7) specifies that each patient's role field, obs, is represented by a combination of the fields nurses and doc declared by the Patient class. The map specifies that the set of observers of any patient is the set of nurse objects currently observing it, plus the doctor object, if any, assigned to it.

Next are the method maps for the specialization. Given that the argument to attach() is an observer, and that instances of both Nurse and Doctor play this role, two mappings are specified for this method (line 9). As specified in the mappings, both addNurse() and setDoctor() play the part of attach(). In each case, the method parameter list corresponds exactly to the parameter list of attach(); no additional argument maps are required. The mappings for detach() and notify() are similar (lines 10-11). In the case of unsetDoctor(), however, the player method does not include the observer argument required by the detach() method. The argument map specifies that this argument is played by the doc field of the Patient class.

Next is the role map used to view instances of Nurse as instances of Observer (lines 13-17). The lead relation clause (line 14) specifies that the object playing the lead role will be defined as a key within the vitals map. (We will consider the motivation for specifying this relation shortly.) When a nurse is viewed as an observer in the context of a particular pattern instance, its sub field references the *lead* object for that instance, that is, the observer's subject. Hence, for a particular pattern instance, the lead object for the instance is mapped to the sub role field. The update() method of Nurse maps directly to the update() method of Observer, excluding the patient argument; this argument is identified as the lead object in any invocation. The role map used to view doctors as observers is analogous.

Finally, consider the auxiliary concept definitions specified in Figure 9. Recall that M*odified*() takes two subject states as argument. In this specialization, only patients play the Subject role. Hence, only one definition is required. The definition (lines 2-3) specifies that the state p2 is *significantly changed* from p1 if either the temp values or hrtRt values are different.

Two definitions are required for the *Consistent*() concept (lines 4-7) because one of its arguments is of type Observer, and this role is played by instances of both Nurse and Doctor. In the first definition, the two arguments are considered *consistent* if the temperature of the patient object is equal to the temperature recorded in the nurse object's vitals map for the patient playing the lead role in the pattern instance under consideration. Note that for this definition to be valid, the lead object must be defined in the vitals map, which is ensured by the lead relation clause specified in the Nurse as Observer role map (Figure 8, line 14). The second definition of *Consistent*() is analogous.

Given the completed subcontract corresponding to a particular system, the design team must show that the specialization satisfies contract requirements. In our ongoing case-study, the first step is to show that the definitions of *Modified*() and *Consistent*() satisfy the appropriate auxiliary concept constraints (Figure 5, lines 5-7). Consider the case when the observer is a nurse. Suppose s1 and s2 are states of a patient p, and o1 is a state of a nurse observing p. Then, given that *Consistent(s1, o1)* is satisfied, we can conclude that s1.temp is equal to o1.vitals.get(p). And, given that ¬*Modified*(s1, s2) is satisfied, we can conclude that s1.temp is equal to s2.temp. Hence, *Consistent*(s2, o1) is satisfied. The case when the observer is a doctor is analogous.

Next, the team must show that Patient, Nurse, and Doctor satisfy the appropriate requirements specified in the pattern contract (e.g., role method requirements, enrollment requirements, etc.), given the field and method maps specified in their respective role maps. The process is similar to showing that a class implementation satisfies its abstract specification (Jones, 1990), except that the team must also account for auxiliary concepts. If the hospital simulation were a safety-critical system, it would be appropriate to use theorem-proving (Owre et al., 1996) or model checking tools (Holzmann, 1997) to verify these properties. If not, an informal or semiformal approach might be appropriate. Alternatively, the team could rely on runtime monitoring tools to check that the appropriate requirements are not violated during system execution. We will return to this last point in the next section.

We conclude this section by considering the system variation proposed at the start of the chapter. In this variation, nurse objects monitor both the temperatures and medication levels of their respective patients. As we discussed, one obvious change required is to extend the state of the Nurse class, and to revise the update() method of the class to retrieve the value of the patient argument's medLvl field. Suppose that this is the only change made by the maintenance team. How would the subcontract (Figures 8 and 9) be revised? The first definition of *Consistent*() would require redefinition to require that both temp and medLvl agree with the values maintained by the nurse object. But now the *constraint* on the auxiliary concepts would no longer be satisfied. If a patient's state were to change from s1 to s2 in such a way that only the medLvl value were changed, a nurse state o1 that was *consistent* with s1, according to the new definition of the concept, would *not* be consistent with s2. The definition of *Modified()* must also be revised to reflect that a change in any of temp, hrtRt, or medLvl is considered a *significant change*. Given this revision, the constraint will be satisfied, but the adjustMeds() method of Patient will no longer satisfy the others clause of the Subject role contract (Figure 6, 11-13). Specifically, when an invocation of the method terminates, ¬*Modified*(#this, this) will not be satisfied, and there is no call to notify() during its execution. Once this is recognized, the solution is straightforward: include a call to notify() in the adjustMeds() method. Thus, simple reasoning based on the pattern contract and subcontract enables the maintenance team to identify this violation, and to safeguard the system's design integrity.

Tool Support

Pattern contracts and subcontracts provide precise implementation guidance, and help to ensure a common understanding of the patterns underlying a design. But descriptive precision alone does not guarantee correctness. Even expert designers occasionally violate specifications that are well-understood. For the benefits of our approach to be fully realized, designers must also have tools that assist in *identifying* and *localizing* contract violations. Such tools are especially important for designers new to our formalism, or who have limited experience working with formal notations.

One approach is to *monitor* a system's behavior using runtime assertion checks, similar to those used in *Eiffel*-based systems (Meyer, 1995), and in Java-based systems developed using *JML* (Leavens, Poll, Clifton, Cheon, & Ruby, 2002). The idea is to check, at relevant points during a system's execution, that the correctness conditions implied by the underlying contracts and subcontracts are satisfied. In the absence of contract violations, the system should behave as usual. If, on the other hand, a contract violation is detected, the system should produce appropriate warning messages that assist designers in identifying the root cause.

As we have seen, the conditions that capture pattern correctness span class boundaries. This is a natural consequence of the fact that a pattern captures a *slice* of a system hierarchy. Or stated another way, pattern implementations are *cross-cutting*, and by consequence, so too are the corresponding correctness conditions. Hence, it is natural to consider an *aspect-oriented* approach to monitoring pattern correctness.

Our approach is based on the use of *aspects*, as exemplified in *AspectJ* (Kiczales, Hilsdale, Hugunin, Kersten, Palm, & Griswold, 2001). The monitoring logic corresponding to a given pattern contract is implemented within an *abstract* aspect. The aspect is applicable to *all* possible applications of the pattern in question. For a *particular* application, the generic monitoring code is specialized by a *derived* aspect based on the corresponding subcontract. The two aspects together realize the complete monitoring code required to check the correctness of the tailored pattern application. The relationships between pattern contracts, pattern subcontracts, and monitoring aspects are illustrated in Figure 10.

Figure 10. Monitoring relationships

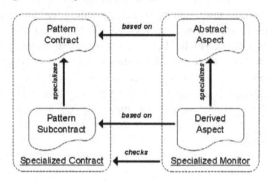

Figure 11. Monitor generation process

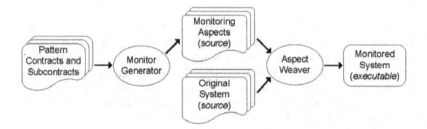

The aspect generation process is automated, imposing no additional burden on users of our formalism. The process is illustrated in Figure 11. As shown in the figure, the aspect-based monitors for a particular system are generated based on the pattern contracts and subcontracts underlying its design.

Consider the monitoring aspects generated for the Hospital system discussed in the previous sections. The abstract aspect corresponding to the Observer pattern consists of five key elements:

1. **State components:** First, the aspect defines state components required to track the pattern instances active in a monitored system, as well as the objects enrolled in each instance. This information is required, for example, to check assertions involving the players vector. The aspect also defines a *stack* of trace vectors used to record information about the calls made during the execution of each method. This information is required to check call sequence assertions.

2. **Pointcut declarations:** Next, the aspect declares *pointcuts* corresponding to the execution points at which correctness conditions must be checked. Hence, the aspect declares pointcuts intended to capture pattern instantiation, role enrollment and disenrollment, role method invocations, and nonrole method invocations. Because, however, the realizations of these execution points vary from one application of the pattern to another, the pointcuts are declared as abstract. Definitions are supplied in

the derived aspect based on the method mappings specified in the Hospital subcontract. The derived aspect defines, for example, a pointcut corresponding to attach() that captures invocations of both addNurse() and SetDoctor() because these are the mappings specified in the subcontract (Figure 8, line 9).

3. **Checking advice:** The advice bound to each pointcut serves two key purposes. First, the advice performs appropriate bookkeeping operations. This includes updating instantiation and enrollment data, as well as recording information about the executing method in the active trace. Second, the advice is responsible for checking the relevant assertions specified in the pattern contract. The advice bound to attach(), for example, checks (1) that the attaching observer was properly added to the observers set, (2) that the target subject was *unmodified*, and (3) that update() was invoked on the attaching observer.

4. **Role field accessors:** Note that the advice bound to attach() checks an assertion involving the role field obs, specified as part of the Subject role contract (Figure 6, line 2). As we have seen, the realization of this field varies from one application of the pattern to another. To accommodate the checking of such assertions, the aspect declares methods corresponding to the role fields defined by the contract. Each of these *role field accessors* returns the value of the appropriate role field when the object passed as argument is *viewed* as an instance of its role. The aspect includes, for example, an accessor function that returns the value of the obs field when the object passed as argument is viewed as an instance of the Subject role. These functions are declared as abstract; appropriate definitions are supplied in the derived aspect based on the field mappings specified in the subcontract (Figure 8, lines 8-11, 16-17). The code generation process is simplified by the fact that the field mappings in the subcontract are defined in terms of code fragments.

5. **Concept functions:** Finally, the aspect declares boolean functions corresponding to the auxiliary concepts declared in the pattern contract. The isModified(s1,s2) function, for example, corresponds to the *Modified()* concept, and returns true if the second subject state is *significantly changed* from the first; it returns false otherwise. The isConsistent(s1,o1) function is defined analogously. These functions are used in checking assertions involving the *Modified()* and *Consistent()* concepts. Again, because the definitions vary from application to application, the functions are declared as abstract, with appropriate definitions supplied in the derived aspect. These definitions are based on the code fragments used to express the auxiliary concepts in the pattern subcontract (Figure 9), again simplifying the code generation process.

When the generated aspects are woven with the original Hospital system, they signal pattern-related defects, and include information about the points at which defects occur. As we will discuss in the final section, when combined with our contract formalism, the approach provides opportunities for amplifying the benefits of Design patterns *across* the system lifecycle.

Related Work

Several other authors have proposed notations for pattern formalization. In the approach presented by Eden (2001), patterns are represented as formulae within a higher-order logic. Each formula consists of a declaration of the participating classes, methods, and inheritance hierarchies, and a conjunctive statement of the relations among them. The formalism enables the specification of rich structural properties, but provides limited support for behavioral properties.

By contrast, the approach proposed by Mikkonen (1998) focuses on behavioral properties. In this approach, patterns are specified using an action-system notation. Data classes model pattern participants, and guarded actions model their interactions. The approach is well-suited to reasoning about temporal properties, but most structural properties cannot be expressed. To address this issue, Taibi and Ngo (2003) describe an approach that combines the formalisms proposed by Mikkonen and Eden. While these various approaches are useful in capturing certain structural and behavioral properties, they do not consider Design pattern *specializations*. As a consequence, the formalisms reduce pattern flexibility, and the resulting specifications are of limited use in reasoning about the systems in which patterns are applied.

Helm, Holland, and Gangopadhyay (1990) propose a *contract* formalism that shares characteristics of our formalism. The formalism allows contracts to be *specialized*, including the definitions of certain relations, similar to our use of auxiliary concepts. It also supports the specification of call sequence conditions, although the expressivity of the formalism is limited in this regard. While the approach has a number of benefits, it is limited in its ability to capture the ways in which contracts may be specialized. It does not, for example, provide constructs for imposing conditions on auxiliary concepts, nor does it consider the requirements that must be satisfied by nonrole methods. As a consequence, even if a pattern implementation satisfies the appropriate contract requirements, incompatibilities between concept definitions and behavioral interference with nonrole methods, can violate the pattern's intent.

Discussion

Design patterns continue to play an important role in software practice, fundamentally impacting the way we design, document, and implement software. While the benefits of patterns are well-established, we have observed, along with several other authors, that their benefits can be extended by supplementing informal pattern descriptions with *precise formalizations*. The point of departure for our work was the observation that any such formalization must satisfy two seemingly conflicting requirements. First, the approach must achieve descriptive *precision*. It must unambiguously capture the implementation requirements and behavioral guarantees associated with the patterns being specified. Second, it must retain the *flexibility* inherent in the patterns, or the very hallmark of their success will be compromised. Further, to maximize practitioner benefits, the approach must admit of tool support to assist in identifying pattern-related defects.

Figure 12. A pattern-centric process model

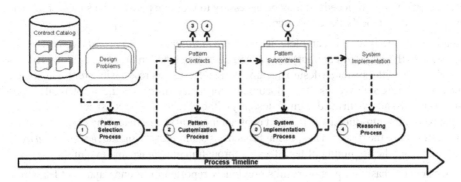

In this chapter, we presented an approach to formalizing Design patterns that satisfies these criteria. The approach is based on the use of *pattern contracts*. Each contract captures the implementation requirements associated with a particular pattern, as well as the system properties that are guaranteed if those requirements are met. And just as individual patterns can be *tailored* for use, so too can the corresponding contracts. A *subcontract specializes* a contract to suit the needs of a particular system. By separating the formalization of properties applicable across *all* instances of a given pattern from those applicable to *particular* instances, our approach achieves precision *and* flexibility. We illustrated our formalism in the context of a simple case study constructed using the *Observer* pattern. Finally, we presented an aspect-oriented approach to *monitoring* a system's runtime behavior to determine whether the pattern contracts and subcontracts underlying its design are respected. Before concluding, we note that the benefits of Design patterns have traditionally been restricted to the early stages of the software lifecycle; specifically, in the early design stages. By combining our formalization approach with the supporting monitoring tools, it is possible to extend pattern benefits *across* the lifecycle, providing the foundation for a *pattern-centric* development process.

Portions of one such process are illustrated in Figure 12. In the first step, we assume the existence of a *contract catalog* that supplements existing informal descriptions. Based on the requirements of the system in question, the design team uses this resource to identify the patterns to be used in the system's design. This reflects current practice, with the important addition of precise pattern specifications. As a result, the selection process is better informed, and the resulting implementation requirements are unambiguously understood.

In the second step, the team determines how the patterns will be customized for use in the system. Based on these customization decisions, the team then develops the subcontracts that characterize the ways in which the patterns will be specialized. These subcontracts, along with their respective contracts, provide the foundation for the third step, in which the system is implemented. This step is guided by the requirements specified in the relevant contracts, as specialized by the mappings and concept definitions defined in the corresponding subcontracts. Although not illustrated in the figure, the contract monitors generated from the pattern contracts and subcontracts provide additional support, serving as valuable tools that assist in identifying pattern-related defects as part of the system testing process. In practice, we can expect steps two and three to be iterated numerous times, because as the implementation proceeds, it may be necessary to redefine parts of the subcontracts and to appropriately modify the implementation.

Finally, once the system is complete, it enters the *maintenance and evolution* phase of the lifecycle. In this step, the contracts and subcontracts developed in the earlier phases serve as key elements of the system's design documentation. Designers responsible for maintenance and evolution are able to consult this documentation to determine whether a potential change would be consistent with the design philosophy of the system. If an inconsistent modification is inadvertently introduced, the relevant contract monitor(s) will detect the error, and notify the designers of the defect. Thus, our approach assists in preserving the *design integrity* of a system from the beginning of the lifecycle through maintenance and evolution.

This chapter is based in part on results previously reported in Soundarajan and Hallstrom (2004), Tyler, Hallstrom, and Soundarajan (2006), and Hallstrom, Soundarajan, and Tyler (2006).

Acknowledgment

This work was funded in part by a grant from the National Science Foundation (CNS-0520222), and a grant from the South Carolina Space Grant Consortium. The authors gratefully acknowledge these agencies for their support.

References

Abrial, J. (1996). *B-book: Assigning programs to meanings.* UK: Cambridge University Press.

Buschmann, F., Meunier, R., Rohnert, H., Sommerlad, P., & Stal, M. (1996). *Pattern-oriented software architecture: A system of patterns.* West Sussex, UK: John Wiley & Sons.

Eden, A. (2001). Formal specification of object-oriented design. In *Proceedings of the International Conference on Multidisciplinary Design in Engineering.*

Gamma, E., Helm, R., Johnson, R., & Vlissides, J. (1995). *Design patterns: Elements of reusable object-oriented software.* Boston: Addison-Wesley Professional.

Hallstrom, J., Soundarajan, N., & Tyler, B. (2006). Amplifying the benefits of Design patterns. In *Proceedings of Fundamental Approaches to Software Engineering* (pp. 214-229). Berlin, Germany: Springer Verlag.

Helm, R., Holland, I., & Gangopadhyay, D. (1990). Contracts: Specifying behavioral compositions in object-oriented systems. In *Proceedings of the ACM Conference on Object-Oriented Programming Systems, Languages, and Applications* (pp. 169-180). New York: ACM Press.

Holzmann, G. (1997). The model checker spin. *IEEE Transactions on Software Engineering, 23*(5), 279-295.

Jones, C. (1990). *Systematic software development using VDM.* Englewood Cliffs, NJ: Prentice Hall.

Kiczales, G., Hilsdale, E., Hugunin, J., Kersten, M., Palm, J., & Griswold, W. (2001). An overview of AspectJ. In *Proceedings of the 15th European Conference on Object-Oriented Programming* (pp. 327-353). Berlin, Germany: Springer Verlag.

Leavens, G., Poll, E., Clifton, C., Cheon, Y., & Ruby, C. (2002). *JML reference manual* (Tech. Rep.). Iowa State University, Department of Computer Science, Ames, IA.

Meyer, B. (1997). *Object-oriented software construction.* Englewood Cliffs, NJ: Prentice Hall.

Mikkonen, T. (1998). Formalizing Design patterns. In *Proceedings of the 20th International Conference on Software Engineering* (pp. 115-124). Washington, DC: IEEE Computer Society.

Owre, S., Rushby, J., Shankar, N., & Srivas, M. (1996). PVS: Combining specification, proof checking, and model checking. In *Proceedings of the 8th International Conference on Computer Aided Verification* (pp. 411-414). Berlin, Germany: Springer Verlag.

Soundarajan, N., & Hallstrom, J. (2004). Responsibilities and rewards: Specifying Design patterns. In *Proceedings of the 26th International Conference on Software Engineering* (pp. 666-675). Washington, DC: IEEE Computer Society.

Taibi, T., & Ngo, D. (2003). Formal specification of Design patterns—A balanced approach. *Journal of Object Technology, 2*(4), 127-140.

Tyler, B., Hallstrom, J., & Soundarajan, N. (2006). Automated generation of monitors for pattern contracts. In *Proceedings of the 21st ACM Symposium on Applied Computing* (pp. 1779-1784). New York: ACM Press.

Chapter XIV

Formalizing Patterns with the User Requirements Notation

Gunter Mussbacher, University of Ottawa, Canada

Daniel Amyot, University of Ottawa, Canada

Michael Weiss, Carleton University, Canada

Abstract

Patterns need to be described and formalized in ways that enable the reader to determine whether the particular solution presented is useful and applicable to his or her problem in a given context. However, many pattern descriptions tend to focus on the solution to a problem, and not so much on how the various (and often conflicting) forces involved are balanced. This chapter describes the user requirements notation (URN), and demonstrates how it can be used to formalize patterns in a way that enables rigorous trade-off analysis while maintaining the genericity of the solution description. URN combines a graphical goal language, which can be used to capture forces and reason about trade-offs, and a graphical scenario language, which can be used to describe behavioral solutions in an abstract manner. Although each language can be used in isolation in pattern descriptions (and have been in the literature), the focus of this chapter is on their combined use. It includes examples of formalizing Design patterns with URN together with a process for trade-off analysis.

Introduction

Patterns document common solutions to recurring problems in a specific context. They enable an efficient transfer of experience and skills. However, many pattern descriptions tend to focus on the solution to a problem, and not so much on how the various (and often conflicting) forces involved are balanced. Therefore, patterns need to be described and formalized in ways that enable the reader to determine whether the particular solution presented is useful and applicable to his or her problem in a given context.

A large body of patterns has been documented to date, and the different efforts are not well-connected. The Pattern Almanac (Rising, 2000) alone, a major effort summarizing and linking the patterns published at patterns conferences and in books prior to the year 2000, lists over 1,200 patterns contained in over 800 different publications. Most of those are publications with a single pattern. The number of patterns has only increased since, but estimates are harder to obtain lacking a similar effort to the Pattern Almanac.

Much work on pattern formalization focuses on the solution domain. For instance, Taibi and Ngo (2001) describe why patterns should be formalized and suggest combining formal specifications of structural and behavioral aspects of Design patterns in one specification. However, the problem domain and relevant trade-offs are seldom handled formally.

In this chapter, we propose a formalization of patterns using the user requirements notation (URN) in a way that supports a rigorous trade-off analysis. In the following sections we first present the background for patterns and the formalization of patterns. Then, we review related work on reasoning about the trade-offs between patterns. We then introduce the user requirements notation, and our explicit model of the forces addressed by a pattern, which provides the basis for the trade-off analysis. The description of the approach is followed by a case study from the literature to which we have applied our approach. Finally, we present future trends and present our concluding remarks.

Formalizing Patterns

Patterns are three-part rules that describe a recurring problem that occurs in a specific context and its solution (Alexander, 1979). They capture important practices and existing methods uncodified by conventional forms of communicating design experience. The structure they capture is usually not immediately apparent. Perhaps the most significant contribution of patterns is that they make the trade-offs between forces explicit.

Each pattern describes the situation when the pattern can be applied in its context. The context can be thought of as a precondition for the pattern. This precondition is further refined in the problem description with its elaboration of the forces that push and pull the system to which the pattern is applied in different directions. Here, the problem is a precise statement of the design issue to be solved. Forces are design trade-offs affected by the pattern. They can be documented in various forms. One popular approach is to document the trade-offs as sentences like "on one hand ..., but on the other hand ...".

The solution describes a way of resolving the forces. Some forces may not be resolved by a single pattern. In this case, a pattern includes references to other patterns, which help resolve forces that were unresolved by the current pattern. Together, patterns connected in this way are often referred to as a pattern language. Links between patterns can be of different types, including uses, refines, and conflicts. Patterns that need another pattern link to that pattern with *uses*. Patterns specializing the context or problem of another pattern *refine* that pattern. Patterns that offer alternative solutions *conflict*.

Current pattern representations are textual. They include the gang-of-four (GoF) form, the Coplien form, and the Alexandrian form. The GoF form (Gamma, Helm, Johnson, & Vlissides, 1994) includes sections for intent, motivation, structure, participants, and collaborations. The emphasis of this format is on the structure of the solution. However, the discussion of the forces is spread out over multiple sections, which makes it challenging for a developer to get an overview of when to apply a particular pattern and the consequences of using it.

Motivated by this drawback of the GoF form, the Coplien form (Coplien, 1996) defines a more rigid pattern structure. It includes explicit sections for forces and consequences, in which the forces and the implications of using the patterns are presented in bullet form. This provides quick access to the reasons for applying a pattern. Variations of this format have been proposed that present the forces and consequences as tables.

Recently, many pattern authors have returned to the Alexandrian pattern form (Alexander, 1979). It resolves the trade-off between the needs to have structure on the one hand, and the desire to create more easily readable pieces of literature, on the other. In practical use for documenting software designs, the Alexandrian form has been adapted to include the concept of explicit lists of forces and consequences from the Coplien form.

Nonetheless, with these formats there are still open issues, such as how to recognize under what conditions a given pattern should be selected, how to compare between different patterns that address the same problem, and how to integrate the consequences of applying a pattern or a combination of patterns into a model of the resulting system. It is with these issues in mind that we propose a formalization of patterns using the user requirements notation (URN) in a way that supports a rigorous trade-off analysis during the application of Design patterns while maintaining the generality of the solution description.

Related Work

Previously, Araujo and Weiss (2002) have proposed an explicit representation of the forces involved in a pattern and their interrelationships. This representation suggests interpreting forces as functional and, mainly, as non-functional requirements, and uses the non-functional requirements (NFR) framework (Chung, Nixon, Yu, & Mylopoulos, 2000) to analyze forces and the trade-offs made by a pattern.

In related earlier work, Ong, Weiss, and Araujo (2003) derived the forces affected by a pattern through a close reading of the textual pattern description. The extended pattern representation enabled them to discover contributions made by the patterns to overall system concerns that were only implicit in their textual descriptions. Their main finding was that the contributions of each pattern to overall system concerns became much more apparent when compared to reading the pattern descriptions alone.

Our approach is similar, at the level of individual patterns, to the work by Gross and Yu (2001), as well as Chung, Supakkul, and Yu (2002). Both present ways of reasoning about patterns using NFRs. However, there are important differences. We are also concerned with the connections between patterns at the pattern language level, as well as with establishing models of the forces and their trade-offs that exist in a particular domain. As a result, we feel that our results are farther-reaching, and will lead to a more objective approach.

Also in related work, use case map scenarios have been used by Andrade and Logrippo (2000) to describe patterns of behavior in wireless systems and by Billard (2004) to capture agent interaction patterns. In addition, such scenarios have been the object of patterns themselves. For instance, Mussbacher and Amyot (2001) proposed use case map modeling patterns for describing and composing features. Our approach also captures pattern solutions with abstract scenarios, but we do so in a context where scenarios are explicitly linked to forces.

User Requirements Notation

Several years ago, the standardization sector of the International Telecommunications Union initiated work toward the creation of a *user requirements notation* (URN) in the Z.150 series of Recommendations (ITU-T, 2003). The purpose of URN is to support, prior to detailed design, the modeling and analysis of user requirements in the form of goals and scenarios, in a formal way. URN is generally suitable for describing most types of reactive and distributed systems and services. It is also a convenient notation for business process modeling and evolution (Weiss & Amyot, 2005). An overview of URN with a tutorial example from the wireless communication domain is presented in Amyot (2003). The appendix at the end of this chapter also includes a summary of the main notation elements.

URN has concepts for the specification of behavior, structure, and goals, which are all relevant for the formalization of pattern forces and solutions, and for trade-off analysis. URN is, in fact, composed of two complementary notations, which build on previous work. The first is GRL, the *goal-oriented requirement language* (URN Focus Group, 2003a). GRL borrows its main concepts from the NFR (Non-functional requirements) framework published in Chung et al. (2000), and complements them with agent modeling concepts from the *i** framework (Yu, 1997). GRL captures business or system goals, alternative means of achieving goals, and the rationale for goals and alternatives. The notation is applicable to functional requirements, but it is especially good for capturing and reasoning about the interaction of non-functional requirements.

The second part of URN is the *use case map* (UCM) notation, described in URN Focus Group (2003b). The UCM notation was developed by Buhr and Casselman (1995) to depict emerging behavioral scenarios during the high-level design of distributed object-oriented reactive systems. It was later considered appropriate as a notation for describing operational requirements and services, at a higher level of abstraction. A UCM model depicts scenarios as causal flows of responsibilities that can be superimposed on underlying structures of components. UCM responsibilities are scenario activities representing something to be performed (operation, action, task, function, etc.). Responsibilities can potentially be allocated to components, which are generic enough to represent software entities (e.g., objects, processes, databases, or servers) as well as nonsoftware entities (e.g., actors or hardware resources). With UCMs, different structures suggested by architectural alternatives that were identified in a GRL model can be expressed and evaluated by moving responsibilities from one component (the UCM equivalent of a GRL actor) to another, or by restructuring (for example, decomposing) components.

Formalizing Forces for Trade-Off Analysis

Our pattern representation uses GRL to add an explicit model of the forces addressed by a pattern, and the rationale behind them. It also allows us to model relationships between patterns. Figure 1 shows the elements of the notation, and their interpretation in the context of representing patterns. The diagram on the left shows how an individual pattern, its contributions to forces, and the desired functionality of the system can be modeled as a goal hierarchy.

Non-functional requirements are represented as softgoals (clouds). The notation suggests that these cannot be achieved in an absolute manner. We use them to represent forces. Functional requirements are represented as (hard) goals (rounded rectangles). They allow us to reason about the functional requirements to which a pattern contributes.

Figure 1. Elements of the notation used to model forces and their resolution

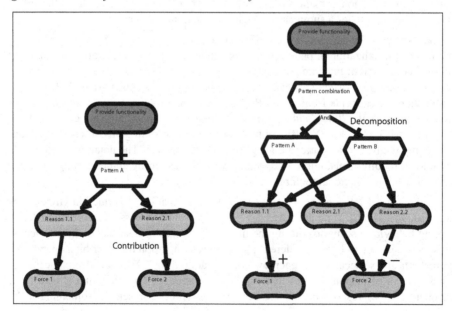

Patterns are modeled as tasks (hexagons), which are ways of achieving a goal or softgoal. The nodes of this goal graph can be connected by different types of links. Direct contributions of a pattern on goals are shown as straight lines. Side effects (indirect contributions called correlations) are shown as dotted lines. Contributions can be labeled with a + (the default value if none is present) or - to indicate that they are positive or negative. Note that GRL also offers a richer set of labels, which allows us to represent different levels of strength of a contribution or correlation (see Figure 12e). Uses, refines, and conflict relationships between patterns are modeled as AND or OR decomposition links between tasks (barred lines).

In order to achieve the desired functional and non-functional requirements, a solution often requires the use of several patterns. Hence, there is a need to model pattern combinations which are also depicted as tasks. The second diagram in Figure 1 indicates that only a pattern combination (which involves the original pattern A) fulfills the functional requirements because only the task describing the pattern combination is connected to the functional requirements goal.

There also exist design situations where more than one individual pattern or pattern combination may have to be considered as alternatives for achieving functional and non-functional requirements. In such a case, additional patterns and pattern combinations are added to the basic GRL graph. Figure 2 extends Figure 1 with an alternative pattern combination. The

Figure 2. Considering alternative pattern combinations

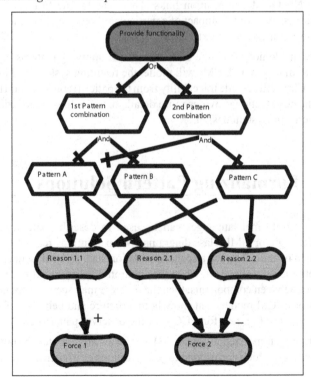

functional goal is now connected to the two pattern combinations with an OR decomposition.

Note that our pattern representation allows contributions to be made by individual patterns as well as pattern combinations. The latter can be modeled with a contribution link from a pattern combination task to any one of the softgoals. This is useful in the case where individual patterns alone cannot balance a force (i.e., softgoal) but only the combined usage of two patterns is able to do so. Finally, even though the examples in Figure 1 and Figure 2 only show one functional requirements goal, our pattern representation is not at all limited to just one such goal. Many different goals describing many different functional requirements may be shown on a GRL graph and may be connected with decomposition links to individual patterns or pattern combinations.

There are several important observations to be made about our representation of patterns. The bottom half of the figures can be derived from other GRL graphs that focus on one individual pattern at a time and show the pattern's contribution to forces. GRL graphs for an individual pattern only need to be created once and establish reusable models of forces applicable to many domains. Several of these focused GRL graphs are then combined into our pattern representation shown above in order to highlight the differences of selected patterns.

Like most goal-oriented languages, GRL supports propagation algorithms to evaluate, for a given *strategy*, to what degree the goals and softgoals in a model are satisfied (URN Focus Group, 2003a). A strategy assigns initial satisfaction values to some of the elements in the model (in our case, the tasks associated with individual patterns in a desired pattern combination) which are then propagated to the other elements connected by contribution, correlation, and AND/OR decomposition links. This enables one to make a qualitative, rapid, and global assessment of the impact of a particular choice and hence to find the most appropriate trade-off in a given context.

Note that GRL graphs do not model the consequences of applying patterns in terms of the architectural design of a system. UCMs will model the resulting system, and links between GRL graphs and UCMs will provide traceability from the pattern representation to the system representation. The next section provides more details on modeling the solution space and the impact of patterns on system design.

Formalizing Pattern Solutions

Many formal and semiformal languages can be used to describe pattern solutions, for instance, first-order logic or UML class diagrams. When solutions require behavioral descriptions, it is often beneficial to use a scenario notation such as UML sequence diagrams or message sequence charts. However, when the solution does not require the definition of message exchanges between components, then the use case map scenario notation becomes an interesting option. UCM models can show both structure and behavior of a solution at an abstract level (e.g., see Figure 3 for a UCM of the observer pattern).

In the UCM notation (summarized in Figure 13), scenarios are initiated at start points, represented as filled circles, which correspond to preconditions or triggering events. Scenarios

Figure 3. Use case map for the Observer pattern

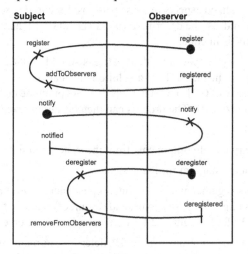

terminate at end points, shown as bars, which correspond to postconditions or resulting events. Paths show the causal relationships between start and end points, and (guarded) alternative and concurrent paths can be expressed. Generic components are shown as rectangles, and they are responsible for the various activities (called responsibilities and indicated by X's on a path) allocated to them. Diamonds are used to represent stubs, which are containers for submaps called plug-ins. Components can also be assigned roles, which further contributes to the reusability and adaptability of the solution in similar contexts. For instance, the two component roles in Figure 3 can be assumed by concrete components when the map is used in a stub.

Similar to GRL graphs for individual patterns, UCMs for individual patterns have to be created only once and can be plugged into any system description with the help of stubs. UCMs for individual patterns can also package different scenario fragments meant to be used by different stubs. For example, in a stub handling the registration phase of the Observer pattern, the "register" start point of the top scenario fragment in Figure 3 is bound to the input segment of a stub and the "registered" end point to the output segment of that stub.

The paths and their elements can easily be allocated to different underlying structures of components, which could represent different architectural alternatives. Different path structures could also share similar component structures. A GRL model could provide the details of the trade-offs involved in choosing one solution over another, in context.

Overview of Proposed Process

The pattern forces and solutions formalized as suggested in the previous sections can be integrated with regular pattern descriptions, independently of the template used. Although such patterns can be useful on their own, this section introduces a process that will take full advantage of the new formalized aspects of these patterns. Essentially, some aspects of the system to be designed should also be described with GRL and UCM, hence enabling global impact and trade-off analysis in context.

A precondition to our process is that individual patterns should include forces formalized with GRL (see first diagram in Figure 1) and solutions formalized with UCM (as in Figure 3). Note that the presence of GRL/UCM models does not preclude the existence of other representations and formalizations. The process can then be summarized as follows:

1.   Extract a preliminary list of components from the system requirements.

2.   Construct a GRL actor diagram for the system:

   a.   Identify actors together with their interdependencies and the objects of these dependencies (e.g., goals, softgoals, and resources). Include the system itself as a GRL actor. Refer to Figure 12 for corresponding notation elements.

   b.   Expand the system's internal goal model, determine its main functional subgoals, and connect the relevant elements to the actor's external dependencies.

3.   For each subgoal, select candidate patterns. Most of the time, a number of patterns can be selected from experience. Additionally, candidate patterns may be found by matching the goals and softgoals identified in the GRL graphs of the candidate patterns to the goals and softgoals found in step 2.b.

4.   For each subgoal, connect alternative candidate patterns or combinations of patterns in an AND/OR graph, as illustrated in Figure 2.

5.   Determine the most suitable pattern or combination of patterns by using trade-off analysis based on GRL strategies.

6.   Assess architectural ramifications based on a UCM model of the system that contains stubs where the selected pattern plug-ins are used.

Application to a Case Study

Feedback Control Framework

Our example is based on a case study from Yacoub and Ammar (2004). In this case study, a reusable framework for feedback control systems is designed by composing Design patterns. In this chapter, we focus on the pattern selection stage of the pattern-oriented design approach advocated by Yacoub and Ammar (2004). We illustrate how URN can be used to support the matching of requirements to patterns.

A schematic representation of a feedback control system is provided in Figure 4. It consists of a feedforward controller, the controlled system or plant, and a feedback controller. The user applies a desired output value (configuration data) to the control system, which is then compared to the actual output observed in the system. The difference between the desired

Figure 4. Schematic representation of a feedback control system

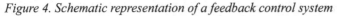
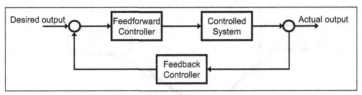

output and the actual output (error) is applied as input to the feedforward controller. In simple systems, an identity function is often used as the feedback controller.

A cruise-control system is a typical example of a feedback control system. It is used to maintain the velocity of a vehicle at a constant speed. Deviations from the desired speed are fed back to the controller as an error, and a corrective action (slowing down, speeding up) is applied to align the actual speed with the desired speed once again. Our goal is to design a generic framework for the development of such feedback control systems.

In Yacoub and Ammar (2004), five high-level components are already identified:

- A feedforward component that applies a control algorithm to the plant;
- A measurement component that collects measurements coming from the plant;

Figure 5. Feedback control system dependencies

Figure 6. Internal goal breakdown of the feedback control system

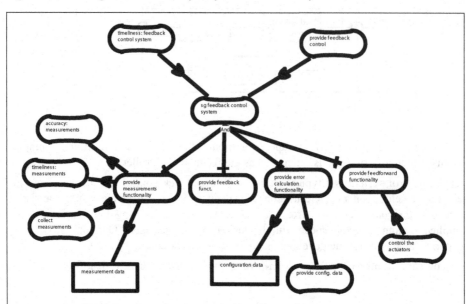

- A feedback component that observes measurements and aggregates them into feedback data representing the actual output measured at the plant;
- An error calculation component that compares the desired output and feedback data and computes the error provided as input to the feedforward component; and
- A plant or the external component controlled by the feedback control system.

The second step of our approach is to map the requirements into an actor diagram that shows the system to be designed as an actor, the external actors using or affected by the system, and the dependencies between the external actors and the system. In the case study, we identify three external actors: the user who applies the desired output to the plant, the plant (controlled entity), as well as the software engineer who develops and maintains the system. Figure 5 shows the resulting actor diagram for the feedback control system. For example, the user depends on the feedback control system to provide feedback control (shown as a goal dependency), and, in turn, the feedback control system depends on the user to provide configuration data (a goal and a resource dependency).

Figure 6 expands the main goal of the feedback control system actor in Figure 5 by showing a high-level breakdown of the goals of the feedback control system, as well as all dependencies from Figure 5 relevant to this diagram. The feedback control system goal is decomposed into subgoals which can be derived from four of the five high-level components identified earlier.

The next step introduces several pattern combinations as design alternatives for each of the four subgoals. It makes use of the pattern representation discussed earlier.

Candidate Patterns for the Case Study

The authors of the original case study (Yacoub & Ammar, 2004) identify three patterns that should be considered during the design of the feedback control framework: Strategy (Gamma et al., 1994), Observer (Gamma et al., 1994), and Blackboard (Shaw & Garlan, 1996). Further exploration, under consultation of the pattern catalogs of Buschmann, Meunier, Rohnert, Sommerlad, Stal (1996) and Avgeriou and Zdun (2005), of the candidate space suggests the following additional patterns: Producer-Consumer (a variation of Publisher-Subscriber), Shared Repository, Active Repository, and Explicit Invocation. Whereas in the original case study, all patterns were used in the design, with the revised list of candidate patterns, there are trade-offs to be made between the patterns. Pattern selection will take into account functional and non-functional requirements and their priorities. Figure 7 shows the

Figure 7. Alternatives for the feedback goal

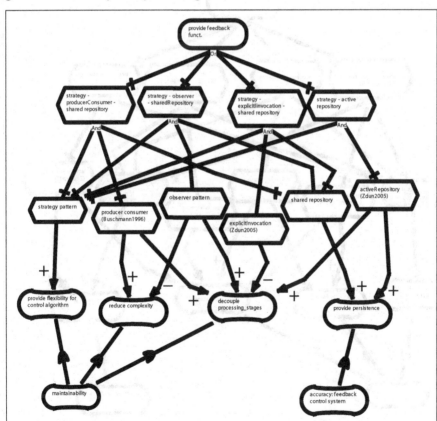

alternatives considered for the design of the feedback component of the system, as well as all relevant dependencies from Figure 5. Four combinations make use of different subsets of five individual patterns. The observer pattern, for instance, has a positive contribution toward the decoupling of processing stages but, on the other hand, it negatively impacts the reduction of the complexity.

Trade-Off Analysis

Two of the four alternatives depicted in Figure 7 are evaluated. The first alternative involves the use of the strategy pattern combined with the observer pattern and a shared repository. The trade-off analysis is done for all subgoals in Figure 6, but only the GRL graph for the feedback subgoal is shown here.

Figure 8. Evaluating one alternative for the feedback goal

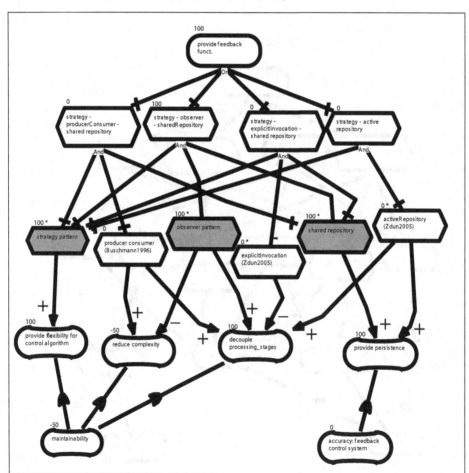

Figure 9. Use case map for first alternative

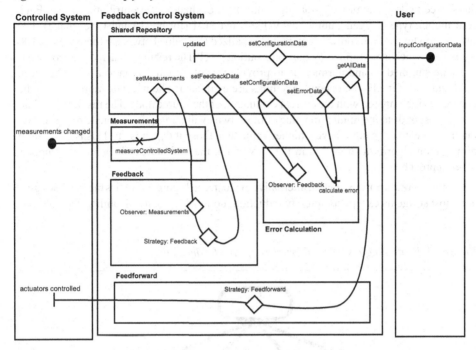

The starting points of the evaluation are the candidate patterns (strategy, observer, and shared repository in this case) which have been assigned an initial satisfaction level. To do so, we have used the jUCMNav tool, an Eclipse-based editor for URN models that supports GRL model evaluation based on GRL strategies and propagation algorithms (Roy, Kealey, & Amyot, 2006). jUCMNav is a generic editor for the URN notation, with no specific support for patterns, and all the diagrams in this chapter were produced with this tool.

We assigned an initial satisfaction value of 100 to the three patterns (Figure 8). The star (*) next to the task symbol indicates that this value was entered by the user. A collection of such initial assignments represents in fact a GRL strategy definition, and these assignments are usually done to a subset of the leaves in the GRL graph (the bottom contributors, that contribute to or refine higher-level goals). In jUCMNav, a positive number between 1 and 100 next to a node indicates the degree of satisfaction achieved for the node. A negative number between -1 and -100 next to a node indicates the degree of dissatisfaction suffered for the node. Zero indicates that there is no evaluation available for the node (the node is undecided). Corresponding GRL satisfaction level icons (Figure 12b) and colors are also used in the diagrams for improved visual feedback.

Based on the decomposition, contribution, and dependency links, the initial evaluation is now propagated to other nodes in the GRL graph. In a nutshell, the propagation procedure from Roy et al. (2006) first considers the decomposition links, as a standard AND/OR graph. For an AND decomposition, the result corresponds to the minimal evaluation of the source nodes, and for an OR decomposition, the result corresponds to the maximal evaluation of the source nodes. The propagation algorithm then evaluates the contribution links. Each contribution type is given a numerical value between -1 (for break) and 1 (for make). The satisfaction level of the source element is normalized to a value between 0 (denied) and 100 (satisfied) which is multiplied by the contribution level. The results of each of the contributions are summed up and normalized to provide the total contribution as a value between -100 and 100. Finally, the dependency links are evaluated. The minimal value among the dependees is compared with the current evaluation of the source node. The resulting evaluation corresponds to the minimum value of those two evaluations, the rationale being that an intentional element cannot have a higher value than those it depends on. This is the default propagation algorithm supported in jUCMNav, but the tool is flexible enough to support other approaches.

Using this algorithm, the particular alternative evaluated in Figure 8 satisfies the feedback goal and most softgoals except complexity reduction, upon which maintainability depends.

Figure 10. Evaluating a second alternative for the feedback goal

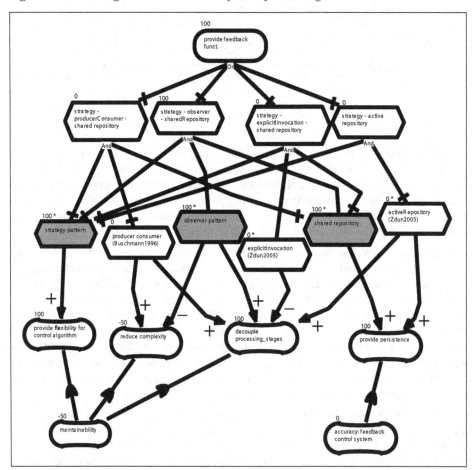

Figure 11. Use case map for second alternative

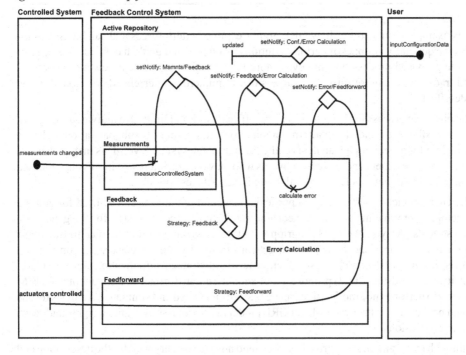

In addition to the GRL graph explaining the impact of the proposed alternative on the forces, a corresponding UCM describes the architectural ramifications. The UCM model in Figure 9 shows the complete system summarizing all design decisions from all four subgoals. It also contains the five components previously discovered for this case study, as well as the actors involved in the use of the feedback control system (namely, the user and the controlled system itself). Links between the GRL graphs and the UCM model ensure traceability. For instance, the strategy pattern task is mapped onto the stub "Strategy: Feedback," the observer pattern task is mapped onto the stub "Observer: Measurements" and "Observer: Feedback," and the shared repository pattern task is mapped to the stub "setFeedbackData" (and many others). The stubs on the UCM can be expanded into submaps which give further details on the application of the pattern in this context. For instance, the middle scenario fragment in Figure 3 is connected to "Observer: Feedback" and the "Error Calculation" component assumes the role of "Observer" while the "Feedback" component assumes the role of "Subject."

The second alternative still uses the strategy pattern but replaces the observer and shared repository with an active repository (Figure 10). Again, the GRL graph is linked to the UCM (Figure 11). The strategy pattern task is mapped onto the stub "Strategy: Feedback" and the active repository pattern maps to the four "setNotify" stubs. In this alternative, the trade-off is different; there is no impact on complexity and maintainability, at the cost of a lower satisfaction level of the decoupling of processing stages. From a maintainability and accuracy point of view, this solution is better than the first one, although there is still room for improvement.

Discussion and Future Trends

This example demonstrates how GRL graphs capture pattern forces and can be used to assess the qualitative impact of various solutions to a functional goal, in context. The benefits of the proposed process become even more interesting as the system gets more complex and trade-offs are more difficult to assess due to numerous interrelated contributions and side-effects.

The proposed process for URN-based trade-off analysis is not limited to individual subgoals. It can easily be extended to pattern combinations addressing all subgoals at once, hence providing for global impact analysis and guidance, at the system level. This may go beyond the needs of designers and system architects who may only be interested in solving a focused design problem, but this level of evaluation is nevertheless possible.

The UCM models resulting from a particular selection of patterns can be used for guiding developers into making low-level decisions, and can be used as a basis for the generation of test goals (Amyot, Weiss, & Logrippo, 2005). They can also help in quantifying some of the performance aspects by providing means to specify more precisely the contribution levels in GRL models and the satisfaction levels in strategy initializations. For instance, Petriu and Woodside (2002) propose a tool-supported transformation from annotated UCM models to performance models that can be formally analyzed and simulated. Analysis results could be fed back to the system-level GRL model to fine-tune some of the weights and reach better conclusions.

Although many graphical approaches often tend not to scale very well for the description and analysis of large systems, this issue is handled to some extent by the high level of abstraction at which URN is used and by several mechanisms such as decomposition (stubs/plug-ins in UCMs, decomposition links in GRL). In addition, URN and jUCMNav distinguish diagrams from models, that is, an element defined in a model can be reused or referenced in many diagrams, which then act like partial views. Complex systems can hence easily be composed of many such diagrams or views, both in UCM and in GRL.

Obviously, in addition to having patterns formalized with URN, the more advanced benefits require additional investments that not all modelers may be willing to make: a system-level GRL model for assessing the global impact of selected patterns, a system-level UCM model (where the pattern solutions will be plugged-in) to perform UCM-level analysis and test generation, and additional performance-level annotations to the UCM model to perform quantitative performance analysis.

There is also a general trend toward formalizing aspects of patterns, whether they are related to the relationships between patterns, or to properties of individual patterns. Often, these efforts have been confined to certain domains, which are more amenable to formalization, such as the area of security patterns. One example is the formalization of security properties that are satisfied by application of a pattern (Wassermann & Cheng, 2003), another is the formalization of security pattern properties in Mouratidis, Weiss, and Giorgini (2005), which allows the authors of a pattern language to assess the completeness of the language. In this work, the pattern solutions are modeled in agent-oriented models in the Tropos modeling framework. A formal language for Tropos models is used to formalize the problems, solutions, and consequences of these patterns. These properties are expressed in logic statements over the components of the solutions. Some of this logic-based formalization could be added to GRL, although it does not appear essential in our current trade-off analysis context.

Aspects, which are concerns that crosscut dominant decompositions, represent another trend identifiable in the software community in general. Aspects have been studied for a decade and are used to compensate several weaknesses of object-oriented programming languages (e.g., scattering and tangling of functionalities and other concerns). Existing Design patterns have been recast for new aspect-oriented languages, for example, see Hannemann and Kiczales (2002), whereas new patterns specific to such languages have started to appear. More recently, aspect-oriented concepts have been included in modeling languages, closer to design and requirements. For instance, Jacobson and Ng (2004) present an approach where aspects are derived from UML use cases, whereas Yu, Leite, and Mylopoulos (2004) present an approach where aspects are inferred from goal models. The impact of the availability of such enhanced modeling languages requires further exploration. For instance, Mussbacher, Amyot, and Weiss (2006) believe aspect-oriented concepts can easily be added to URN. This could help close the gap between aspect-oriented modeling and programming languages and, at the same time, open the door to new types of patterns that are more abstract or closer to requirements than the current generation of Design patterns.

Conclusion

In this chapter, we have presented an approach where Design patterns are formalized with the user requirements notation, which combines the goal-oriented requirements language (GRL) and the use case map (UCM) scenario notation. Our main objective is to describe patterns in a way that the various and conflicting forces involved can guide, in a given context, the selection of the most suitable patterns or combinations of patterns among many alternatives.

Forces and contributions for individual patterns are captured using GRL. Combinations and side effects (correlations) are described with AND graphs, and alternative combinations for a given (functional) goal are represented with an OR graph. With the help of strategies (i.e., initial selections of candidate patterns) and propagation rules, designers can assess the impact of their selection on the forces and find a suitable solution in their context. This context can itself be modeled with GRL, first at the actor/dependency level, and then at the level of intentional elements (goals, softgoals, tasks, etc.) for the system. This enables global and rigorous assessments to be made, even when many functional subgoals are considered.

Pattern solutions are formalized at an abstract level with UCM. Such models package many scenario segments that can be plugged into stubs belonging to a description of the system's main operational scenarios (also a UCM model). The availability of such a scenario model enables further analysis and transformations, including simulation, performance evaluation, and test goal generation.

To take full advantage of URN-based formalization of Design patterns, a process was briefly introduced and illustrated with a case study where many combinations of patterns could be used to achieve the same functionality while leading to different trade-offs involving non-functional aspects, such as maintainability and accuracy. A prototype tool, which was used to create and evaluate the URN models presented here, already exists to support such process, and is still evolving to support new types of analyses and transformations, including patterns-oriented ones.

We believe this formalization approach will provide means to get rapid and global trade-off analysis results in context and make better use of current and future Design patterns.

References

Alexander, C. (1979). *A pattern language*. Oxford University Press.

Amyot, D. (2003). Introduction to the user requirements notation: Learning by example. *Computer Networks, 42*(3), 285-301.

Amyot, D., Weiss, M., & Logrippo, L. (2005). UCM-based generation of test purposes. *Computer Networks, 49*(5), 643-660.

Andrade, R., & Logrippo, L. (2000, July). Reusability at the early development stages of the mobile wireless communication systems. In *Proceedings of the 4th World Multiconference on Systemics, Cybernetics and Informatics (SCI 2000)*, Orlando, FL (Vol. VII, Part I, pp. 11-16).

Araujo, I., & Weiss, M. (2002). Linking non-functional requirements and patterns. In *Proceedings of the 9th Conference on Pattern Languages of Programs (PLoP)*. Retrieved November, 16, 2006, from http://jerry.cs.uiuc.edu/~plop/plop2002/final/PatNFR.pdf

Avgeriou, P., & Zdun, U. (2005, July). Architectural patterns revisited: A pattern language. In *Proceedings of the 10th European Conference on Pattern Languages of Programs (EuroPlop)*, Irsee, Germany.

Billard, E.A. (2004, August). Patterns of agent interaction scenarios as use case maps. *IEEE Transactions on Systems, Man, and Cybernetics. Part B, Cybernetics, 34*(4), 1933-1939.

Buhr, R.J.A., & Casselman, R.S. (1995). *Use case maps for object-oriented systems*. Prentice Hall.

Buschmann, F., Meunier, R., Rohnert, H., Sommerlad, P., Stal, M. (1996). *Pattern-oriented software architecture*. Wiley.

Chung, L., Nixon, B., Yu, E., & Mylopoulos, J. (2000). *Non-functional requirements in software engineering*. Kluwer Academic Publishers.

Chung, L., Supakkul, S., & Yu, A. (2002, July 8-11). Good software architecting: Goals, objects, and patterns. In *Proceedings of the Information, Computing & Communication Technology Symposium (ICCT- 2002), UKC'02*, Seoul, Korea.

Coplien, J. (1996). *Software patterns*. SIGS. Retrieved November 16, 2006, from http://users.rcn.com/jcoplien/Patterns/WhitePaper/SoftwarePatterns.pdf

Gamma, E., Helm, R., Johnson, R., & Vlissides, J. (1994). *Design patterns: Elements of reusable object-oriented software*. Addison-Wesley.

Gross, D., & Yu, E. (2001). From non-functional requirements to design through patterns. *Requirements Engineering, 6*(1), 18-36.

Hannemann, J., & Kiczales, G. (2002, November). *Design pattern implementation in Java and AspectJ. In Proceedings of the 17th OOPSLA* (pp. 161-173).

ITU-T (2003). *Recommendation Z.150 (02/03), user requirements notation (URN) – Language requirements and framework.* Geneva, Switzerland.

Jacobson, I., & Ng, P.-W. (2004). *Aspect-oriented software development with use cases.* Addison-Wesley.

Mouratidis, H., Weiss, M., & Giorgini, P. (2005). Security patterns meet agent oriented software engineering: A complementary solution for developing secure information systems. *Conceptual modeling (ER)* (LNCS 2716, pp. 225-240). Springer-Verlag.

Mussbacher, G., & Amyot, D. (2001, October 3-5). A collection of patterns for use case maps. In *Proceedings of the 1st Latin American Conference on Pattern Languages of Programming (SugarLoafPLoP 2001)*, Rio de Janeiro, Brazil.

Mussbacher, G., Amyot, D., & Weiss, M. (2006, September 11). Visualizing aspect-oriented requirements scenarios with use case maps. In *Proceedings of the International Workshop on Requirements Engineering Visualization (REV 2006)*, Minneapolis/St. Paul, Minnesota.

Ong, H., Weiss, M., & Araujo, I. (2003, March). Rewriting a pattern language to make it more expressive. *Hot topic on the expressiveness of pattern languages, ChiliPLoP.* Carefree, USA.

Petriu, D., & Woodside, M. (2002). Software performance models from system scenarios in use case maps. *Computer performance evaluation / TOOLS 2002* (LNCS 2324, pp. 141-158). Springer-Verlag.

Rising, L. (2000). *Pattern almanac 2000.* Addison-Wesley.

Roy, J.-F., Kealey, J., & Amyot, D. (2006, May). Towards integrated tool support for the user requirements notation. In *Proceedings of the Fifth Workshop on System Analysis and Modelling (SAM'06)*, Kaiserslautern, Germany.

Shaw, M., & Garlan, D. (1996). *Software architecture: Perspectives on an emerging discipline.* Prentice Hall.

Taibi, T., & Ngo, D.C.L. (2001). Why and how should patterns be formalized. *Journal of Object-Oriented Programming (JOOP), 14*(4), 8-9.

URN Focus Group (2003a, September). *Draft Rec. Z.151 – Goal-oriented requirement language (GRL).* Geneva, Switzerland.

URN Focus Group (2003b, September). *Draft Rec. Z.152 – Use case map notation (UCM).* Geneva, Switzerland.

Wassermann, R., & Cheng, B. (2003). *Security patterns* (Tech. Rep. No. MSU-CSE-03-23). Michigan State University.

Weiss, M., & Amyot, D. (2005, July-September). Business process modeling with URN. *International Journal of E-Business Research, 1*(3), 63-90.

Yacoub, S., & Ammar, H. (2004). *Pattern-oriented analysis and design: Composing patterns to design software systems.* Addison-Wesley.

Yu, E. (1997, January 6-8). Towards modelling and reasoning support for early-phase requirements engineering. In *Proceedings of the 3rd IEEE International Symposium on Requirements Engineering (RE'97)* (pp. 226-235). Washington, DC.

Yu, Y., Leite, J.C.S.P., & Mylopoulos, J. (2004, September). From goals to aspects: Discovering aspects from requirements goal models. In *Proceedings of the 12th IEEE International. Conference on Requirements Engineering (RE 2004)* (pp. 38-47). Kyoto, Japan.

Appendix

Figure 12. Summary of the GRL notation

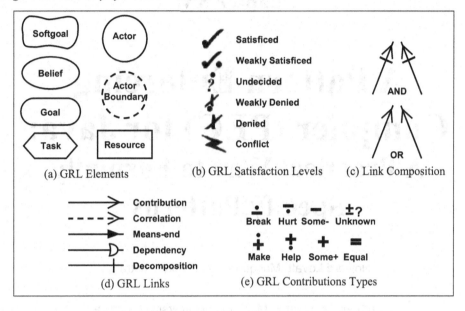

(a) GRL Elements   (b) GRL Satisfaction Levels   (c) Link Composition

(d) GRL Links   (e) GRL Contributions Types

Figure 13. Summary of the UCM notation

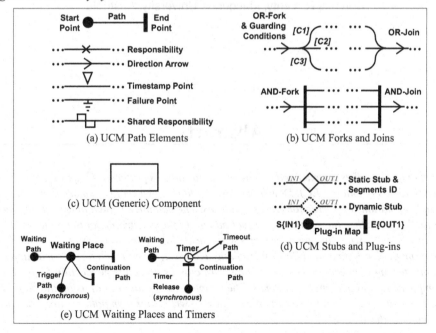

(a) UCM Path Elements   (b) UCM Forks and Joins

(c) UCM (Generic) Component   (d) UCM Stubs and Plug-ins

(e) UCM Waiting Places and Timers

Chapter XV

A Pattern Enforcing Compiler (PEC) for Java:
A Practical Way to Formally Specify Patterns

Howard Lovatt, Macquarie University, Australia

Anthony M. Sloane, Macquarie University, Australia

Dominic R. Verity, Macquarie University, Australia

Abstract

This chapter describes an extended compiler that formalizes patterns, which we call a pattern enforcing compiler (PEC). Developers use standard Java syntax to mark their classes as implementations of particular Design patterns. The compiler is then able to use reflection to check whether the classes do in fact adhere to the constraints of the patterns. The checking possible with our compiler starts with the obvious static adherence to constraints such as method presence, visibility, and naming. However, we go much further and support dynamic testing to check the runtime behavior of classes and code generation to assist in the implementation of complex patterns. The chapter gives examples of using the patterns supplied with our PEC and also examples of how to write your own patterns and have our PEC enforce these.

Introduction

Formalization techniques for Design patterns vary in the extent to which mathematical formalisms are employed. While it is possible to model many aspects of patterns in a very precise way with mathematical techniques, the result is often methods that have restricted scope to deal with systems on a real-world scale or tools that are unlikely to be integrated into developers work practices due to unfamiliarity and training requirements. This observation has been made a number of times in the more general area of formal methods for software development.

This chapter is based on our research in using compiler technology to automatically enforce Design patterns in Java code. This approach provides many of the benefits of more mathematical approaches, such as mechanized checking, but also enables us to integrate the checking with standard developer practices. For example, our approach supports standard compilation and build tools as used by modern Integrated Development Environments.

Our approach achieves pattern formalization via an extended compiler, which we call a pattern enforcing compiler (PEC). Developers use standard Java syntax to mark their classes as implementations of particular Design patterns. The compiler is then able to use reflection to check whether the classes do in fact adhere to the constraints of the patterns. The checking possible with our compiler starts with the obvious static adherence to constraints such as method presence, visibility, and naming. However, we go much further to support dynamic testing to check the runtime behavior of classes and code generation to assist in the implementation of complex patterns. We have a robust implementation, structured as a transparent back-end to any standard Java compiler, and it is freely available by download (http://pec.dev.java.net) under the Lesser GNU General Public License (Lovatt, 2004). In the standard distribution we support a number of standard Design patterns, but developers can easily extend the system.

The chapter is structured as follows:

- Review the literature on related work to give background to the work and to tease out problems with current approaches.

- Introduce the idea of a PEC and outline the philosophy and motivation behind our approach to pattern formalization to show why this approach solves many of the problems highlighted when reviewing literature.

- Give some examples of simple patterns to illustrate how developers can formalize their own patterns.

- Introduce a more complex pattern that is derived from a formal specification.

- Briefly describe the patterns that our PEC currently supports.

- Suggest future trends.

- Conclude and summarize the chapter.

The main thrust of this chapter is to demonstrate how a contract for a Design pattern can be enforced using our compiler; but before getting into details it is useful to provide an example of writing a class that is enforced, so that context is provided for subsequent discussions.

Using a Formal Pattern Specification

Using our PEC patterns are enforced at the class level, that is, the class has to be written by the programmer to conform to the pattern and has to be declared as an implementation of the pattern. For example, a Singleton is:

```
import pec.compile.singleton.*;
public final class SingletonClass implements Singleton {
    private final static SingletonClass instance = new SingletonClass();
    private SingletonClass() {
        if ( instance != null )
            throw new IllegalStateException( "Singleton!" );
    }
    public static SingletonClass instance() { return instance; }
    // other methods
}
```

The key to the above code is the implements Singleton clause[1] that tells:

- Our PEC that the class should conform to the Singleton pattern.

- The programmer maintaining SingletonClass that it is a Singleton.

- The user of SingletonClass, via its Javadoc, that it is a Singleton. If the user of the class wishes to find out more about a Singleton, they can click on the Singleton link in the Javadoc and they will be taken to our PEC's Singleton page (Lovatt, 2004) which gives a detailed explanation.

Note the natural reading of the declaration class SingletonClass implements Singleton, it describes the exact relationship between SingletonClass and Singleton, that is, SingletonClass is an implementation of the Singleton pattern. This reading of the clause extends the interface to not only mean that the class contains specified methods, but also that the class conforms to the specified *contract*. We have not found in practice that this dual use of interfaces, defining method signatures and pattern contracts, is a problem; even though there is nothing specific to distinguish one from the other. This has not been a problem for three reasons: the names of patterns tend to be different from typical interface names and therefore not confused, the Javadoc links identifies the patterns by their package name which begins with **pec** and by linking to our Web site, and Java centric IDEs easily allow interrogation to find package names, Javadocs, class hierarchies, and so forth.

The checks our Singleton pattern performs are:

- The class:
  - Must be final.

- Must have a single, private, no argument, constructor that throws IllegalStateException if it is called more than once.
- If the class is serializable then it should have a readResolve method that returns the "Singleton."
- Cannot be clonable.
- Must have a method called instance.
- This instance method must:
  - Return the same object when called twice.
  - Have no arguments.
- Be static.
- Have either package or public access.

This example demonstrates how both static testing (e.g., class must be final), and dynamic testing (e.g., instance returns the same object) can be supported. The example also shows:

- The detail at which a pattern can be enforced, for example, class and method modifiers like final and private and the exact signature of a method including argument and return types.
- The usual pattern enforcement criteria like "must contain a given method," in this case instance[2].
- Detailed dynamic testing, for example if the constructor is called twice it throws an exception.

Not shown in this particular example, but demonstrated below, is how our PEC deals with patterns that rely on the cooperation of multiple classes. In the case of multiclass patterns each class is marked by an interface and the interface names the role that the class plays in the pattern.

Literature Review

Our PEC is believed to be unique in combining static testing, dynamic testing (unit testing), and code generation in one utility and is also unusual in having an extension mechanism. Although the whole is unique, the individual elements predate our PEC in general computer science and in the context of patterns both static and dynamic testing are known. This section supports this view of uniqueness by reviewing the literature.

All of the following papers have influenced our PEC for the better; in particular, features of these systems have been "borrowed!" Only positive influences on our PEC work are included below because the body of literature is too large to include everything.

Patterns in General

A good introduction to patterns is Coplien (1998), which gives a description of software Design patterns and their use. General "catalogues" of patterns exist (e.g., Gamma, Helm, Johnson, & Vlissides, 1995, which did much to popularize patterns), details of how to implement patterns in Java are available (e.g., Bloch, 2001), and the standard library contains many examples of pattern usage (Sun Microsystems, 2003).

Supporting patterns with a tool is difficult because there are a lot of patterns and some of these are domain specific (Chambers, Harrison, & Vlissides, 2000). In Chambers et al. (2000) the authors discuss the problem of supporting many patterns and note that it is undesirable to build language support for all the possibilities into a language. This is a similar argument to Steele (1998) and this argument led to the design of an extensible system rather than adding new language syntax for our PEC.

Hedin (1996) notes the impracticality of supporting all patterns by syntax extensions, but has a further useful observation that many domain specific languages are little more than an API of useful functions, some syntax to make the API easy to use, and a compiler that enforces the correct patterns required by the API. This last point, of pattern enforcing, is often not emphasized when discussing domain specific languages. A goal of our PEC is to enable development of APIs that require particular usage patterns and to enforce these. An example of such an API that requires a usage pattern is the interaction of ValueArrayList and ImmutableArrayList, which interact via our immutable value conversions pattern.

Some patterns have direct language support; for example, the OO pattern is supported directly in many languages. Other patterns are supported by code generation systems that customize the "boiler plate" code, for example, Budinsky, Finnie, Patsy, and Vlissides (1996) and Maplesden, Hosking, and Grundy (2002). The customized "boiler plate" is then compiled and maintained as normal. Contrast this with our PEC, that in the case of involved patterns like Multiple Dispatch, generates the compiled code automatically.

The desirability of reducing the "boiler plate" code is noted by Hannemann and Kiczales (2002). They use AspectJ to reduce the amount of "boiler plate." However AspectJ requires new syntax itself and their system does not incorporate static or dynamic testing unlike our PEC.

In specialized domains, particularly using enterprise JavaBeans (EJBs) in a client-server application, high level development environments use patterns and generate code (Hammouda & Koskimies, 2002). But these systems are very domain specific, whereas our PEC is intended as a general purpose tool crossing all domains.

Our PEC provides a means of documenting the use of the pattern via the Javadoc for the class. The need for documentation is recognized by Cornils and Hedin (2000) and they also note the undesirability of trying to support patterns with syntax extensions. The Cornils and Hedin system differs from our PEC in that the documentation is provided via a separate file linked to the source code using a special editor. Our PEC uses marker interfaces and the standard utility Javadoc to document the use of a pattern and hence does not require a special editor or viewer.

Pattern Checking Systems

One of the more complete systems in the literature is Pattern Lint, Sefika, Sane, and Campbell (1996), which as its name suggests[3], processes source files and identifies patterns. The program does not require any new syntax for the patterns and performs both static and dynamic tests and in these regards is similar to our PEC. Sefika et al. (1996) emphasize how unusual combining both static and dynamic testing is and gives a good list of references to systems that perform either static or dynamic testing. However Pattern Lint does not generate code or generate documentation and is not a "drop in" replacement for the compiler.

Pattern Lint uses heuristics to determine the patterns used and is also interactive to confirm its heuristics. This interactive nature is unusual in checking or compilation systems. Contrast this with our PEC that extends the type checking in an explicit manner, via a declaration, to identify the pattern. This contrast between heuristics and declarations is similar to the contrast between type checking by inference (e.g., Haskell) and type checking by declaration (e.g., Java). Both checking systems have their advantages and disadvantages and one of the reasons for choosing by-declaration for our PEC is that it is more consistent with the Java language.

A disadvantage of our current PEC compared to pattern lint is that antipatterns, or bad patterns, are not automatically detected. This negative pattern checking could be added to our PEC because much of the necessary infrastructure is present. However, antipattern detectors produce many false warnings, unlike our PEC that passes or fails a class (Rutar, Almazan, & Foster, 2004).

A feature of Pattern Lint is that it uses heuristics to "guess" the patterns used. This approach has much in common with reverse engineering systems that use similar approaches to aid understanding of programs either during program maintenance or for documentation. Murphy, Notkin, and Sullivan (1995), for example, describes a system that visualizes patterns in C source code. These postanalysis systems differ from our PEC in that our PEC extends the type checking in an explicit manner and documents the use of the pattern via a declaration.

As already noted, there are many static checking systems that for reasons of space are not reviewed in this chapter. One system, CoffeeStrainer, however, deserves special mention because it provides many more facilities than typical systems and because it has much in common with our PEC. Bokowski (1999) describes CoffeeStrainer, which has in common with our PEC the use of marker interfaces to cause a class to be checked, the use of Java as the specifying language, no new syntax, and user extensible, and also it is a "drop in" replacement compiler. The Bokowski paper contains a good discussion of the pros and cons of using Java to specify a pattern compared with a domain-specific language. However it differs from our PEC in only providing static testing and not dynamic and also in that it does not automatically generate code for the pattern (you need to hand code the pattern; it only enforces it). Our PEC will generate most of the "boiler plate" code associated with the pattern Multiple Dispatch, for example.

Compared to CoffeeStrainer, the number of patterns that our PEC currently supports is much smaller, but the patterns tend to be much higher level, for example, Multiple Dispatch.

Motivation and Philosophy

A common method of using a Design pattern is to cut and paste "boiler plate" code and then manually edit to suit a particular application. Boiler plate code is example code that lacks details, for example, method bodies, that the programmer uses as a starting point and "fills in the blanks." Another method is to use a wizard in an integrated development environment (IDE). These "ad-hoc" approaches have a number of disadvantages, including:

- There are variations on a given pattern and it is unclear exactly what the programmer intended (Noble & Biddle, 2002).
- Mistakes when manually editing the "boiler plate" or when maintaining the code means the code no longer conforms to the pattern.
- The use of the pattern is not clearly documented to either the maintainer of an application programming interface (API) or to the user of the API ("Using a Formal Pattern Specification" describes how our PEC documents pattern usage).
- The exact implementation of the pattern may vary from one usage to the next in the same code because different programmers used different a "boiler plate."
- The "boiler plate" can be impractically complicated.

Our PEC eliminates the above problems and, in addition, gives the following advantages:

- The compiler is easy to use.
- The compiler does not require syntax extensions to Java and is therefore compatible with existing IDEs, pretty printers, and so forth.
- The resulting code from our PEC is backwardly compatible with old Java code and our PEC can be used to compile any Java file, not just files that use patterns.
- A conventional compiler statically checks source code and generates binary code; our PEC has these functions and also dynamically checks (unit tests) code.
- Our PEC is extensible, that is, you can write your own patterns and have our PEC enforce them.
- You specify patterns at the class level, not at the instance level. This insight, enforcement at the class level, has proven to be valuable, as it is often impractical to retrospectively apply a pattern. For example, how do you enforce singularity at the instance level?

Our PEC can also be used in novel ways:

- **To Refactor Code:** An alternative to using "boiler plate" or a wizard to write a pattern conforming class is to take existing code and refactor it. For example, you may have a class that you want to turn into a singleton: add "implements Singleton," compile with our PEC, and follow the error messages given by our PEC that will guide you in refactoring the class.

- **To Maintain Code:** Another alternative way of using our PEC is for code maintenance. If you find a class you think is a Singleton, but singularity is not documented and therefore not clear, you can convert it into a Singleton by adding "implements Singleton" and refactoring, as above. This use of our PEC aids understanding, you test your hypothesis that the class is a Singleton, and makes future code maintenance easier because the action of the class is now clearly documented.

How to Write Enforceable Patterns

Up to this stage in the chapter, only the use of the patterns using our PEC is discussed, but as noted, it is advantageous to write your own patterns. The first stage in writing a pattern is to design the pattern, and then the pattern can be enforced. You also need an appreciation of how our PEC works.

How to Design Patterns

Some skill is required in designing the pattern to be enforced; if it is too pedantic, it will find few applications, and if it is too loose, it will add little to the formal correctness of the code. This is often an issue with unit testing, for example, our Singleton pattern calls the instance method twice. This is a compromise between calling the method an infinite number of times to absolutely ensure the method is correct, and not calling it at all, which would not test that it returned the same object on successive calls at all.

When designing a pattern, you need to be very familiar with Java; for example, how will the pattern interact with inner classes, serialization, multiple class loaders, or cloning? The level of protection offered by the pattern should be documented. For example, our Singleton pattern does not protect against multiple class loaders, and this is documented for the pattern.

A good technique for designing patterns is to start with a formal specification (e.g., Taibi & Ngo, 2003), and then convert this specification into a formal check ("Complete Example of Pattern Checking Code"). Also, we are proposing to add the ability to specify the patterns more formally ("Future Work").

Like any piece of software, it is possible that our pattern enforcing code contains bugs, either in its specification or in its implementation. We combat this problem by adopting the best industry practice, for example, unit testing, using code coverage to ensure our testing is thorough, and releasing the code so that people outside of our group use the code, perhaps in a manner we had not thought of, and therefore find bugs that we had not found. Also with patterns you can show example code, which is passed by our PEC, to people that are familiar with that pattern and ask them to comment on the implementation of that pattern. Similarly, an automatic pattern detection tool, for example Pattern Lint, could be used instead of a person on PEC passed code.

How our PEC Works

Our PEC works by testing, inspecting, and modifying an intermediate representation of the programmer's code, the class file. The class file is easy to manipulate and only contains the information required for manipulation. For example, it does not contain the literal text from the programmer, so information like the layout of the programmer's text and comments in the code are not represented, thus simplifying the task.

As discussed above, there are a number of advantages from the fact that our PEC requires no new syntax. A further advantage not discussed above is that an existing compiler can be used to generate a class file. This class file is easily tested, inspected, and modified, for example:

- It can be unit tested or inspected using the java.lang.reflect API (Sun Microsytems, 2003).
- It can be modified or inspected using the javassist API (Chiba, 2004) and Javassist can also create new class files.

Thus, the class file is used as an intermediate representation of the programmer's intent, like the intermediate language used in many compiler implementations. It is not surprising that the class file is a good intermediate representation of the program because its function is to represent the programmer's intent in a machine independent manner that is easy to process further, in particular to be processed further by a Java virtual machine (JVM) into native code for the processor in use. This is very similar to the requirement of an intermediate language in a conventional compiler. The biggest difference is that conventional intermediate languages are generally only available internally in the compiler and not written out to disc.

The Patterns for Writing Pattern Checks

As you might expect from a pattern enforcing compiler, the method of enforcing patterns follows a pattern! An interface that acts as a marker for checking extends CompilerEnforced, and just like a normal interface, can or cannot contain methods or static (class) fields. For example, Singleton (minus Javadoc comments) is:

```
package pec.compile.singleton;

import pec.compile.*;
import pec.compile.creational.*;
import pec.compile.staticfactory.*;

public interface Singleton extends Creational,StaticFactory,CompilerEnforced {
    // Empty

}
```

This declaration of the marker interface Singleton shows a number of interesting features.

- The name of the interface, Singleton, is the name of the pattern.

- The interface directly (not by inheritance from a base interface) extends CompilerEnforced. This tells our PEC that Singleton is a pattern checking marker interface.

- The interface is in a named package; see below for the significance of this.

- The pattern is categorized under the heading Creational (it extends Creational). All our patterns are categorized, following Gamma et al. (1995), under the headings Behavioral, Creational, or Structural. The purpose of the categorization is to act as an index. You can look at the Javadoc entry for Behavioral, for example, and it will list all the Behavioral patterns because their marker interfaces extend Behavioral. The use of interfaces to aid documentation is suggested by Wallace (2003).

- The pattern interface Singleton extends the pattern interface StaticFactory. This is because our Singleton pattern is a specialized type of our Static Factory pattern (one that only allows one instance to be created by the factory). This extension of a pattern by simply extending a pattern's marker interface is very convenient. There is no need for our Singleton pattern to enforce the characteristics it has in common with our Static Factory pattern. This is because any class that implements Singleton will also implement StaticFactory (Singleton extends StaticFactory), and therefore the class implementing Singleton will also be checked for conformance to our Static Factory pattern.

In the same package as the interface there is a class called {interface name}Utility, where {interface name} is the name of the interface that acts as the marker. The "utility" class needs to be in the same package as the interface and conform to the naming convention given so that our PEC can find the class. Our PEC finds the class using reflection, a.k.a. run-time type identification (RTTI). This allows the user of our PEC to add their own patterns; simply write an interface and "utility" that follow the pattern described in this section, and our PEC will enforce the new pattern if the new pattern is in its search path for classes (classpath). Our PEC reports error if this pattern for writing pattern checks is not adhered to, for example, it reports a missing "utility" class.

These "utility" classes contain either the method:

```
public static void compileTimeCheck( Class clazz )
throws CompilerEnforcedException
```

or

```
public static void compileTimeCheck( CtClass clazz, JavaCompiler pec )
throws CompilerEnforcedException
```

These "check" methods are called by our PEC with the class to check given as an argument. This second method signature is explained below. Our Singleton pattern uses the first method signature and this is explained first. For example, the class SingletonUtility (just showing declarations) is:

```
package pec.compile.singleton;

import pec.compile.noinstance.*;

public abstract class SingletonUtility implements NoInstance {
    public static void compileTimeCheck (Class clazz) throws

    SingletonException {

        ...

    }
}
```

The above code snippet from SingletonUtility shows a number of interesting features:

- It is in the package pec.compile.singleton.
- It uses a pattern itself, NoInstance, which ensures that no instance of the class can be made.
- The class is compiled with our PEC, which enforces our No Instance pattern.
- It uses the first of the "check" method signatures given above.
- It throws SingletonException, which extends CompilerEnforcedException.
- SingletonException provides convenience constructors or static factories for making the exception and also gives an informative name, SingletonException. The exception is created when the "check" method has found an error and it is created with a message that is used as the error message by our PEC. The exception is thrown by the "check" method, is caught by our PEC, and the message reported.
- The method compileTimeCheck is called by our PEC for each class that implements Singleton with the argument clazz set to the corresponding Class instance for the class to be checked for conformance to the pattern.

The reason for having two possible method signatures for the "check" method is that there are three aspects to checking a pattern and two different APIs, java.lang.reflect (Sun Microsystems, 2003) and javassist (Chiba, 2004), are used to cover the three aspects. The two signatures given above correspond to the two APIs listed, respectively. The required aspects for a PEC are:

1. The obvious aspect of pattern checking is static type checking, for example, finding the signature of methods. This is possible using either API, and therefore either method signature can be used.

2. Dynamic testing is achieved using the java.lang.reflect API. For the Singleton example, part of the testing is to use java.lang.reflect to call instance twice and to check that it returns the same object on both calls and therefore our Singleton pattern dynamically tests Singleton classes ("Dynamic/Unit Testing").

3. Some patterns are impractically complex to rely on hand editing of "boiler plate" code, for example, Multiple Dispatch. For these the "utility" method must generate extra code and the javassist API can do this.

Simple Examples of Pattern Checking Code

Static testing is quite straightforward using either of the two APIs. Typical static tests are quite declarative in nature and are therefore easy to code and understand.

Static Testing

To statically test that all fields are private, define the marker interface. For example:

```
package pec.example.compile;
import pec.compile.*;

public interface AllFieldsPrivate extends CompilerEnforced {/* Empty */}
```

Then the utility class:

```
package pec.example.compile;

import static java.lang.reflect.Modifier.*;
import static pec.compile.Utilities.*;
import pec.compile.noinstance.*;

public abstract class AllFieldsPrivateUtility implements NoInstance {

    private AllFieldsPrivateUtility() {}

    public static void compileTimeCheck( Class clazz )
                                    throws AllFieldsPrivateException {
        final Field[ ] fields = getAllFields( clazz );
```

```
    for ( final Field field : fields )
        if ( !isPrivate( field.getModifiers() ) )
            throw new AllFieldsPrivateException(
                "Field " + Utilities.toString( field ) + " isn't private" );

    }

}
```

The highlighted code is very close to how the specification might be written in a mathematical notation, particularly if the code is read as: for each field in the list of fields test if it is private and if it is not then throw an exception. An important aspect of this code is not only that it specifies the pattern, but it also generates a meaningful error message. It does not simply state that the class does not conform to the pattern, but explains exactly what the problem is.

The exception class, as is typical of our PEC's exception classes, is trivial:

```
package pec.example.compile;

import pec.compile.*;

public class AllFieldsPrivateException extends CompilerEnforcedException{
    AllFieldsPrivateException( final String message ) { super( message );
    }
}
```

Dynamic/Unit Testing

An important aspect of pattern checking is that many patterns need to be tested dynamically; the Singleton example above is an example of a pattern requiring dynamic testing. The pattern requires that multiple calls to instance return the same object. The relevant code for this test is:

```
// Unit test instance method
// Which is called using reflection via variable instance
final Object s1 = instance.invoke( null, null );
final Object s2 = instance.invoke( null, null );
if ( s1 != s2 )
    throw new SingletonException(
        "Must have an 'instance' method that returns the same instance " + "on each call, first
        call gave an object with a " + "'System.identityHashCode' of " + System.identityHash-
        Code( s1 ) + " and second " + System.identityHashCode( s2 ) );
```

The above code calls the Singleton class' instance method twice (using reflection) and then checks that the returned object is the same. If the objects are not equal then an informative error message is given via throwing an exception. As with the field testing example, the code is straightforward and declarative in style.

As with any form of dynamic/unit testing the testing is not exhaustive. For example, the test that the method instance returns the same object only calls instance twice, suppose on the third call it returned a different object? As is normal with this type of testing, it is necessary to accept that coverage will not be 100%, because an exhaustive test would take infinite time, for example, calling instance an infinite number of times!

Some patterns require more extensive unit testing and also require examples to use for testing because the compiler can not create and initialize arbitrarily complicated objects. Value semantics are an example of this. An object has Value semantics if its equals, hashCode, and toString methods are based on field values rather than its memory location. For the unit testing of Values, the programmer needs to include in the definition of the class an inner class that gives examples that can be used for testing. For example, for a Value Integer:

```
class ValueInteger implements Value {

    ...

    private static abstract class Values implements NoInstance {
        static final ValueInteger value1a = new ValueInteger( 1 );
        static final ValueInteger value1b = new ValueInteger( 1 );
        static final ValueInteger value2 = new ValueInteger( 2 );
    }

}
```

Using these values the testing checks that value1a and 1b are equal, that they have the same hash code and string representation, and that they are both not equal to value2, which also has a different hash code and string representation. The use of an inner class to give the example values ensures that outside of testing this inner class plays no part in execution. It is not even loaded!

Transforming Code

The programming style for transforming code is less declarative than simply testing code because by its very nature it changes code and therefore is not simply a list of assertions. The code is, however, still straightforward. For example, consider a pattern that automatically writes a toString method for a class that implements the pattern. The resulting toString returns a string with the format:

<short class name>{<field 1 name>=<field 1 value>, <field 2 name>=<field 2 value>, ...}

To implement the pattern define the pattern marker interface (note it extends ModifiesClass-File):

```
package pec.example.compile;
import pec.compile.*;
public interface ToString extends CompilerEnforced, ModifiesClassFile {}
```

Then the utility class:

```
package pec.example.compile;

import javassist.*;
import static pec.compile.Utilities.*;
import pec.compile.javacompiler.*;
import pec.compile.noinstance.*;

public abstract class ToStringUtility implements NoInstance {

  private ToStringUtility() {}

  public static void compileTimeCheck(
          CtClass clazz, JavaCompiler pec ) throws ToStringException {
    try {
      clazz.getDeclaredMethod( "toString", null );
       return; // Already has a toString declared in this class
    } catch ( NotFoundException notUsed ) {
      // Add a toString
      final StringBuffer body = new StringBuffer(
                        "public String toString() {\n return \"" );
      body.append( clazz.getSimpleName() );
      body.append( "{" );
      final CtField[] fields = getAllFields( clazz );
      for ( int f = 0; f < fields.length; f++ ) {
          final CtField field = fields[ f ];
          // For each field add name=value
          body.append( field.getName() );

          body.append( "=\" + " );
          body.append( field.getName() );
          if ( ( f + 1 ) < fields.length )
```

```
        body.append( " + \", " );

    }

    if ( fields.length > 0 )
        body.append( " + \"" );
    body.append( "}\";\n}" );
    try {
        final CtMethod toString =
        CtNewMethod.make(body.toString(),clazz);
        clazz.addMethod( toString );
    } catch ( Throwable e ) {
        throw new ToStringException( e );
    }
    }
  }
}
```

The above code demonstrates the simplest method of using the Javassist API, namely generating the required method as a text string and adding the method to the class. In the above code, the class CtClass is the Javassist equivalent of the reflective class Class. The above code gets all the fields using getAllFields, and then steps through the fields building up the Java source code to implement the toString method, and finally adds the new method to the class. (The exception class is, again, trivial and therefore not shown.)

Complete Example of Pattern Checking Code: The Composite Pattern

The following sections demonstrated how a formal specification can be taken as a starting point for writing a pattern check method. The steps illustrated are:

1.   Write an example of the pattern using our PEC. This highlights any issues if the PEC is suitable and if code generation is necessary. The example will normally follow the formal specification quite closely; except that the formal specification is written from the point of view of discovering if an application uses a pattern, whereas for our PEC you explicitly declare that you intend to use the pattern.

2.   Write the required marker interfaces; these are usually simple. The interfaces all extend CompilerEnforced and those that modify code also extend ModifiesClassFile.

3.   Write the corresponding utility classes for each of the marker interfaces. These utilities enforce the pattern and hence code the logic given in the specification. Usually, the

utility classes go into more detail than the formal specification does and they usually generate error messages.

Composite Example Using Our PEC

In Taibi and Ngo (2003) the Composite pattern is described, the UML diagram is given as in Figure 1 and this is translated in the chapter into a formal specification as in Table 1. The specification means:

- **Line 1:** There are classes that are given the labels: *application, component, leaf,* and *composite* and a method given the label *operation.*
- **Line 2:** Method *operation* is defined in class *component.*
- **Line 3:** Class *application* contains a reference to an instance of class *component.*
- **Line 4:** Class *composite* has a reference to one or more instances of class *component.*
- **Line 5:** Class *leaf* inherits from *component.*
- **Line 6:** Class *composite* inherits from *component.*

Figure 1. UML for Composite pattern

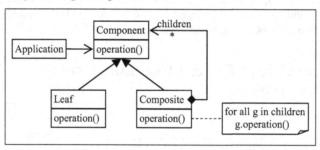

Table 1. BPSL specification for Composite pattern

∃ application, component, leaf, composite ∈ *C;* operation ∈ *M*
Defined-in (*operation, component*) ∧
Reference-to-one (*application, component*) ∧
Reference-to-many (*composite, component*) ∧
Inheritance (*leaf, component*) ∧
Inheritance (*composite, component*)

In the above specification, "class" is used to mean class or interface, in terms of Java terminology. Using our PEC, an example of a Composite is:

```
import pec.compile.composite.*;
interface PrintComponent extends Component { void print(); }
class PrintLeaf implements PrintComponent, Leaf {
    private final int value;
    PrintLeaf( final int value ) { this.value = value; }
    public void print() { System.out.println( value ); }
}
class PrintComposite implements PrintComponent, Composite {
    private final PrintComponent[] components;
    PrintComposite( final PrintComponent[] components ) {
        this.components = components;
    }
    public void print() { throw new AssertionError(); }
}
```

The key points with reference to the formal specification (including in braces the relevant line of the specification) are:

- Our PEC is a compiler that uses explicit typing of classes to mark them as conforming to a pattern, not a discovery system, whereas the specification is written from the point of view of discovering if an application uses the composite pattern. In particular, the specification is concerned if there is an *application* class that references an instance class *component*. For our PEC, which does not attempt to discover and instead enforces the pattern, this part of the specification is not relevant (Line 1, Table 1).

- Import the Composite pattern specification; this is the first stage of enforcement.

- Interface PrintComponent is marked as a *component* in a Composite pattern by extending Component (Line 1, Table 1).

- Interface PrintComponent defines method *print,* which is an *operation* method (Lines 1 and 2, Table 1).

- Class PrintLeaf is marked as a *leaf* in a Composite pattern by extending Leaf and its *component* is PrintComponent. The class simply prints its value (Lines 1 and 5, Table 1).

- Similarly class PrintComposite is marked as a *composite* in a Composite pattern by extending Composite and its *component* is PrintComponent (Lines 1 and 6, Table 1).

- The field components is the *components* reference in the Composite pattern. (Line 4, Table 1)

- The body of method print in PrintComposite is a dummy body. This body is replaced by our PEC with a loop that calls print on each element in components. (This looping over *components* is not part of the formal specification in Table 1, but is an informal annotation shown in the UML diagram in Figure 1.)

The composite example shows a number of interesting features of our PEC, including how a pattern can be made from multiple classes and how a class can participate in multiple patterns or multiple instances of the same pattern.

A composite is a collection of classes, PrintComponent, PrintLeaf, and PrintComposite, which as a whole make the pattern, but not a single class that makes the pattern, for example, ASingleton. As described below, this complicates the testing because the classes need to be cross referenced via their common base, PrintComponent. At first site, it would appear that the programmer cannot tell which instance of the Composite class a particular class belongs to, for example, if the classes in the example did not have a common beginning to their name, *PrintXXX*, then it would seem that it is not obvious to which composite they belonged. However, the Javadoc for the classes links them; PrintLeaf and PrintComposite link to PrintComponent, which in turn links to the other two. Therefore, finding the other members of the composite is at most one link away. Java specific IDEs often provide a class hierarchal view or give a UML style diagram, which also shows inheritance. Because our PEC uses standard Java the standard tools, like Javadoc, IDEs, and so forth, can be used, and this shows the advantage of retaining standard syntax.

The linking of the classes together via inheritance also allows a class to participate in multiple patterns or even multiple instances of the same pattern. For example, a Composite class could implement two Components and have two Component arrays and our PEC can write the appropriate methods looping over the correct array and the programmer can see that the Composite is in two instances of the Composite class via the Javadoc.

Writing the Enforcement Code

The code for Component enforcement is:

```
public interface Component extends Structural,CompilerEnforced {
                                                 /* Empty */ }
```

Component is the marker interface and therefore extends CompilerEnforced and the Composite pattern is classed as Structural. The utility to enforce Component is:

```
public abstract class ComponentUtility implements NoInstance {
    private ComponentUtility() {}
    public static void compileTimeCheck(Class clazz)throws
    ComponentException {
        Class[ ] interfaces = clazz.getInterfaces();
        for ( final Class interface : interfaces )
```

```
        if ( interface == Component.class )
            throw new ComponentException(
"Component cannot be directly implemented by a class, it must be " +
"implemented by implementing an interface that extends Component. ..." );
    }
}
```

The utility tests that no class implements Component directly; it should only be implemented by inheritance from another interface. The error reporting is straightforward and therefore not shown (Lovatt, 2004).

The classes for Leaf are similar to those for Component:

```
public interface Leaf extends Structural, CompilerEnforced {/* Empty */}
```

Like Component, Leaf is a simple marker. The utility class is more involved.

```
public abstract class LeafUtility implements NoInstance {
    private static final CtClass component = Utilities.get(
                                "pec.compile.composite.Component" );
    private LeafUtility() {}

    public static void compileTimeCheck(
                        final CtClass clazz, final JavaCompiler notUsed )
                            throws LeafException, ComponentException {
        if ( getComponents( clazz ).size() == 0 )
            throw new LeafException();
    }

    static Set getComponents( final CtClass clazz ) throws
ComponentException {
        CtClass[ ] interfaces = Utilities.getAllImplementedInterfaces(clazz);
        final Set posComponents = new HashSet();
        try {
            exclusions( posComponents, interfaces );
            excludeSuperInterfaces( posComponents );
            testForCommonBases( posComponents );
            return posComponents;
        } catch ( NotFoundException e ) {
            throw Utilities.assertionError("...", e );
        }
```

```
    }
}
```

The utility class tests if there are any Components and, if not, throws an exception. The code to find Components is quite involved and therefore only partially presented (Lovatt, 2004 gives the full listing). The getComponents method:

- Gets all the interfaces.
- Removes those that do not implement Component and Component itself.
- Removes super components (it does not make sense in a Composite to include both the super and derived components because the derived component is used throughout).
- Checks if two components have the same base (it is an error to have the same base twice because the composite cannot be written—for a method in the base component which components array would be used?).

This scheme is more involved than the checking in the formal specification given in Table 1 (e.g., checking if two components have the same base); however, this extra checking increases the certainty that the Composite is correctly implemented.

The most complicated item is Composite:

```
public interface Composite
                extends Structural, CompilerEnforced, ModifiesClassFile {
    // Empty - just a marker interface
}
```

Composite is a simple marker interface. Note that it extends ModifiesClassFile because classes that implement this interface are modified by our PEC. The utility class is:

```
public abstract class CompositeUtility implements NoInstance {
    private static final CtClass componentClass = Utilities.get(
                            "pec.compile.composite.Component" );
    private static final CtClass voidClass = Utilities.get( "void" );

    private CompositeUtility() {}

    public static void compileTimeCheck( CtClass clazz, JavaCompiler pEC )
            throws CompositeException,ComponentException,NotFoundException{
        final Set components = LeafUtility.getComponents( clazz );
        if ( components.size() == 0 )
            throw new CompositeException(
```

"A Composite class must implement an interface that extends Component, ...");

```
    final Map componentArrays = getComponentArrays(clazz, components );
    modifyComponentMethods( clazz, pEC, components, componentArrays );

}
```

The check method gets the *components* (see getComponents listed for Leaf above) and checks that the class has some components. It then makes a map that associates a component with a field that is an array of corresponding component instances. Then, it modifies the class file by writing the methods that loop over the components. The getComponentArray method is:

```
private static Map getComponentArrays(CtClass clazz, Set components )
                            throws CompositeException, NotFoundException {
    final Set possibleFields = getPossibleFields( clazz );

    if ( possibleFields.size() == 0 )

        throw new CompositeException(
                "A Composite class must have a Component array for " + "each Component; this class
                has no such arrays." );
    final Map arrays = new HashMap();
    for ( CtClass component : components ) {
        CtField field = null;
        for ( CtField possibleField : possibleFields )
            if (
        possibleField.getType().getComponentType().subtypeOf( component ) )
                if ( field == null )
                    field = possibleField;
                else
                    throw new CompositeException(
                            "There must be a one-to-one correspondence " +
                            "between Components and Component arrays ..." );
        if ( field == null )
            throw new CompositeException(
                    "There must be a one-to-one correspondence " +
                    "between Components and Component arrays; ..." );
        arrays.put( component, field );
    }
    return Collections.unmodifiableMap( arrays );

}
```

The method gets all fields that are arrays of Components, checks that there is at least one such field, checks that there is a one-to-one correspondence between components and component arrays, and maps the component to the corresponding field. The method getPossibleFields is straightforward; it returns the set of fields that are Component arrays, and therefore this method is not listed (Lovatt, 2004, gives the full listing). The most interesting method in CompositeUtility is:

```
private static void modifyComponentMethods(
CtClass clazz, JavaCompiler pEC, Set components, Map componentArrays )
throws CompositeException, ComponentException, NotFoundException {
   if ( pEC.isVerbose() )
      pEC.message( "modifying class " + clazz.getName() +
                                       ": writing composite methods" );
   for ( final CtClass component : components ) {
      final CtMethod[ ] componentMethods =
                         Utilities.getAllMethods( component, false );
      if ( componentMethods.length == 0 )
         throw new ComponentException( "Component " +
         Utilities.toString(component)+"doesn't have any methods. ..." );

      for ( final CtMethod componentMethod : componentMethods ) {
         final String methodName = componentMethod.getName();
         final CtMethod classMethod =
               getClassMethod( clazz, componentMethod, methodName );
         if ( classMethod == null )
            continue; // method is in superclass
         final CtField field = (CtField) componentArrays.get(component );
         final String fieldName = field.getName();
         final StringBuffer body = new StringBuffer( "{\n  if ( " );
         body.append( fieldName );
         body.append( " == (" );
         body.append( field.getType().getComponentType().getName() );
         body.append( "[])null ) return;" );
         body.append( "\n  for ( int i = 0; i < " );
         body.append( fieldName );
         body.append( ".length; i++ ) " );
         body.append( fieldName );
         body.append( "[ i ]." );
         body.append( methodName );
         body.append( "( $$ );\n}" );
         try {
            classMethod.setBody(body.toString() );
         } catch ( CannotCompileException e ) {
            throw new CompositeException(
```

"Cannot write composite loop for " + Utilities.toString(classMethod) +
". See cause below for compiler error message.", e);
               }
          }
     }
}

The method prints out some debugging information if the verbose flag to the compiler is set, gets the methods associated with each component (the method getClassMethod is trivial except that it checks that the method return type is void and is therefore not shown—Lovatt (2004) lists the method), checks that there is at least one method, and then for each method in the component it finds the corresponding method in the class hierarchy. If the corresponding method is in this class (not a superclass) then it writes the method body. The written method body, except for formatting and with $$ replaced with the list of arguments for the method[4], is:

```
{
  if ( <fieldName> == (<fieldType>[ ])null )
    return;
  for ( int i = 0; i < <fieldName>.length; i++ )
    <fieldName>[ i ].<methodName>( <arguments> );
}
```

Our PEC's API and Its Patterns

The available patterns are summarized in Table 2 and are briefly described below. Fuller descriptions are in Lovatt (2004), including advice on when and how to use each pattern.

An important observation in Gamma et al. (1995) (GOF) is that the language that is used to encode the pattern influences the relevance and details of the patterns themselves:

Table 2. Patterns supplied with our PEC (categorized)

Behavioral	Creational	Structural
Immutable	No Instance	Immutable Value Conversions
Value	Singleton	Composite
Multiple Dispatch	Static Factory	
	Instance Factory	

The choice of programming language is important because it influences one's point of view. Our patterns assume Smalltalk/C++ level language features, and that choice determines what can and cannot be implemented easily. If we assume procedural languages, we might have included Design patterns called "Inheritance", "Encapsulation", and "Polymorphism". Similarly, some of our patterns are supported directly by less common object-oriented languages. CLOS has multi-methods, for example, which lessen the need for a pattern such as Visitor.

Our PEC provides facilities beyond those available in typical OO languages, for example Java, and this is why the patterns from GOF are not all directly implemented in our PEC's patterns. For example, Multiple Dispatch instead of Visitor is provided.

Another reason why some of the patterns from GOF are not currently supported in our PEC is that Java or its standard library uses and defines some common patterns already, for example:

- Prototype (called Cloneable in Java)
- Flyweight (Java 5 uses enum for a fixed set of flyweights)
- Proxy (static inner classes are used in Java – Bloch 2001, Item 48)
- Command (Java 5 uses enum that implements an interface – Bloch, 2002)
- Iterator (Java has iterators for its collections)

Note: the patterns in the standard library are not formally checked. They are, however, presumably well debugged because they are widely used and because of in-house testing from the compiler vendor. It would be possible to write classes that extend these library interfaces and add in a formal pattern check using our PEC. However, this is currently not a priority because other patterns have no support in standard Java ("Future Work" gives our planned future work).

In the summaries of each pattern, references are given to three common "catalogues" of patterns: Bloch, (2001), Gamma et al. (1995), and Sun Microsystems (2003). These references are not meant to imply that our PEC enforces a pattern that is identical to those described in these references.

No Instance

A No Instance class cannot have an instance of it made. In many ways it is similar to a Singleton, and the two are often interchangeable. The use of No Instance classes is procedural instead of OO in nature. No Instance classes are described by Bloch (2001) and Sun Microsystems (2003) (e.g., System). The main features of No Instances classes are that they contain only static methods and static fields and they have a private constructor.

Static Factory

A Static Factory class has a static (class) method, named xxxInstance or instanceXXX, which creates a new object or returns an existing object and which is called instead of calling a constructor. Static factories are described by Bloch (2001) and Sun Microsystems (2003) (e.g., Boolean). Static Factories are not to be confused with Factories described by Gamma et al. (1995), which are called Instance Factory in our PEC's terminology.

Singleton

Our Singleton class is a variation of our Static Factory class; it differs from a Static Factory because each call to its static instance method returns the same instance (object). Singletons are described by Bloch (2001), Gamma et al. (1995), and Sun Microsystems (2003) (e.g., Runtime). The Singleton marker interface extends the StaticFactory marker interface and therefore any class that implements Singleton also implements StaticFactory and is therefore checked against both our Singleton and our Static Factory patterns. "Using a Formal Pattern Specification" gives a description of the tests we perform to check for Singularity.

Instance Factory

Instance Factories are called Factories in Gamma et al. (1995), but the term Instance Factory is used here to clearly distinguish them from Static Factories. Like Static Factories, an Instance Factory class has a method, named xxxInstance or instanceXXX, which creates a new object or returns an existing object and which is called instead of calling a constructor. The difference between Static and Instance Factories is that as the name suggests, the factory method for a Static Factory is a static (class) method and for an Instance Factory is an instance method. The two types of factory have different uses (Lovatt, 2004).

Value

A Value class has equals, hashCode, and toString methods that use the values of its fields instead of using the memory address of the instance. Value classes are described by Bloch (2001) and Sun Microsystems (2003) (e.g., Color). Our Value pattern comes with a useful class, ValueArrayList, which interacts with ImmutableArrayList via our Immutable Value Conversions pattern.

Immutable

Our Immutable pattern is a variation of our Value pattern; it differs by not changing its value once the instance is created. Immutable classes are described by Bloch (2001) and Sun Microsystems (2003) (e.g., String). Our Immutable pattern comes with a useful class,

ImmutableArrayList, which interacts with ValueArrayList via our Immutable Value Conversions pattern. Immutable types are a proposed extension to Java (Lovatt, 2001).

Immutable Value Conversions

An Immutable class can have a performance penalty because of excessive object creation and it can be advantageous to link an immutable class with a Value class that has a super-set of its interface. This pattern allows conversions between our Value and Immutable classes.

There is no direct equivalent of this pattern in the literature[3], but String and StringBuffer in Sun Microsystems (2003) are similar. Immutable Value Conversions class's main feature is that they have toValue and toImmutable methods. An example of the interaction between a Value class and an Immutable class are the classes ValueArrayList and ImmutableArrayList (see above).

Composite

As described in "Complete Example of Pattern Checking Code".

Multiple Dispatch

In most OO languages, the method called depends on the *runtime* type of the receiver and the *declared* type of the arguments, that is, single dispatch is used. In some circumstances this is insufficient; Gamma et al. (1995) suggest the Visitor pattern as a solution; however, this is a difficult to follow pattern. As noted by Gamma et al., Multiple Dispatch is an alternative. Our Multiple Dispatch does not require new syntax; all other solutions for Java are believed to require new syntax (i.e., Bonniot, 2004 and Relaxed MultiJava, 2004). Multiple Dispatch classes contain static (class) methods that are invoked like an instance method (i.e., *{receiver}.{method}* (*{arguments}*)). This pattern is an example of our PEC generating considerable code to minimize the amount of "boiler plate" code that the programmer needs.

A description of how our Multiple Dispatch pattern works and what code it generates is too long for this chapter (Lovatt, 2004 or Lovatt, Sloane, & Verity, 2005, give the generated code and even a most cursory glance at these texts will convince the reader of the impracticality of "boiler plate" code for Multiple Dispatch and hence the need for code generation).

Future Work

This chapter describes version 2 of our PEC. We are currently working on version 3, and when this work is sufficiently advanced, this compiler will also be made available on the Web site (Lovatt, 2004). The new compiler uses annotations and interfaces. Annotations have some advantages and disadvantages in the context of pattern enforcement:

1. **Advantages:**

   - Annotations are the standard method in Java of conveying extra linguistic information.

   - Annotations can annotate any declaration, not just class declarations; with interfaces you are forced to use naming conventions for fields and methods, for example, a factory method called instance.

   - Annotations can be removed completely from the compiled code, thus reducing the size of the compiled code and eliminating the need to ship the PEC library with the compiled code.

2. **Disadvantages:**

   - By default, annotations can be applied to any declaration (not just a class); they are not inherited, and they are not documented. All these can be overcome to some extent by additional metaannotations (annotations applied to annotations).

   - If an interface is annotated, a class that implements the interface is not annotated. This is inconvenient because you may wish to define a set of operations that are only applicable to a given pattern, for example, Immutable Value Conversions is only applicable to Value types.

   - An annotation cannot be extended, which makes it difficult to build patterns in stages, for example, Immutable builds upon Value.

   - An annotation is not a type. For example, it is advantageous to make Immutable a type, so that an Immutable list of Immutables is possible and hence an annotation and an interface are used.

   - Annotations cannot declare methods, which makes it inconvenient when you have a standard way of accessing a feature in a pattern, for example, Immutable Value Conversions defines methods toImmutable and toValue, and hence an annotation and an interface are used.

However, they are part of standard Java because Java 5, and hence a Java programmer, would expect their use. This is the overriding factor that convinced us that annotations and interfaces should be used together instead of just interfaces.

A further change in version 3 is that instead of manipulating the class file, PEC 3 manipulates the source. The reasons for this change are threefold: the changes made by our PEC are more transparent and thus easier to comprehend, there are some limitations to the manipulations that the chosen byte code manipulator (Chiba, 2004) allows, and the chosen source code manipulator (Ball, 2005) is more powerful, and by changing source, the code is easier to follow when using a source code debugger.

After the immediate goal of releasing PEC 3, we plan to add more patterns. The immediate candidate patterns are Not Null, Adapter, Iterator, Proxy, and Decorator. With the added features that come as part of the source code manipulation library, in addition to the features taken from version 2, that is, static and dynamic testing, it is not envisaged that any these patterns will be beyond the capabilities of the system. The version 2 PEC had the limitation that patterns that needed to be enforced at the instance level, for example, Not

Null, were problematic. But a side effect of the change to manipulating source code is that the full abstract syntax tree is available and therefore finding and enforcing at the instance level is possible.

Another aspect of the future work is to look at incorporating parts of a formal specification directly. For example writing a routine that checks that a method exists in a class and is suitably annotated via pattern matching, so that the string pattern "@pec.six.staticfactory. Factory" could be used to find all methods annotated as factories. This formal specification might be achieved with Design by Contract like specifications, that is, pre, post, and invariant conditions on classes, fields, and methods that are enforced by our compiler at compile time rather than at runtime, as are common with most Design by Contract like systems.

However, incorporating formal specifications that are completely language independent is not possible. The definition of a given pattern differs in detail from one language to the next, as noted by Gamma et al. (1995), Coplien (1998), and Noble and Biddle (2002). For example, a Singleton in Java uses a private constructor, whereas in languages like O'Caml, Scala, and Fortress, the constructor has the same access as the class and therefore a different technique is used. In all languages though the clear marking of the programmer's intent is advantageous, particularly to someone new to that language who may be unfamiliar with the Singleton idiom in the language but familiar with the Singleton concept.

Conclusion

This chapter has shown how pattern checks may be written using our Pattern Enforcing Compiler (PEC). In addition the philosophy behind our PEC and the motivation for our PEC were discussed. This discussion brings out the desirability of enforcing patterns at the class level as opposed to the instance level, and the necessity for an extensible system. Our PEC is contrasted with other systems in the literature and is shown to build on these systems and to be unique in providing a compiler that generates code, provides the boiler plate for complex patterns, is extensible, statically checks code, and dynamically checks code (unit tests code).

A further contribution of this work is to extend the notation of "*implements X.*" In standard Java this means that the class implements the interface X, and in our PEC the statement means it implements *contract X*. Where a contract is an interface plus other conditions placed on a class, for example, only one instance of the class in the case of contract Singleton.

An aspect of the research in this project is to find out which patterns can be usefully and practically enforced and how this impacts the design of the compiler. For example, it is not particularly useful to "enforce" a Singleton pattern without checking that multiple calls to the constructor cause an exception or that the instance method always returns the same object (hence the need for unit testing). Another example is that it is not practical to require the user to cut and past boiler-plate code for a Multiple Dispatch pattern, hence the need for code generation.

Although we have found unit testing to be necessary, like any form of unit testing we cannot guarantee that our test coverage is 100% comprehensive. In practice the unit testing has worked well, and we propose to retain the testing in future work.

This chapter describes version 2 of our PEC. The work is ongoing and version 3 is currently under development, and will also be released on our Web site when suitable progress has been made. The version 3 PEC primarily addresses two issues with our current PEC: it uses a combination of annotations and interfaces (instead of just marker interfaces), and it transforms source code instead of class files (so that the transformations are more transparent and compatible with source code debuggers).

Version 2 of our PEC can enforce many types of patterns, including multiclass patterns. However, it is difficult in 2 to enforce patterns that require testing at the instance level, for example, Not Null. This issue of instance level enforcement is addressed in PEC 3. We are currently not aware of any patterns that PEC 3 will not be able to enforce, even if that coverage uses dynamic tests which, as noted, cannot be 100% comprehensive. However, there are an infinite number of patterns and so we cannot say with certainty that all can be covered!

Acknowledgment

The work reported in this chapter was shaped by interactions within the Programming Language Reading Group at Macquarie University's Computing Department (Sloane, 2004).

Trademarks

Java, JVM, jar, and Javadoc are trademarks of Sun Microsystems, Inc., Design by Contract is a trademark of Eiffel Software, Inc., UML is a trademark of The Object Management Group, and Pattern Enforcing Compiler and PEC are trademarks of Howard Lovatt.

References

Ball, T. (2005). *Jackpot module home.* Retrieved November 16, 2006, from http://jackpot. netbeans.org/

Bloch, J. (2001). *Effective Java™: programming language Guide.* Boston: Addison-Wesley Publishing. ISBN 0201310058.

Bloch, J. (2002). *A Typesafe Enum facility for the Java^tm programming language.* Retrieved November 16, 2006, from http://www.jcp.org/aboutJava/communityprocess/jsr/tiger/enum.html

Bokowski, B. (1999, September). CoffeeStrainer: Statically-checked constraints on the definition and use of types in Java. In *Proceedings of the Software Engineering - ESEC/FSE'99: 7th European Software Engineering Conference, Held Jointly with the 7th ACM SIGSOFT Symposium on the Foundations of Software Engineering* (pp.

355-374). Toulouse, France. Lecture Notes in Computer Science, 1687. Berlin/Heidelberg: Springer.

Bonniot, D. (2004). *The nice programming language*. Retrieved November 16, 2006, from http://nice.sourceforge.net/

Budinsky, F., Finnie, M., Patsy, Y., & Vlissides, J. (1996) Automatic code generation from Design patterns. *IBM Systems Journal, 35*(2), 151-171.

Chambers, C., Harrison, W., & Vlissides, J. (2000, January). A debate on language and tool support for Design patterns. In *Proceedings of the 27ᵗʰ ACM SIGPLAN-SIGACT Symposium on Principles of Programming Languages* (pp. 277-289). Boston.

Chiba, S. (2004). *Javassist home page*. Retrieved November 16, 2006, from http://www.csg.is.titech.ac.jp/~chiba/javassist/

Coplien, J.O. (1998, January). Software Design patterns: Common questions and answers. In L. Rising (Ed.), *The patterns handbook: Techniques, strategies, and applications* (pp. 311-320). New York: Cambridge University Press. ISBN 0-521-64818-1.

Cornils, A.., & Hedin, G. (2000, June). Statically checked documentation with Design patterns. In *Proceedings of the Technology of Object-Oriented Languages and Systems (TOOLS) Europe 33* (pp. 419-431). Mt. St. Michel, France. IEEE Computer Society Press.

Gamma, E., Helm, R., Johnson, R., & Vlissides, J. (1995). *Design patterns: Elements of reusable object-oriented software*. Boston: Addison Wesley.

Hammouda, I.., & Koskimies, K. (2002, August 26-29). Generating a pattern-based application development environment for enterprise JavaBeans. In *Proceedings of the 26ᵗʰ International Computer Software and Applications Conference on Prolonging Software Life: Development and Redevelopment (COMPSAC 2002)* (pp. 856-866). Oxford, UK: IEEE Computer Society.

Hannemann, J., & Kiczales, G. (2002, November). Design pattern implementation in Java and AspectJ. In *Proceedings of the 17ᵗʰ ACM SIGPLAN Conference on Object-Oriented Programming, Systems, Languages, and Applications,* Seattle, Washington (pp. 161-173).

Hedin, G. (1996, May). Enforcing programming conventions by attribute extension in an open compiler. In *Proceedings of the Nordic Workshop on Programming Environment Research (NWPER'96),* Aalborg, Denmark.

Lovatt, H.C. (2001). *Bug ID: 4617197 RFE: Add immutable types to Java*. Retrieved November 16, 2006, from http://bugs.sun.com/bugdatabase/view_bug.do?bug_id=4617197

Lovatt, H.C. (2004). *pec: Pattern enforcing compiler (TM) (PEC(TM)) home page*. Retrieved November 16, 2006, from http://pec.dev.java.net/

Lovatt, H.C., Sloane, A.M., & Verity, V.R. (2005. January-February). A pattern enforcing compiler (PEC) for Java: Using the compiler. In *Proceedings of The Second Asia-Pacific Conference on Conceptual Modelling (APCCM2005)* (pp. 69-78). University of Newcastle, Australia. Conferences in Research Practice in Information Technology, 43.

Maplesden, D., Hosking, J., & Grundy, J. (2002, February 18-21). Design pattern modelling and instantiation using DPML. In *Proceedings of Technology of Object-Oriented Languages and Systems (TOOLS) Pacific 2002*, Sydney, Australia. In J. Noble & J. Potter (Eds.), *Conferences in research and practice in information technology (CRPIT)* (vol. 10).

Murphy, G.C., Notkin, D., & Sullivan, K. (1995, October). Software reflexion models: Bridging the gap between source and high-level models. In *Proceedings of the 3rd ACM SIGSOFT Symposium on Foundations of Software Engineering* (pp. 18-28). Washington, DC.

Noble, J., & Biddle, R. (2002 June 10-14). Patterns as signs. In *Proceedings of the 16th European Conference on Object-Oriented Programming (ECOOP2002)*, Malaga, Spain (pp. 368-391). Lecture Notes in Computer Science, 2374. Berlin/Heidelberg: Springer.

Rutar, N., Almazan, C.B., & Foster, J.S. (2004, November). A comparison of bug finding tools for Java. In *Proceedings of the 15th International Symposium on Software Reliability Engineering (ISSRE '04)* (pp. 245-256). IEEE Computer Society Press.

Sefika, M., Sane, A., & Campbell, R.H. (1996). Monitoring compliance of a software system with its high-level design models. In *Proceedings of the 18th International Conference on Software Engineering (ICSE)* (pp. 387-396). Berlin, Germany.

Sloane, A.M. (2004). Programming languages reading group home page. Retrieved November 16, 2006, from http://www.comp.mq.edu.au/plrg/PLRG/Reading%20Group/Reading%20Group.html

Steele, G.L. (1998, October). Growing a language. *Object-Addendum to the 1998 Proceedings of the 13th Annual Conference on Object-Oriented Programming, Systems, Languages, and Applications (Addendum to OOPSLA '98)*, Vancouver, BC, Canada.

Sun Microsystems Inc. (2003). *Java™ 2 platform, standard edition*, v 1.4.2 API specification. Retrieved November 16, 2006, from http://java.sun.com/j2se/1.4.2/docs/api/index.html

Taibi, T., & Ngo, D.C.L. (2003, March). Formal specification of Design pattern combination using BPSL. *Elsiever Journal of Information and Software Technology, 45*(3), 157-170.

Wallace, B. (2003). PolyGlot, Inc. design markers. Retrieved November 16, 2006, from http://www.polyglotinc.com/DesignMarkers/

Endnotes

[1]   Relaxed MultiJava (2004). The MultiJava project. Retrieved November 16, 2006, from http://multijava.sourceforge.net/

An alternative to implementing a marker interface would be to use annotations. Currently, a version 3 compiler that uses annotations and interfaces is under development ("Future Work").

[2]   In the future, we intend to allow the method to be annotated instead of using a naming convention ("Future Work").

[3]   Lint is a C language utility that performs extra static type checks beyond those of a *traditional* C compiler.

[4] $$ is the shorthand used in Javassist to mean all the arguments.

[5]   The Value/Immutable/Immutable-Value-Conversion patterns are proposed as an extension to Java by one of the authors, Lovatt 2001.

Chapter XVI

LePUS:
A Formal Language for
Modeling Design Patterns

Epameinondas Gasparis, University of Essex, UK

Abstract

We present LePUS, a formal language for modeling object oriented (O-O) Design patterns. We demonstrate the language's unique efficacy in producing precise, concise, generic, and appropriately abstract specifications that effectively model the Gang of Four's Design patterns. Mathematical logic is used as a main frame of reference: LePUS is defined as a subset of first-order predicate calculus and implementations (programs) are modeled as finite structures in model theory. We also demonstrate the conceptual framework in which the verification of implementations against pattern specifications is possible and our ongoing endeavour to develop effective tool support for LePUS.

Introduction

Design patterns have been a significant step forward in the contemporary software engineering community. According to Gamma, Helm, Johnson, and Vlissides (1995, p. 3) Design patterns are *"descriptions of communicating objects and classes that are customized to solve a general design problem in a particular context."* Unfortunately, patterns are commonly illustrated using UML Class Diagrams which lack the means to model certain Design pattern attributes. We believe that it is appropriate for a Design pattern specification to capture only the pattern's generic properties at the appropriate level of detail and deliberately ignore various implementation specific details that do not belong to the level of abstraction Design patterns are concerned with.

Early versions of LePUS (Eden, 2007), such as LePUS (Eden, 2001) and LePUS2, were originally developed as formal languages for modeling Design patterns. LePUS is a mathematical language specifically designed to overcome the shortcomings of existing modeling languages and notations. It has been successfully used to model a wide range of Design patterns, O-O applications and application frameworks. Specifications in LePUS can be expressed visually (*LePUS Charts*) or symbolically (*Class-Z Schemas*) in a form which borrows syntactical notions from the Z specification language (Spivey, 1992). LePUS features a simple syntax defined as formulas in the classical first-order predicate calculus and their semantics (implementations) are defined in terms of model-theoretic structures (design models) that have been axiomatized to reflect constraints on O-O design. LePUS is designed to pick out the building-blocks of Design patterns, as a result of which it simplifies the search for relations between patterns, and thanks to its commitment to predicate calculus, formulates these relations.

In this presentation of LePUS, we will intentionally focus on a subset of LePUS, namely the visual language. Our current discussion brings to light certain qualities of the language, including its unique abstraction capability, solely for the purpose of modeling the sample Design patterns quoted in this chapter. The comprehensive definition of the language is available in Eden (2007).

We begin by presenting the Iterator pattern (Gamma et al., 1995, pp. 257-271). We proceed to discuss a semantics, which represents the category of Java™ implementations that agree with ("satisfy") the Iterator pattern. We then present the LePUS language which is used to specify the Iterator pattern. The discussion is followed by a more general discussion on the applications of LePUS, including reasoning on Design patterns, verification, and tool support. We conclude with a summary of this chapter.

Motivation

Modeling a Design Pattern in UML

We motivate our discussion using the Iterator pattern (Gamma et al., 1995, pp. 257-271). According to Gamma et al. (1995) the Iterator pattern introduces the following participants (p. 259):

- **Iterator:** Defines an interface for accessing and traversing elements.
- **ConcreteIterator:** Implements the Iterator interface, keeps track of the current position in the traversal of the aggregate.
- **Aggregate:** Defines an interface for creating an Iterator object.
- **ConcreteAggregate:** Implements the Iterator creation interface to return an instance of the proper ConcreteIterator.

And collaborations (Gamma et al., 1995, p. 260):

- A ConcreteIterator keeps track of the current object in the aggregate and can compute the succeeding object in the traversal.

Object modeling technique (OMT) (Rumbaugh, Blaha, Premerlani, Eddy, & Lorenson, 1991) and the various dialects of unified modeling language (UML) (Booch, Rumbaugh, & Jacobson, 2004) have been the de-facto industry standard notations for the visual modeling of Design patterns. Both notations define a large vocabulary of symbols allowing one to create diagrams which depict minute implementation details but fail to deliver means for representing generic notions of "design motifs," such as variables, sets of classes, sets of

Figure 1. OMT Class Diagram of the Iterator pattern (Adapted from Gamma et al., 1995, p. 259)

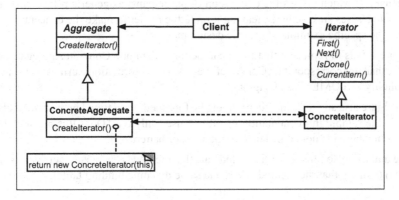

Table 1. An instance of the Iterator pattern in java.util *(Adapted from Sun Java J2SE version 1.4.2)*

public interface Collection { ...
    public Iterator iterator();
    ...
}
	public interface Iterator { ...
	    Object next();
	}

public interface List
    extends Collection {...}
	public interafce ListIterator
	    implements Iterator {...}

public class LinkedList
    implements List ... {
    public Iterator iterator() { ...
    // create and return
    // an instance of ListItr
    }
}
	private class ListItr
	    implements ListIterator {
	    public Object next() { ...
	    // Return the next object
	    // in the list
	    }
	}

methods, and constraints on their relationships. This makes existing notations only appropriate for visualizing the particulars of specific implementations, but inadequate for delivering the abstract perspective essential for modeling software design. Let us illustrate some of the inadequacies of UML with relation to the Iterator Design pattern.

Figure 1 attempts to depict the participants of the pattern and some of the relations between them. Gamma et al. further illustrate the pattern using sample code. A Java™ implementation that satisfies the Iterator Design pattern in package java.util is outlined in Table 1. We say that package java.util contains an *instance* of the Iterator pattern.

We observe the following inadequacies of Figure 1 as a specification of the Iterator Design pattern:

1. Each one of the boxes marked "ConcreteAggregate" and "ConcreteIterator" does not represent a specific class, but rather it merely serves as a placeholder for a respective participant. We conclude that UML lacks variable symbols, or the generalisation mechanism which allows the expression of participants as generic roles rather than specific classes and methods, leaving it up to the reader to make the conceptual leap from the specific example to generic design motif.

2. Figure 1 fails to represent that there can be more than one ConcreteAggregates and more than one corresponding ConcreteIterators. This information can not be visualised explicitly in a UML Class Diagram.

3. The figure also suggests that there should be four methods defined in the Iterator class, while the sample implementation in Table 1 uses only one. Does this mean that the implementation is not an instance of the Iterator pattern?

4. The diagram also fails to explicitly indicate that method ListItr.next() overrides Iterator. next() (namely that the methods share the same dynamic binding table).

5.   Gamma et al. had to resort to the popular pseudo-code annotation to express that each ConcreteAggregate.iterator() method creates and returns an instance of the appropriate ConcreteIterator. While such annotation seems intuitive, its precise interpretation is a matter of guesswork: Should the method create the instance of the ConcreteIterator in its body or does it only return such an instance? Can there be multiple instances of the ConcreteIterator? Can the source code annotation be clearly understood by developers using various O-O programming languages?

Based on the various limitations of the UML family of notations, we can formulate the following desiderata for a formal language capable of capturing the generic properties of design motifs:

- (Req. 1) *Genericity*, the ability to express a class or method as a variable.
- (Req. 2) *Scalability*, the ability to represent abstract building blocks of OOD such as inheritance hierarchies and isomorphic relations.
- (Req. 3) *Rigour*, the ability to maintain well-defined mappings from specifications to possible implementations and verify their correctness at any point in time.

Almost everyone who builds computing systems is convinced that all systems design—software or hardware—needs to be done within a rich conceptual frame, which is articulated by rigorous methodologies…. The conceptual frame provided just by programming languages is too narrow; a wider frame is needed in which to understand the specifications of systems and the methodology which articulates this understanding must be based on some form of logic. (Milner, 1986)

This motivates our use of mathematical logic for the specification of Design patterns and their verification, as follows. The semantics of implementations (demonstrated below using Java™ implementations) are delivered using finite structures in mathematical logic ("design models"). Specifications in LePUS are taken to be representations of statements in first-order predicate calculus.

Semantics

Every O-O program is perceived as a universe inhabited by classes, methods and relations between them (Eden, 2002). The semantics of a program is distilled from its textual representation (the "source code") into a more abstract representation, known in LePUS as *design model*. Design models closely resemble relational databases because all information about a program is logically organised into tables, analogous to tables found in relational databases.

Design models constitute a first step toward an abstract representation of programs, as various minute details of the implementation such as loops, error handling, and conditional

Table 2. Design model extracted from program in Table 1

Class	Method		Signature
{Collection, Iterator, List, LinkedList, ListIterator, ListItr}	{Collection.iterator, LinkedList.iterator, Iterator.next, ListItr.next}		{iterator(), next()}

Inherit	Abstract
{(LinkedList, List), (ListItr, ListIterator)}	{Collection, Iterator, Collection.iterator, Iterator.next}
SignatureOf	*Return*
{(Collection.iterator, iterator()), (LinkedList.iterator, iterator()), (Iterator.next, next()), (ListItr.next, next())}	{(Collection.iterator, Iterator), (LinkedList.iterator, Iterator), (Iterator.next, Object), (ListItr.iterator, Iterator)}
Produce	*Hierarchy*
{(LinkedList.iterator, ListItr)}	{Collections = {Collection, LinkedList}, Iterators = {Iterator, ListItr}}

statements are intentionally ignored. A design model focuses on information about classes, methods, and their signatures, which we refer to as *ground entities*, and the possible relations between them, which we refer to as *ground relations*. Ground relations include unary relations (such as *Abstract*) and binary relations (such as *Call, Inherit, Return, Produce, Member*). Table 2 details such a design model that abstracts the program in Table 1.

Each ground entity and ground relation corresponds to some static property of an O-O program and can be directly traced to statements or expressions in the program itself. For example, the pair ⊠LinkedList . . List⊠ in the table *Inherit* (Table 2), abstracts statement "public class LinkedList implements List" found in program source code (Table 1) and represents an *Inherit* relation between LinkedList and List.

To satisfy scalability and rigour, the notion of the design model is extended to include representations of nonempty sets of entities, such as set of classes and class hierarchies. LePUS allows the grouping of conceptually related classes (or methods) into *higher-dimensional classes* (or methods). For this reason, we would call an individual class "a class of dimension *0*" and a set of individual classes "a class of dimension *1*." Similarly, we can group together class ListItr (that indirectly inherits from Iterator) and class Iterator into "a hierarchy of dimension *1*" (named Iterators in Table 2). A LePUS hierarchy is a special case of a set of classes (a class of dimension *1*) that contains one root class such that all other classes in the set inherit (either directly or indirectly) from.

LePUS

Genericity

We observed that the Iterator pattern (Gamma et al., 1995, p. 259) defines four participants: Aggregate, ConcreteAggregate, Iterator, and ConcreteIterator. Therefore, the boxes marked with these symbols in Figure 1 do not represent specific classes, as the language of UML Class Diagrams suggests, but any class that can play the respective role in the context of the pattern. In LePUS, participants are more adequately represented using *variables*. Variables are contrasted with *constants* which represent specific elements of a particular implementation. For example, UML Class Diagrams only allow for the representation of constants. The inadequacy of UML in this respect can therefore be attributed to the absence of variables from the language, namely the lack of support in genericity.

LePUS variables are analogous to variables in algebraic expressions. For example, the expression $c=2\pi r$ describes the relation between a circle's radius r with its circumference c in any circle. But when a specific value is assigned to r, the expression describes only a specific circle.

Chart 1 depicts a LePUS specification that partially models the Iterator Design pattern. Each of the pattern's participants is modeled as a 0-dimensional class. A 0-dimensional class variable is represented as a rectangle, and a 0-dimensional signature is represented as an ellipse. Methods are represented in LePUS by superimposing signature variables over class variables. The reasons for this choice are as follows.

Signatures represent the names and argument types of methods. The superimposition of a signature s over a class c is a superimposition term (also written as $s \otimes c$) which uniquely models a specific method m, such that m is a member of c with the signature s. Because each class defines at most one method with a given signature, each superimposition term models a specific method. For example, the signature variable *iterator* superimposed on the

Chart 1. Not quite the Iterator Design pattern

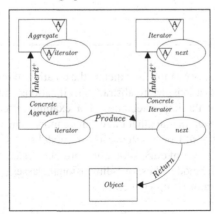

Table 3. Another ConcreteAggregate and ConcreteIterator in java.util *(Adapted from Sun Java J2SE version 1.4.2)*

public class ArrayList
    implements List ... {
    public Iterator iterator() { ...
    // create and return
    // an instance of Itr
    }
}
	private class Itr
	    implements ListIterator {
	    public Object next() { ...
	    // Return the next object
	    // in the list
	    }
	}

class variable *Aggregate* in Chart 1 forms a superimposition term that models the method *Aggregate.iterator.* The same signature is used again in Chart 1 as, superimposed on the class variable *ConcreteAggregate* models the method *ConcreteAggregate.iterator.*

LePUS relations are also an important aspect of the language, as they model relationships between LePUS entities. A unary relation is represented by its initial letter contained in an inverted triangle, which we positioned over the LePUS term it is applied to. For example, the *Abstract* relation in Chart 1 includes the class variables *Aggregate* and *Iterator*, as well as the methods *iterator⊗ Aggregate* and *next⊗ Iterator.* The same chart includes binary relations such as *Produce* and *Return.* Each of these relations is represented by a single-arrow that joins its domain with its respective range. For example, the chart asserts that method implied by term *iterator⊗ ConcreteAggregate* produces (creates and returns) an instance of *ConcreteIterator.*

The symbol *Inherit⁺* in Chart 1 indicates that *ConcreteAggregate* may *indirectly* inherit from *Aggregate*, through an arbitrary number of intermediate classes. In general, a transitive relation $\mathcal{R}^{\boxplus}$ represents the transitive closure of a ground binary relation $\mathcal{R}$.

Note that Chart 1 only partially captures the Iterator Design pattern. It fails to indicate that there can possibly exist more than one class assigned to the roles of *ConcreteAggregate* and *ConcreteIterator.* For example, the classes outlined in Table 3 participate in the same instance of the Iterator pattern depicted in Table 1.

To allow the representation of sets of participants in a single pattern, we move to consider the scalability mechanisms provided by LePUS.

Scalability

The needs of large-scale software modeling dictate the creation of highly complex, concise, and yet meaningful specifications. More abstract specifications should allow us to model larger numbers of parts of the implementation. For example, a correct depiction of the Iterator pattern must represent the fact that there can be more than one ConcreteAggregate and a corresponding number of ConcreteIterators. To model sets of entities, LePUS offers *higher dimensional terms* (terms of dimension *1* or more). For instance *ConcreteAggregate* and *ConcreteItrator* can be modeled using *1*-dimensional classes (sets of classes), thereby correctly depicting the Iterator Design pattern.

Chart 2. Iterator Design pattern in LePUS

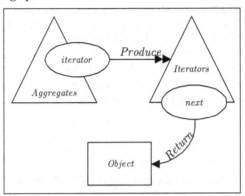

Hierarchies

To avoid the limitations of Chart 1 we can use LePUS hierarchies. A hierarchy variable represents a set of classes which contain one class such that all others inherit from. For example, *Aggregates* is a hierarchy variable in Chart 2 which collectively models the set of all ConcreteAggregate classes and the Aggregate class. Similarly, *Iterators* is a hierarchy variable which collectively models the set of all ConcreteIterator classes and the Iterator class.

Clans

Chart 2 raises a possible question: What is the intended meaning of the superimposition term *iterator ⊗ Aggregates*? This superimposition term collectively models all the iterator() methods that are defined in each one of the classes modeled by *Aggregates* hierarchy. In LePUS we say that *iterator ⊗ Aggregates* forms a *Clan*.

Predicates

It is common in LePUS to encounter the need to model relations between higher dimensional terms, such as sets of classes, sets of signatures, and hierarchies. Each of these relations may have different possible interpretations. To render their meaning precise, *Total* and *Isomorphic predicates* are provided. We demonstrate their use by considering the following examples.

The *Total* predicate represents a total functional relation. For example, the expression *Total(Return, next ⊗ Iterators, Object)*, is represented in Chart 2 as a single-arrow edge marked *Return*, which connects the term *next ⊗ Iterators* with *Object*. It indicates that each one of the (non abstract) methods represented by term *next ⊗ Iterators*, returns an instance of *Object*.

The *Isomorphic* predicate represents an isomorphic functional relation. For instance, the expression *Isomorphic(Produce,iterator⊗ Aggregates,Iterators)*, represented in Chart 2 as a double-arrow edge marked *Produce*. The relation asserts that the body of each one of the (non abstract) methods represented by term *iterator⊗ Aggregates* produces an instance of a unique (non abstract) class in the hierarchy represented by *Iterators*. In other words, it indicates that for every ConcreteAggregate *ca* in *Aggregates* there exists exactly one ConcreteIterator *ci* in *Iterators* such that *Produce(iterator⊗ ca, ci)*.

Rigour

Programmers usually regard design specifications as statements that imply certain desirable properties for the implementation, or introduce constraints imposed on it. There is also an expectation that a corresponding implementation agrees with the specification, but usually there are no means to verify their agreement. This problem can be rephrased as follows: Given a specification Ψ (e.g., Chart 2) and an implementation (e.g., Table 1) modeled by a design model $\mathfrak{M}$ (e.g., Table 2), how do we verify that $\mathfrak{M}$ agrees with Ψ? In mathematical logic, this question is represented by asking whether:

$$\mathfrak{M} \vDash \Psi$$

holds (read: $\mathfrak{M}$ satisfies Ψ).

For example, let $\Psi_{Iterator}$ represent the specification of the Iterator pattern in Chart 2. Let us also define the design model $\mathfrak{M}_{JavaUtil}$ with the revised `Collections` and `Iterators` hierarchy entities as shown in Table 4.

To find out whether java.util satisfies the Iterator pattern, we ask whether the following proposition holds:

$$\mathfrak{M}_{JavaUtil} \vDash \Psi_{Iterator}$$

To establish that design model $\mathfrak{M}$ satisfies specification Ψ we must find an *assignment function g* from each one of the free variables in Ψ to an entity in $\mathfrak{M}$. In our example, we define g to assign every variable from Chart 2 to an entity of the same type and dimension from Table 4 as follows:

Table 4. Design model $\mathfrak{M}_{JavaUtil}$

Class, Method, Signature, Inherit, Abstract, SignatureOf, Return:
Similar to Table 2 with additional information from Table 3 needed (but omitted).
Hierarchy
{Collections = {Collection, LinkedList, ArrayList},
Iterators = {Iterator, ListItr, Itr}}

Chart 3. Is this an implementation of the Iterator pattern?

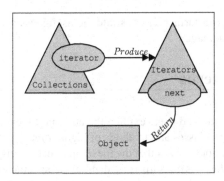

- *Aggregates* is assigned to `Collections`
- *Iterators* is assigned to `Iterators`
- *next* is assigned to `next()`
- *iterator* is assigned to `iterator()`

Thus, for example, $g(Aggregates)$=`Collections` and $g(next)$=`next()`. The consistent replacement of each free variable $x_1,\dots x_n$ in the specification $\Psi/x_1,\dots x_n/$ with the entity assigned thereto is written as $\Psi/g(x_1)\dots g(x_n)/$. The result of substituting the variables from Chart 2 with the names of the entities from Table 4 assigned thereto can be illustrated using constant terms, as demonstrated in Chart 3.

To conclude the verification process, we must establish that Chart 3 is true in Table 4. This proposition is written in mathematical logic as follows:

$$\mathfrak{M}_{JavaUtil} \vDash_g \Psi_{Iterator}$$

At this point, the problem of verification is reduced to the much simpler problem of looking up the design model tables to determine whether the design model $\mathfrak{M}_{JavaUtil}$ satisfies each one of the statements represented by Chart 3. This proposition evidently holds in our example. Therefore, we say that the program in Table 1 and Table 3 satisfies the Iterator pattern.

More generally, the problem of verifying that program p satisfies a LePUS specification Ψ can be reduced to the problem of searching for a design model $\mathfrak{M}_p$ for p and an *assignment function* g from the free variables in Ψ to the entities in $\mathfrak{M}_p$ such that $\mathfrak{M}_p \vDash_g \Psi$. We shall return to this problem in our discussion in tool support.

Applications

In this section we attempt to further demonstrate the usefulness of LePUS by presenting two applications of the language.

Reasoning on Patterns

LePUS is designed to capture and make explicit the building-blocks of O-O design, and in particular class hierarchies, classes and methods of higher dimensions (sets of any dimension), and isomorphic relations. Given that the meaning of each translates into the classical first order predicate calculus, it is not surprising that LePUS specifications pick out relations between O-O Design patterns that are not otherwise obvious. To demonstrate this quality, consider the specification of the factory method (Gamma et al., 1995, pp. 107-116) Design pattern depicted in Chart 4 and contrast it with the specification of the Abstract Factory (Gamma et al., 1995, pp. 87-95) Design pattern depicted in Chart 5.

It is surprising to find the striking resemblance between the two Design patterns. Most likely, this resemblance only becomes apparent thanks to consistently employing the same level of abstraction in representing each, for example, by abstracting the set of factory classes using the *Factories* hierarchy variable. Gamma et al. (1995, p. 95) did observe that the Abstract Factory is "implemented using the Factory Method." Our comparison shows that the two patterns have a lot more in common. In fact, they are identical except that $PRODUCTS$ is a *2*-dimensional hierarchy (a set of class hierarchies) rather than a *1*-dimensional hierarchy and that *FactoryMethod* is a *2*-dimensional method (a set of sets of methods) rather than a *1*-dimensional method. This example demonstrates the contribution of LePUS specifications to the comprehension of and reasoning about Design patterns (Eden, 2001).

Chart 4. Factory method (Source: Gamma et al., 1995, pp. 107-116) in LePUS

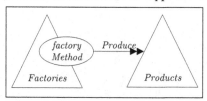

Chart 5. Abstract Factory (Source: Gamma et. al., 1995, pp. 87-95) in LePUS

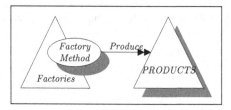

Tool Support

As the semantics of LePUS specifications is defined in terms of design models, the verification of a specification is computable. Because the ground relations in LePUS (such as *Produce* and *Return*) represent obvious static properties of programs in Java™ and in most other O-O programming languages, automatically verifying that a particular Java™ program implementation satisfies a given specification is straightforward. Proof of concept of such a tool (Iyaniwura, 2003) and implementations of modules thereof have been completed. The "Specifier" (Liang, 2004) reads LePUS specifications in XML format. The "Generator of semantic representations" (Bo, 2004) extracts design models directly from Java™ byte code.

More recently, we at the two-tier programming project (Eden, Kazman, & Fox, 2003) at the University of Essex are working to create a toolkit for generating LePUS specifications and verifying them against any Java™ program that is integrated with the Eclipse development environment (Eclipse, 2006). The TTP toolkit, although it is still work in progress, is a set of tools which does not interfere with existing developments tools and compilers and is not constrained to any specific domain of application. In particular, tool support for the verification of LePUS specifications against their respective Java™ along the lines of the process described in the previous section is of particular interest.

After we have achieved the short term objectives of the TTP toolkit, we intend to extend its functionality to include the following:

1. *Recognition*, the process that searches for possible instances of a given Design pattern in a program (Kraemer & Prechelt, 1996).

2. *Discovery*, a method which uses efficient search heuristics to detect recurring constructs in a program's design model and aims to identify possible candidate Design patterns therein.

3. *Design mining*. Starting from a Java™ program's design model, we are working to determine the set of abstraction operators required in an automated process of generating increasingly more abstract representations in LePUS. This process of reverse engineering, which can be referred to as *design mining*, seeks to detect correlated entities in the design model and abstract them by introducing higher dimensional entities and relations between them. Ideally, the design mining process shall be able to generate a small number of "good" LePUS models of the program, where a chart is "good" if it is maximally informative and minimally verbose in modeling a particular program.

Design mining is distinguished from *design recovery* as it does not attempt to reconstruct the intended design of a given program, but rather to detect those "design building-blocks" that LePUS can effectively represent. We expect design mining to promote program comprehension, as it aims to free the developer from the tedious task of manually examining the source code of the entire program before they can understand its structure.

Conclusion

We presented the capabilities of LePUS for modeling O-O Design patterns. We identified some of the shortcomings of UML and demonstrated how they can be overcome using LePUS. We demonstrated how LePUS is capable of capturing the abstract perspective that modeling Design patterns requires. Our presentation of the language's visual dialect, LePUS charts, focused on an easy-to-use, small set of visual primitives, and on its abstraction capabilities which allow the creation of concise, scalable, generic, and yet informative specifications. The sample specifications of various Gang of Four (Gamma et al., 1995) Design patterns demonstrated that the mathematical definitions of the language and their meaning do not limit the language's usability or expressiveness. Finally, we indicated the range of applications of LePUS, such as reasoning and tool support, and examined ways in which LePUS can benefit the average object-oriented programmer.

Acknowledgment

The work presented in this chapter is exclusively based on Dr. Amnon H. Eden's work on both LePUS and Class-Z. Had it not been for his contributions toward LePUS, this presentation would not have been possible. The author would also like to thank Christina Maniati for her generous moral support.

References

Bo, G. (2004). *An analysis tool for java programs*. Unpublished master's dissertation, University of Essex, UK.

Booch, G., Rumbaugh, J., & Jacobson, I. (2004). *The unified modelling language reference manual* (2nd ed.). Reading, MA: Addison-Wesley.

Eclipse Foundation. Retrieved November 16, 2006, from http://www.eclipse.org

Eden, A.H. (2001). *Formal specification of object-oriented design*. Paper presented at the International Conference on Multidisciplinary Design in Engineering CSME-MDE 2001, Montreal, Canada.

Eden, A.H. (2002). A theory of object-oriented design. *Information Systems Frontiers, 4*(4), 379-391.

Eden, A.H. (2007). *Object-oritented modelling, abstracting and visualizing the building blocks of object-oriented design*. UK: Essex.

Eden, A.H., Kazman, R., & Fox , C.J. (2003). *Two-tier programming* (Tech. Rep. No. CSM-387). UK: University of Essex, Department of Computer Science.

Gamma, E., Helm, R., Johnson, R., & Vlissides, J. (1995). *Design patterns: Elements of reusable object-oriented software.* Indianapolis, IN: Addison-Wesley.

Iyaniwura, O.A. (2003). *A verification tool for object-oriented programs.* Unpublished master's dissertation, Department of Computer Science, UK.

Kraemer, C., & Prechelt, L. (1996). Design recovery by automated search for structural Design patterns in object-oriented software. In *Proceedings of the 3rd Working Conference on Reverse Engineering,* Monterey, California (pp. 208-215).

Liang, M.T. (2004). *Specification module for the TTP toolkit.* Unpublished master's dissertation, Chalmers University of Technology, Sweden.

Milner, R. (1986). Is computing an experimental science? *Transcript of the Inaugural Lecture of the Laboratory on Foundations of Computer Science* (Tech. Rep. No. ECS-LFCS-86-1). UK: University of Edinburgh, Department of Computer Science.

Rumbaugh, J., Blaha, M., Premerlani, W., Eddy, F., & Lorenson, W. (1991). *Object-oriented modelling and design.* Englewood Cliffs, NJ: Prentice Hall.

Spivey, J.M. (1992). *The Z notation: A reference manual.* Hertfordshire: Prentice Hall.

Appendix: Quick Reference of LePUS Visual Primitives

Constants

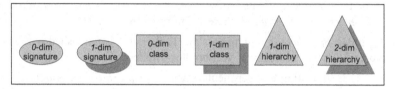

Variables

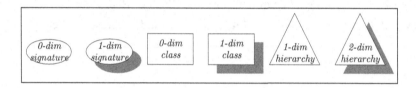

Methods

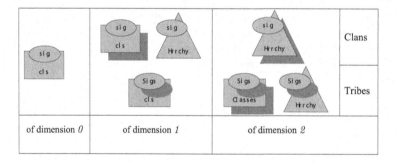

Predicates

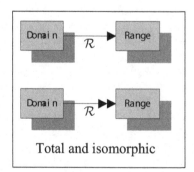

About the Authors

Toufik Taibi received the PhD in computer science from Multimedia University, Malaysia, in 2003. He is currently an assistant professor at the College of Information Technology at United Arab Emirates University, UAE. Dr. Taibi has more than 10 years of teaching and research experience. His research interests include formal specification of Design patterns, distributed object computing, and component-based software engineering. He has been in the program committee of numerous conferences and has chaired several sessions in conferences. He is a member of the IEEE.

***

Paulo Alencar is currently a research associate professor of computer science in the David R. Cheriton School of Computer Science at the University of Waterloo, Canada. His research, teaching, and consulting activities have been directed to software engineering in general, and his current research interests specifically include software design, architecture, composition, evolution, software processes, Web-based and hypermedia systems, and formal methods. Dr. Alencar has received international research awards from organizations such as Compaq (Compaq Award for best research paper in 1995 for his work on a theory of evolving software systems) and IBM (IBM Innovation Award, 2003). He has been the principal or coprincipal investigator in projects supported by NSERC, IBM, Bell, Sybase, Rogers, and funding agencies in Germany, Argentina, and Brazil. He has been a visiting professor at the University of Karlsruhe, at the Imperial College of Science and Technology (London), and at the University of Waterloo. He has also held faculty positions at the University of Brasilia, Brazil. He has published more than 100 technical papers, and is a member of the IEEE, the IEEE Computer Society, and the ACM.

Daniel Amyot is an assistant professor at the University of Ottawa, Canada, which he joined in 2002 after working for Mitel Networks as a senior researcher in software engineering. His research interests include scenario-based software engineering, requirements engineering, formal methods, and feature interactions in emerging applications. Daniel is Rapporteur for requirements languages (MSC and URN) at the International Telecommunication Union. He has a PhD and an MSc from the University of Ottawa (2001 and 1994), as well as a BSc from Laval University (1992). He is also the father of three energetic children.

Gabriela Aranda is an assistant professor and a member of the Research Group on Software Engineering (GIISCO: http://giisco.uncoma.edu.ar) at the University of Comahue, Argentina. In addition, she is a member of the MAS (Agile Systems Maintenance) Research Project, at the University of Castilla-La Mancha, Spain; under the direction of Dr. Macario Polo Usaola. Her interests are centred on improving the requirements elicitation process in distributed environments, and developing strategies for selection of groupware tools and elicitation techniques according to the cognitive aspects of stakeholders. She is currently a PhD candidate at the University of Castilla-La Mancha, Spain.

Alex Blewitt holds a PhD and MSc from Edinburgh University, UK, as well as an MA from Cambridge. He has been interested in Java and Design patterns since 1995, and also contributes to a number of open-source projects, such as Eclipse and Apache. He currently works in London for a major investment bank, and lives in Milton Keynes, UK, with his wife Amy, son Sam, and two dogs, Milly and Kea.

Alejandra Cechich is an associate professor and head of the Research Group on Software Engineering (GIISCO: http://giisco.uncoma.edu.ar) at the University of Comahue, Argentina. Her interests are centred on object and component technology and their use in the systematic development of software systems. She received a European PhD in Computer Science by the University of Castilla-La Mancha, Spain, and an MSc in Computer Science by the University of South, Argentina.

Sivakumar Chinnasamy is currently a software architect with Verizon Information Services, USA. He holds a master's degree in computer science, where his research involved formalizing Design pattern specifications. As part of his graduate research done under Professor Raje, he developed eLePUS, an extension to the already existing LePUS (Language for Pattern Uniform Specification). In the industry side, he has lead the architecture, design, and development of many large-scale, object-oriented, component-based Web applications. His other technical interests include distributed and high performance computing.

Donald Cowan is distinguished professor emeritus at the University of Waterloo, Canada, Director of the Computer Systems Group, and holds appointments in the David R. Cheriton School of Computer Science and the Department of Biology. He was the founding chairman of the Computer Science Department at the University of Waterloo. He also has an appointment in the Faculty of Computer Science at Dalhousie University in Halifax, Canada.

Jens Dietrich is a senior lecturer in software engineering in the Institute of Information Sciences and Technology at the Turitea (Palmerston North) Campus of Massey University in New Zealand. He has a master's in mathematics and a PhD in computer science from the University of Leipzig. Between 1996 and 2003, he has worked as IT consultant in several European countries and Namibia, before joining Massey University in 2003. His research interests are in the areas of agile software engineering, rule-based systems, business rule automation, collaborative software engineering, semantic Web technology and object-oriented software design. Jens is the founder of two popular open source projects, Mandarax (derivation rules integrated into Java), and the WebOfPatterns (a suite of tools to publish, share, and detect Design patterns).

Jing Dong is an assistant professor in the Computer Science Department at the University of Texas at Dallas, USA. He received a PhD in computer science from the University of Waterloo. He has been in the program and organization committee of various international conferences and workshops. His research interests include Design patterns, UML/MDA, component-based software engineering, and formal methods. He has published more than 50 technical papers. He is a member of the ACM, the IEEE, the IEEE Computer Society, and the IEE.

Chris Elgar is a Java developer at SolNet Solutions Ltd. in Wellington, New Zealand. He has a Bachelor of Software Engineering and a Master in Computer Science from Massey University. As a keen field hockey player, his current interest is in the application of software within sports. Chris was a committer to the open source project, WebOfPatterns, while conducting his honours year project.

Andrés Flores is an assistant professor and a member of the Research Group on Software Engineering (GIISCO: http://giisco.uncoma.edu.ar) at the University of Comahue, Argentina. In addition, he is a member of the MAS (Agile Systems Maintenance) Research Project, at the University of Castilla-La Mancha, Spain; under the direction of Dr. Macario Polo Usaola. His interests are centered on component-based system testing, software architectures, and object-oriented applications. He holds an MSc in computer science from the University of South, Argentina, and is currently a PhD candidate at the University of Castilla-La Mancha, Spain.

Epameinondas Gasparis is a research student, supervised by Dr. Amnon H. Eden, at the Department of Computer Science at the University of Essex, UK. In 2000, he received a BSc in computer science and an MSc in computer science (Distributed System) in 2004. His current work is mainly in the area of the Two Tier Programming (TTP) project, which intends to provide tool support for the Class-Z formal specification language. His practical contributions to the TTP toolkit include the implementation of several of its modules. His research work focuses on the domain of reverse engineering, and particularly design mining.

John Grundy is a professor of software engineering at the University of Auckland, New Zealand. His interests include software engineering methods and tools, automated software engineering, software architecture and component-based systems, domain-specific visual languages and environments, user interfaces and object technologies. He is interested in Design patterns tool support at both the implementation-level and in helping improve software requirements and architecture practice.

Jason O. Hallstrom is an assistant professor of computer science at Clemson University, USA. He holds the BS and MA degrees from Miami University in systems analysis and economics, respectively. He also holds the MS and PhD degrees from Ohio State University in computer and information science. His research spans both software engineering and wireless sensor network design. In the former area, he considers specification and reasoning questions in the context of object-oriented development. In the latter area, he works to enable the reliable design, deployment, and management of long-lived applications at scale.

Joni Helin (MSc 2000, Tampere University of Technology, Finland) is currently finishing his dissertation research on formal methods at the Institute of Software Systems at Tampere University of Technology. In addition to his academic aspirations, he does consultation and subcontracting work as an entrepreneur in industrial software projects, specializing in conceptual, architectural, and object-oriented design and generative programming to deliver generic, adaptable solutions.

Angel Herranz is an assistant professor at Facultad de Informática of the Universidad Politécnica de Madrid, Spain. His current research interests are in the area of formal specifications of computer systems and formal methods. His PhD thesis is an in-progress work in the design of an object-oriented formal specification language. He is teaching abstract data types and concurrent programming. He became assistant professor in 1993 after finishing a 6-year software and electrical engineer's degree at Universidad Politécnica de Madrid.

William Higdon earned the MS degree from Purdue University (at Indianapolis, USA) in 2003. His master's project, which was overseen by Professor Rajeev Raje, is titled: "Formal Representation of Distributed Computing Design Patterns with LePUS". He is also interested in mathematics, particularly analysis, and earned the PhD in mathematics at Michigan State University in 1997. He performed his doctoral dissertation under the supervision of Professor Joel H. Shapiro. Dr. Higdon is an associate professor in the Department of

Mathematics and Computer Science at the University of Indianapolis, where he has been a faculty member since 1998.

John Hosking is a professor of computer science at the University of Auckland, New Zealand. His interests include visual languages and environments, software engineering and software engineering tools, model driven design approaches, software architecture, user interfaces, Design patterns, and pattern languages. He has authored or coauthored more than 150 refereed publications across this range of interests.

Pertti Kellomäki received his MSc degree in 1991 and Dr.Tech. degree in 1998, both from Tampere University of Technology, Finland. He currently works as a research fellow with the Academy of Finland. Kellomäki has worked on formal specification and verification of distributed behavior using theorem-proving techniques.

Dae-Kyoo Kim received the PhD in computer science from Colorado State University in 2004. He is currently an assistant professor in the Department of Computer Science and Engineering at Oakland University, Michigan, USA. Previously, he worked as a software engineer at McHugh Software International, Wisconsin, for three years, and had an internship at NASA/Ames Research Center, California. His research interests are access control modeling, pattern formalization, model refactoring, aspect-oriented modeling, and component-based software development. He was a cochair of the Workshop on Using Metamodels to Support Model-Driven Development of Complex Systems, ICECCS 2005. He is a member of the IEEE.

Kevin Lano was one of the originators of formal object-oriented techniques, and developed a combination of UML and formal methods in a number of papers and books. He was one of the founders of the Precise UML group, who influenced the definition of UML 2.0. His most recent book is "Advanced Systems Design with Java, UML and MDA" (Elsevier, 2005).

Howard C. Lovatt studied at Nottingham and Leeds Universities in the UK, obtaining his first PhD in electrical and electronic engineering in 1992. Dr. Lovatt has worked in private industry, academia, and currently at CSIRO, the largest government research organization in Australia. At CSIRO he won the organization's highest medal, the Chairman's Medal. The medal was awarded in 2000 for work on hybrid vehicles. In 2003, Dr. Lovatt started a second, part time, PhD at Macquarie University in Australia; his work is tentatively titled a Pattern Enforcing Compiler (PEC) for Java.

David Maplesden is a senior software architect for Orion Health, an international health IT integration and product development company. Maplesden's Master of Science thesis was based on the design and development of DPML and associated tool support. Having completed this, he joined the staff at Orion Health working on a range of product lines, including the Rhapsody integration engine and Symphonia messaging products. Starting in

2002, he spent 2 years working as a consultant for Orion Health in the UK before returning to NZ to take up a leading position in the development of Orion Health's next generation of clinical workflow products.

Tommi Mikkonen (MSc 1992, Lic. Tech. 1995, Dr. Tech 1999, Tampere University of Technology, Finland) works on distributed systems, software architectures, and formal methods at the Institute of Software Systems at Tampere University of Technology. Over the years, he has written a number of research papers on formal specification, software engineering and architectures, and their relation, as well as supervised a number of theses and research projects on these subjects.

Juan José Moreno-Navarro received his PhD degree in computer science from the Technical University of Madrid (UPM), Spain in 1989. Since 1996, he has been full professor in the Computer Science Department at the UPM. Currently, he is also deputy director of the IMDEA-Software (Madrid Research Institute for Software Technologies). His main research area concerns all the aspects related to declarative technology and software development. On these topics, he has published more than 60 refereed papers. He has also participated in several EU-funded and other national and international research projects. He is a member of the editorial board of the *Electronic Journal of Functional and Logic Programming*. He has organized, served in program committees, and given invited talks and tutorials in many conferences in the ICT field. He is the director of SpaRCIM (Spanish Research Consortium on Informatics and Mathematics)—the Spanish member of ERCIM (European Research Consortium on Informatics and Mathematics), member and founder of the Spanish Technological Platform on Software and Services INES, member of the Steering Committee of the European Technological Platform on Software and Services NESSI, and vice-chair of the Spanish Software Engineering Research Association.

Gunter Mussbacher has a PhD candidate in computer science at the University of Ottawa, Canada, since 2005. He previously studied as an undergraduate at the Technische Universität Graz in Austria, and then received his MSc from Simon Fraser University in 1999. After spending almost 2 years in industry as a research engineer with Strategic Technology at Mitel Networks, he flung a backpack on his shoulders and donned the suit of his alter ego, the traveler, for a 3-year travel adventure. Now back in academia, his research interests include scenario-based requirements engineering, the user requirements notation, and aspect-oriented software development.

Andrew M. Olson is professor emeritus at Indiana-University/Purdue-University, Indianapolis, USA, and an ACM and SIAM member. He currently investigates component-based design engineering of distributed systems. Additional publications include Human/Machine Interaction, Visual Programming and Symbolic-Numeric Computation. The U.S. Offices of Naval and Army Research, NSF, and Indiana Corporation for Science & Technology have funded Andrew's research projects, some of which were collaborative. He authored or coauthored several book chapters and numerous journals, conference papers, workshop papers, and reports. Andrew was a key organizer of three international conferences. He reviews for scientific journals, international workshops, international conferences, books, and proposals to governmental organizations. Washington University, St. Louis, awarded his engineering doctorate.

Rajeev R. Raje is an associate professor in the Department of Computer and Information Science at Indiana University, Purdue University, Indianapolis, USA. Raje holds degrees from the University of Bombay (BE) and Syracuse University (MS and PhD). His research interests are in distributed-object computing, component-based systems and software engineering. Dr. Rajes current and past research has been supported by the U.S. Office of Naval Research, National Science Foundation, Indigo Foundation, Eli Lilly and Company, and Microsoft Corporation. Raje is a member of the ACM and IEEE.

Anthony M. Sloane is an associate professor and the head of department in the Department of Computing at Macquarie University in Sydney, Australia. He has received degrees from the University of Colorado, Boulder, USA, and the Australian National University. His research interests are in compiler generation, programming language implementation, programming environments and tools. Notable recent projects include the Eli Language Processor Generation System and a major domain-specific language survey. Current interests include abstraction mechanisms for compiler generation, pattern-based calculi for computation, and software generation for handheld computing devices.

Neelam Soundarajan is an associate professor of computer science at The Ohio State University, USA. He holds the BS and MS degrees in physics, and the PhD degree in computer science, all from the Bombay University. His research interests lie primarily in reasoning about program behavior. In this area, he works to develop techniques for specification and verification of program properties, as well as methods for testing programs against their specifications.

Jason Smith is a software engineering researcher at IBM T.J. Watson Research Center, USA. His interests are the description, comprehension, and validation of software design. His industry experience inspired his practical, tool-oriented focus on results, while his mathematics and physics studies drive him to insist on proper formalizations. He envisions software production as a true engineering discipline, with repeatable results, comparative experimentation, and a comprehensive model that spans syntax and semantics. Dr. Smith received his PhD in computer science from the University of North Carolina at Chapel Hill in 2005.

David Stotts received the PhD in computer science from the University of Virginia in 1985 and has been at UNC Chapel Hill since 1992. His areas of research include hypermedia, collaborative systems, HCI, and software engineering. Recent work includes an interoperability framework for creating scientific model federations, a formal method and system for finding Design patterns in object-oriented source code, and Facetop, a system that integrates semitransparent video teleconferencing with PC desktop information. Dr. Stotts teaches courses at UNC on programming languages, software design, and agile software development methods.

Dominic R. Verity is an associate professor and is the director of postgraduate programs in information technology and allied sciences at Macquarie University in Sydney, Australia. He completed his bachelor's and doctoral studies in pure mathematics at Cambridge University in the United Kingdom, and has recently held an appointment there as a visiting professorial fellow of its Fitzwilliam College. Aside from his continuing involvement in pure mathematics, his research interests lie in the field of compiler construction, programming language semantics, and formal verification. Having started his career in 1981 as a software developer for the now legendary British technology pioneer Acorn Computers, his experience in the practice of software engineering extends over some 25 years.

Michael Weiss is an associate professor at Carleton University, Canada, which he joined in 2000 after a 5-year stint in industry following his PhD in computer science in 1993 (University of Mannheim, Germany). In particular, he led the Advanced Applications Group within the Strategic Technology group of Mitel Corporation. His research interests include service-oriented architectures, software architecture and patterns, business model design and evolution, and open source development.

Index

Single Journal Articles and Case Studies
Are Now Right
at Your Fingertips!

Purchase any single journal article or teaching case for only $25.00!

Idea Group Publishing offers an extensive collection of research articles and teaching cases in both print and electronic formats. You will find over 1300 journal articles and more than 300 case studies on-line at **www.idea-group.com/articles**. Individual journal articles and cases are available for only $25 each. A new feature of our website now allows you to search journal articles and case studies by category. To take advantage of this new feature, simply use the above link to search within these available categories.

We have provided free access to the table of contents for each journal. Once you locate the specific article needed, you can purchase it through our easy and secure site.

For more information, contact cust@idea-group.com or 717-533-8845 ext.10

Databases, Data Mining & Data Warehousing

Distance Learning & Education

E-Commerce and E-Government

E-Government

Healthcare Information Systems

Human Side and Society Issues in IT

Information Technology Education

IT Business Value, Support and Solutions

IT Engineering, Modeling & Evaluation

Knowledge Management

Mobile Commerce and Telecommunications

Multimedia Networking

Virtual Organizations and Communities

Web Technologies and Applications

IDEA GROUP INC.   www.idea-group.com